SUFIS OF BIJAPUR (1300-1700)

SUFIS OF BIJAPUR (1300-1700)

Social Roles of Sufis in Medical India

Richard Maxwell Eaton

KALPAZ

ISBN: 978-93-5128-340-9 (HB)

First Published in 1978
Indian Reprint in 2017

Published by

Kalpaz Publications
C-30, Satyawati Nagar,
Delhi – 110052
E-mail: kalpaz@hotmail.com
Website: kalpazpublications.com
Ph.: +91-9212142040

SUFIS OF BIJAPUR
1300-1700

Sufis of Bijapur
1300-1700

SOCIAL ROLES OF SUFIS
IN MEDIEVAL INDIA

By
Richard Maxwell Eaton

To my mother and father

CONTENTS

PART TWO: Reformers and Writers

PART THREE: Sufis of the Late ʿAdil Shahi Period

LIST OF FIGURES

LIST OF CHARTS

LIST OF TABLES

NOTE ON TRANSLATION AND TRANSLITERATION

The writer is responsible for all translations quoted in this study except for those otherwise credited in the footnotes. Middle Eastern and Indian terms not in common usage in the English language have been italicized when used in the text. It seemed neither necessary nor desirable to burden the reader with diacritical markings over and under such words each time they should appear. To serve the interests of exactness, however, a glossary has been appended to the study in which all such terms are given their full diacritical markings. An explanation of the system of transliteration used in this study will also be found in the Glossary.

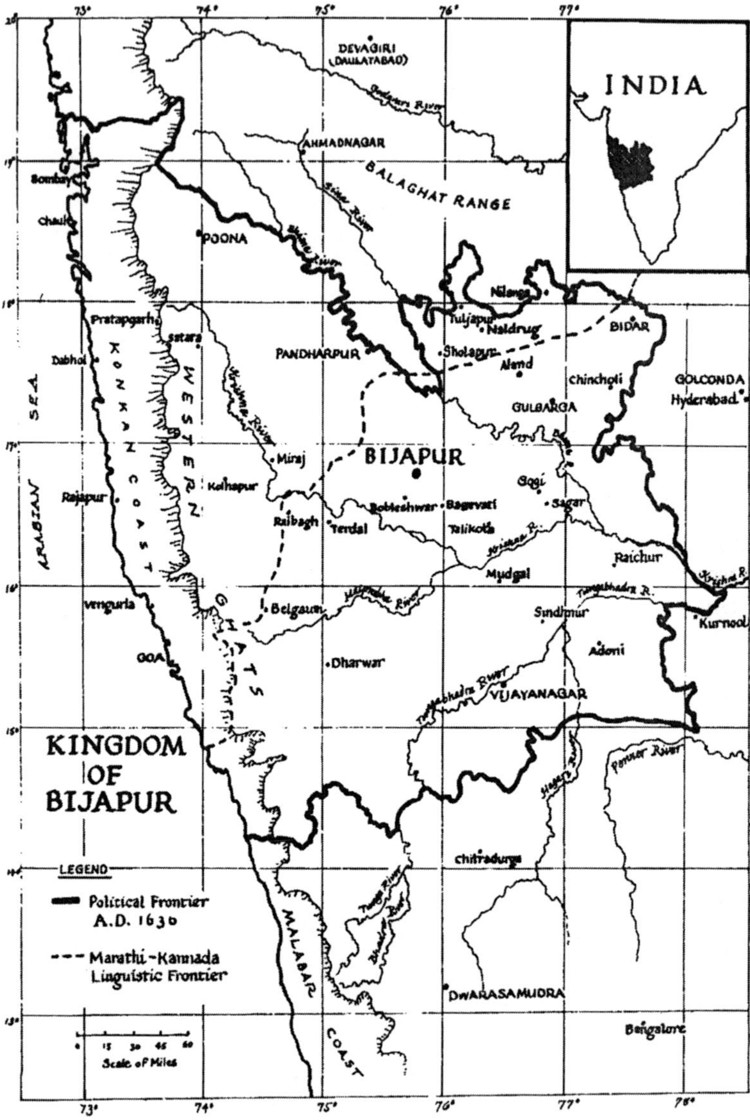

INDIA
DEVAGIRI (DAULATABAD)
AHMADNAGAR
BALAGHAT RANGE
Bombay
Chaul
POONA
Bhima River
Pratapgarh
Satara
Dabhol
KONKAN COAST
WESTERN GHATS
PANDHARPUR
Tuljapur
Naldrug
Nilanga
BIDAR
Sholapur
Alend
Chincholi
GOLCONDA
Hyderabad
GULBARGA
ARABIAN SEA
Miraj
BIJAPUR
Kolhapur
Rajapur
Gogi
Sagar
Bagevati
Talikota
Terdal
Raibagh
Krishna R.
Raichur
Mudgal
Krishna R.
Tungabhadra R.
Vengurla
Belgaum
Sindhnur
Kurnool
Adoni
GOA
Dharwar
Tungabhadra River
VIJAYANAGAR
KINGDOM OF BIJAPUR
Pennar River
Chitradurga
LEGEND
Political Frontier A.D. 1630
Marathi-Kannada Linguistic Frontier
MALABAR COAST
DWARASAMUDRA
Bengalore
Scale of Miles
0 15 30 45 60
73° 74° 75° 76° 77° 78°

PREFACE

This study seeks to identify the social roles played by the Sufis, heirs to a tradition of Islamic mysticism, who lived in the medieval city-state of Bijapur in South India. The Sufis examined in this work have been regarded as an integral part of an evolving society in which an Indo-Muslim ruling establishment was superimposed on an indigenous non-Muslim population. Within this framework the present study explores not only how Sufis of various social types interacted with the main components of the society in which they lived—the upholders of Islamic orthodoxy, the court, and the non-Muslim population—but also how these types evolved and changed over time. The shaping of this study into its present form is attributable both to the kinds of sources that I uncovered in the course of my research and also to the many individuals and institutions that have, in countless ways, guided and assisted my studies and research through their various phases. An explanation of these sources and an acknowledgment of my gratitude to these individuals and institutions are therefore in order.

The primary sources used in this study consist mainly of Persian manuscripts preserved in various institutions in Hyderabad, Andhra Pradesh, and may be classified under four broad headings: works written about the Sufis, works written by the Sufis, official documents of the Bijapur government, and court chronicles, memoirs, and travel accounts contemporary with the period under review. In my quest to learn from the primary sources who the Sufis of Bijapur were and what they did, the first type of source material to come to my attention was the biographical literature on the Sufis, known formally as hagiographies. While going through catalogues of Persian manuscripts in Hyderabad libraries I found reference to the *Rauzat al-Auliya'-i Bijapur*, originally entitled *Tazkira-yi Auliya'-i Dar al-Zafar Bijapur*. This important manuscript consists of biographical notices on the Sufis of Bijapur compiled in the early nineteenth century by one of the most reliable historians of the area, Muhammad Ibrahim Zubairi. Having learned of this manuscript, of which the only copies in the world are found in Hyderabad, I journeyed to that city and was lead by Zubairi's important work to a great many other manuscripts dealing with the Sufis of Bijapur, which seem never to have been utilized by Indian or Western scholars.

Locating such materials, however, and utilizing them to arrive at an accurate understanding of the historical personalities they describe, are two different matters. Compiled anywhere from one generation to several hundred years after the lives of the Sufis they mention, these sources vary a great deal from one to the next. The best of them, such as Zubairi's, diligently utilize and cite earlier works sometimes no longer available to modern researchers. At their worst, however, they indulge in laudatory embellishments to the point of the most fanciful miracle-mongering. For the popular veneration of the Sufis, and more importantly their tombs, has led to the rise of countless popular stories about them that, with the compilation of these biographies, passed from oral to written traditions. Hence it has always been necessary, when trying to find the kernel of truth from which these traditions grew, to consider such factors as the time lag between the life of the Sufi and the date of compilation of his biography, the relationship (spiritual, familial, or social) between the Sufi and the compiler who mentions him, and the tendency of both oral and written traditions to conform to certain archetypes of Indo-Muslim saints and therefore to tell us how they *should* have acted in Indian history.

But the biographies, or *tazkirat*, are not the only type of source material that I found valuable. Another type is the discourses (*malfuzat*), or the sayings of a Sufi as recorded by one of his disciples. Though few in number for Bijapur's Sufis, the discourses have immense value since, written during a Sufi's lifetime by his close associates, they are generally free from miracle-mongering or other forms of embellishment. Indeed, they provide perhaps the most candid pictures of how Sufis lived.

Extensive research in various institutions in Hyderabad, both private and public, eventually led me to another broad category of primary sources. This is the works written by the most prominent Sufis, which in turn fall into two classes: mystical literature and popular literature. Although the mystical literature differs little in substance from the classical statements of Islamic mysticism that had emerged in the Islamic heartland during the first five centuries A.H. and are well known to students of Sufism, the literature composed by Sufis for the common folk of the Bijapur region represents a unique find. For it was this literature, composed in the vernacular language of Dakhni and not in the high languages of Islamic culture, Arabic and Persian, that brought one section of Bijapur's Sufis into direct contact with the region's lower classes.

The third and fourth categories of primary sources used in this study were non-Sufi in origin but proved of immense value in painting in the background against which the principal subjects of this study were viewed. Many state documents, consisting chiefly of *farmans* or orders issued by the Bijapur government, pertained to Sufis or the institutions that grew up around their tombs, and provided valuable information on the relations between the court and certain sections of the Sufi community. Finally there were the contemporary histories, memoirs, and travel accounts, which shed a good deal of indirect light on the Sufis of this study. I have relied extensively upon two historians in particular: Muhammad Qasim Firishta and Muhammad Ibrahim Zubairi, mentioned above as the author of the *Rauzat al-Auliya*. Though less well known than the work of Firishta, whose narrative for Bijapur goes up to the year 1596, Zubairi's account takes on special importance because of its breadth. Although it was compiled as late as 1811, his *Basatin al-Salatin* was based on a number of contemporary sources that it superseded and others that no longer exist. It is, moreover, the only comprehensive history of the entire 'Adil Shahi dynasty (1490-1686) whose reign over Bijapur coincides with most of the period under review in this study.

My sincere thanks are due to the many individuals and institutions without whose assistance and patience this work would not have appeared. I owe a deep indebtedness to Professor Robert E. Frykenberg who, during my early graduate career at the University of Wisconsin, urged me to apply my knowledge of Persian to the study of Indian history. It was also he who pointed out to me the gross imbalance in the historiography of medieval India in favor of the northern part of the subcontinent, particularly the Mughal Empire, and suggested that I pursue the study of the Deccan in general, and the Kingdom of Bijapur in particular. To the extent that this study may partly redress the present imbalance between the study of medieval North India and the Deccan, I am obliged to Professor Frykenberg for his initial encouragement. I am also deeply indebted to the members of the University of Wisconsin's Comparative World History program, particularly Professors Philip D. Curtin and John R. W. Smail, for directing my attention and interests to social history and the study of culture contact. It was this approach that led me to focus on the Sufis as possible pivotal individuals standing between Muslim and non-Muslim groups in medieval Indian society.

Professor John F. Richards of the University of Wisconsin directed the doctoral dissertation upon which this study is based. I am deeply indebted to him for the advice he freely rendered during all phases of my graduate career and for the careful criticisms he gave during the research and writing phases of my work. Without the encouragement based on his own expertise in the field of medieval Indian history this work would not have been completed.

I am particularly grateful to the many institutions in England, India, and Pakistan whose willing assistance made my research possible. My research in India, conducted between October 1969 and January 1971, was supported by a grant from the American Institute of Indian Studies. I am much obliged to the men who were at that time the organization's officers in India—particularly Dr. D. D. Karve, the co-director, and Dr. P. R. Mehendiratta, the deputy executive officer—for all that they did in facilitating my stay in India. In London the British Museum and the India Office Library made available many manuscripts that I used both in the initial phases of my work before embarking for India, and over a year later in the final phases of my research while returning from India. In India itself, five institutions whose manuscripts or documents were made available to me deserve special mention. These include, in Hyderabad, the State Archives of Andhra Pradesh, the Asafiyah Library (State Central Library), the Salar Jung Museum, and the Idara-e-Adabiyat-e-Urdu; and in Bijapur, the Archeological Museum. In 1976 I consulted relevant manuscripts in Karachi at the Anjuman-i Taraqqi-yi Urdu, whose collection is currently preserved in the National Museum of Pakistan. I am much obliged to the directors, archivists, and librarians of these institutions for the patience and kindness they showed in allowing me to utilize their collections. For granting me permission to make photographs of certain miniature paintings in their collections, I acknowledge thanks to the Salar Jung Museum in Hyderabad (Figures 7, 8, and 12), the Idara-e-Adabiyat-e-Urdu in Hyderabad (Figure 3), the Archeological Museum of Bijapur (Figure 9), and Mr. Aqa Haidar Hasan of Hyderabad (Figure 2).

While conducting my research in India I was fortunate in having conversations with a number of noted scholars in the field of medieval Indian history. In Hyderabad I had useful talks with Dr. H. K. Sherwani, Dr. P. Saran, Dr. Rafi'a Sultana, Professor M. Akbaruddin Siddiqi, and Bishop John A. Subhan. I have also benefited a great deal from personal conversations with Dr. P. M. Joshi of the Deccan College, Poona, and Dr. K. A. Nizami of the Aligarh Muslim University, Aligarh. Contact with scholars of this high caliber, coming as it did in the formative stage of my research in India, proved of immense value in directing my energies to fruitful sources of inquiry.

A number of individuals provided me with expert skills that assisted my research. I am most indebted to Mr. Safdar Shafeeq Ahmad for his invaluable services in helping locate relevant documents in Hyderabad and Bijapur, and in assisting me in their interpretation. Mr. Ziauddin Ahmed Shakeb, an archivist at the State Archives of Andhra Pradesh, was most helpful in locating manuscripts in private collections in Hyderabad as well as in the State Archives. And for their fine work in making clear and accurate transcriptions of certain Persian manuscripts I am grateful to Mr. 'Abd al-Karim Mahir and Mr. Rahmat Allah Khan, both of Hyderabad.

There are numerous other individuals who helped me while I was in India and whose acquaintance I shall always treasure. I am greatly indebted to Professor M. Akbaruddin Siddiqi, formerly of the Urdu Department, Osmania University, Hyderabad, for making available to me his fine collection of Dakhni manuscripts and for helping me in their translation. Messrs. Burhan al-Din Husaini, Faruq Husaini, and Saiyid Murtaza Qadiri, all of whom are residents of Bijapur and descendants of prominent Sufis there, kindly provided me with many rare manuscript sources handed down to them by their forefathers. More than that, numerous and lengthy talks with them gave me a feel for the subject of my research that no amount of reading could ever have accomplished.

Finally, I would like to express my deep gratitude to my colleagues and good friends Mrs. Jane Ragsdale, Dr. Joseph Brennig, and Miss Katherine Ewing, whose careful reading and critical comments of various drafts of this study proved of immeasurable value.

Tucson, Arizona R. M. E.

INTRODUCTION

In 1890 an English archeologist for the government of India, Henry Cousens, described his trip across the barren, flat Deccan plateau and his arrival at the ruined city he was about to survey. "Not many years ago," wrote Cousens,

> the way was not altogether free from Maratha freebooters; and when the city was reached it was found a lonely and deserted extent of ruins, the haunt of the jackal, the wolf, and the hyaena, and an elysium of bats and owls. Very few families lived within the walls: it had remained a desolate waste from the time of its fall to within the last half century.[1]

The magnificent palaces, mausoleums, mosques, and other structures surveyed by Cousens once graced the medieval city of Bijapur, capital of the kingdom of the same name.[2] At its height in the mid-seventeenth century the Kingdom of Bijapur was, after the Mughal Empire, one of the largest and most powerful states of the Indian subcontinent. In 1686, however, the Mughal Empire itself swallowed up this Deccan kingdom, which precipitated the city's rapid decline into the ruined specter Cousens described.

What particularly strikes today's visitor to Bijapur is the extraordinary number of tombs scattered both inside and outside the city walls. Of course, the most imposing of these are the great mausoleums built by and for the kingdom's sultans, who once ruled over the entire western Deccan. Other tombs, less grandiose than those for the monarchs, were constructed for members of the upper nobility, talented artists, architects, and musicians. But all these are numerically insignificant compared with the number of tombs and graves of Sufis, the Muslim saints of Bijapur. Varying from large mausoleums twenty feet in height with cupola or dome, to simple tombstones raised only several

1 Henry Cousens, *Notes on the Buildings and Other Antiquarian Remains at Bijapur* (Bombay: Government Central Press, 1890), p. 1.

2 See Cousens, *Notes on the Buildings*; see also Cousens, *Bijapur and Its Architectural Remains* (Bombay: Government Central Press, 1916).

feet off the ground, the structures built to consecrate the burial places of Bijapur's Sufis number almost three hundred. Of these about one third are located within the city's great, circular walls, which measure about two miles in diameter, and the rest lie scattered about the countryside outside the walls.[3]

Although the city today is again inhabited by a thriving population, most of these Sufi burial sites, especially the smaller ones, lie in the same neglected condition that Cousens saw when he made his surveys at the end of the nineteenth century. On the other hand some of the larger tombs, called *dargahs*, have become centers of a living popular religion. On any Thursday afternoon crowds of common people—both Hindus and Muslims, and mostly women—can be seen giving gifts to and taking blessings from a *pirzada*, a descendant of the Sufi buried beneath the *dargah*.[4] Especially illustrating the living nature of the *dargahs* are the festive celebrations that annually commemorate the Sufis' death dates (*'urs*, or "marriage with God"). Thousands of pilgrims from all over the Deccan plateau will, on these occasions, throng to Bijapur and join local devotees in the celebrations that have made such *dargahs* the focus of popular Islam throughout India.

But who were the Sufis that were buried in these *dargahs*? In the eighteenth century, a time when a series of natural and political disasters denuded Bijapur of its once-bustling population and transformed its palaces into the refuge of jackals and wolves, there was a great hiatus in the city's history. Although their tombs are central to the devotional lives of thousands today, very little is remembered of the lives of the Sufis of Bijapur. The aim of this study, then, is to bridge the hiatus and to discern, to the extent possible, who these Sufis were and what kind of social roles they played in medieval Indian society.

Three fundamental questions guide the inquiry. First, what was the Sufis' relationship to Bijapur's *'ulama*, or the upholders of Islamic orthodoxy in its exoteric sense? This study explores with

[3] A complete list of the Sufis buried in and around the city can be found in Saiyid Muhyi al-Din bin Mahmud Qadiri, *Sahifat-i Ahl-i Huda*, trans. and ed. M. Akbaruddin Siddiqi (Hyderabad: National Fine Printing Press, 1966), pp. 12-16 (hereafter cited *Sahifat*, Urdu edn.). This source mentions ninety-six burial sites of Sufis within the city walls, and one hundred eighty-nine outside the walls.

[4] See Figures 13 and 14.

reference to medieval Bijapur the extent of doctrinal incompatibility and social hostility that in other contexts are frequently said to have existed between Sufis and the *'ulama*. Second, what was the Sufis' relationship to the Bijapur court and how can it be explained? Although some modern writers on Sufism have noted the variety of relationships between Sufis and medieval Indo-Muslim courts, ranging from mutual patronage to bitter hostility, there has appeared no attempt to explain the variables that influenced these different relationships. Third, what was the Sufis' relationship to the non-Muslim population that surrounded them? Although we often hear the rather glib assertion that medieval Indian Sufis were primarily responsible for converting Hindus to Islam, the issue has not been at all closely examined. Are we to assume that all of Bijapur's Sufis concerned themselves with converting Hindus? Even if only some of them were so inclined, how and why might they have done it? How could highly developed traditions of Middle Eastern mysticism have been translated in terms meaningful to illiterate non-Muslims of the Deccan? In sum, what social roles did the Sufis of Bijapur play in relation to the *'ulama*, the court, and the non-Muslim population?

It is necessary here to define the spatial, chronological, and conceptual limits of this study. The spatial unit we are concerned with is primarily the city and immediate environs of Bijapur, though we shall frequently have occasion to refer to other cities and towns within the kingdom. There are in the Indian subcontinent a number of centers of Islamic civilization which, for purposes of analyzing the social roles of medieval Sufis in the Hindu environment, might appear to have served as satisfactorily as the one used. But the city-state of Bijapur is preferable for several reasons. The first stems from the disproportionate amount of research that has already been done on North Indian history in contrast to that on South India generally or the Deccan plateau in particular. Notwithstanding the remarkable extent of Bijapur's power in the sixteenth and seventeenth centuries, most historians have continued to write of Bijapur from a northern viewpoint, seeing the kingdom as merely one of the Deccan obstacles against which the Mughals, and particularly Aurangzeb, so doggedly struggled. Probably also as a result of this northern-centric bias, the kingdom has tended to remain neglected; historians to date have generally confined themselves to Bijapur's political history, and the kingdom's cultural history has been all but completely ignored.[5] Thus this kingdom presented not only a relatively uncharted area of research, but also one needing to be interpreted and understood on its own terms. Second, the existence of a once-thriving Sufi tradition in and around the city, manifested by the sheer number of Sufis who lived there as well as by the extent of written sources concerning them, made Bijapur a particularly fruitful area for research of this kind.

The chronological limits of this study extend from the early fourteenth century to the end of the seventeenth century, that is, when the first Sufis appeared on the Bijapur plateau until the sudden depopulation of the city following the Mughal conquest of 1686. Within a generation of that conquest a plague, a famine, a flood, and repeated raids by foreign armies combined to sever any continuous tradition of Sufism in Bijapur, so that by the mid-eighteenth century only the tombs remained. The greater part of the study, however, concerns Sufis of the seventeenth century, as most of them lived during the height of the 'Adil Shahi dynasty (1490-1686).

The conceptual framework of this study depends a great deal on the use of the word "Sufi" and whom it is taken to include. Many scholars of Sufism, including in this century such eminent authorities as A. J. Arberry, L. Massignon, and R. A. Nicholson, have concerned themselves mainly with the philosophical and doctrinal aspects of Islamic mysticism and have consequently

[5] The best comprehensive study of Bijapur's history in a Western language is P. M. Joshi's dissertation, "The Kingdom of Bijapur," submitted in 1935 to the University of London. Based on Persian and Marathi sources as well as extensive use of travelers' accounts, Joshi's work has recently appeared in a revised and reorganized form in the first volume of the *History of Medieval Deccan* edited by H. K. Sherwani and Professor Joshi. Another recent study of the 'Adil Shahi Sultanate, D. C. Verma's *History of Bijapur*, is a political and diplomatic narrative. Three other writers have treated more specialized aspects of the kingdom's history. I. H. Ghauri, using mainly Persian sources, has written a number of articles on the kingdom's administrative organization, and H. Fukazawa, using mainly Marathi sources, has treated the same topic in somewhat greater depth. Finally there is the work of G. H. Khare, who has performed a great service to the study of Bijapur by publishing and interpreting a number of old Marathi documents he has found in Maharashtra. Among historians of North India Sir Jadunath Sarkar has contributed most significantly to our understanding of Bijapur. See bibliography for references.

understood the Sufi primarily as a mystic who, within the framework of Islam, attempts to achieve direct communion with God.[6] In this, what might be called the classical approach to Sufi studies, the individual Sufi has been examined not as an organic part of his society but as a practitioner and transmitter of esoteric Islam, standing, as it were, above or beyond the social order. Of course, this approach is quite legitimate as long as interest in Sufis is confined to the development of mystical doctrines. To analyze, for example, the philosophy of the Spanish-Arab Sufi Ibn ʿArabi or that of the Persian Sufi Jalal al-Din Rumi requires little knowledge of the society of medieval North Africa or Iran. The classical approach, in a word, stresses not the Sufi but Sufism, not the man as a social component but the doctrine as conveyed by the man.

As used in this study, however, the word "Sufi" denotes any person integrated into the organizational structure of the Islamic mystical tradition. This involved a person's taking a vow of spiritual allegiance (*baiʿat*) from another, who in turn had taken a similar vow from still another, so that an institutionalized "spiritual" chain linked any Sufi with some earlier master who, in turn, very probably claimed a spiritual lineage extending from the Prophet himself. This understanding of the term "Sufi" is considerably broader than that of the classical approach to Sufi studies since it includes not only the true mystics of Islam, but many nonliterate individuals who may have had little training in or even understanding of Islamic mysticism. For in its later form, the institutionalized vow of allegiance had begun carrying with it an increasing amount of ritual and a diminishing amount of mystical knowledge. Nonetheless, people who took the vow considered themselves Sufis and were considered as such by their contemporaries. Furthermore, certain objective criteria in the literature would seem to substantiate their claim. One of them is biographical reference to a person's having taken the *baiʿat* from another, an act usually accompanied and consecrated by a formal ceremony. Another is recorded reference to the passing from one to another of a written certificate (*khilafat-nama*), a patched frock (*khirqa*), or other objects symbolizing spiritual succession (*khila-*

[6] The leading works of these authors are listed in the bibliography. For an excellent survey of the history of the study of Sufism, see A. J. Arberry, *An Introduction to the History of Sufism* (New York: Longmans, Green and Co., 1942).

fat). Such ritualistic acts did not necessarily make a man a mystic; nor did they necessarily join him with a Sufi brotherhood. Yet they did, in his own estimation, make him a Sufi.

This interpretation of the word "Sufi" can best be understood when placed in the context of the historical evolution of Sufism and Sufi brotherhoods. In his important study, *The Sufi Orders in Islam*, J. S. Trimingham has identified three distinct stages through which Sufism in its organizational aspect has passed: the *khanaqah* stage, the *tariqa* stage, and the *ta'ifa* stage.[7] The first or *khanaqah* stage of Sufism was the true golden age of Islamic mysticism in terms of the creativity of thought, the quantity of original mystical literature produced, and the simplicity of the Sufis' social organization. Shocked by the extravagant wealth and power of the Abbasid caliphate and struck by the apparent contradiction between the imperial worldliness of an opulent Caliph of Islam and the stern commandments of the Prophet Muhammad, the first Sufis were true ascetics. In both lower Iraq and Khurasan, Sufis like Hasan al-Basri (d. 728), Ibrahim b. Adham (d. 777), Shaqiq of Balkh (d. 810), and ʿAbd Allah b. al-Mubarak (d. 797) led quietistic and highly ascetic lives of withdrawal from the mundane society of the Abbasid caliphate. The ascetics of the eighth century were followed in the ninth by the early mystics, such as Muhasibi (d. 837), Dhu'l-Nun (d. 861), Bayazid Bistami (d. 875), Abu'l-Qasim al-Junaid (d. 910) and Mansur al-Hallaj (d. 922), whose emphasis was placed much more on love of God and spiritual affinity with God than on fear of God. Insofar as the attainment of such affinity involved a discipline or method to be learned and followed, a tradition of the master and his circle of pupils soon characterized this early phase.

But it is important to stress the loose and unstructured nature of this phase of Sufi development. There was no formal bond between the master and his pupils, the latter frequently being itinerant dropouts from the orthodox society of the Abbasids. Nor did the master in any way pose himself as an intermediary between the pupil and God. Whether masters or pupils, all Sufis were generally undifferentiated and unspecialized, and the physical structure upon which early Sufism centered was equally unspecialized and simple. This was the *khanaqah*, the humble rest-

[7] Oxford: Oxford University Press, 1971. The following discussion draws from chapters one through three of Trimingham's study.

house or convent where wandering Sufis could lead a devotional life under the tutelage of some master. From the ninth through the twelfth century such *khanaqahs* could be found all over the Islamic world, especially on the Islamic frontier, where they played important roles in integrating non-Muslims into the Islamic community. Thus Sufism's earliest stage of development, like that of so many social movements in history, saw a burst of creativity and vigor unencumbered by organizational or doctrinal elaboration.

From about the thirteenth century the Sufi movement underwent a profound change with respect to its doctrinal evolution and social organization. This stage (the *tariqa* stage) saw the formation of mystical schools that had begun to coalesce around one or another master. From a doctrinal standpoint this second phase of Sufi development was characterized by the gradual systemization of mystical techniques designed to bring the Sufi into direct communion with God. These systems of techniques gradually crystallized into schools in which the method, consisting of a structured set of spiritual exercises to be learned and mastered, became the focal point of the Sufis' concentration. Also in this phase the principle of the transmission of the method from one Sufi to another became explicit, resulting in the formation of spiritual lineages or *silsilas* (literally, "chain") that corresponded to each school and that could be traced back to the founder of each school. Thus the Qadiri order (*silsila-tariqa*) is traced to its founder, ʿAbd al-Qadir Jilani (d. 1166), the Rifaʿi order to Ahmad al-Rifaʿi (d. 1182), the Yasavi order to Ahmad al-Yasavi (d. 1166), and so on.

From the standpoint of social organization, too, the *tariqa* phase was characterized by greater systemization, differentiation, and specialization. The *silsila* principle implied new sets of social relationships between Sufis. Differentiated schools of discipline meant that Sufis now belonged to one or another order, as opposed to the freer *khanaqah* phase when they were socially undifferentiated. Moreover the formation of orders introduced the phenomenon of initiation. Sufis were now allowed to practice the method of an order in return for a pledge of spiritual allegiance to the local director or representative of that order. This also altered the relationship between the Sufi and his master. In the *khanaqah* phase both teacher and pupil were essentially equal in their capacities to attain their spiritual goal. But in the second phase of institutional evolution a distinction became discernible between the *pir* (or *murshid*), who was the director, and the *murid*, or disciple. Although the *murid* might eventually attain the spiritual heights of his *pir*, he was in the first instance obliged to surrender himself completely to the *pir* and to the whole complex of exercises, terminology, and disciplines that his *pir* taught. There also emerged in this phase another category of disciple besides the *murid*. This was the *khalifa*, literally "successor," who was closer to the *pir* than the *murids* in that unlike the latter he was deputized to initiate other *murids* into the order of the *pir*. In sum, the *tariqa* phase may be regarded, as Trimingham noted, "as the beginning of the process whereby the creative freedom of the mystic was to be channelled into an institution."[8]

Sufism evolved into its third and final stage from the fifteenth century onward, the exact timing of the transition varying widely from order to order and from place to place. To be a Sufi now came to mean more the belonging to a cult-association called a *ta'ifa* than the submitting to a method of discipline. Moreover Sufism's mystical element, which in its unrestrained abundance had characterized the *khanaqah* phase and which in the *tariqa* phase was subjected to a good deal of systemization, now played a minor role in the movement. In this stage a Sufi's direct communion with God was replaced by the veneration and even worship of a *pir* who now occupied the position of spiritual intermediary between the disciple and God. *Pirs* thus became saints (*wali*, literally, "friend of God"), and Sufi orders which in the second stage had been schools of spiritual discipline now became saint-cults centered on the spiritual power, or *barakat*, of a single individual. Moreover the headship of most *ta'ifas*, particularly in India, became mainly hereditary as blood replaced merit as the chief criterion of succession. This in turn gave rise to a whole new class of individuals who by virtue of their blood descent from a saint could claim special spiritual status. For it was now believed that the spiritual power possessed by a saint passed on to his own familial descendants, in India called *pirzadas* (literally, "born of a *pir*").

Barakat, that intangible capacity of a saint to wield spiritual power and to attract devotees, was transmitted not only to a saint's descendants, but also to his tomb. These tombs, in India

[8] Ibid., p. 11.

called *dargahs*, generally replaced *khanaqahs* as the physical structures upon which Sufi movements were based. Correspondingly, Sufism now became more a devotional than a mystical movement. Although there was still an inner circle of *murids* or adepts who studied with the *pir* or the *pirzada*, a much larger circle of devotees was now brought into informal association with the order as devotees in the saint-cult. Whereas in its earlier phases of evolution Sufism had been confined to a tiny spiritual elite, it had now broadened to become a popular movement in which the unlettered masses could freely participate. Devotion to some saint, exercised through the veneration of his descendants and his tomb, exerted a powerful appeal among common folk whose goal was not the mystic's goal of spiritual affinity with God, but the simpler one of achieving relief from worldly anxieties or attaining possession of worldly desires. It was mainly through the intercession of the saint that God's help could be secured in attaining these goals. This was perhaps the reason that this phase witnessed the introduction of astrology, magic, belief in talismans and charms, and other forms of superstition as means of preserving the flow of *barakat* from the saint, who occupied the central position in the cult, to the devotee. As Trimingham summed it up, if Sufis in the *khanaqah* phase surrendered to God, and in the *tariqa* phase to a method of discipline, in the *ta'ifa* stage they surrendered to a person, the *barakat*-possessing saint of whose cult they were members.[9]

If we apply Trimingham's three-phase theory to the Sufis of Bijapur we will find that most of them fell into phases two and three. Indeed, for some Sufi groups the transition from the second to the third stage was a clearly observable phenomenon occurring in sixteenth- and seventeenth-century Bijapur. But though Trimingham's scheme represents an important contribution to our understanding of the internal changes that occurred within institutional Sufism from the eighth century to the present, it is insufficient to answer the main questions of this study respecting the Sufis' interaction with those social components external to them—the *ʿulama*, the court, and the non-Muslim population. Nor is it feasible in this study to take the Sufi order as the unit of analysis. Although affiliation with orders sometimes differentiated Sufis from each other, this was not found to be a consistent variable. Some belonged to two or more orders simultaneously; others

[9] Ibid., pp. 72, 102.

belonged to the same order but interacted in opposite ways with the key elements of their society. Still others belonged to no order at all.

On the other hand, the various social functions performed by Sufis have seemed to provide a far more meaningful way of differentiating the various individuals encompassed in this study. In his examination of the social organization of medieval Middle Eastern cities, Ira Lapidus has distinguished three types of Sufis: those who were well integrated into the social and religious world of the *'ulama*, those who represented a fanatically puritanical element waging personal wars on vice, and, their opposite, those who represented the "low life" of the cities and were, from the viewpoint of the *'ulama*, dangerously unorthodox.[10] This study seeks to extend and elaborate Lapidus's distinctions and to suggest a typology of Bijapur's Sufis based on what appear to have been their dominant roles. For the explicit assumptions of this investigation, implicit in Trimingham's study and absent in the classical approach to Sufi studies, are that Sufis formed an integral part of the social order in which they lived, that society acted on them at least as much as they acted on it, and that an understanding of the socio-historical milieu in which they lived is therefore crucial to our understanding of the Sufis themselves.

The plan of the study is based on this conceptual groundwork and follows a chronological as well as topical organization. This is because social types were not static entities, but seem to have changed and evolved over time along with the context of Bijapur's socio-historical development. Therefore, the broadest organizational principle of the study is chronology—the three parts treat the early, middle, and late periods respectively—while the chapters are topical in organization, most of them being devoted to one or another social type of Sufi. One of the pervading themes of this study is the interaction between the changing social context in which Sufis lived and the changing social functions they performed. It is, however, only by understanding the nature of the historical context and how it changed that we can understand the Sufis' responses to their environment and why these responses, reflected in their social roles, changed over time.

[10] Ira M. Lapidus, *Muslim Cities in the Later Middle Ages* (Cambridge, Mass.: Harvard University Press, 1967), p. 106.

one

ARRIVAL AND SETTLEMENT OF SUFIS

Chapter One

HISTORICAL SETTING: THE BIJAPUR PLATEAU TO THE COMING OF ISLAM

MAHARASHTRA AND KARNATAKA, 1100-1300

Except for its wooded northwestern region where knotted, twisted hills rise to the Western Ghats, the Bijapur plateau is uniformly flat and barren.[1] Three principal rivers, all rising in the Western Ghats and flowing to the east, drain this plateau—in the north the Bhima, in the center the Krishna, and in the south the Tungabhadra—and along their shallow valleys deep black soils permit extensive cultivation.[2] The black soils support the cultivation of cotton, a cash crop that provided the Kingdom of Bijapur with its export textile industry.[3] The main food crop produced is *juwar*, or millet, as rice and wheat are seldom grown in the area. All agriculture on the Bijapur plateau, however, depends upon a short and capricious summer monsoon, resulting

[1] As used in this study, the Bijapur plateau refers to that portion of the western Deccan plateau that had been most persistently administered by the 'Adil Shahi dynasty of Bijapur (1490-1686). It is bounded on the north by the Balaghat Range, on the west by the Western Ghats, on the south by the Tungabhadra River, and on the east by the 78th meridian, there being no natural barrier between the Kingdom of Bijapur and the neighboring Kingdom of Golconda to the east.

[2] In 1561 a Jesuit priest, writing to his superior in Goa, made the following assessment of the land between Belgaum (50 miles northeast of Goa) and Bijapur city: "Having left Belgaum, we made our way in our journeys through very good lands that spread before the eyes. In places may be found some good streams, extensive areas, much cattle: bulls, cows, buffaloes, sheep and goats; plenty of supplies: corn, jowar, grains, oils, cotton. And the land that yields this, very black and fertile, very flat" (John Correia-Afonso, "Bijapur Four Centuries Ago as Described in a Contemporary Letter," *Indica*, 1, No. 1 [March 1964], pp. 82 f.).

[3] See P. M. Joshi, "Some Notes on the Textile Industry and Trade of the Kingdom of Bijapur," *Proceedings, 7th Indian Historical Congress* (1944), pp. 262-65.

in a most precarious, dry climate. Situated in the "rain shadow" of the Western Ghats whose towering spurs trap most of the rain carried by the southwestern monsoon,[4] the Bijapur plateau averages only 20 to 25 inches of rainfall yearly, and is notorious as one of the most drought-prone regions of India.[5]

The cultural geography of the Bijapur plateau might best be described with reference to what modern geographers have called "core" or "nuclear" areas.[6] These areas, such as coastal Andhra, coastal Tamilnadu, deltaic Bengal or the Delhi Doab, generally exhibit highly developed and relatively stable cultural patterns. These include a fairly persistent political tradition, a nexus of trading routes and commercial markets, a considerable measure of social stratification based on a surplus agricultural base, and perhaps most crucial, a high degree of linguistic unity between all strata of the society. Between such core areas can be found what Bernard Cohn has called "shatter zones," or "the traditional regions through which large numbers of people passed either in military or peaceful invasion. In these areas, which in effect connect the nuclear regions, there is no persistent political tradition. Socially and culturally the area tends to be more of a mosaic than a relative unitary kind of social structure."[7]

With respect to its political heritage, its linguistic distribution, and its religious history over the past seven hundred years, the Bijapur plateau can be designated a shatter zone. From about the thirteenth century two distinct core areas formed on both the northern and southern extremities of the plateau. On the northern edge, from the Bhima River north to the upper Godavari basin,

[4] Stations in the higher altitudes of the Ghats have recorded over 200 inches yearly, while some stations only fifty to one hundred miles away on the lee side record only 20 to 40 inches a year (Raye R. Platt, *India: A Compendium* [New York: American Geographical Society, 1962], p. 24).

[5] See C. D. Deshpande, *Western India, A Regional Geography* (Dharwar, India: Students' Own Book Depot, 1948), p. 111; B. N. Sathyan, ed., *Mysore State Gazetteer, Bijapur District* (Bangalore: Government Press, 1966), pp. 164-66.

[6] See Platt, *India*, pp. 120-26; O. H. K. Spate, *India and Pakistan: A General and Regional Geography* (3rd edn.; London: Methuen & Co. Ltd., 1967), pp. 175-79.

[7] Cohn, "Regions Subjective and Objective: Their Relation to the Study of Modern Indian History and Society," in Robert I. Crane, ed., *Regions and Regionalism in South Asian Studies: An Exploratory Study* (Durham, N. C.: Duke University Press, 1967), p. 12.

there arose the nucleus of the Marathi-speaking core region now known as Maharashtra. Similarly, from the Tungabhadra River on the southern edge of the plateau south to the Kaveri River, Kannada-speaking peoples formed the nucleus of what is now called Karnataka.[8] Thus the center of the Bijapur plateau, especially the upper Krishna region including Bijapur city itself, straddled a cultural fault zone between Maharashtra and Karnataka, its inhabitants being fully integrated into neither Marathi nor Kannada culture, but only partially into one or the other.[9]

From the year 973 to 1190 a single Hindu state, the Western Chalukya Empire, had sprawled over the entire western half of the Deccan plateau from the upper Godavari basin down to the upper Kaveri region, thus linking Maharashtra politically with Karnataka. But in the late twelfth century this empire broke up, representing one of the early cases of an Indian political entity crumbling before the forces of linguistic regionalism. For in 1190 a Marathi-speaking family, the Yadava dynasty, delivered a *coup d'état* to the rapidly dissolving Chalukya power by declaring full authority over the northern, Marathi-speaking portion of the empire, and by establishing its capital in the nucleus of what was becoming the Marathi core region, i.e., in Devagiri in the upper Godavari basin.[10] Coinciding with this political development was the rise of vernacular Marathi, which provides us with an early example of the union of language and politics. The earliest known Marathi record (1187)[11] appeared almost simultaneously with the founding of the Yadava dynasty (1190). Moreover, as soon as they had achieved independence from the Chalukyas, the Marathi-speaking Yadavas established their mother tongue as the official

[8] The terms "Maharashtra" and "Karnataka" are used here not in a political sense but in a cultural, or more precisely, linguistic sense: Maharashtra as a primarily Marathi-speaking area, and Karnataka as a primarily Kannada-speaking area. Since the 1956 States Reorganization Act used linguistic boundaries as its criterion of political demarcation, these areas are currently represented by the states of the same names.

[9] This is reflected in the cartographic research of Raye R. Platt. See his map "India: Cultural-Political Core Areas and Boundaries," in Platt, *India*, p. 122.

[10] K. A. Nilakanta Sastri, *A History of South India* (3rd edn.; Madras: John Brown, Oxford University Press, 1966), pp. 197-99.

[11] A. S. Altekar, "The Yadavas of Seunadesa," in G. Yazdani, ed., *The Early History of the Deccan* (2 vols.; London: Oxford University Press, 1960), II, p. 571.

language of their dominion.[12] It was during the thirteenth century, too, that this area, specifically the upper Godavari region around Devagiri, produced the earliest poets to employ the Marathi vernacular as a vehicle for expression. Poets such as Jnanadeva (fl. 1290) and Namdev (fl. 1400) are widely acclaimed as among the finest writers in the history of Marathi literature. It is possible to conclude, then, that the widespread popularity of vernacular Marathi poetry and the official acceptance of that language by the government must have gone far in integrating Marathi-speaking peoples living outside the upper Godavari core region into the entity now known as Maharashtra.

Shortly after the Yadava dynasty proclaimed its rule in the North, a Kannada kingdom under the Hoysala dynasty likewise established its rule over the southern, or Kannada-speaking, portion of the former Chalukya Empire.[13] Thus were formed two regional kingdoms in the western Deccan, each claiming sway over, but not extending beyond, a given linguistic area. In this way linguistic frontiers between Maharashtra and Karnataka were given, by the beginning of the thirteenth century, political reenforcement. Since the breakup of the Chalukyas, writes the French anthropologist G. A. Deleury, "unity was never achieved again, Maharashtra and Karnataka being destined to undergo their evolutions separately."[14]

Further distinguishing these two cultural regions was the rise of regional *bhakti* movements, or popular devotional cults, which swept over the Bijapur plateau in the twelfth and thirteenth centuries. The rise of *bhakti* cults, which first appeared around the sixth century in the Tamil country and from there spread throughout much of the subcontinent, represents a crucial phase in the evolution of Hinduism. Often voicing popular opposition to the impersonal and ritualistic aspect of what has been called "the haughty Vedant creed" monopolized by the priestly Brahmin

[12] G. A. Deleury, *The Cult of Vithoba* (Poona: Deccan College, 1960), p. 9.

[13] As the Yadava capital had been established in the Marathi core region of Devagiri, far to the north of the Bijapur plateau, likewise the Hoysala capital was established far to the south of the Bijapur plateau, in the Kannada core region. This was Dwarasamudra, located about 100 miles west of the modern city of Bangalore.

[14] Deleury, *Vithoba*, p. 31.

caste,[15] *bhakti* devotional cults fostered the growth of an intense theism marked by a fervid devotion to a personal god. The goal of the *bhakta* (devotee), "to attain and enjoy for all time the blissful company of a personal god,"[16] contrasts sharply with the Vedic aim of merging in the unconsciousness of Brahman, or the Absolute.

The ardent theism of *bhakti* cults usually found expression in popular devotional hymns. One such collection of popular hymns, and one of the most influential devotional texts used by various *bhakti* sects since the ninth century, was the *Bhagavata Purana.* Composed around A.D. 850 in the Tamil country, this text reflects a nearly complete break with traditional religious ceremonies based on the Vedas, an absence of any qualification of birth or status for participation in devotional worship, and an identification of the wealthy and learned supporters of the status quo as the prime opponents of *bhakti.*[17] The intensely fervent *bhakti* of the *Bhagavata Purana* focused on the deity Krishna, whose devotees served him "by gazing at the images of Krishna, singing his praises, remembering him in meditation, keeping company with his devotees, touching their bodies, serving them lovingly, hearing them tell the mighty deeds of Krishna, and talking with them about his glory and his love."[18] The object of the *bhakta's* adoration did not always focus on Krishna, as it did in the *Bhagavata Purana*, though certainly the some twenty incarnations of Vishnu, including especially Krishna and Rama, provided the most popular objects of *bhakti* worship.[19]

Through their use of vernacular languages, as opposed to Sanskrit, *bhakti* movements in Maharashtra and Karnataka played important roles in both defining and distinguishing the Marathi

[15] Nicol MacNicol, *Psalms of Maratha Saints* (Calcutta: Association Press, 1919), p. 24.

[16] K. A. Nilakanta Sastri, *Development of Religion in South India* (Madras: Orient Longmans Ltd., 1963), p. 44.

[17] Thomas J. Hopkins, "The Social Teaching of the *Bhagavata Purana*," in Milton B. Singer, ed., *Krishna: Myths, Rites, and Attitudes* (Honolulu: East West Center Press, 1966), pp. 6, 11, 21.

[18] J. N. Farquhar, *An Outline of the Religious Literature of India* (London: Oxford University Press, 1920; reprinted Delhi: Motilal Banarsidass, 1967), p. 230.

[19] Max Weber, *The Religion of India*, trans. and ed. by Hans Gerth and Don Martindale (New York: The Free Press, 1967), p. 306.

and Kannada cultural traditions. One of the factors that had historically given the Brahmin community and Brahminical teachings their pan-Indian character was their common use of Sanskrit as the medium of religious intercourse. *Bhakti* movements, on the other hand, tended not to cut across linguistic lines precisely because of their capacity to reach non-Brahmin commoners in the vernacular idiom of particular linguistic regions. Far from integrating peoples of different cultural traditions, or core areas, *bhakti* movements tended to be regional phenomena that reinforced peoples' identity with particular regions.[20]

The *bhakti* cult that grew up among the Marathi people, the cult of Vithoba, was one of those devotional sects in which the deity worshipped, Vithoba, represented a form of Vishnu. This Vaisnavite cult, to this day an important force in Maharashtrian cultural life, grew around a temple to Vithoba on the banks of the Bhima River at Pandharpur. First mentioned in a 1249 grant made in its favor, the temple became, in Professor A. S. Altekar's words, "the most famous centre of popular worship in the Deccan towards the end of the thirteenth century."[21] An explanation for this popularity might be found in the social context in which the cult grew, a society in which caste rigidity and Brahmin supremacy had apparently become highly advanced. For in thirteenth-century Maharashtra both the Kshatriyas and Vaishyas had been brought down to the level of Sudras, and it was at this time that untouchability took on its present form and character.[22] Drawing its followers mainly from among lower class Maharashtrians,[23] the Vithoba cult, argues Deleury, "can be considered as a reaction against the overwhelming domination of the Brahmin community and their esoteric language, Sanskrit."[24]

In the earliest period of the cult's known history pilgrims to Pandharpur were not exclusively Maharashtrians, as many Kannadiga pilgrims also joined in Vithoba *bhakti*. This changed,

[20] For a discussion of this theme as it relates to Saivite *bhakti* and the growth of Tamil regionalism, see George W. Spencer, "The Sacred Geography of the Tamil Shaivite Hymns," *Numen*, 17 (December 1970), pp. 232-44.

[21] Altekar, "Yadavas," p. 566.

[22] Ibid., p. 567.

[23] R. G. Bhandarkar, *Vaisnavism, Saivism and Minor Religious Systems* (Varanasi: Indological Book House, 1965), p. 89.

[24] Deleury, *Vithoba*, p. 202.

however, at the end of the thirteenth century when the poet Jnanadeva (d. 1296), perhaps the greatest poet-saint of Marathi *bhakti*, migrated from the Maharashtrian heartland of the upper Godavari region to Pandharpur, thus linking the temple cult there with the cultural movement of the North. Deleury has described the poet's coming to Pandharpur as the greatest event in the history of the Vithoba movement, adding: "By working in Marathi, he brought within reach of the common people the understanding of their Sanskrit heritage, and also made it possible for them to realize their national culture which had been taking shape at the [Yadava] court of Devagiri."[25] It was Jnanadeva who first translated the devotional work *Bhagavad Gita* to vernacular Marathi. Indeed it is chiefly to the poet-saints who sang of Vithoba, especially Jnanadeva and Namdev, that early Marathi literature owes its development.[26] What is perhaps more important, the replacement of Sanskrit by the vernacular speech for devotional purposes brought language and religion together, no doubt strengthening a sense of unity among the masses of Vithoba *bhaktas*.[27]

South of Pandharpur, in the Kannada-speaking region of the Bijapur plateau, there arose another *bhakti* cult which, though differing from the Vithoba cult in significant respects, resembled the latter in its capacity to integrate many non-Brahmin peoples of its own linguistic area. This was the Lingayat movement, also known as Virasaivism.[28] Although there is some controversy over the antiquity and ultimate origin of Lingayat *bhakti*, scholars are agreed that it received its greatest momentum in the late twelfth century at the Chalukya capital of Kalyani. A reformer named Basava (ca. 1169) is credited with having initiated and expanded

[25] Ibid., p. 10.

[26] G. A. Grierson, *Linguistic Survey of India* (11 vols.; Calcutta: Government Printing, 1927), IV, pp. 12 f.; Deleury, *Vithoba*, p. 6. For biographical notices on these poet-saints, see the translations of Marathi folk stories about them in C. A. Kincaid, trans., *Tales of the Saints of Pandharpur* (Bombay: Oxford University Press, 1919). For translations of the poetry itself see MacNicol, *Psalms*.

[27] See M. G. Ranade, *Rise of the Maratha Power* (Bombay: University of Bombay, 1961), chap. 8.

[28] In common usage the term "Virasaivism" usually refers to the movement's religious aspect, and "Lingayat" to its social aspect. That is, Virasaivism essentially denotes the belief, and Lingayat the believer.

the revolutionary ideals of Lingayat *bhakti* amidst the collapsing social and political order of the Western Chalukya Empire.[29] In his teachings, Basava rejected the caste system, Brahmin supremacy, Brahminical rituals (sacrifices, pilgrimages, fasts, etc.), polytheism, and even the authority of the Vedic texts. In their place was substituted the Lingayat creed, open to all persons, which accorded absolute devotion to Siva. Lingayat *bhakti* was therefore Saivite, while most other *bhakti* movements, such as the Vithoba cult, were Vaisnavite. The most distinguishing feature of Lingayat *bhakti* was that, unlike Marathi *bhakti*, the deity's form was not represented in any temple image, but in the emblem or *linga* (hence the sect's name) invested upon the follower on initiation into the sect and carried by him, usually around the neck, at all times. The *linga* was the moving deity, the abode of Siva.[30] It was also a social leveller, enabling the wearer, theoretically at least, to achieve social equality with other Lingayats despite the rank of the caste from which he converted.[31] As in the case of the Vithoba cult at Pandharpur, the movement was propagated mainly by poets who devised vernacular literary forms to reach the commoners. In Marathi *bhakti* this was the *abhang*, a short lyrical utterance expressing religious longing;[32] in Lingayat *bhakti* it was the *vachana*, a type of popular Kannada verse that commended the Lingayat creed and, requiring no learning to understand, flooded the Kannada-speaking countryside.[33] Owing to the vernacular nature of its early propagation, Lingayat *bhakti* was an almost exclusively Kannada phenomenon.

Despite the egalitarian and anti-Brahminical fervor that char-

[29] Some writers, in fact, see this movement as a major cause of the empire's collapse. See R. G. Bhandarkar, *Early History of the Dekkan* (Calcutta: Susil Gupta Pvt. Ltd., 1957), p. 100.

[30] Hence the Lingayats have no spatial point of reference equivalent to Pandharpur, which is the focal point of Vithoba *bhakti* and the goal of the cult's pilgrimage. Lingayat doctrine explicitly denies sanctity not only to temples, but also to rivers, mountains, or any fixed shrine, and thus rejects the need for pilgrimages *per se*. The only "shrine" for the Lingayats is their own *linga*, carried with them constantly.

[31] Edgar Thurston, *Castes and Tribes of Southern India* (7 vols.; Madras: Government Press, 1909; reprinted London: Johnson Reprint Co. Ltd., 1965), IV, p. 249.

[32] MacNicol, *Psalms*, p. 11.

[33] Edward P. Rice, *History of Kanarese Literature* (London: Oxford University Press, 1921), p. 56.

acterized Lingayat *bhakti* when it expanded in the twelfth century, social distinctions gradually crept into the movement. Older converts began placing newer converts on a lower social scale than themselves, while great privileges were accorded a priestly class within the Lingayat community, the Jangams, who had asserted for themselves the right to define Lingayat "orthodoxy" in terms of certain rites and ceremonies in which they officiated.[34] In short, the *bhakti* aspect of personal devotion to the god Siva steadily gave way to the hierarchal and exclusive qualities of the very type that Lingayat *bhakti* had set out to oppose, and in the process Lingayats passed from a sect to a caste.[35]

The point at which this change occurred is difficult to determine. Although some authorities have placed it at the end of the seventeenth century,[36] the change would seem to represent a more prolonged process. While it is true that the Jangams had probably not become a closed and privileged caste until around the seventeenth century, there were other social institutions among the Lingayats that had achieved definite shape before that time. One such institution was the *math*, or the local monastery to which all *linga* wearers were affiliated, which formed a basic unit of Lingayat *bhakti* since the twelfth century.[37] Headed usually by a pious Lingayat *guru*, or teacher, the village *math* formed the center of the sect in terms of spiritual guidance, dis-

[34] R. E. Enthoven, *Tribes and Castes of Bombay* (3 vols.; Bombay: Government Central Press, 1920), II, pp. 371 f. The most important ceremony assuring the Jangam's status was the rite of initiation into the Lingayat fold, which the Jangam officiated by confirming the *linga* on the wearer.

[35] So far has institutionalization advanced today, that the only Lingayats now considering themselves "devotees" (*bhaktas*) are the Lingayat ascetics (*viraktas*), who themselves come from the priestly Jangam caste. The masses of non-Jangam Lingayats, on the other hand, consider "Lingayat" to refer simply to anyone who wears the *linga* and practices strict vegetarianism (William McCormack, "Lingayats as a Sect," *Journal of the Royal Anthropological Society*, 93 [January-June 1963], p. 61).

[36] See Herbert H. Risley, *The People of India*, ed. by William Crooke (2nd edn.; Delhi: Oriental Books Reprint Corporation, 1969), p. 78. See also Thurston, *Castes and Tribes*, IV, p. 250.

[37] The fervent spread of Lingayat *bhakti* in northern Karnataka evidently swallowed up several other Saivite sects in its wake. There is evidence that the *mathas* of some of these sects were simply transformed into Lingayat *mathas* (S. C. Nandimath, *A Handbook of Virasaivism* [Dharwar: Literary Committee, L. E. Association, 1942], pp. 9 f.).

tribution of food to the hungry, and Lingayat education.[38] It was to these *maths* that local poets who disseminated Lingayat teachings in their vernacular poems (*vachanas*), were attached. Linked together by affiliation with one of the five original monasteries, the local Lingayat *math* thus extended deep into many aspects of village life in Karnataka.

An equally important early Lingayat institution was the *guru* in his all-important capacity as mediator between a Lingayat devotee and the god Siva. At a very early time, it had become axiomatic among Lingayats that each follower must belong to a *math* and must have a *guru*.[39] This *guru*, furthermore, was to be accorded limitless reverence by the devotee. He was held in greater esteem not only than one's natural father, but also than the deity Siva, because, as one writer put it, "it is he who leads the soul to unity with Siva."[40] The *guru* also linked the devotee to the *math*, or monastery. As head of the *math*, the *guru* had absolute authority in all matters concerning the institution, including that of succession to its leadership.[41] In recent centuries the rights of the *guru* have become hereditary, just as the larger class of Jangams from which *gurus* come has developed into a closed caste that neither dines nor marries with non-Jangam Lingayats. But the broad and integrative social roles of the village *math* as well as the immense spiritual and social importance of the *guru* certainly predated the seventeenth century, and were ongoing traditions when Sufis first came to Bijapur.

By the fourteenth century, then, two core regions differentiated by two languages, two political traditions, and two *bhakti* movements, had crystallized both to the north and to the south of the central Bijapur plateau. The city of Bijapur itself and its surrounding countryside thus occupied the shatter zone between Maharashtra and Karnataka. Politically, the city was aligned with the North. First mentioned in inscriptions of 1074[42] and 1091[43] as a provincial seat (*rajadhani*) of the Chalukyas, Bijapur city

[38] Sastri, *Development of Religion*, pp. 116-18.

[39] Farquhar, *Religious Literature*, p. 261.

[40] Nandimath, *Virasaivism*, p. 54.

[41] Nilakanta Sastri, *Religion in South India*, p. 129.

[42] J. F. Fleet, "Sanskrit and Old-Canarese Inscriptions," *The Indian Antiquary*, 10 (May 1881), p. 129.

[43] J. F. Fleet, *Dynasties of the Kanarese District* (Bombay: Government Central Press, 1896), pp. 449 f.

became after 1190 the southernmost provincial seat of the Yadava dynasty.[44] For a long period after that, the city remained dominated by northern capitals.[45] Linguistically, on the other hand, the city is mainly Kannada-speaking and lies just to the south of the line demarcating Karnataka from Maharashtra. The city also occupies an intermediary position between the centers of Marathi and Kannada *bhakti*. Pandharpur, the focus of the Vithoba cult, is located just sixty-five miles northwest of Bijapur, while the birthplace of Basava, the great Lingayat reformer, is located just twenty-five miles southeast of Bijapur.[46]

Straddling this fault zone between Maharashtra and Karnataka, the Bijapur area eventually became not only the basis of Muslim political power under the 'Adil Shahi dynasty, but also the area of perhaps the highest Sufi settlement in the Deccan. This suggests that Muslim influence either in the form of political power or the settlement of Sufis could find the most fertile soil in such a shatter zone where Islam represented a third culture system located between the nuclei of two non-Muslim cultures.

Early Muslim Penetration of the Bijapur Plateau

Islam in western peninsular India first arrived with peaceful enclaves of Arab merchants, who settled along the Konkan and Malabar coasts. In A.D. 916-17 the Arab traveler Mas'udi described a settlement in Chaul (25 miles south of modern Bombay) of ten thousand Muslims whose ancestors had come from Arabia and Iraq to engage in the pepper and spice trade. This settlement, granted a degree of political autonomy by a local raja, was composed mainly of Arabs who had been born in Chaul and had intermarried considerably with the local population.[47] The pat-

[44] The southern boundary of the Yadava kingdom extended beyond Bijapur to the Malprabha River and the Krishna from the point where the Malprabha joins it (Fleet, *Dynasties*, p. 503).

[45] The Yadava Kingdom, the Delhi Sultanate, the Bahmani Sultanate, and after the Kingdom of Bijapur the Mughal Empire, the Maratha Confederacy, and the Bombay Presidency—all consecutively dominated the central Bijapur plateau from northern capitals.

[46] Basava's birthplace was Bagevadi, today the headquarters of the *taluk* of the same name.

[47] Mas'udi, *Les Prairies d'Or*, trans. into French by C. Barbier de Maynard and Pavet de Courteille (9 vols.; Paris: l'Imprimerie Imperiale, 1861-1917), II, pp. 85 f.

tern seems to have become well established along the coastal littoral, for in 1342 the renowned world traveler Ibn Battuta described much the same sort of Muslim colonies further south, in Malabar.[48] Thus, long before any Muslim government was planted on the Bijapur plateau, a tradition of Arab settlement had become firmly established along the western seaports of the peninsula. The significance of this trading tradition as an important type of Muslim influence in the Deccan was to be seen in the impact these seaports subsequently exerted on the economic and religious history of the Kingdom of Bijapur.[49]

The first Muslim military expeditions to the Bijapur plateau were sent by the Delhi Sultanate under the Khalaji dynasty (1290-1320). In 1296 'Ala al-Din Khalaji raided the Yadava capital of Devagiri, sacked it of its treasures, imposed tributary status on the Hindu kingdom and, after marching back to North India, seized the Delhi throne. This opened an era of repeated raids on the Deccan by armies of the Delhi Sultanate. In 1307 'Ala al-Din dispatched his favorite slave, Malik Kafur, to Devagiri to punish the Yadavas for not having sent several years' tribute to Delhi. This accomplished, he used Devagiri as a base for the sultanate's thrusts still deeper into the Deccan. In 1309 Malik Kafur raided and sacked Warangal in the eastern Deccan, and in 1311 he launched the most ambitious expedition yet: a march completely across the Bijapur plateau down to Dwarasamudra, the Hoysala capital, and to the Pandya dominions in Ma'bar adjacent to Sri Lanka. Between 1296 and 1311, then, both the Yadava and the Hoysala dynasties, as well as another contemporary dynasty in the eastern Deccan, the Kakatiyas of Warangal, had been defeated and pillaged, though not yet annexed, by the Delhi Sultanate.

The above invasions were essentially looting expeditions. Delhi made no initial effort to impose direct administrative control over any part of the Deccan. This policy changed in 1312, however,

[48] Ibn Battuta, *Travels in Asia and Africa, 1325-54*, trans. by H. A. R. Gibb (London: Routledge & Sons, 1929), pp. 230-34.

[49] Horses imported from Arabia through these ports maintained the Bijapur cavalry, which formed the backbone of the kingdom's military system. Textiles and peppers exported from the ports sustained the kingdom's economy to a great degree. Bijapur's social history was greatly affected by the influx of Iranians, Abyssinians and Arabs coming through these ports from the Middle East. The ports were also important for Bijapur's religious history in that they facilitated the influx of theologians and Sufis as well as the heavy pilgrim traffic going to and from Mecca.

when Ramadeva, the Yadava monarch who had acquiesced in the sultan's authority, died and was succeeded first by his son and later by his son-in-law, both of whom tried to sever all connections with Delhi. Full annexation of Maharashtra to the Delhi Sultanate, finally extinguishing the last remnants of the Yadava dynasty, was ultimately effected by 'Ala al-Din's successor, Sultan Qutb al-Din Khalaji (1316-20). Determined to impose direct administrative control over Maharashtra, the new sultan marched to Devagiri in 1318 and, after beheading the refractory son-in-law of Ramadeva, established a tradition of lasting Muslim political rule in the Deccan.

It seems to have been at this time that the city of Bijapur, formerly the southernmost provincial seat of the Yadavas and called by that dynasty Vijayapura (City of Victory), passed from Hindu to Muslim rule. In 1318, wrote the historian Barani, Sultan Qutb al-Din "appointed feudatories, rulers, and revenue-collectors over the territories of the Mahrattas,"[50] and Firishta adds that the sultan ordered the establishment of a number of garrisons extending as far south as Dwarasamudra.[51] An inscription on Bijapur's oldest mosque, the Karim al-Din Mosque, clearly indicates that from about 1318 the city of Bijapur had become one of the sultanate's provincial seats referred to by these historians.[52] Written

[50] Ziya al-Din Barani, *Tarikh-i Firuz Shahi*, ed. Saiyid Ahmad Khan. Persian printed edition (Calcutta: Asiatic Society of Bengal, 1862), p. 390. (Abridged English edition: H. M. Elliot and J. Dowson, eds., *The History of India as Told by its Own Historians* [8 vols.; Allahabad: Kitab Mahal, 1964], III, p. 215.)

[51] Muhammad Qasim Firishta, *Tarikh-i Firishta*. Persian lithograph (2 vols.; Lucknow: Nawal Kishor, 1864-65), I, p. 125. (Abridged English edition: John Briggs, trans., *History of the Rise of Mahomedan Power in India* [3 vols.; London, 1829; reprinted Calcutta: Editions Indian, 1966], I, p. 222.)

[52] A translation of the inscription is as follows: "Hail. In the *Saka* (year) 1242 [A.D. 1320] on (an auspicious?) day in the victorious reign of the illustrious Khudubudin [Sultan Qutb al-Din Khalaji], Malik Krimidin [Karim al-Din], the Governor (literally, 'appointed by him'), had a spacious mosque made at Vijayapuri (Bijapur) the Benares of the south. Revaiya, the carpenter from Salehautage (modern Salotgi near Bijapur) built the mosque. The Malik gave him a field, at the village of Bitur, (the measurement being) 24 *nitans* with 24 cubits and made it free from taxes and obstructions. (May there be) great prosperity" (Muhammad Nazim, "Bijapur Inscriptions," *Memoirs of the Archeological Survey of India*, No. 49 [Delhi: Manager of Publications, 1936], p. 25).

1. Karim al-Din Mosque, constructed c. 1320

in Old Marathi and dated 1320, or just two years after the coming of Qutb al-Din to Devagiri, this inscription states that a certain Malik Karim al-Din had been appointed governor of Bijapur by Sultan Qutb al-Din Khalaji.[53] It adds that this Karim al-Din had ordered the mosque to be constructed. But the tenuous nature of Muslim rule in Bijapur at this early date and the degree to which Islam had accommodated itself to indigenous forms is suggested by the very architecture of the Karim al-Din Mosque, certainly

[53] The archeologist Henry Cousens wrote, without citing his authority, that Karim al-Din was the son of the Khalaji general Malik Kafur, and that the latter had settled in Bijapur for some time before he died (Cousens, *Architectural Remains*, p. 42).

one of the most fascinating structures in Bijapur.[54] Its low squat pillars supporting long beams, not arches or domes, reflect the style of a Hindu temple more than anything Islamic, and betray what is obvious to the viewer and is also recorded in the inscription: that it had been built by local Hindu craftsmen.[55]

At the time Malik Karim al-Din was beginning to consolidate his governorship at Bijapur, important events were taking shape to the immediate south of the Muslim governor's jurisdiction. The repeated raids from Delhi that culminated in the extinction of Yadava sovereignty over Maharashtra and Delhi's annexation of that region in 1318 had provoked profound social and political repercussions. Since 1296 these raids had been steadily pushing Maharashtrian and Telugu warriors from defeated dynasties in the northern Deccan to the southern Deccan, especially the region immediately south of the Tungabhadra River in Karnataka. There these transplanted warriors began reestablishing themselves as the ruling elite for new warrior-states.[56]

One such warrior-state, the Kingdom of Kampili, was founded by a Maharashtrian chief who had fled from Devagiri to the Tungabhadra Valley following Malik Kafur's 1307 raid on the Yadava capital.[57] Centered on the southern banks of the Tungabhadra River and extending as far north as the Krishna River, this frontier state briefly functioned as a refuge for warriors retreating from the North until 1327, when the sultanate's armies finally conquered it.[58] The extinction of Kampili was followed

[54] See Figure 1.

[55] So extensive is the Hindu influence in this mosque that one of the first English scholars to visit Bijapur, James Bird, believed that it had originally been a Brahminical College (*agrahar*) which the Muslims converted to a mosque simply by adding a pulpit and inscribing the Islamic credo over it. (James Bird, "On the Ruined City of Bijapur," *Journal of the Bombay Branch, Royal Asiatic Society*, 1 [May 1884], p. 373). Henry Cousens, on the other hand, concluded that it was "a purely Muhammadan building erected from a miscellaneous lot of material obtained from one or more odd temples" (Cousens, *Architectural Remains*, p. 43).

[56] See Burton Stein, "Agrarian Integration in South India," in R. E. Frykenberg, ed., *Land Control and Social Structure in Indian History* (Madison: University of Wisconsin Press, 1969), p. 189.

[57] N. Venkata Ramanayya, *Kampili and Vijayanagara* (Madras: Christian Literature Society's Press, 1929), p. 15.

[58] The Raja of Kampili provided protection not only to Telugu warriors fleeing before Malik Kafur's armies in the upper Deccan, but even to Mus-

nine years later by the establishment of another and far more powerful warrior-state, the Vijayanagar Empire. Also centered on the upper Tungabhadra River, Vijayanagar accomplished what Kampili had failed to do: namely, to seal off South India below the Krishna from further attacks by the sultan's armies. Ruled predominantly by Telugu warriors, Vijayanagar was, in Nilakanta Sastri's words, "perhaps the nearest approach to a war-state ever made by a Hindu kingdom."[59] The kingdom remained a stalwart foe on the southern frontier of several Muslim sultanates, including the Kingdom of Bijapur.

As the Krishna River formed the boundary between Malik Karim al-Din's governorship at Bijapur and the new warrior-states to the south, Bijapur thus represented in the early fourteenth century a turbulent and remote outpost of the Muslim political frontier. It remained as such from 1296 to 1347, when a new Muslim state, the Bahmani Kingdom, opened a period of a closer, deeper, and more permanent Islamic rule over the plateau. This fifty-year span witnessed the rather turbulent period of transition in Bijapur from *Dar al-Harb* ("the abode of war") to *Dar al-Islam* ("the abode of peace"). It also witnessed the coming of Bijapur's earliest Sufis.

---

lim rebels who themselves had turned against the sultan's viceroy in Devagiri and had sought refuge in the South. See N. Venkata Ramanayya, *The Early Muslim Expansion in South India* (Madras: University of Madras, 1942), pp. 129-43; see also Venkata Ramanayya, *Kampili*, p. 18.

[59] Nilakanta Sastri, *History of South India*, p. 307.

Chapter Two

SUFIS AS WARRIORS

WARRIOR SUFIS OF BIJAPUR, 1296-1347

The first Sufis to enter the Bijapur plateau are designated in Muslim hagiographic literature as the "chalk of the dawn" of Islamic civilization in the Deccan.[1] They are the ones who are remembered as having first carried Islamic culture into the area. Yet such individuals are also generally pictured in the same literature as militant champions of Islam. Placed in a disturbed social and political context, namely *Dar al-Harb*, these Sufis usually emerge waging *jihad* (holy war), slaying countless infidels against overwhelming odds and, more often than not, being themselves slain and martyred in the process. The context, according to this body of literature, is the expanding Islamic frontier, the unit the armed Sufi, and the theme an ideological-military struggle. To what extent is this an accurate portrayal of the early Sufis of Bijapur?

Of all the Sufis of Bijapur those who appeared in the late thirteenth and early fourteenth centuries are perhaps the most difficult to understand. This is due in the first instance to the greater amount of time that elapsed between their lives and the recording of their lives in hagiographic literature, much of which was not compiled until as late as the nineteenth century. A second hindrance in interpreting these Sufis is the image of pious quietism commonly (and mistakenly) associated with Sufis in general, which conflicts with the militancy of the Sufis considered in this chapter. The first problem, the gap between the Sufi and his recorder, is heightened by the nature of the recorded sources themselves. In learning about the lives of Bijapur's earliest Sufis we are nearly entirely dependent upon a single class of literature, the *tazkiras* or biographies. These frequently amount to written versions of oral traditions that had been passed down for many

[1] *Rauzat al-Auliya, Tazkira-yi Auliya'-i Dar al-Zafar Bijapur*, comp. by Muhammad Ibrahim Zubairi. Persian MS (Copy A, Hyderabad: Asafiyah Library, Tazkira no. 266), p. 38. Hereafter cited as *Rauzat*, copy A.

generations among people associated with a *ta'ifa*, or saint-cult. As Trimingham observed, "the difficulty of utilizing the lives of the saints as historical sources is well recognized. Hagiographia is simply biography designed, and consequently distorted, to serve the cult of the saints. It forms an essential aspect of any study of the orders since these qualities, deeds, and manifestations are real to the believer, but they obscure the historical personality."[2]

Trimingham's caveat is worthwhile to bear in mind as indicating the worst dangers of using the *tazkira* literature. But it is by no means necessary to dismiss as inspired fiction the entirety of this literature. One must in the first place discern the presence or absence of a saint-cult around the Sufi described in the *tazkira*. If the Sufi whose life is being described forms the center of a living saint-cult having masses of devotees who regularly participate in the social functions associated with his tomb, it is fair to guess that *tazkiras* written about that Sufi, as Trimingham wrote, would exist primarily to serve that cult, and would consequently be distorted. There might be even more distortion if the compiler were related to either the familial or spiritual descendants of the saint. On the other hand, if there existed no saint-cult around the tomb of a Sufi whose life was compiled, the compiler would probably have had to rely upon surviving oral traditions that had no reference to a cult. While such traditions may still be distorted, they would not contain the same type of distortions that are typical of such cults. The point is that while all *tazkiras* consist of oral traditions that at some time were written down and that require, therefore, the same caution with which one approaches any oral tradition, it is not true that all *tazkiras* served a saint-cult and were distorted on that count.

Even in *tazkiras* that did serve a cult, present or past, there is still much information whose accuracy is highly probable. These biographies did not recount the lives of Sufis as if they had lived in an historical vacuum isolated from the world of sultans and rajas, of wars and famines, and all the other events or personages that form a part of a people's collective past and that serve as time-markers in that past. The *tazkiras* invariably make reference to events, persons, or places that were not necessarily intrinsic to the lives of the Sufis but that can be checked against other, non-hagiographic, sources for their accuracy. When this data—the

[2] Trimingham, *Sufi Orders*, p. 31.

setting against which the Sufis lived—has been accurately preserved intact through generations of oral transmission, it is reasonable to assume that the focal point of these traditions, the lives of the Sufis themselves, must likewise contain a kernel of accuracy. Moreover, even the *tazkiras*' information concerning the lives of the Sufis themselves can often be correlated with similar information found in the nonhagiographic sources. When such cross-verification of data is found—the occurrence of accurate historical information in the hagiographic literature or of hagiographic information in the historical literature—the researcher can assume that the accounts of the lives of the Sufis have been preserved in an accurate form.

In the case of the earliest Sufis of Bijapur our primary biographical source is the *tazkira* written by the historian Muhammad Ibrahim Zubairi, who compiled his work in 1825-26 from a number of written records, including earlier *tazkiras* and discourses (*malfuzat*) of Sufis, as well as from oral traditions given him by descendants of some of Bijapur's more prominent Sufis.[3] Whether or not Zubairi intended to append his biography of Bijapur's Sufis to his history of Bijapur, it seems that the author wrote the *Rauzat al-Auliya* with the same desire for historical accuracy and objectivity as he did his *Basatin al-Salatin*, a work described by one leading authority as "the most valuable chronicle of the kingdom of Bijapur."[4] When, for example, certain events of a Sufi's life were entered as traditions (*naql*) he indicated this to the reader and did not try to weave such traditions, some of which may be of doubtful authenticity, into the narrative. On the other hand, Zubairi, in common with all the other *tazkira*-writers encountered in this study, seldom sifted and weighed the various traditions he found in an effort to determine the relative accuracy of each. This was normally left for the readers to do. The remaining *tazkiras* mentioning Bijapur's earliest Sufis are Urdu works compiled in the early twentieth century by local scholars. One of these is the *Waqi'at-i Mamlakat-i Bijapur* ("Events of the Kingdom of Bijapur"), compiled by Bashir al-Din Ahmad in 1913-1914. The author, while in the service of the Nizam of

[3] Zubairi gives details of his sources in his preface. See *Rauzat*, copy A, p. 5.

[4] P. M. Joshi, "The Kingdom of Bijapur," Dissertation, University of London, 1935, p. iv.

Hyderabad as collector in Raichur District, gathered a good deal of oral and written information about both the Kingdom of Bijapur and its Sufis and published it in gazetteer form.[5] A similar such source is the *Tazkira-yi Auliya'-i Dakan* ("Biographies of the Saints of the Deccan"), compiled by 'Abd al-Jabbar Mulkapuri in 1912-1913.[6] The author was an inveterate biographer of prominent Muslims of the Deccan, having also compiled large biographical accounts of local scholars and nobles.

Bearing in mind the above comments on the sources, it may be possible to examine Bijapur's earliest and most militant Sufis. The life of the first Warrior Sufi of Bijapur, Shaikh Sufi Sarmast (d. 1281), is summarized in the following biographical account:

> He came to the Deccan from Arabia in the seventh century A.H. [thirteenth century A.D.] at a time when the Deccan was a land of unbelievers with no sign of Islam or correct faith anywhere. His companions—mendicants (*faqir*), disciples (*murid*), and soldiers (*ghazi*)—numbered over seven hundred. He settled in Sagar in Sholapur [District]. There, a zealous and anti-Muslim raja named Kumaram wished to expel him. . . . [Sufi Sarmast] and his companions having also prepared for a struggle, a bitter fight ensued. Heroes on both sides were slain. Finally the raja was slain by the hand of his daughter. Countless Hindus were killed, and at this time Lakhi Khan Afghan and Ni'mat Khan came from Delhi to assist him. Hindus were defeated and the Muslims were victorious. The rest of the Hindus, having accepted tributary status, made peace. Since by nature he was fundamentally not combative, Sufi Sarmast spread the religion of Muhammad and befriended the hearts of Hindus. Having seen his fine virtues and uncommon justice, many Hindus of that time became Muslims. . . . Finally he died in the year A.H. 680 [A.D. 1281].[7]

There are a number of problems with this account, not the least of which is that the compiler did not reveal his own sources for

[5] The author gives details of his sources in his preface. See *Waqi'at-i Mamlakat-i Bijapur*, comp. by Bashir al-Din Ahmad. Urdu lith. (3 vols.; Agra: Mufid-i 'Am Press, 1915), I, pp. 18-22. Hereafter cited as *Waqi'at*.

[6] *Tazkira-yi Auliya'-i Dakan*, comp. by 'Abd al-Jabbar Mulkapuri. Urdu lith. (2 vols.; Hyderabad: Hasan Press, 1912-13). Hereafter cited as *Tazkira-yi Auliya*.

[7] *Tazkira-yi Auliya*, I, pp. 460 f.

the narrative. The chronology of the events described here also contains problems. We know that Sufi Sarmast is buried in Sagar,[8] a hill fort located approximately seventy miles east of Bijapur, and that according to this passage he died in the year 1281. It is also stated in this passage that Sufi Sarmast received military assistance from officers of the Delhi Sultanate, suggesting that the Sufi was in some way associated with the sultanate's early military expeditions in the Deccan. And we can also use nonhagiographic sources to check certain points mentioned in the *tazkira*. The historian Zia al-Din Barani, who lived from the 1280s to about 1360 and was therefore contemporary with the events he described, wrote that Lakhi Khan Afghan, who was one of the sultanate's officers mentioned in the *tazkira*, was appointed viceroy of the Deccan in the year 1318.[9] This is the first mention in the historical literature of this officer's service in the Deccan; the other officer mentioned in the *tazkira*, Ni'mat Khan, is not mentioned at all in this literature. This means that the Sufi's death, which according to the *tazkira* occurred in the year 1281, would have taken place fifteen years before the earliest raids of the upper Deccan by the sultanate's armies, and a full thirty-seven years before the annexation of Maharashtra, including the Bijapur and Sagar region, by the sultanate. If, then, Sufi Sarmast received any assistance from officers of the Delhi Sultanate, it could not have been before 1318, which was when such armies first penetrated as far south as Sagar.

This chronological discrepancy might be resolved in several ways. One interpretation would be that Sufi Sarmast lived at a slightly later time than that given in this account, and that he was actually associated with an expedition to Sagar led by Lakhi Khan in the 1320s. Although there is no historical record of such expeditions having been carried out, such expeditions would certainly have fallen within the province of a Deccan governor's normal activities, particularly since Sagar was located on the remote frontier where the collection of tribute would likely have demanded the governor's military intervention. In support of this interpretation one could cite the likelihood that the date of the

[8] G. Yazdani, "Inscriptions of Shahpur, Gogi, and Sagar," *Epigraphia Indo-Moslemica* (1931-32), p. 10.

[9] Barani, *Tarikh-i Firuz Shahi*, p. 390. (Elliot and Dowson, *History of India*, III, p. 215.)

Sufi's death, being a figure, has been more susceptible to distortion through generations of oral transmission than have matters of factual content such as the Sufi's association with Lakhi Khan Afghan. Moreover, the Sufi's association with Delhi prior to his coming to Sagar can be further sustained by an earlier passage in this *tazkira* that identifies him as belonging to the Chishti order of Sufis, which at that time was primarily associated with North India, especially the city of Delhi.[10] And a local tradition at Sagar, his place of burial, identifies him as a disciple of the well-known saint Nizam al-Din Auliya (d. 1325),[11] a leading member of the Chishti order, many of whose disciples migrated to the Deccan.

While the above data would point to Sufi Sarmast's origins in northern India and his affiliation with the Delhi Sultanate's early raids in the Deccan, it could be argued that the chronology given in the narrative is correct and that his expedition to Sagar actually did precede the sultanate's Deccan invasions. If he were not affiliated with the armies of Delhi it is possible that he had spilled over on the Bijapur plateau from Arab trading enclaves on the Konkan Coast. The statement that "he came to the Deccan from Arabia" would seem to support this conjecture. However, the Arab colonies on the Konkan Coast, well established since at least the ninth century, seem to have been peaceful throughout their existence; there are no references in the historical literature to Arab colonists invading the upland Deccan plateau from these coasts. Moreover, we need not assume that Sufi Sarmast arrived in Sagar directly from the Middle East. The only other *tazkira* treating the biography of Sufi Sarmast extensively, the *Waqi'at-i Mamlakat-i Bijapur*, also gives him an Arab origin, in fact locating his origins in Samaria where he is said to have been a noble, and giving him a lineage stretching back to the Caliph 'Umar. From Samaria this account traces his travels to Mathura in North India, and from there to Sagar, adding that he was accompanied on this last journey by 1,407 palanquins of Sufis—certainly a hyperbolic expression indicating his affiliation with the general movement of settlers and armies from North India to the Deccan in the early fourteenth century.[12] This seems to be the most likely interpretation of the Sufi's origin and means of arriving in the Deccan,

[10] *Tazkira-yi Auliya*, I, p. 460.

[11] Yazdani, "Inscriptions," p. 10 fn.

[12] *Waqi'at*, III, p. 363.

even though the *Waqi'at*, like the *Tazkira-yi Auliya*, fixes his death date in 1281. This must certainly be an error since, as noted above, the first penetration of the Sagar region by Northerners did not occur until 1318.

The above discussion of Sufi Sarmast's origins and means of arrival in Sagar is useful in the more important matter of determining the nature of his activities vis-à-vis the area's non-Muslim population. The passage quoted above from the *Tazkira-yi Auliya* has apparent contradictions. We first see him locked in mortal combat with a local Hindu raja named "Kumaram." Then he is portrayed as a gentle and peace-loving paradigm of virtue on whose account many Hindus were won over to Islam. One way to resolve these contrasts is to dismiss the historicity of most of the account and interpret what resulted in the written narrative as a garbled confusion of hagiographic and political traditions. According to such an interpretation certain facts and legends pertaining to the officers or sultans of Delhi, particularly 'Ala al-Din Khalaji, Malik Kafur, and Muhammad bin Tughluq, became through centuries of oral transmission attributed to some real or fictitious Sufi. Sanctified as a saint, this Sufi thus became a folk Indo-Muslim archetype whose historical function was to render a degree of religious legitimacy to Delhi's military conquest of the Deccan. Such an interpretation might explain the identity of the hundreds of followers that in both *tazkiras* were said to have accompanied Sufi Sarmast: though called "Sufis" in the hagiographic tradition for purposes of legitimacy, they in fact might have been the body of armed retainers or mercenaries in service to some Muslim military adventurer. One might also argue that Sufi Sarmast's residence in the well-fortified hill fort of Sagar represents another confusion of the Sufi with some Muslim officer. Or, one could observe that "Kumaram" (Kumara Ram or Ramanatha in the non-Muslim sources), who in the Muslim hagiographic version was murdered by the Sufi's daughter, was according to one of the Kannada versions murdered by the officers of the sultan of Delhi.[13] This represents a clear confusion of the Muslim hagiographic tradition with political history as remembered by Hindus of the area, and one authority has re-

[13] K. A. Nilakanta Sastri and N. Venkataramanayya, *Further Sources of Vijayanagara History* (3 vols.; Madras: University of Madras, 1946), I, pp. 28 f.

cently noted that already by the sixteenth century "Kumara Ram had become an almost legendary figure, whose exploits against the Muslims in particular figure in works still read in Karnataka."[14] If Sufi Sarmast's adversary has become a semi-legendary figure among Hindus of the Deccan, it seems reasonable to suppose that Sufi Sarmast himself might likewise have become a semi-legendary figure among Muslims of the region.

From another perspective, however, it can be cogently argued that a real Sufi Sarmast did in fact exist apart from fourteenth-century Muslim officers or legends of such officers, but that he was not independent from the Muslim armies. If the Sufi had been associated with one of the early armies of Delhi, both his having settled in the hill fort of Sagar and his having received military assistance from several Afghan commanders become plausible. Moreover, if this narrative were entirely legendary, there would be no need for it to have gone beyond a description of his *jihad* or holy war against Kumara Ram with perhaps some elaborations and embellishments built around that event. But the *Waqi'at* version, for example, briefly relates the lives of his four sons, an addition that would seem to serve no utility in establishing the valor or sanctity of Sufi Sarmast and is therefore not likely to be legendary. In fact this is one aspect of the account that accords perfectly with what one might expect to find operating in a political and social frontier zone such as the fourteenth-century Bijapur plateau. One son was murdered by non-Muslims in Sagar, one fled to Gulbarga, and the other two to Awadh.[15] These facts, extraneous to the legend, point to the chaotic situation of Sagar at that time as against the safer, more established centers of Muslim population further to the north.

Viewing the historical Sufi Sarmast as having combined the qualities of both warrior and Sufi, as opposed to seeing none but a legendary Sufi Sarmast emerging from a garbled confusion of two separate traditions, helps in resolving other apparent contradictions in the narrative. According to the *Tazkira-yi Auliya'-i Dakan*, his seven hundred companions were composed of soldiers (*ghazis*), Sufi disciples (*murids*), and mendicants (*faqirs*). Assuming that the "*faqirs*" referred to any or all of the undifferentiated

[14] J. Duncan Derrett, *The Hoysalas* (London: Oxford University Press, 1957), p. 159.

[15] *Waqi'at*, III, p. 363.

camp-followers that accompanied the expeditions of those days, it remains to reconcile the presence of both *ghazis* and *murids* among Sufi Sarmast's followers—the former usually connoting fighters and the latter mystics. Upon close examination, however, these terms are found to be not at all mutually exclusive, but in fact identical when placed in proper context. For while "*ghazi*" generally means a soldier, it refers more specifically to a religious fighter in the cause of Islam, and is therefore a term closely identified with the early period of Islamic history, the period of its military-political expansion. Similarly, while "*murid*" refers generally to a disciple of a Sufi, by the thirteenth century when the development of Sufi orders was passing into its *tariqa* phase, the term also denoted a man who granted a quasi-mystical, quasi-militant leader an unquestioning and even fanatical obedience. Hence, it is possible not only that *ghazis* and *murids* both accompanied Sufi Sarmast to the Deccan, but also that in the context of the early fourteenth-century Islamic frontier in India the two terms refer to the same persons. On the one hand they were, as *ghazis*, fighters for Islam; on the other they were, as *murids*, fanatically devoted followers of their *pir*.

This interpretation might clarify the nature of Sufi Sarmast's alleged role in the conversion of Hindus to Islam. Given what we know of the initial reaction to other Muslim armies in the Deccan during the late thirteenth century, it is reasonable to assume that some sort of military engagement did take place between Sufi Sarmast's group of warrior-followers and the indigenous peoples of the Bijapur plateau. In this case the Sufi's purported role in the peaceful conversion of Hindus to Islam would seem highly unlikely, and probably represents an embellishment that accrued to the tradition over centuries of oral transmission. On the other hand it is quite possible that Sufi Sarmast, as an armed Sufi adventurer accompanying a North Indian army, did attempt conversions in the manner often considered typical for Islam—by the sword. But his success in this endeavor must certainly have been limited. For there appears a suicidal quality about the penetration of a militant Sufi in territory which, though politically fragmented, was still dominated by non-Muslims.

There exists more information about another Warrior Sufi of Bijapur, Pir Ma'bari Khandayat. This Sufi, who died in Bijapur in the early fourteenth century, clearly illustrates the case of a

Sufi accompanying one of Delhi's military expeditions to Bijapur and participating in the struggle for Muslim control of that city. In his *Rauzat al-Auliya*, Muhammad Ibrahim Zubairi wrote,

> It is known that he was born and raised in Ma'bar . . . on the coast of the salty sea. During the period of 'Ala al-Din Khalaji, the Shah of Delhi, he accompanied the camp of the army of Islam in the year A.H. 710 [A.D. 1310-11] when buried treasures of gold and silver came to the hands of the Muslims and the victory of Islam was effected.[16]

In this instance there is no chronological confusion between the hagiographic and the political narrative traditions. For it was in the year 1311 that Sultan 'Ala al-Din Khalaji sent Malik Kafur on an expedition to the extremity of South India to bring the Kannadiga and Tamil peoples under the suzerainty of Delhi. Having seized Dwarasamudra in the spring of 1311, the Malik's army then moved on Ma'bar, the Arab term for the southern Coromandel coast adjacent to Sri Lanka. We know from Arab accounts written around the turn of the fourteenth century that flourishing colonies of Muslim merchants then lived along this coast.[17] Furthermore, the contemporary historian Amir Khusrau wrote that while in Ma'bar Malik Kafur's army "was joined by some Musulmans who had been subjects of the Hindus, now no longer able to offer them protection."[18] Hence it is most likely that Pir Ma'bari Khandayat, whose very name verifies his origin in Ma'bar, joined the army of Malik Kafur in the Tamil country in 1311 and moved with it back north as far as Bijapur, where the Sufi evidently remained while the army continued on its return to Delhi.[19]

[16] *Rauzat*, copy A, p. 40.

[17] 'Abd Allah Wassaf, *Tazjiyat al-Amsar wa Tajriyat al-Asar* (*Tarikh-i Wassaf*). Persian lithograph (Bombay, 1853), pp. 301 f. (Abridged English edition: Elliot and Dowson, eds., *History of India*, III, pp. 32 f.). See also S. Krishnaswami Aiyangar, *South India and Her Muhammadan Invaders* (London: Oxford University Press, 1921), pp. 69-73.

[18] Amir Khusrau, *Khaza'in al-Futuh*, ed. Syed Moinul Haq. Persian lithograph (Aligarh: Muslim University, 1927), pp. 161 f. (Abridged English edition: Elliot and Dowson, eds., *History of India*, III, p. 90).

[19] According to S. Krishnaswami Aiyangar, Malik Kafur's southern route to South India passed through Bijapur. Presumably, too, the army returned north via the same route. (See Krishnaswami, *South India*, p. 102.)

2. Ma'bari Khandayat

It is not clear why Pir Ma'bari Khandayat remained in Bijapur while Malik Kafur's huge army, laden with treasures seized from further south, rumbled north on its triumphant return to Delhi. Watching this formidable army with all its camp pass through their city—an army known to be returning from having sacked some of the richest temples of South India in the name of an alien religion—the local residents of Bijapur must have felt a sullen bitterness. Furthermore, the year was 1311, seven years before Bijapur was finally brought under the Muslim governorship of Malik Karim al-Din. It is therefore likely that when Pir Ma'bari Khandayat separated himself from the army with which he was so clearly associated, the local population would hardly have welcomed him. The hagiographic literature relates the conflict that followed his arrival at Bijapur:

> It is said that in the time that arrogant infidels, surly Hindus and powerful and vain rajas ruled [Bijapur] by force, he came here and waged *jihad* against the rajas and rebels. And with his iron bar he broke the heads and necks of many rajas and drove them to the dust of defeat. Many idolators who by the will of God had guidance and blessings, repented from their unbelief and error, and by the hand of [Pir Ma'bari] came to Islam. [Nonetheless] by the hands of wretched idolators and erring unbelievers, he and a group of his sons and friends drank the cup of martyrdom.[20]

A local oral tradition collected in 1844 further attributed to Pir Ma'bari Khandayat the expulsion of a group of local Brahmins from their *agrahar*, or Brahmin village, at Bijapur.[21]

Notwithstanding this portrayal of Pir Ma'bari as a fierce wager of *jihad* wielding an iron bar,[22] some recent works have interpreted the Sufi in a peaceful light. The *Bombay Gazetteer* for 1884 stated that around 1305 he came to the Deccan as a "missionary" and converted to Islam a large number of Jains whose descendants are among the cultivating classes of Bijapur District.[23]

[20] *Rauzat*, copy A, p. 39.

[21] Bird, "Ruined City of Bijapur," p. 374.

[22] His name, Khandayat, literally means "blunted bar." A miniature painting of the Sufi is reproduced in Figure 2.

[23] *Gazetteer of Bombay Presidency. Bijapur District* (Bombay: 1884), 23, p. 282.

This passage was cited by Thomas W. Arnold in his *Preaching of Islam* to support his contention that the most important agents in the spread of Islam in the Deccan were peaceful Muslim saints.[24] While Arnold's general argument may have a good deal of validity, an argument that will be explored in greater depth in the present study, it would seem that in the case of Pir Ma'bari he chose the wrong example to illustrate it. For the question arises: why did Arnold cite a tradition, the 1884 *Bombay Gazetteer*, which presented only one side, the "peaceful missionary" side, of Pir Ma'bari's life? One possibility is that the hagiographic traditions such as the one quoted above were unknown to Arnold and that he had available to him only the *Gazetteer* version. Another possibility is that Arnold was aware of the Sufi's militancy in the hagiographic traditions but chose to ignore it, an interpretation that would accord with the general effort in his books to revise the simplistic nineteenth-century image of Islam as a religion of the sword. But it does not suffice to correct one distorted view by presenting an equally distorted, if opposite, view. If the Sufi's peaceful character can be supported by both written and oral traditions, so can his militancy. In view of the tendency of both oral and written traditions to extol or even fabricate the pious qualities of Sufis, it is most likely that Pir Ma'bari, like Sufi Sarmast, was in reality a militant Sufi and only acquired the reputation of a peaceful missionary through generations of oral transmission of his life story.

Although Sufi Sarmast and Pir Ma'bari Khandayat shared in common an affiliation with Muslim armies in the Deccan, there were other Sufis who appeared in the Bijapur plateau in the late thirteenth and early fourteenth centuries who, though not directly linked with any known military expedition, are nonetheless remembered for their combative prowess and martyrdom. Shaikh 'Ali Pahlavan, a companion of Sufi Sarmast, migrated to a town near Kurnool where he and his followers became engaged in a struggle with Hindus, again described as a *jihad*, and were killed.[25] Shaikh Shahīd (d. 1272-73), who was a disciple (*khalifa*)

[24] Arnold, *The Preaching of Islam: A History of the Propagation of the Muslim Faith* (2nd edn.; London: Constable & Company, Ltd., 1913), p. 271.

[25] *Waqi'at*, III, p. 377. Kurnool is located about 150 miles east by southeast of Bijapur on the Tungabhadra River near the point where that river joins the Krishna.

of Sufi Sarmast, is said to have migrated with four companions to Talikota, a town fifty miles southeast of Bijapur. There, he and his companions engaged a number of Hindus in combat and, after killing "countless numbers" of them, were themselves slain. Their burial place in Talikota is named *ganj-i shuhada*, or "treasure of martyrs."[26] Still another early Sufi, Pir Jumna (d. 1304), is said to have come to Bijapur city "in the time of flourishing unbelief," i.e., immediately before the governorship of Karim al-Din, and waged *jihad* which "cleansed the area of idol-worship."[27] Another source adds that despite the Sufi's many virtues, in the year 1304 Hindus persecuted and killed both him and his forty or fifty followers.[28]

Even the titles of many of these Sufis, given to them after their deaths, suggest their essentially martial character. *Shahīd* means "martyr." Sufi Sarmast's title was *asad al-auliya*, or "lion of the saints." Another Sufi who might have been a Warrior Sufi was Saiyid Husam al-Din Tigh Barahna (d. 1281) who, after having become a disciple of his father, migrated from Delhi to Gulbarga long before that city was settled by Muslims.[29] Although one writer[30] has associated Husam al-Din with the peaceful expansion of Islam in the Deccan, his title *tigh barahna*, which means "naked sword," would suggest otherwise.[31]

What, in sum, can be said of the Warrior Sufis? It is instructive to note where they appeared and the timing of their arrival and disappearance in Deccan history. By the beginning of the fourteenth century the Bijapur plateau represented not only a fluid shatter zone located between the stable Marathi and Kannada core regions, but also a volatile frontier zone located between an aggressive, expanding Islamic state to the north and a new state to the south—the Vijayanagar Empire—which owed its existence mainly to Hindu reaction to the movements to the North. "The

[26] *Tazkira-yi Auliya*, I, pp. 410 f.

[27] *Rauzat*, copy A, p. 38.

[28] *Tazkira-yi Auliya*, I, pp. 222 f.

[29] Ibid., pp. 393 f.

[30] Mohammad Abdul Aziz, "The Deccan in the Fifteenth Century," *Journal and Proceedings of the Asiatic Society of Bengal*, NS 21 (1925), p. 570.

[31] He acquired this title from the fact that he always carried in his hand a naked sword. (*Tazkira-yi Auliya*, I, p. 394.)

foundation of the empire," wrote Nilakanta Sastri, "was the culmination of a strong wave of religious revival and political excitement caused by the Sultanate of Delhi seeking to impose its sway on the Deccan and farther south in the early fourteenth century."[32] Rulers of Vijayanagar generously patronized the whole spectrum of Hindu thought and practice. On the one hand they commissioned scholars to write commentaries on the Vedic classics; on the other they supported the *bhakti* movements of the central Deccan—Lingayatism and Vaisnavism—by making frequent journeys to popular shrines and by granting both shrines and temples lavish endowments in land and cash.[33] This anti-Muslim bulwark south of the Tungabhadra River thus placed the Bijapur plateau, as the southernmost frontier of the Delhi Sultanate's authority, in a position of social instability and created ripe conditions for communal confrontation.

The timing of the Warrior Sufis' arrival and disappearance in Deccan history provides further clues to the nature of their role. They began to arrive around the time of the first invasions from Delhi, and began to disappear around the time of the establishment of the Bahmani Kingdom (1347-1489). The fifty-year period encompassed by these two events, from 1296 to 1347, thus saw the passing of the Bijapur plateau from *Dar al-Harb* to *Dar al-Islam*. This suggests that these Sufis were not able to exist entirely independent of some kind of Muslim military presence in the Deccan. It also suggests that their existence was not necessary after Islam had achieved full political expression in a region that theretofore had been a Muslim frontier. The Warrior Sufi thus appears as the most typical kind of Sufi during the intervening half century when this part of the Deccan was subjected to repeated raids by armies from the North and was experiencing the social turmoil that accompanied the transition from Yadava to Muslim rule.

The vehicle that brought most of the Warrior Sufis to this part of India was the large-scale Muslim military expeditions to the Deccan, which began in 1296 and continued regularly through the first half of the fourteenth century. Sufis like Pir Ma'bari Khandayat probably formed a part of the vast entourage that so

[32] Nilakanta Sastri, *Development of Religion*, p. 125.
[33] Ibid., pp. 125 ff.

often accompanied large armies in those days, just as it has been argued that Sufis settled the islands of Southeast Asia by accompanying merchant ships sailing across the Indian Ocean to Java, Sumatra, and the Spice Islands.[34] As Sufis in the latter instance stepped off the ships and formed their own local following and institutions, so also did Warrior Sufis of the early fourteenth century splinter off from the main armies of the North and form their own bands, or simply bring with them the nucleus of followers that they had already mobilized within those armies.

It would be convenient here to place the Warrior Sufis in the broader context of Islamic history as it had evolved by the fourteenth century. Sir Hamilton Gibb has made some significant observations regarding the relationship between the *ghazi*, or holy warrior, and the Sufi in the fourteenth century. He has noted that the Arabic word *ribat*, which originally meant the forts or fortified lines (literally, "pickets") staffed by fighting *ghazis* along the Muslim frontier, came to mean for the Sufis the hospices where devotees congregated to lead their religious life (equivalent to *khanaqah* in Persian).[35] This development was not coincidental, for in the early years of Islamic history the fighting life of the *ghazi* had temporarily merged with the rise of the ascetic and mystical movement within Islam. "Early Muslim asceticism," writes Gibb, "was dominated by fear of Hell. Since death on Jihad was the only sure passport to Paradise, it came about that in the early days ascetics had generally taken a prominent part in the frontier warfare."[36] The term *jihad*, like *ribat*, also reflects this development. Early Sufis applied the term to the inward and spiritual struggle against the temptations of this world as well as to the war against non-Muslims, although with the stabilization of the Islamic frontiers Sufis gradually withdrew from frontier warfare.

There is considerable evidence, however, that by the thirteenth and fourteenth centuries certain groups of Sufis living along the worldwide Muslim frontier had not yet withdrawn from active participation in frontier warfare. For example in Anatolia some Sufis, or "*ghazi-babas*," conferred a measure of religious legitimi-

[34] Anthony H. Johns, "Sufism as a Category in Indonesian Literature and History," *Journal of Southeast Asian History*, 2 (July 1961), pp. 13-17.

[35] H. A. R. Gibb, Introduction to Ibn Battuta, *Travels*, pp. 33 f.

[36] Ibid., p. 33.

zation on the acts of the fighting *ghazis* living with them on the frontier.[37] Paul Wittek, the historian of early Ottoman history, has written,

> We find in the biographies of the Mevlevi shaikhs, by Eflaki, written about the middle of the fourteenth century, clear traces of a ceremony of granting the title of Ghazi, comparable to that of investure with knighthood in the West. We are told how one of the emirs of the house of Aydin was designated as "Sultan of the Ghazis" by the shaikh of the Mevlevi darvish order. From the hands of the shaikh he received the latter's war-club, which he laid on his own head and said: "With this club will I first subdue all my passions and then kill all enemies of the faith." This ceremony means that the emir accepted the shaikh as his "senior," and his words show that the quality of Ghazi also involved ethical obligations.[38]

The *ghazi* and the *ghazi-baba*, the two ideal types of the Anatolian frontier, are also seen in the exploits of *ghazi*-led Turkoman tribes and a certain Sari Saltuk, a thirteenth-century Sufi whose heroic deeds were expounded in a fifteenth-century hagiography, the *Saltuk-nama*. Here, Sari Saltuk is portrayed as exhorting the Turkomans of Anatolia to take up war against the Christians, and his exhortations generally led to war and resulted in victory.[39] This phenomenon of Anatolian *ghazi-babas* consecrating the warlike activities of *ghazis* has been explained in terms of the *ghazis'* need to find religious legitimization in an area where formal Islamic institutions had not yet been established. Thus the early *ghazis* of Anatolia and the states they founded "linked themselves with the only Islamic organization available in the marches which possessed any dynamic element—the wandering Turkish *dara-*

[37] In using the term "*ghazi-baba*" I am following the discussion of Huriçihan Ghaznavi in her "The Kizilbas Sect and its Relationship to the Ottoman Central Government," M.A. thesis, University of Wisconsin, 1972, p. 16.

[38] Wittek, *The Rise of the Ottoman Empire* (London: Luzac and Co. Ltd. for The Royal Asiatic Society of Great Britain and Ireland, 1971), p. 39.

[39] Halil Inalcik, *The Ottoman Empire: the Classical Age, 1300-1600*, trans. by Norman Itzkowitz and Colin Imber (New York: Praeger Publishers, 1973), p. 187.

wish, the *bavas* from Central Asia who accompanied, followed, and fortified the warriors."[40]

Another case of Sufis actively participating in frontier warfare is seen in northwestern Iran during the late fifteenth century, when the Safawi order of Sufis based at Ardabil became militantly transformed into a dynamic force from which grew the Persian Safawi dynasty that ruled Iran from 1501 to 1722. Michel Mazzaoui, who thus far has made the most exhaustive inquiry into the origins of the Safawi state, noted the geographic position of Ardabil straddling the frontier between Islam and the predominantly Christian Caucasus. "For all of a sudden now," wrote Mazzaoui referring to the period around 1456, "the *murids* of the Order became the *guzat-i sufiya* [Sufi *ghazis*], and under the leadership of Gunaid and Haidar we see them fighting in large numbers against the Christian enclave of Trapezund, or against the Georgians of the Caucasus. It is no more the heart of the Muslim world which attracts them . . . it is no more the *Dar al-Islam* but the *Dar al-Harb*. Overnight they have become *gazis* fighting the unbelievers along the Muslim frontiers of the north."[41]

[40] Trimingham, *Sufi Orders*, p. 68.

[41] Michel M. Mazzaoui, *The Origins of the Safawids: Si'ism, Sufism, and the Gulat* (Wiesbaden: Franz Steiner Verlag, GmbH, 1972), p. 74. The contemporary chronicler Fazl Allah bin Ruzbihan Khunji, though a Sunni and a critic of the Safawi movement, confirms that the movement was seized by a *ghazi* spirit. With reference to Shaikh Haidar, the chronicler wrote: "I have heard that he made several thousand pikes, coats of mail, swords, and shields . . . because he wished to teach his adepts (*murid*) as their leader (*murshid*). When all these things were ready according to his wishes, innumerable crowds rallied around him—outwardly sufis and *murids*, but inwardly rebellious demons; he issued to them arms from his arsenal, and they were all obedient to him—youths, robust and warlike, sword-slashers in clever fighting." We also find in Haidar the double use of the word "*jihad*" referred to above. In requesting from his Turkoman overlord safe conduct in his fight against the Christians, the Sufi leader noted that his men, "having exerted themselves (*ijtihad*) in various religious exercises and duly completed the great *jihad*, which is the assault of one's own soul, they now . . . claimed the right to distinguish themselves in the lesser *jihad* [to fight the infidel]. Should the sovereign permit, they would begin the holy war against the Cherkes. . . . Let (the ghazis) acquire a great recompense, a handsome reward (in the other world) and an exalted companionship" (V. Minorsky, ed. and trans., *Persia in A.D. 1478-1490: An Abridged Translation of Fadlullah b. Ruzbihan Khunji's Tarikh-i*

It is clear that the frontier environment in which the movement flourished was fundamental in shaping the fanaticism on the part of the Safawi *murids*, as was the role of certain Sufi institutions. As for the first of these, one may note that it was not only its location on the frontiers of Islam that gave the movement its *ghazi* aspect, but also that its main adherents were rural and illiterate Turkoman tribesmen whose vision of Islam differed vastly from that held in the Islamic metropolis. By assuming the role of a living embodiment of the line of imams, noted Professor Minorsky, Junaid "conquered the hearts of the nomads . . . who had little interest in the pious doctrines and practices of the city-dwellers but were enthusiastic at the thought of being able to touch the hand of a being who incarnated the divine holiness and even omnipotence."[42] As for the role of Sufi institutions in the movement, it appears that Shaikh Junaid, Haidar, and above all Shah Isma'il (ruled 1501-24), were the witting or unwitting benefactors of the *pir-murid* relationship as it had evolved in the second stage of institutionalized Sufism. This relationship had by then become one of complete dependence of the *murid* on his *pir*, even to the point of the *murid's* going to battle and martyring himself if demanded by his *pir*. Thus we find that Shah Isma'il, in his own poetry written in the dialect spoken by his Turkoman followers, addressed his supporters as a community of militant dervishes, whom he called *ghazi, sufi, akhi*.[43] It is significant that Isma'il used both the term "*ghazi*" and "Sufi" when referring to his *murids*, thus explicitly recognizing that Islam's militant and mystical traditions could converge in the same individuals.

The Turkish and Iranian cases mentioned above indicate that the Warrior Sufis of Bijapur were not unique in the militant roles they played in the early fourteenth century. In common with both the Anatolian *ghazi-babas* and the Safawi leaders and their *murids*, the Warrior Sufis declared *jihad* and thereby performed

---

'Alam-Ara-yi Amini [London: Luzac and Co., Ltd. for The Royal Asiatic Society of Great Britain and Ireland, 1957], p. 68).

[42] V. Minorsky, "Iran: Opposition, Martyrdom, and Revolt," in G. E. von Grunebaum, ed., *Unity and Variety in Muslim Civilization* (Chicago: University of Chicago Press, 1955), p. 194.

[43] V. Minorsky, "The Poetry of Shah Isma'il I," *Bulletin of the School of Oriental and African Studies*, 10, No. 4 (1942), p. 1027. "*Akhi*" means "brother."

a function later reserved for jurists. For the earliest Sufis of Bijapur inhabited a remote frontier region far from the established centers of Muslim culture. Moreover the relationship between Pir Khandayat, Sufi Sarmast, Shaikh 'Ali Pahlavan, and Pir Jumna on the one hand, and their *murids* on the other seems to have resembled that of Isma'il and his followers in the *murids'* double role of spiritual disciples and warriors. Both instances indicate the potential of the *pir-murid* relationship, when it is one of absolute subservience of the *murid* to the *pir* and when the latter is placed in conditions of extreme social and political instability, to become a commander-soldier relationship.

In sum, the Warrior Sufi may be seen as one of the earliest products that arose from the contact between Arab Islamic and Indic civilizations. In their psychological appeal, philosophical underpinnings, and historical development, these two civilizations are diametrically opposed. Where the one is ardent, dogmatic, and austere, the other is reflective, syncretic, and sentimental. Where Arab Islam centers upon the submission to a single discipline and perceives society, the universe, and the divine principle in terms of unity, Indic Hinduism diffuses into an elusive aggregate of metaphysical systems, folk beliefs, customs, symbols, and traditions that collectively perceive society, the universe, and the divine principle in terms of plurality. By the early fourteenth century the Arab Islamic and Indic traditions had only just begun their long and tortuous process of fusing into what later was to become "Indian Islam." Hence the Warrior Sufi did not represent a synthesis of the Islamic and Indic traditions, but only a transplant of the former into the world of the latter. Clifford Geertz has depicted the style of Moroccan civilization, which is in some ways an extension of Arab Islam in northwest Africa, as "strenuous, fluid, visionary, devout, and unsentimental, but above all, self-assertive. It was a society in which a very great deal turned on force of character and most of the rest on spiritual reputation. In town or out, its leitmotivs were strong-man politics and holy-man piety, and its fulfillments, small and large, tribal and dynastic, occurred when in the person of a particular individual, they momentarily fused. The axial figure, whether he was storming walls or building them, was the warrior saint."[44]

[44] Geertz, *Islam Observed: Religious Development in Morocco and Indonesia* (Chicago: University of Chicago Press, 1971), p. 8.

If the force of the warrior and the virtue of the saint remained the twin leitmotivs of Moroccan civilization, pointing perhaps to the lasting imprint that Arab Islam has made on North Africa, these austere themes did not survive the mid-fourteenth century in the Bijapur plateau. The Warrior Sufi appeared only briefly in the subcontinent's Islamic frontier, being the product of unique historical circumstances. The disappearance of the Warrior Sufi may be credited partly to the assimilative character of Hindu civilization, which has usually succeeded in at least modifying if not fully absorbing the many foreign elements that have been introduced into the subcontinent, and partly also to the establishment from the mid-fourteenth century of stable Indo-Muslim states on the Bijapur plateau. The emergence of such states, initially the Bahmani Kingdom (1347-1489) and subsequently the Kingdom of Bijapur (1490-1686), removed the unsettled social and political conditions which had made the Warrior Sufi's appearance possible. In the first instance, the rise of Indo-Muslim city-states meant that members of the orthodox Muslim establishment, and not wandering Sufis, could be called upon to declare *jihad* if and when battles of state required such legitimization. The Warrior Sufi's function of providing religious legitimacy to raids carried out by Muslim generals from the North was thereby removed. More than this, insofar as the new Indo-Muslim states were to become reconciled to and embedded within existing Hindu social and political structures, the new conditions that prevailed under these states precluded the very possibility of holy war. For with the coming of the Bahmani and Bijapur kingdoms there came a period that was mainly peaceful, at least by contrast to the intense chaos that had characterized the Bijapur plateau in the early fourteenth century. It is, then, to the formation of these states that our attention must now turn.

Establishment of Muslim Power in the Bijapur Plateau

There were several processes of Muslim penetration in peninsular India: the process of peaceful settlement arising from trade along the west coast, the process of military invasion, which provoked in stiff reaction the formation of the Vijayanagar Empire, and the process of Muslim settlement occurring after the invasions. The earliest settlers—soldier-adventurers and their slaves, camp-followers, merchants, etc.—had originally accompanied the invading armies. Instead of returning north with the armies, however, this group remained and settled in the upper Deccan. A later wave of settlers came as a result of Sultan Muhammad bin Tughluq's abortive attempt in 1327 to compel the entire population of Delhi to migrate to Devagiri (renamed Daulatabad), as part of his efforts to secure a firmer grip over the newly acquired Deccan provinces. Over the course of the first half of the fourteenth century, however, both waves of migrants seem to have lost their ties with North India, which in part led to their declaration of independence from the Delhi Sultanate in 1347.

The new sultanate thus established was the Bahmani Kingdom (1347-1489), which held sway over most of the Deccan plateau north of Vijayanagar from the Arabian Sea to the Bay of Bengal. The Marathi-speaking northwestern, the Kannada-speaking southwestern, and the Telugu-speaking eastern Deccan were all ruled from the center of the plateau, another shatter zone, at the point where these three cultural regions converged.[45] When this kingdom began disintegrating at the end of the fifteenth century, each of its five provincial divisions, the most important of which was the province of Bijapur in the southwestern portion of the kingdom,[46] declared its independence from Bahmani authority. Ruling over the Bijapur plateau from 1490 to 1686 under the ʿAdil Shahi dynasty, the Kingdom of Bijapur inherited from six generations of Bahmani rule political and cultural traditions that were quite distinct from those of the Delhi Sultanate and its successor in the North, the Mughal Empire. Because this independent tradition of medieval Deccan culture provided the environment in which the Sufis of Bijapur lived, several salient aspects of that culture should be emphasized. One is the social composition of the Muslims themselves. Another is the degree and quality of synthesis or accommodation achieved by them with the indigenous Hindu population among whom they lived, a subject examined in detail in chapter four of this study.

The Muslims of the Bahmani Kingdom as well as of the Kingdom of Bijapur can be divided into two major and generally

[45] The first capital was at Gulbarga, located 80 miles northeast of Bijapur; the second was at Bidar, located 60 miles northeast of Gulbarga.

[46] H. K. Sherwani, *The Bahmanis of the Deccan* (Hyderabad: Manager of Publications, 1953), pp. 80, 258.

antagonistic groups: the Deccanis and the Foreigners. In contrast to the Foreigners, who were usually first- or second-generation immigrants from overseas, the Deccanis always represented those Muslims whose ancestors had inhabited the Deccan the longest, or who for political or social reasons identified with that group. Four groups of Deccanis can be distinguished.[47] The first, a small one, was composed of descendants of the early Arab traders who between the tenth and fifteenth centuries had been spilling over on the Deccan plateau from the Konkan Coast. Having lived on the coasts and the plateau for many centuries and having intermarried considerably with indigenous peoples, they naturally regarded the Deccan as their home. The second and numerically most important group of Deccanis was composed of settlers from North India. This group had come to the Deccan with the first armies and remained, or had migrated as a result of Muhammad bin Tughluq's attempt in 1327 to settle the Deccan, or had deserted the Delhi Sultanate to seek better fortunes in the Deccan. Descended mainly from the same Turkish peoples who had founded the Khalaji and Tughluq dynasties in Delhi, these settlers, like the Arabs, were generally Sunni Muslims. A third group of Deccanis consisted of the Abyssinians (or Habashis), the black slaves brought by sea from Ethiopia to the Konkan Coast and sold there by Arab traders, and after 1500 by Portuguese traders, to Muslim nobles on the plateau.[48] Strictly speaking, the Abyssinians were Foreigners insofar as they had come from overseas, but racial and sectarian discrimination on the part of the Foreigner nobility caused them to identify with other Deccanis.[49] The fourth and final group of Deccanis consisted of Hindu converts

[47] The following discussion on the Deccanis follows I. A. Ghauri, "Muslims in the Deccan: A Historical Survey," *Islamic Literature*, 13 (May 1967), pp. 28-35.

[48] For a description of this slave trade, see the notes of the famous Dutch traveler Linschoten, who visited the Konkan Coast in the 1580s. John Hughen von Linschoten, *The Voyage of John Hughen von Linschoten to the East Indies*, vol. 1 ed. by A. C. Burnell (2 vols.; London: Hakluyt Society, 1884; reprinted New York: Burt Franklin, 1970), 1, pp. 264-67. See also C. F. Buckingham, "Amba Gesen and Asirgarh," *Journal of Semitic Studies*, 2 (April 1957), pp. 182-88.

[49] The Muslims among the Abyssinians were invariably Sunni, although Linschoten noted that some Abyssinians were Christians (Linschoten, *Travels*, 1, p. 264).

to Islam. They, of course, fully considered the Deccan their home. Like the Abyssinians, Hindu converts were never fully accepted by the elitist Foreigner class, and so they also identified with other Deccanis.

The Foreigners comprised the other broad class of Muslims in the Bahmani and Bijapur sultanates. The political separation of the rebel Bahmani dynasty from the Delhi Sultanate had cut off the handful of settlers in the Deccan from the Iranian plateau, to which sultans and emperors of Delhi traditionally looked for recruiting Muslim administrators. Hence two alternatives were open to the Deccani rulers for staffing their military and civil bureaucracies: either they could employ indigenous Hindus to fill these positions, or they could look for recruits direct from the Persian Gulf. For the first fifty years of Bahmani rule (1347-97), the original colonists and their sons administered the kingdom quite independent of either foreign immigrants or indigenous non-Muslims. But with the accession of Sultan Firuz Bahmani (1397-1422) a change occurred. Whether because of feelings of dependence on the Persian courtly model, or because of depletion among the ranks of the original settlers, or both, Firuz vigorously sought recruits from overseas. Yearly he sent a number of empty ships to the Persian Gulf for the purpose of bringing soldiers, artists, and administrators to serve at his court.[50]

Those recruits who came, mainly Iranians and Arabs from the Persian Gulf region, were accorded great prestige and political power by both Firuz and his successor, Ahmad. But the rapid rate with which the original settlers and other Deccanis had absorbed indigenous habits prevented these newcomers from easy social assimilation with more established residents of the Deccan. Deccanis of whatever ultimate ethnic origin—Arab, Turkish, Abyssinian, or indigenous Hindu—had been cut off from both Delhi and the Middle East sufficiently long to have identified the Deccan as their homeland. Iranians and Arabs coming directly from the Persian Gulf, on the other hand, tended to retain their attachments to the Middle East. Foreigners, for example, tenaciously cultivated the Persian language and despised the Marathi and Kannada vernaculars, while the Deccanis developed their own dialect, Dakhni, with little regard for the purity of Persian. Sectarian differences also kept the groups apart, for the Iranians,

[50] Ghauri, "Muslims," p. 30.

who composed the most numerous and prestigious group among the Foreigners, were predominantly Shi'a, though Deccanis of all types were Sunni Muslims. Furthermore, the Iranian newcomers seem to have taken full advantage of the Persianized cultural orientation of the court, revived by Sultans Firuz and Ahmad, by flaunting a feeling of superiority over the Deccanis.[51]

For all of these reasons there was generated between the Foreigners and the Deccanis a bitter elite-non-elite cleavage that was to weaken and ultimately destroy the internal stability of the Bahmani Kingdom. As Foreigners filled the nobility and the civil bureaucracy, the original settlers and others who were beginning to consider themselves "Deccanis" found themselves by the end of Ahmad's reign (1422-36) wholly shut out of ranking social and political positions.[52] Open hostilities between the two groups eventually erupted in 1447 when an Arab general and his followers publicly blamed their Deccani troops for a certain defeat suffered during a Bahmani campaign against the Gujaratis. From this point on, wrote Wolsely Haig, "the feud thus begun was not confined to intrigues for place and power, but frequently found expression in pitched battles and bloody massacres, of which last the Foreigners were usually the victims. Thence-forward the history of the domestic affairs of the Deccan is mainly a record of this strife, which contributed in no small measure to the disintegration of the [Bahmani] kingdom and afterwards to the weakness of the states which rose on its ruins."[53]

SUMMARY

By the fourteenth century, when waves of Muslim settlers first moved into the Bijapur plateau, both the Marathi and Kannada core areas had already begun to crystallize. As these areas had developed on either side of the central Bijapur plateau, Islam was able to flourish along the resulting cultural fault line. Linguistically, this meant that the Dakhni language was able to flourish

[51] Sri Ram Sharma, *Dakani Zaban ka Aghaz aur Irtiqa*, trans. into Urdu by Ghulam Rasul (Hyderabad: Andhra Pradesh Sahitia Academy, 1967), p. 29.

[52] Sherwani, *Bahmanis*, p. 194.

[53] H. H. Dodwell, ed., *The Cambridge Shorter History of India* (Cambridge: University Press, 1943), pp. 289 f.

more brilliantly at Bijapur than anywhere else, for this area had previously experienced little linguistic integration. Politically, it meant that Muslims were able to rule the area until the chaotic eighteenth century when, among other things, a resurgence of Marathi culturalism swept over the region. Socially, it meant that the Deccanis, with their greater capacity to assimilate indigenous culture than the Foreigners, were able to swell in numbers such that by 1583 they could dislodge the Foreigners from their position of political and social preeminence. And religiously, it meant that Sufis would appear having an altogether different nature than their warlike predecessors who had initially smashed into the Bijapur plateau as religious auxiliaries to Khalaji and Tughluq imperialists. Unlike the Warrior Sufis, the later Sufis of Bijapur were able to wield considerable influence in an area where neither Vaisnavite *bhakti* (the Vithoba cult) nor Saivite *bhakti* (Lingayatism) was altogether dominant, and where their own variant of devotionalism could find room for accommodation.

Chapter Three

LATER SETTLEMENT OF SUFIS IN BIJAPUR

Early Development of the Chishti, Qadiri, and Shattari Orders in India

From about the mid-fourteenth century through the seventeenth century there migrated to the city of Bijapur and the surrounding region a good number of Sufis who were affiliated with one or another of the Sufi orders that had been developing throughout the Muslim world. In Trimingham's scheme, Sufism had by now entered its second phase, the *tariqa* phase, in which individual Sufis identified themselves as initiates or masters of one of the schools of mystical discipline. While this development occurred in all parts of the Islamic world, it did not occur simultaneously. There was somewhat of a time lag between the formation of the earliest orders in the Islamic heartland and the appearance of these orders on the Islamic frontier. This in part explains why it was only after the mid-fourteenth century that Sufis belonging to orders had become common in Bijapur. Then, too, by the mid-fourteenth century the city of Bijapur was beginning to pass from a remote outpost on the edge of the Islamic frontier to a small center of Islamic culture in its own right. For this reason also it was attracting an entirely different sort of Sufi than the Warrior type.

Most of the Sufis of Bijapur who migrated to the city from the mid-fourteenth century belonged to the Chishti, the Qadiri, or the Shattari orders, each of which had already undergone considerable development in various parts of the Indian subcontinent before becoming significant in Bijapur. The Chishti order, which was the earliest Sufi order introduced in India, had flourished in Delhi since the early thirteenth century. Although its founder in India, Mu'in al-Din Chishti (d. 1236), had come to India from Khurasan, from which he traced his own spiritual lineage, the order was essentially an indigenous Indian and not a Middle Eastern order.[1] Mu'in al-Din himself taught and died in Ajmer, Rajasthan, and his order was continued in Delhi by a line of indigenous Sufis whose names are familiar to millions of Indians today.[2]

Because the Chishti Sufis of Bijapur could claim no familial descent and only indirect spiritual lineage from the Chishtis of Delhi, a detailed review of the latter is not necessary here. The Chishti Sufis of Delhi did, however, develop several unique characteristics that were retained by Chishtis of Bijapur and therefore merit some attention. First among them was the Chishti tradition of avoiding the court and courtly affairs.[3] "My room has two doors," one fourteenth-century Chishti said, "if the Sultan comes through one door, I will leave by the other."[4] This sentiment reflected a uniform policy of the order, and the Chishti Certificate of Succession (*khilafat-nama*) strictly forbade its followers to accept grants in land from the court.[5] A corollary to this detachment from political affairs was the Chishti ideal of ascetic poverty, to which each *murid* pledged himself when initiated into the order. Inmates at the Chishti *khanaqahs* lived a communal life,

1 Khurasan included what is today northeastern Iran, western Afghanistan, and Soviet Central Asia south of the Oxus River. The town in which the Chishti order originated, Khwajachisht, is located in western Afghanistan 90 miles east of Herat in the Hari Rud valley.

2 The most eminent of the early Chishti Sufis of Delhi formed a chain linking from Mu'in al-Din Chishti (d. 1236): Bakhtiyar Kaki (d. 1235), Farid al-Din Ganj-i Shakar (d. 1265), Nizam al-Din Auliya (d. 1325), and Nasir al-Din Chiragh-i Delhi (d. 1356). Of the many writings on the early Chishti Sufis of Delhi, see especially K. A. Nizami, *Some Aspects of Religion and Politics in India during the Thirteenth Century* (Aligarh: S. Nural Hasan, 1961), ch. 6; Aziz Ahmad, "The Sufi and the Sultan in Pre-Mughal India," *Der Islam* (1955), pp. 142-53; Mohammad Habib, "Chishti Mystics Records of the Sultanate Period," *Medieval India Quarterly*, 1 (October 1950), pp. 1-42; Mohammad Habib, "Shaikh Nasir al-Din Mahmud Chiragh-i Delhi as a Great Historical Personality," *Islamic Culture*, 20 (1946), pp. 129-53; Saiyid A. A. Rizvi, *Muslim Revivalist Movements in Northern India in the Sixteenth and Seventeenth Centuries* (Agra: Agra University, 1965), ch. 1.

3 See Mohammad Salim, "The Attitude of the Chishti Saints towards Political Power," *Proceedings, Pakistan Historical Conference*, 2 (1952), pp. 225 f.

4 Statement of Shaikh Nizam al-Din Auliya about Sultan 'Ala al-Din Khalaji, quoted in Habib, "Nasir ud-din," p. 137.

5 Aziz Ahmad, "The Sufi and the Sultan," p. 143.

sleeping, praying, studying, and sharing food when available. Tasks were also distributed among inmates: collecting wood for fuel, preparing food, writing out documents such as amulets (*ta'wiz*), or attending the *pir*, around whom all affairs of the *khanaqah*, both spiritual and temporal, revolved.[6] Thus one aspect of the Chishti *khanaqah* life related to the disciples by providing them with an atmosphere for concentration on their spiritual life as guided by the *pir*. Another aspect related to the non-Sufi public. Remaining open until midnight each day, the Chishti *khanaqahs* received all sorts of people—scholars, politicians, soldiers, Hindu yogis—who would come to receive blessings or guidance from the *pir*, or simply to tell him their worldly concerns.[7]

In both Delhi and Bijapur, the Chishti order was distinguished from others by its ecstatic practices and controversial doctrines. One of their practices, which harked back to the ascetic ideal of the earliest Muslim mystics, was the *chilla*, or spending forty days of isolation in prayer and meditation with little food or drink. Far more notorious because they were thought by some to conflict with Islamic orthodoxy were the practices of *sama'* (musical sessions) and *raqs* (dancing). Both music and dance were immensely popular among Chishtis and were used either individually or collectively to induce states of spiritual ecstacy. It is said, in fact, that one of the early Chishti Sufis of Delhi, Shaikh Bakhtiyar Kaki (d. 1235), actually died under the spell of a couplet recited musically in a *sama'*.[8] Chishti thought, which was as liberal as its practices were ecstatic, centered on the doctrine of the Unity of Being (*wahdat al-wujud*), the doctrine that all Reality is a borrowed fragment from the being of God. Derived mainly from the Spanish-Arab mystic Ibn 'Arabi (d. 1240), this doctrine most significantly distinguished the Chishti Sufis from the upholders of Islamic orthodoxy, or *'ulama*,[9] for by stressing that

[6] Nizami, *Religion and Politics*, pp. 208-10.

[7] Ibid., p. 214.

[8] Rizvi, *Muslim Revivalist Movements*, p. 16.

[9] The world *'ulama* is commonly used in two senses. As a general term it refers to a number of learned Muslims, as it is the Arabic plural of *'alim*, a learned person. More specifically, the term refers to the class of state-supported doctors of Islam who were collectively concerned with upholding Islamic orthodoxy in the state in which they served. The class con-

nothing exists but God ("all is He"). Chishti Sufis clashed with the transcendental aspect of Koranic theology ("all is *from* Him"). And although Chishtis were by no means the only Indian Sufis to emphasize this doctrine, it was they who were most consistently identified with it. This, plus their states of rapture associated with the practice of *sama'* and *raqs*, tended to keep them at arm's length from, and often in conflict with, the *'ulama* and the political authorities that supported the *'ulama*.

The brilliance of the Chishti tradition in Delhi, most eminently represented by Shaikh Nizam al-Din Auliya (d. 1325), was virtually extinguished in the mid-fourteenth century. The Chishti policy of maintaining an aloofness from the court developed into an open and mutual hostility that resulted from conflicting notions in the court and the *khanaqahs* about the Sufis' proper role in society. For their part, the Chishtis under Nizam al-Din Auliya had fallen under the mystical influence of Ibn 'Arabi, which involved, among other things, a withdrawal from the affairs of the world and a devotion to "spiritual splendour and concentration on the individual soul."[10] But Sultan Muhammad bin Tughluq, though he had visited the assemblies of Nizam al-Din as a young man, became influenced by rationalist philosophers who rejected Ibn 'Arabi's doctrine of the Unity of Being and stressed instead a strict conformity to the *shari'at* (Islamic Law). The sultan thus came to believe that Sufis, instead of devoting themselves to a cult of personal worship of God, should be active in the propagation of Islam among non-Muslims.[11] His attempt to harness the Sufis to state service even extended to requiring them to discard their patched frock (*khirqa*), one of the outward symbols of membership in the order, and to wear the silken gown and broad waistband of government officers.[12] Tension between the court and the Sufis culminated in 1327 when Muhammad bin Tughluq ordered all Sufis to disperse from their *khanaqahs* and to migrate to the Deccan as part of his policy of shifting the inhabitants of Delhi to the new capital in the Deccan, Daulatabad. "So complete was the destruction of *khanaqah* life in Delhi,"

sisted mainly of expounders of Islamic Law (*muftis*), judges (*qazis*), and prayer-leaders (*imams*).

[10] Aziz Ahmad, "The Sufi and the Sultan," p. 146.

[11] Ibid., p. 151.

[12] Habib, "Nasir-ud-din," p. 139.

wrote K. A. Nizami, "that with the exception of the tombs of Shaikh Qutb al-Din Bakhtiyar Kaki and Shaikh Nizam al-Din Auliya, no tomb or hospice in Delhi had even a candle lamp."[13]

Delhi's loss, however, was to a great extent the Deccan's gain, as many of the leading disciples of Shaikh Nizam al-Din Auliya migrated to the new capital at Daulatabad.[14] In 1347, just twenty years after the migration southward, the rebel Deccanis revolted against Delhi's rule and founded the Bahmani Kingdom at Gulbarga. In this new political situation several Chishti Sufis gravitated to Gulbarga, but in doing so they, unlike their spiritual forefathers in North India, developed close relations with the court. The most likely explanation for this lies in the needs of the court, for it was generally the Bahmani sultans that took the initiative in forging alliances with Muslim divines. As the founder of a rebel kingdom in the Deccan detached from his ancestral roots in North India, the first Bahmani sultan, 'Ala al-Din Hasan (1347-58), needed any support he could muster for consolidating his initially tenuous hold over the Deccan plateau. Accordingly, he and his successors actively solicited the support and cooperation of any Sufi who, because of his popularity with large numbers of non-elite groups, was thought to be capable of carrying the roots of Bahmani power deeper in public confidence.[15]

One of the first Sufis to become closely associated with the Bahmani court was Shaikh Siraj al-Din Junaidi (d. 1380). Born in Peshawar, Siraj al-Din had accompanied Muhammad bin

[13] K. A. Nizami, *Studies in Medieval Indian History and Culture* (Allahabad: Kitab Mahal, 1966), p. 96.

[14] Habib, "Chishti Mystics Records," pp. 2-6; H. K. Sherwani and P. M. Joshi, eds., *History of Medieval Deccan, 1295-1724* (2 vols.; Hyderabad: Government of Andhra Pradesh, 1973-74), II, pp. 178-82.

[15] See Sherwani and Joshi, *History of Medieval Deccan*, II, p. 182. There is a story, perhaps apocryphal, which also explains Bahmani support of Chishti Sufis. One day Ulugh Khan, the future Muhammad bin Tughluq, went to the *khanaqah* of Nizam al-Din Auliya in Delhi. As the prince left, another visitor, 'Ala al-Din Hasan, the future founder of the Bahmani Kingdom, was waiting at the gate. The shaikh turned to one of his disciples and remarked, "One king has left and another is waiting at the door. Bring him in." The shaikh then gave 'Ala al-Din a loaf of bread, saying that it represented the umbrella (*chatr*) of the kingdom he would found in the Deccan. See ibid., p. 177; Saiyid 'Ali Tabataba'i, *Burhan-i Ma'asir*. Persian edn. (Delhi, 1936), p. 12; Firishta, *Tarikh-i Firishta*, I, p. 274. (Briggs's translation, II, p. 176.)

Tughluq to the Deccan and settled in the city of Bijapur in 1330. About this time, too, he became the spiritual guide to the future founder of the Bahmani Kingdom, 'Ala al-Din Hasan.[16] It was Siraj al-Din, in fact, who crowned the new king at the royal coronation on 3 August 1347. In return for the Sufi's continued blessings and prayers for the sultan's long life, Siraj al-Din received what was perhaps the first land grant ever given to a Deccani Sufi—the village of Korchi, which has continued into this century in the hands of his descendants.[17] Shortly after his coronation the new sultan distributed four hundred pounds of gold and a thousand pounds of silver in the name of Nizam al-Din Auliya, the great Chishti of Delhi.[18] So close were Sufi-court relations during the early Bahmani period that 'Ala al-Din's successor, Muhammad Shah Bahmani, was able to obtain a declaration of allegiance from virtually all the Sufis of his kingdom.[19]

Chishti association with the Bahmani court was intensified by another prominent Sufi of the time, indeed the best known Muslim divine of Deccan history, Saiyid Muhammad Husaini Bandanawaz Gisudaraz (d. 1422, pictured in Figure 3). The activities of this famous Sufi and saint indicate the degree to which certain Chishti ideals of fourteenth-century Delhi had been compromised in fifteenth-century Gulbarga. Born in Delhi in 1321, Gisudaraz moved to Daulatabad with his father when Muhammad bin Tughluq ordered the Sufis of Delhi to migrate there. When his father died in Daulatabad, Gisudaraz, then sixteen years of age, returned to Delhi where he became attracted to the one Chishti Sufi who had defied the sultan's orders by remaining in Delhi, Nasir al-Din Chiragh-i Delhi (d. 1356).[20] But in 1398 when rumors of Tamerlane's invasion of India prompted him again to abandon Delhi for the Deccan, Gisudaraz veered radically from the ideals of his *pir* with respect to the traditional Chishti policy of avoid-

16 Sherwani, *Bahmanis*, p. 46, fn. 83.

17 *Tazkira-yi Auliya*, I, p. 392; *Armaghan-i Sultani*, or *Sair-i Gulbarga*, comp. by Muhammad Sultan. Urdu lithograph (Agra: Mufid-i 'Am, 1902), p. 161. The latter source states that it was 'Ala al-Din's successor, Muhammad, who gave him the grant.

18 Firishta, *Tarikh-i Firishta*, I, p. 277. (Briggs's translation, II, p. 180.)

19 Ibid., p. 294. (Briggs's translation, II, p. 200.)

20 *Mishkat-i Nubuwat*, comp. by 'Ali Musawi al-Qadiri. Persian MS (Copy A, Hyderabad: Asafiyah Library, Tazkira no. 21), fol. 4a-b. Hereafter cited as *Mishkat*, copy A.

3. Saiyid Muhammad Husaini Bandanawaz Gisudaraz (d. 1422)

ing the court. When Gisudaraz arrived at Gulbarga the reigning monarch, Sultan Firuz Bahmani (1397-1422), sought him out and granted him several villages in *in'am* (tax-free land),[21] which the Sufi apparently accepted. Gisudaraz's popularity with the urban population at Gulbarga evidently lent considerable political importance to his support of one or another political rival at the court,[22] for relations between the sultan and the Sufi broke down when Gisudaraz threw his support to the sultan's brother Ahmad as successor to the Bahmani throne, in preference to Firuz's son, who was the sultan's own choice. Angered, Sultan Firuz ordered Gisudaraz to move his *khanaqah* away from the proximity of the court, complaining of the excessive mobs of people who thronged around the *khanaqah*.[23] Ahmad, on the other hand, regularly attended Gisudaraz's musical sessions and lavished great sums of money on his *khanaqah*. When he eventually did succeed in obtaining the throne on Firuz's death (1422), Ahmad went even further by transferring the court's traditional support of the family of Siraj al-Din Junaidi to Gisudaraz, as well as by granting the Sufi even more towns and villages in the Gulbarga region.[24]

It was a normal pattern in the history of Indian Sufism that as a Sufi's political sympathies merged with those of the court, his doctrinal position generally became more orthodox. This was certainly true in the case of Gisudaraz. We have noted above that under Nizam al-Din Auliya the Chishti Sufis of Delhi had incorporated many of the pantheistic and monistic ideas of Ibn 'Arabi, and that this development provoked the stern condemnation of Sultan Muhammad bin Tughluq as well as of the *'ulama*. Unlike the Chishtis of Delhi, however, Gisudaraz aligned himself squarely with the *'ulama* by declaring the supremacy of Islamic Law (*shari'at*) over all Sufi stages and by launching a tirade not only against Ibn 'Arabi but also against the liberal Persian Sufis Farid al-Din 'Attar and Jalal al-Din Rumi, all of whom he denounced as enemies of Islam.[25]

[21] Tabataba'i, *Burhan-i Ma'asir*, p. 44.

[22] The *Mishkat-i Nubuwat*, an important biography of Deccani Sufis, records that Gisudaraz drew his followers not only from among saiyids, nobles, princes and shaikhs, but also from among tailors, cobblers and ironsmiths. *Mishkat*, copy A, fol. 7a-b.

[23] Firishta, *Tarikh-i Firishta*, I, p. 316. (Briggs's translation, II, p. 240.)

[24] Ibid., p. 319. (Briggs's translation, II, p. 245.)

[25] Rizvi, *Muslim Revivalist Movements*, p. 54. Rizvi maintains that Gisudaraz never had thoroughly imbibed Chishti monistic traditions, "other-

No Chishti Sufis of note succeeded Gisudaraz at Gulbarga. In the year that he died, 1422, the Bahmani court shifted its capital from Gulbarga to Bidar, thereby removing the political center on which Sufis in Gulbarga had come to depend. Before leaving Gulbarga, however, Sultan Ahmad built a great shrine (*dargah*) over the grave of the Sufi who had helped him to power.[26] As was true generally in all parts of the Muslim world and at all times, a vibrant tradition of Sufi teaching frequently terminated with the construction of a great mausoleum over a Sufi's grave. For it was roughly at this point that the institutions of the Sufis became replaced by the institutions of the *dargah*, or, in Trimingham's scheme, that the *tariqa* phase of Sufi development passed to the *ta'ifa* phase. As the tomb became a renowned focal point of popular devotionalism in the Deccan, the descendants of Gisudaraz became too occupied administrating the affairs of the *dargah* as well as the vast estates bestowed upon their illustrious ancestor to turn their attention to teaching Chishti doctrine.[27] Taken together, these developments effectively killed any living tradition of Chishti Sufism in Gulbarga.

If the Chishti tradition had ceased functioning in Delhi by being too unyielding before a hostile court, it ceased functioning in Gulbarga by being too pliant before a generous court. In both cases the Chishti *khanaqahs* were located in such close proximity to the seats of political power that Sufis could not remain entirely uninfluenced by the court and its conception of the Sufis' proper role in the Muslim state. Clearly, if the Chishti order were to survive in India in its vibrant *tariqa* phase it could not follow the examples provided by the Sufis of Delhi and Gulbarga. We shall see that the Chishti Sufis who achieved such eminence in Bijapur in the sixteenth and seventeenth centuries drew their inspiration from local influences quite independent of the Delhi and Gulbarga traditions, and that they maintained a safe physical distance from the seat of political power.

---

wise there was no reason for his having been denied in the *Khirqa* [*khilafat*] by his preceptor, Shaikh Nasir ud-Din Chiragh" (ibid., p. 339).

26 Sherwani, *Bahmanis*, pp. 179 f.

27 In 1609 the historian Firishta wrote that "in the present day, though the country has passed from the family of Bahmuny to that of the kings of Beejapoor, yet most of the estates given by the former princes are still in possession of the Syud's descendants" (Firishta, *Tarikh-i Firishta*, I, p. 320. [Briggs's translation, II, p. 245]).

Nurtured mainly by southward emigration from its parent home in Delhi, the Chishti order had dominated Sufi activity in the Deccan throughout the fourteenth century. In the fifteenth century another Sufi order, the Qadiri order, became firmly entrenched in the Deccan plateau. This order differed from the Chishti tradition in several important respects. The Qadiri order was a pan-Islamic order, its members being spread throughout the Muslim world from India to Morocco. Moreover, its point of origin and spiritual center of gravity was Baghdad, where its founder, ʿAbd al-Qadir Jilani (d. 1166), had taught and died. This lent to the order a distinctly Arab character and led its members in India to emphasize the Middle Eastern more than the Indian aspect of their spiritual (and often familial) ancestry. By contrast, the Chishti order is represented chiefly in India and its major spiritual center is in Ajmer, Rajasthan, location of the shrine of Muʿin al-Din Chishti. Thus, while Chishti Sufis were generally more conscious of their Indian heritage, Qadiri Sufis looked more to the Arab world for spiritual nourishment.

A second distinction between the two orders is the more orthodox orientation of the Qadiri *tariqa*. While Chishti doctrine rested fundamentally on the pantheistic monism of Ibn ʿArabi, a doctrine never in line with strict Islamic orthodoxy, the Qadiri order espoused from its beginning the orthodox point of view within Sufism. In the writings of the order's founder, ʿAbd al-Qadir Jilani, the Sufi emerges clearly subordinate to the Prophet and ecstatic behavior subordinate to conformity to the *shariʿat*.[28] Qadiri Sufis, at least those living in the medieval Deccan, generally upheld this tradition and frequently embraced doctrinal positions hardly distinguishable from those of the regular Islamic clergy, or the *ʿulama*. But the Chishti Sufis of Bijapur—though not those of Gulbarga—tended to deviate from Islamic orthodoxy in terms of both doctrine and practice to an extent nearly and sometimes wholly incompatible with Muslim Law.

These differences between the Chishtis and Qadiris of Bijapur can be viewed in terms of a distinction Sir Hamilton Gibb has made between "urban" and "rustic" Sufi orders. "Urban" orders, wrote Gibb, were "founded and maintained by elements of the

[28] A. J. Arberry, *Sufism* (5th edn., London: George Allen and Unwin, Ltd., 1969), p. 85; G. E. von Grunebaum, *Classical Islam: A History, 600-1258*, trans. by Katherine Watson (London: George Allen and Unwin Ltd., 1970), pp. 195 f.

city population which were in fairly close association with the Ulama and the madrasas, [while] 'rustic' orders . . . spread chiefly in the villages, and being less open to [urban] influence were liable to diverge more widely from the strict tenets of orthodoxy."[29] The extent to which the Chishti or any other Sufis of Bijapur represented a "rustic" order is a subject to be examined in a later chapter. The point to emphasize here is that the Qadiri Sufis of Bijapur generally espoused the same ideals that caused Gibb to single out that order as Sufism's most typical urban order.[30] For Sufis, an urban orientation generally corresponded to compatible relations with the *'ulama*, the upholders of Islamic Law. These three qualities—religious orthodoxy, urbanism, and a distinct Arab identity—characterized Bijapur's Sufis of the Qadiri order.

The first Qadiri Sufis to journey from the Arab Middle East to India appeared in the Bahmani capital of Bidar from about the mid-fifteenth century. The timing of their migration to Bidar is noteworthy, for the year 1422 represented a significant turning-point in both the political and religious history of the Bahmani Kingdom. Politically, it inaugurated an era of a century and a half of domination by the Foreigner class. Symbolizing the government's determination to shake off traditions of Deccani or North Indian origin and assert its foreign (i.e., Iranian and Arab) nature, the seat of government was moved from Gulbarga to Bidar with the accession of Sultan Ahmad in 1422.[31] Gulbarga, the old Bahmani capital from 1347 to 1422, had evidently become too closely identified with the Deccani Muslims who had built and inhabited the city, and was thenceforward destined to fade from the political history of India and become a city of tombs. On the other hand the Foreigner class that established the new city of Bidar patronized Persian and Arab culture as resolutely as it had tried to suppress the Deccani traditions of Gulbarga, as can be witnessed in its pronounced attempts to reproduce Persian art and architectural forms in Bidar.[32]

[29] H. A. R. Gibb, *Mohammedanism: An Historical Survey* (2nd edn., London: Oxford University Press, 1961), p. 154.

[30] Ibid., p. 155.

[31] Sherwani, *Bahmanis*, pp. 181 f.

[32] An example of Iranian influence in Bidar is the tiled representation of the ancient symbol of Persian monarchy—the Lion and Sun—found in the Throne Room (*Takht Mahal*). See G. Yazdani, *Bidar, Its History and Monuments* (Oxford: Oxford University Press, 1947), plate 37.

As the political complexion of the Bahmani Kingdom changed with the transfer of government from Gulbarga to Bidar, so also did the Sufi tradition. We have noted that the renowned Chishti Sufi of Gulbarga, Saiyid Bandanawaz Gisudaraz, died in the same year that the Bahmani government moved its capital to Bidar, and that the Chishti tradition in Gulbarga died with him. In addition to the causes already cited for this development, one can conjecture that the Bahmani court at its new capital of Bidar felt the Chishtis to be "too Indian" for their pro-Foreigner, anti-Deccani bias. The court no longer patronized Chishti Sufis. Instead, it actively encouraged the immigration of foreign Sufis from the Middle East, a policy very much in line with its desire to seek Foreigner administrators from the Arab and Iranian area around the Persian Gulf.[33] Sufis of the Qadiri order, with their urban and religiously orthodox orientation, and especially with their prestigious claim to spiritual successorship from 'Abd al-Qadir Jilani of Baghdad, were perfectly suited to help give the Bahmani court an air of religious legitimacy and piety.

From 1422 the city of Bidar thus became the first, and until the seventeenth century perhaps the most important, Qadiri center in India. Most of these Sufis arrived directly from the Arab world,

[33] The bargaining that took place between the court and foreign Sufis could almost be seen as a special branch of diplomacy. Firishta relates that Sultan Ahmad Bahmani (1422-1436), the monarch responsible for shifting the capital from Gulbarga to Bidar, sent two holy men from his court to the Iranian city of Kerman for the purpose of soliciting a renowned Sufi by the name of Shaikh Ni'mat Allah (d. 1430-31) to return with them to Bidar. The shaikh declined, but sent in his place his favorite disciple. Sultan Ahmad, pleased with this gesture but still not satisfied, sent two more holy men to Kerman to solicit the shaikh's sons to come to Bidar. Shaikh Ni'mat Allah again declined, pleading that he had but one son. He did agree, however, to send his grandson to Bidar. Although both missions from Bidar fell short of their aim, the extent to which the Bahmani court valued foreign Sufis can be seen in the lavish treatment accorded to Shaikh Ni'mat Allah's grandson. He was carried from the Konkan seacoast to Bidar on the monarch's personal palanquin, escorted by two venerable religious men. And in the vicinity of the capital the monarch personally went out to welcome the newcomer, and directed that on that spot be built a mosque and village, which he named after the man's grandfather still in Kerman, Shaikh Ni'mat Allah (Firishta, *Tarikh-i Firishta*, I, pp. 328 f. [Briggs's translation, II, pp. 258 f.]).

especially from Baghdad, via the Persian Gulf and Arabian Sea.[34] One of the first Qadiri Sufis to arrive at Bidar from Baghdad was Shah Zain al-Din Ganj Nishin (d. 1457), whom the reigning sultan personally welcomed to the city.[35] About the same time, the mid-fifteenth century, another Qadiri Sufi from Baghdad, Shah Isma'il Qadiri (d. 1456-57), arrived at Bidar where he and his three sons furthered the teachings of their order.[36] One of the most popular Sufis of Bidar, whose tomb is still visited by a large number of devotees daily, was Shaikh Muhammad Multani (d. 1529).[37] In his archeological survey of Bidar, G. Yazdani listed and described the large number of Sufi *khanaqahs* in the city, noting that Bidar "was at one time a great centre for the teaching of the Qadiriya school of Islamic doctrine, since there are several monasteries of the votaries of this order in the town."[38] The Sufiya School, Sufiya Mosque, and Sufiya Arch, all located close to the shrine of Shaikh Muhammad Multani, attest to this tradition.[39] In the mid-sixteenth century a group of seven Qadiris of Baghdad known in the hagiographies as the Exalted Seven migrated to Bidar where they established their *khanaqahs*.[40] Some of the most prominent Sufis of seventeenth-century Bijapur were descended from members of this group.

The fortunes of Qadiri Sufis in the Deccan generally followed the fortunes of the Muslim sultanates in whose capitals they lived. Hence the decline of Bidar and the rise of Bijapur as an important urban center saw the migration of many Qadiri Sufis from the former to the latter city. At the same time, many of Bijapur's Qadiri Sufis began, from the late sixteenth century, coming to Bijapur directly from Arab lands rather than by way of Bidar.

[34] Control of this route by Arab merchants and seamen until the arrival of the Portuguese in the beginning of the sixteenth century naturally facilitated this movement.

[35] Yazdani, *Bidar*, p. 174.

[36] *Tazkira-yi Auliya*, I, p. 131.

[37] Yazdani, *Bidar*, p. 107.

[38] Ibid., p. 111. For a discussion of the archeological remains of this tradition see pp. 106 ff.

[39] Ibid., p. 109 fn.

[40] *Mishkat-i Nubuwat*, comp. by 'Ali Musawi al-Qadiri. Persian MS (copy B, Hyderabad: Asafiyah Library, Tazkira no. 194), fols. 482b and 493b. Hereafter referred to as *Mishkat*, copy B.

But the rise of Bidar as a major Qadiri center in the fifteenth century marked an important phase in the evolution of the order in the Deccan, for it clearly established a tradition of orthodox, urban Sufism that could be merely transplanted to Bijapur with the rise of that city as a center of Islamic political power.

The third Sufi order to attain significance in Bijapur, though to a somewhat lesser degree than either the Chishti or Qadiri orders, was the Shattari order. While Qadiri Sufis traced their origins to Baghdad and Chishti Sufis to North India, the Shattari order arose in Iran. Brought to India by Shaikh ʿAbd Allah Shattar (d. 1485) in the mid-fifteenth century, this order seems to have passed through several phases of doctrinal development by the time it settled down in Gujarat, whence it was brought to Bijapur. Included in the Shattari spiritual genealogy is the Persian mystic, Shaikh Bayazid Bistami (d. 845).[41] This spiritual heritage may account for the liberalism that pervades much of the later Shattari writing, for Bayazid was one of the first of the "intoxicated" Sufis. "Transported upon the wings of mystical fervour," wrote Arberry, Bayazid "found God within his own soul and scandalised the orthodox by ejaculating, 'Glory to Me! How great is my Majesty!' "[42] This was the concept of *fana*, first expressed by Bayazid, which signified the passing away of individual self in Universal Being.[43] From the standpoint of orthodox Islamic theology this concept was blatantly heretical since it denied the essentially transcendental nature of God. Hence Bayazid came to represent those elements in Sufism that stressed antischolasticism, rapture, and pantheism—indeed the very antithesis of orthodox Sufism as represented by the Qadiri order, which accepted the transcendentalism revealed in the Koran and the supremacy of "sobriety" over "intoxication."

After arriving in India from Iran, Shattari Sufis showed a remarkable capacity to absorb non-Islamic ideas and practices while eventually, by the sixteenth century, becoming firmly rooted in Gujarat. The Sufi most responsible for these developments, prob-

[41] K. A. Nizami, "The Shattari Saints and Their Attitude towards the State," *Medieval India Quarterly*, 1 (October 1950), p. 56.

[42] Arberry, *Sufism*, p. 54.

[43] R. A. Nicholson, *The Mystics of Islam* (London: Routledge and Kegan Paul Ltd., 1966), p. 17.

ably the most eminent of the order, was Saiyid Muhammad Ghaus of Gwalior (d. 1563). After spending thirteen years meditating in the hills near Benares under severely austere conditions, he emerged to spend the remainder of his life teaching a most eclectic variety of Sufism. A student of Sanskrit, Muhammad Ghaus wrote one book combining Islamic mystic thought with astrological theories, and another on the methods of self-discipline and breath control as practiced by the yogis.[44] This was the first treatise on the yogis written by an Indian Muslim.[45]

Muhammad Ghaus's instructions to his followers indicate the eclectic position the Shattari order had adopted by the late sixteenth century. As recorded by a later biographer they are, *inter alia*:

1. See the One, know the One, say the One, seek the One; and whatever you see regard as Him.
2. Attain sufficient knowledge (*'ilm*) to recognize deceit, and be a strict Sunni.
3. Pattern your conduct on that of the Prophet.
4. Do not seek truth in books, but in what your *pir* has told you.
5. Report dreams to your *pir*, without exaggeration.
6. Do not associate with illiterate people.
7. Do not associate with "worldly" people, lest you lose your faith.[46]

In the first of these instructions one notes a pantheistic concept, possibly inherited direct from the tradition of Bayazid and filtered through the ecstatic poetry of Jalal al-Din Rumi.[47] The next two points, on the other hand, place Muhammad Ghaus squarely on the side of orthodoxy, not only because of his emphasis on one's ethical behavior following the Prophet's, but also because the knowledge he advocates here is not the esoteric knowledge (*ma'rifat*) of the Sufis, but the exoteric knowledge (*'ilm*) of the *'ulama*. Also significant is his stress on being a strict Sunni,

[44] M. Mujeeb, *The Indian Muslims* (London: George Allen and Unwin Ltd., 1967), p. 301.

[45] Aziz Ahmad, *Studies in Islamic Culture in the Indian Environment* (Oxford: Clarendon Press, 1964), p. 137.

[46] *Mishkat*, copy B, fol. 422b.

[47] Compare Rumi's "One I seek, One I know, One I see, One I call" (R. A. Nicholson, ed. and tr., *Selected Poems from the Divani Shamsi Tabriz* [Cambridge: Cambridge University Press, 1898], p. 127).

evidence of the order's partisanship in the sectarian conflict within Islam between Sunnism and Shi'ism. The fourth and fifth points reflect a characteristic that was becoming common to most Sufi orders in their full-blown *tariqa* phase: what had begun in the *khanaqah* phase as a *murid*'s respect for his *pir* was now developing into a slavelike submission to the master.

The final two points concern Muhammad Ghaus's instructions on social ethics. Here, as in some of the other points, one sees how fine can be the line between eclecticism and contradiction. The admonition to avoid "worldly" people is not unique to Muhammad Ghaus, nor for that matter to the Shattari order. It was an admonition frequently voiced and almost as frequently violated by many Sufis of various orders, including Muhammad Ghaus himself. But his frank advice to avoid illiterate people,[48] seldom stated in such blunt terms, betrays the Shattari order's later tendency toward elitism and association with the rich and the powerful. Muhammad Ghaus's own close association with monarchs and nobles set the precedent. It was his attachment to the Mughal court of Humayun, in fact, that forced him to flee to Gujarat when Humayun was overthrown by Sher Shah in 1539.[49]

In Gujarat Muhammad Ghaus established various centers of Shattari teaching, most importantly at Ahmedabad and Broach. But his followers, instead of adopting his ascetic or syncretistic qualities, retained only his scholastic and socially elitist qualities. The most eminent among his followers in Gujarat, Shah Wajih al-Din 'Alawi (d. 1589) of Ahmedabad, is remembered for having been a distinguished scholar, an author of some three hundred tracts, and the founder of a great *madrasa* (religious school) in Ahmedabad, which existed until as late as 1820.[50] But Wajih al-Din did not indulge in mystic "intoxication" as did Bayazid; nor did he engage in ascetic or yogic practices as did his own *pir*, Muhammad Ghaus. On the contrary, he allowed no place for non-Muslim influence in his teachings and in fact rejected the

48 The text reads *na-jins* ("ignoble," "rude") and *jahilan* ("ignorant," "illiterate").

49 Nizami, "The Shattari Saints," p. 63.

50 John A. Subhan, *Sufism, Its Saints and Shrines* (Lucknow: Lucknow Publishing House, 1960), pp. 319 f.

possibility of Hindus becoming followers of Shattari *pirs*.[51] Not surprisingly Shah Wajih al-Din endorsed the position of orthodox Sufis that the mystic path (*tariqat*) must be subordinate to Islamic Law (*shari'at*).[52]

In Gujarat during the sixteenth century, then, the Shattari order because of its urban nature and its stand on Muslim orthodoxy, was moving ever closer to the posture of the Qadiri Sufis of Bidar. Shattari Sufis were also beginning to resemble the Qadiris in their increasingly close association with the state. It was Muhammad Ghaus's identification with the Mughals that forced his flight to Gujarat in the first place. When Akbar restored Mughal authority in India, Muhammad Ghaus returned from Gujarat to Agra where he renewed his association with the Mughal court, even becoming the spiritual guide for Akbar's famous court musician, Tan Sen.[53] As for Wajih al-Din 'Alawi, although he never coveted state help, he never refused it when offered.[54] During one of Gujarat's periods of political turmoil he even advised his followers to place their faith and prayers in one of the nobles of the time, I'timad Khan.[55] Reliance on the state reached its culmination for many of the successors and descendants of Wajih al-Din when they began, in the early seventeenth century, accepting endowments and land grants from the Mughal court.[56]

[51] *Malfuzat-i Shah Wajih al-Din Gujarati*, comp. uncertain, Persian MS (Hyderabad: Asafiyah Library, Tasawwuf no. 547), p. 3.

[52] Ibid., p. 1.

[53] Aziz Ahmad, *An Intellectual History of Islam in India* (Edinburgh: University Press, 1969), p. 148.

[54] Nizami, "The Shattari Saints," p. 68.

[55] *Samarat al-Quds min Shajarat al-Uns*, comp. by Mirza La'l Beg. Persian MS (2 vols.; Hyderabad: Salar Jung Museum, Tarajim-i Sufiya no. 5), II, fol. 574a.

[56] In 1619, thirty years after Wajih al-Din's death, the Mughal Emperor Jahangir visited Ahmedabad and afterwards wrote the following in his memoirs: "As it was the anniversary of Shaikh Wajih-d-din, 1,500 rupees were given to Shaikh Haidar [the Sufi's grandson and successor to the *dargah*] for the expenses of the anniversary, and I bestowed 1,500 rupees more on the band of fakirs who were present in the monastery, with my own hand in charity, and made a present of 500 rupees to the grandson (?) of Shaikh Wajih-d-din. In the same way I gave something for expenses, and land to each of his relatives and adherents according to his merit." (Jahangir, *The Tuzuk-i-Jahangiri, or Memoirs of Jahangir*, trans. by Alexander Rogers, ed. by Henry Beveridge [2 vols., 2nd edn.; Delhi: Munshiram Manoharlal, 1968], I, p. 426.)

Shah Wajih al-Din 'Alawi is said to have had fourteen hundred *khalifas* or successors,[57] but not all of them remained in Gujarat, nor did all become bound to Mughal charity. Many Shattaris of Gujarat claiming spiritual lineage from Wajih al-Din or Muhammad Ghaus migrated to Bijapur about the same time that Sufis of the Qadiri order were migrating to Bijapur from Bidar, that is, during the late sixteenth and early seventeenth centuries. By that time, Shattari Sufis of Gujarat had adopted a doctrinal and social posture quite similar to that of Qadiri Sufis in spite of the different origins of the two orders. Sufis of both orders resided in cities, were well integrated with Islamic orthodoxy, and had accommodated themselves with local political authority. In Gibb's terminology they were both urban orders.

Settlement in the Shi'a Period of 'Adil Shahi Rule, 1490-1583

It would be impossible to guess the total number of Sufis who lived in Bijapur at any one time. The hagiographic literature simply and understandably does not include anything like a census; this literature, after all, is more concerned with establishing and transmitting the quality of Sufis' lives than the quantity of Sufis. But this does not make the situation hopeless. Although hagiographers were not at all concerned with demographic statistics, we find that they generally did record the fact, if not the precise date, of an immigrant Sufi's arrival from outside the Bijapur area. From this information, given in Table 1, it is possible to make several broad generalizations.[58] First, although centers of Sufi brotherhoods had already appeared in Bidar and Gujarat

[57] *Rauzat*, copy A, p. 153.

[58] The figures for Sufi migrants given in this table have been culled from *tazkiras* listed under "Contemporary Works about Prominent Sufis" in the bibliography of this study. It should be noted that the figures given here are probably incomplete owing to the uneven attention to detail one finds among the various hagiographies. In any case, the figures would necessarily be small since the Sufis of Bijapur at all times represented only a tiny elite class in the society in which they lived. Unfortunately, only in a fraction of cases was the actual date of a Sufi's arrival recorded in the hagiographies, while the reign in which he arrived more readily survived oral tradition. Notwithstanding these allowances, however, the table clearly suggests certain trends in the migration patterns of Sufis to Bijapur.

by the beginning of the sixteenth century when the ʿAdil Shahi Sultanate of Bijapur asserted de facto control over the Bijapur plateau, few Sufis migrated to the kingdom throughout most of that century. As the table indicates, it was only after 1580, and continuing into the seventeenth century, that Bijapur attracted Sufis from various parts of India and the Middle East. While our sources do not permit a guess at the total number of Sufis living

TABLE 1

MIGRATION OF SUFIS TO BIJAPUR IN THE ʿADIL SHAHI PERIOD

Sultan	*Dates of Reign*	*Number of Sufi Migrants*
Yusuf	1490-1510	1
Ismaʿil	1510-1534	0
Mallu	1534-1535	0
Ibrahim I	1535-1558	1
ʿAli I	1558-1580	1
Ibrahim II	1580-1627	27
Muhammad	1627-1656	11
ʿAli II	1656-1672	4
Sikandar	1672-1686	0

in Bijapur at any one time—a figure that would include native-born Deccanis as well as migrants—it may be presumed that even though the number of migrants decreased toward the end of the dynasty, the total number of Sufis living in Bijapur must have continued to increase. The very nature of the *pir-murid* system, by which disciples could become *khalifas* who in turn could make more disciples, insured that the total number would multiply. Thus it would seem fair to conclude that while Bijapur remained relatively barren as a center for Sufism prior to the reign of Ibrahim II, the post-1583 period saw Sufism flourish in Bijapur to a significant degree.

Two factors inhibited the immigration of Sufis in the first half of ʿAdil Shahi history, covering the period 1490 to 1583. One was the absence of the sort of Muslim urban environment in which either the Qadiris or the Shattaris, both urban orders, could thrive. Another was the emergence of the *isna-ʿashari* Shiʿa sect of Islam, which was generally hostile to Sufis and Sufi doctrines, as Bijapur's state religion during most of the sixteenth century.

Although the establishment of Bahmani rule over the Deccan in 1347 had removed Bijapur's status as a remote frontier post, the city under the Bahmanis never possessed the economic or political importance of Gulbarga or Bidar, the two Bahmani capitals. Nor did Bijapur's de facto independence from Bahmani authority in 1490 suddenly transform the city into a notable center of Islamic civilization.[59] Situated in the center of a flat plateau with no hills or escarpments to provide it with natural defenses, the city remained exposed to enemies from all sides. Consolidation of the kingdom was further hampered by the chaotic pattern of Deccani politics in the sixteenth century. The reigns of Bijapur's first four monarchs (1490-1558) saw a period not only of intense internal strife between the antagonistic Deccani and Foreigner classes, but also of the gravest threats by external powers to the kingdom's survival. Repeated wars with sister successor kingdoms to the Bahmanis, especially Golconda and Ahmadnagar, were compounded by struggles with the hostile Vijayanagar Empire to the immediate south and the rise on the Konkan Coast of the Portuguese, to whom the port of Goa was permanently lost in 1510.

Further discouraging Sufi immigration was the promulgation of state Shi'ism of the *isna-'ashari* variety as the official religion of Bijapur during most of the sixteenth century. For both theological and historical reasons Muslims of the Shi'a sect have at various times opposed the propagation of Sufi brotherhoods. From a theological standpoint there would appear to exist some affinity between Shi'ism and Sufism, for both trace their spiritual lineage back to the Prophet's son-in-law 'Ali, to whom both Shi'as and Sufis believe the Prophet revealed his esoteric knowledge. However, doctrinal Shi'ism, as Gibb has observed, "was still more hostile to Sufism than were the early Sunnis, since by laying stress on the immediate relation between God and man the Sufis

[59] Bijapur became effectively independent from the Bahmani Sultanate in 1490 under Yusuf 'Adil Khan, its first monarch, and the other four successor states to the Bahmanis likewise achieved de facto independence about the same time. The kingdom did not assume full titles of sovereignty, however, until after the last of the Bahmani royal family died *c.* 1538. By 1539 Ibrahim I, the fourth of the 'Adil Shahi line, had given up all pretensions of loyalty to Bidar and styled himself "Shah" instead of "Khan" as his three predecessors had done. See Sherwani and Joshi, *History of Medieval Deccan*, I, pp. 292, 316.

denied the distinguishing tenet of Shi'ism, that salvation depends upon devotion to an Imam of the house of 'Ali."[60]

Although the historical basis of Shi'a-Sufi enmity lies deep in the history of Islam, its immediate origins can be found in the rise of the Safawi dynasty in Iran (1501-1722) and the hostility that this dynasty exhibited toward Sufi brotherhoods. It is known that the heterodox Turkoman tribesmen who propelled the dynasty to power were both zealous Shi'as and members of the Safawi Sufi order, and that Shah Isma'il had risen to power mainly by virtue of his identification as a semi-divine *pir* among his Turkoman *murids*. But the Sufi bond of Isma'il to his followers was snapped, it has been argued, when the Ottomans inflicted upon Isma'il and his Turkoman armies a crushing defeat in 1514 (Battle of Chaldiran). Because of this defeat Isma'il sank into a state of despondency from which he never fully recovered, and the very term "Sufi" became a pejorative in Iran.[61] Moreover, as the Safawi political machinery, after Shah Isma'il, fell under increasing Persian (and Arab) influence, those Sufis who were Turkoman tribesmen belonging to the Safawi order lost their former official favor. "The basic *qizilbash* [Turkoman] Sufi organization obstinately refused to be merged with the Persian bureaucracy," wrote Roger Savory, "and became an increasingly meaningless survival of the past."[62]

A more important factor leading to the Safawi government's growing hostility toward the Turkoman Sufis was the rise of doctrinal Shi'ism to the status of state religion and the emergence of a class of Shi'a *'ulama* that served the new Safawi government. Although both Shah Isma'il's Turkoman followers and the *'ulama* of the government were Shi'a, a sharp distinction must be drawn between the types of Shi'ism exhibited by each group. The Shi'ism of the Turkoman tribes was of an extreme variety (*ghulat*) which frequently embraced the heretical notions that 'Ali and the imams descended from him, or indeed any particularly charis-

[60] H. A. R. Gibb and H. Bowen, *Islamic Society and the West*, I, pt. 2 (London: Oxford University Press, 1957), p. 181, fn. See also Trimingham, *Sufi Orders*, pp. 135 f., 164.

[61] Roger M. Savory, "The Principal Offices of the Safawid State during the Reign of Isma'il I (1501-24)," *Bulletin, School of Oriental and African Studies*, 23 (1960), pp. 91 f.

[62] Roger M. Savory, "The Office of *Khalifat al-Khulfa* under the Safawids," *Journal of the American Oriental Society*, 85 (1965), p. 498.

matic individual, were incarnations of God. On the other hand, the type of Shi'ism of the Safawi *'ulama*, the *isna-'ashari* type, was theologically more moderate in that while it accorded great respect to 'Ali and the Twelve Imams, such *ghulat* notions as incarnation (*hulul*) or metempsychosis (*tanasukh*) were vigorously rejected. These differences of doctrine were powerfully reinforced by sociological and political factors. Although the Turkoman Shi'as were rural and tribal in orientation, and as bands of armed tribesmen represented a potential threat to the stability of the state, the official Shi'a *'ulama* class was urban and state oriented, and represented above all the very stability of the Safawi theocracy. The power of this class became especially formidable, moreover, through the influence of Arab Shi'a scholars and divines who migrated to Iran and found government employment where their sect had been declared the official creed.[63] In this situation, as the fortunes of *isna-'ashari* Shi'ism became tied to those of the new Iranian state, state Shi'ism evolved into a conservative ideology, and those very Turkoman elements that had propelled the dynasty to power were now regarded as doctrinally and politically dangerous.

The association of the Turkoman tribesmen not only with extreme Shi'ism (*ghulat*) but also with Sufism had serious results. We find immediately after the reign of Shah Isma'il an increasing tendency on the part of the Safawi monarchs to dissociate themselves from the Sufi order that had in fact given its name to the dynasty. Stimulated by the increasing influence of the *isna-'ashari 'ulama*, particularly those Arab immigrants who were imbued with a traditional Shi'a enmity to Sufism, official hostility toward Sufi brotherhoods became more manifest throughout the sixteenth century. The government came to persecute non-Turkoman as well as Turkoman Sufi orders, culminating in frequency and severity with the reign of Shah 'Abbas I (1588-1629). Sunni orders such as the Naqshbandi were suppressed soon after the Safawi consolidation of power in Iran, while suppression of Shi'a orders such as the Ni'mat Allahi followed somewhat later.[64]

[63] Hamid Algar, "Some Observations on Religion in Safavid Persia," *Iranian Studies*, 7, Nos. 1-2 (Winter-Spring, 1974), p. 291.

[64] One Iranian scholar has written that with regard to Sufis particularly, the Safawi state "employed every kind of severity and vexation, whether by exile, expulsion, slaughter or reprimand, slaying or burning many of them

As a result of this situation many Sufis, reflecting an age-old response to religious persecution on the Iranian plateau, emigrated to India. It appears, however, that they did not migrate to Bijapur as long as that kingdom, like Safawi Iran, was under *isna-'ashari* Shi'a domination. During most of the sixteenth century, from 1502 to 1534 and again from 1558 to 1583, the Kingdom of Bijapur was ruled as a Shi'a state, reflecting the domination in those periods of the Foreigner class of which the most prominent component was Iranian Shi'as. The kingdom's founder, Yusuf 'Adil Khan (1490-1510), exercised caution in declaring Bijapur a Shi'a state, waiting until 1502 when news arrived that Shah Isma'il had already done so in Iran. Yusuf's successor, Isma'il 'Adil Khan (1510-34), more stridently promulgated the Shi'a sect, pushing aside all Deccanis from the army and even requiring his soldiers to wear the same Shi'a caps as did the followers of his Safawi namesake.[65] During the reign of Bijapur's fourth monarch, Ibrahim I (1535-58),[66] the Sunni sect was for a while installed as the state religion, reflecting the growing influence of Deccanis in Bijapur—i.e., Muslims descended from the early settlers of the Deccan, Abyssinian slaves, and converted Hindus.

But with the accession of 'Ali I (1558-80), Bijapur's fifth monarch and greatest conqueror, the Shi'a Foreigners vigorously reasserted their former hegemony. This occurred, however, only after a dramatic armed clash in which the Foreigners laid seige to Bijapur's old Jami' Mosque, fortified by the Sunni Deccanis.[67] Thereafter during 'Ali I's reign, not only were the Friday prayers

---

with their own hands or by their sentence. . . . Hence it was that under this dynasty learning, culture, poetry and mysticism completely deserted Persia, and the cloisters, monasteries, retreats and resthouses (of the *darwishes*) were so utterly destroyed that there is now throughout the whole of Persia no name or sign of such charitable foundations." (Mirza Muhammad Qazvini, quoted in Edward G. Browne, *A Literary History of Persia* [4 vols.; Cambridge: Cambridge University Press, 1953], IV, p. 27).

65 Muhammad Ibrahim Zubairi, *Basatin al-Salatin.* Persian lithograph (Hyderabad: Saiyidi Press, 1892-93), pp. 32 f. Hereafter referred to as *Basatin.*

66 Bijapur's third monarch was the profligate and incompetent Mallu 'Adil Khan, who after a brief reign of seven months in 1534-35 was deposed and blinded by his younger brother, Ibrahim I.

67 *Basatin*, pp. 77 f. The Deccanis held out long enough that 'Ali yielded and allowed the mosque to remain a Sunni preserve.

(*khutba*) read in the Shi'a form, but three thousand Shi'as were employed to revile the first three caliphs, whom Shi'as do not accept, by publicly cursing their names in the court, through the streets, and in the bazaars.[68] Nor did 'Ali I direct his Shi'a fanaticism only against the Deccani class, which was Sunni. While campaigning in Karnataka following the fall of Vijayanagar 'Ali I's armies destroyed two to three hundred Hindu temples, and the monarch himself was said to have smashed four to five thousand Hindu images.[69] And in Mudgal, a town located 75 miles southeast of Bijapur, 'Ali I tore down two temples and replaced them with *'ashura-khanas*, or houses used in the celebration of Shi'a festivals.[70]

The kingdom's religious and intellectual atmosphere seems to have been remarkably sterile during most of the sixteenth century. The absence not only of Sufis, but also of poets, musicians, historians, calligraphers, and other men of cultivated skills would suggest that doctrinal Shi'ism cast a shadow of stifling austerity over the cultural life of pre-1583 Bijapur, as also happened in Safawi Iran.[71] The career of a certain Shah Tahir (d. 1549), who was a learned Shi'a scholar of Iran having connections with the Isma'ili sect,[72] illustrates this point in the cases of both Iran and Bijapur. Having aroused the jealousy of the Safawi monarch Isma'il I owing to his excessive popularity and possibly also his sectarian connections, Shah Tahir was forced to flee Iran in 1519 and was chased by the king's men even to the shores of the Persian Gulf. But Tahir was able to board a ship bound for India just hours before his pursuers arrived at the port. Reaching India via Goa, Shah Tahir traveled straight to Bijapur and the court of Isma'il 'Adil Khan. Bijapur's Shi'a monarch, however, extended scarcely more welcome to the scholar than had the Safawi monarch. An account of Shah Tahir's life recorded that "Isma'il only

[68] Ibid., p. 77.

[69] Rafi' al-Din Ibrahim Shirazi, *Tazkirat al-Muluk*. Persian MS (Hyderabad: Salar Jung Museum, Tarikh no. 142), fol. 55b. See also *Basatin*, p. 129.

[70] *Waqi'at*, III, p. 575.

[71] See Browne, *Literary History*, IV, pp. 24-28. For a discussion of this point as it relates to the Safawis, see Ehsan Yar-Shater, "Safavid Literature: Progress or Decline," *Iranian Studies*, 7, Nos. 1-2 (Winter-Spring, 1974), pp. 217-70.

[72] Muhammad Ma'sum 'Ali Shah, *Tara'iq al-Haqa'iq* (3 vols.; Teheran: Kitabfurushi-yi Barani, 1345 solar), III, pp. 133-37.

wanted Shi'a soldiers who could fight for him in battles and had little concern with scholars and spiritual leaders." The frustrated scholar accordingly resolved to leave Bijapur and visit Mecca, Medina, and the holy shrines of the Shi'a Imams.[73]

A biographical notice of one of the only Sufis who lived in the kingdom during its entire Shi'a phase illustrates the friction then existing between state Shi'ism and Sufis and makes comprehensible the paucity of Sufis in sixteenth-century Bijapur. The notice relates that a certain Saiyid Chanda Husaini had migrated from the coasts of Arabia to Bidar in the late fifteenth century, that is, during the dissolution of the Bahmani Kingdom into five sultanates.[74] After a while, the narrative continues, "Chanda Husaini joined the cavalry of Yusuf 'Adil Khan and accompanied him to Gogi [a town 65 miles east of Bijapur]. Then Yusuf 'Adil Khan everywhere proclaimed the Shi'a faith in 1504-5 [sic], and Chanda Husaini renounced their friendship, becoming absorbed in the remembrance of God."[75] We have no more details than these. There can be no mistaking, however, the narrative's causative inference between Yusuf's promulgation of state Shi'ism and Chanda Husaini's renunciation of their friendship. Moreover, the fact that Chanda Husaini was Arab and not Iranian suggests that doctrinal tensions between Sufism and Shi'ism did indeed run deep, quite apart from the hostilities generated when Shi'ism became the state religion of Iran.

In sum, an environment conducive to the flourishing of Sufi brotherhoods did not obtain in Bijapur as long as the Foreigner class, which was nearly exclusively Shi'a, dominated the political and religious life of the kingdom. Until the last third of the sixteenth century, moreover, Bijapur had remained a small and in-

[73] M. Hidayat Hosein, "Shah Tahir of the Deccan," in S. M. Katre and P. K. Gode, eds., *E. Denison Ross Presentation Volume* (Bombay: Karnatak Publishing House, 1939), pp. 149-51.

[74] The exact date of Chanda Husaini's death is not known. A chronogram over his tomb in Gogi puts it at 1454 (Yazdani, "Inscriptions of Shahpur," p. 5). This, however, conflicts with what we know of his connections with Yusuf 'Adil Khan fifty years later. One of the hagiographies states that he died in the reign of 'Ali I (1558-80), which is chronologically more plausible. (*Tazkirat al-Qadiri*, comp. by Munshi Qadir Khan Bidari. Persian MS [Hyderabad: Asafiyah Library, Tazkirat Jadid, no. 1086], fol. 74b.)

[75] Ibid., fol. 73b.

secure city-state, struggling incessantly with its neighbors as well as with its own quarreling factions, commanding little political authority over the plateau, and governing more by personality than by institution. In these circumstances Bijapur did not attract foreign Sufis, at least not those belonging to urban orders.

SETTLEMENT IN THE SUNNI PERIOD OF 'ADIL SHAHI RULE, POST-1583

It was not until the reign of 'Ali I's successor, Sultan Ibrahim II (1580-1627), that an atmosphere of intellectual liberalism and Sunni Islam flourished in Bijapur. This new atmosphere resulted partly from the substitution of Sunni for Shi'a Islam as the state religion, partly from the liberal and charismatic personality of Ibrahim II himself, and partly from the emergence of a new political elite ushered in when the Foreigner class, which had throughout the sixteenth century dominated Bijapur's political and cultural life, finally gave way to the more socially heterogeneous Deccani class, a process encouraged and presided over by Ibrahim II himself.

Having no son when he died in 1580, 'Ali I had named as heir-apparent his nine-year-old nephew, the future Ibrahim II. But as the new monarch did not begin ruling in his own right until 1590, Bijapur lapsed into a ten-year period, virtually an interregnum, when the state was ruled by four successive regents. With no mature monarch on the throne, struggles for the regency allowed the sociopolitical conflicts between the Foreigners and the Deccanis, long submerged under 'Ali I's firm rule, to rise to the surface. Between 1580 and 1583 no less than three regents were pulled down from power amidst these factional struggles. Finally in 1583 a fourth regent, Dilawar Khan Habashi, an Abyssinian slave, rose to an undisputed and autocratic supremacy that lasted seven years. This development allowed the Deccani class, of which the Abyssinian blacks were one part, to entrench themselves in positions that the Foreigner class would never again recover. The phenomenon of slave mobility, by which palace bodyguards rose to usurp the power of their masters, was not uncommon in medieval Muslim history. But because Abyssinian slaves, through their contact with Arabs in East Africa, were for the most part Sunni Muslims and generally hostile to Iranians, the rise of Dilawar Khan worked deep changes in the kingdom's ruling structure. Upon gaining power, Dilawar Khan forthwith expelled from the kingdom ʿAli I's bodyguard of five or six thousand Foreigner soldiers and replaced them with fellow Abyssinians. More significantly, he officially terminated state Shiʿism and installed as the kingdom's official creed orthodox Sunni Islam, which was to remain paramount throughout the rest of the dynasty's history. Members of the Sunni *ʿulama* were also recruited by Dilawar Khan, not from overseas, but from Gujarat and the Punjab.[76] Thus, while no complete social revolution occurred during the ten-year regency for Ibrahim II, the rise of the Abyssinians and the overthrow of state Shiʿism prepared the way for changes that would be made more complete later in Ibrahim II's reign.

Ibrahim II ousted Dilawar Khan Habashi from power in the summer of 1590 and shortly thereafter devoted himself to the establishment of Bijapur as a center of Indo-Muslim culture in which a synthesis of Islam and indigenous Marathi and Kannada culture could take place. His conception of Islam in India held no room for religious bigotry, much less the physical replacement of Hindu temples by mosques or *ʿashura-khanas* as had happened in his predecessor's reign. For where ʿAli I had been a strict and militant Shiʿa, Ibrahim II was a Sunni of the most liberal sort. And where ʿAli I had been a soldier, Ibrahim II was primarily a lover of poetry and music, as contemporary paintings of him indicate.[77]

The liberal and eclectic atmosphere prevailing in Bijapur by the turn of the seventeenth century, presided over and personified by the monarch himself, doubtless stimulated Sufi immigration. We hear, for example, that during Ibrahim II's reign "thousands of musicians" were attracted to the sultanate, in addition to numerous Sufis, learned scholars, poets, calligraphers, and master artists.[78] According to one contemporary biography of Bijapuri Sufis, Ibrahim II personally sent letters to Sufis and scholars of Gujarat requesting them to settle in Bijapur.[79] Shaikh ʿAlam Allah Muhaddis, a Sufi residing in the northern Deccan city of Burhan-

[76] *Basatin*, pp. 190, 213.

[77] Compare Figures 7 and 8, which reflect sharply opposing aspects of the two monarchs.

[78] *Basatin*, pp. 274 f.

[79] *Sahifat*, Urdu edn., p. 112.

pur, likewise received a letter from Ibrahim II personally requesting him to migrate to Bijapur.[80]

Apart from internal developments within Bijapur that attracted Sufis to the sultanate, another set of forces drove Sufis to Bijapur from the outside. We have already noted the hostility that state Shiʿism in Safawi Iran harbored for Sufis. This hostility increased during the sixteenth century and culminated with Shah ʿAbbas I, who began sending to the executioners Sufis affiliated with Shiʿa as well as Sunni orders. As it happened, the reign of Shah ʿAbbas I (1588-1629) coincided almost exactly with that of Sultan Ibrahim II (1580-1627), whose enthusiasm to adorn his capital with Sufis of all orders has already been mentioned. Therefore, since both the Chishti and the Shattari orders had originated in Khurasan, in northeastern Iran, it may safely be presumed that state Shiʿism in Safawi Iran was in part responsible for their removal to India.

In Gujarat toward the end of the sixteenth century a number of political and social disorders seem to have caused many Sufis to abandon that province. The wars that accompanied Akbar's Mughal conquest of Gujarat in 1573 probably caused considerable dislocation. Political conquest was followed the next year by a famine all over the province. "From the severity of these calamities," wrote one contemporary historian, "the inhabitants, rich and poor, fled the country, and were scattered abroad."[81] Then between 1583 and 1592 the ex-sultan of the erstwhile independent Sultanate of Gujarat rose in rebellion against Mughal authority. "The formidable insurrection which was thus brought about," wrote M. S. Commissariat, "plunged Gujarat—both the mainland and the peninsula—into another ten years of bloodshed and disorder, and, for a time, shook to its foundations the newly established imperial power."[82] Several biographies of Bijapuri Sufis, moreover, mention that chaotic conditions in Gujarat prompted Sufis of Ibrahim II's period to migrate to Bijapur.[83] These were mainly Shattari Sufis since Sufis of that order were well represented in sixteenth-century Gujarat.

[80] *Rauzat*, copy A, p. 213.

[81] Nizam al-Din Ahmad, *Tabaqat-i Akbari*. Persian lithograph (Lucknow: Nawal Kishor, 1879), p. 323. (Abridged English edition: Elliot and Dowson, eds., *The History of India*, v, p. 384.)

[82] M. S. Commissariat, *History of Gujarat* (2 vols.; Bombay: Orient Longmans, 1957), II, p. 17.

[83] See *Sahifat*, Urdu edn., p. 112; *Rauzat*, copy A, p. 154.

In Bidar the dominant order of the sixteenth century had been the Qadiri order, and in that city, like Gujarat, internal developments probably played some part in Sufis quitting the area for Bijapur. The city's decline commenced with the collapse of the Bahmani Sultanate, of which Bidar had been the capital. After the Battle of Talikota (1565) the city's decline progressed more rapidly, while its neighbors—Bijapur, Golconda, and Ahmadnagar—became so powerful that they frequently fought for possession of Bidar as a potential *jagir*.[84] Eventually, in 1619, Ibrahim II annexed Bidar to the Kingdom of Bijapur. This political connection might also have stimulated Qadiris to migrate to Bijapur, given the tendency of Sufis of that order to ally themselves with centers of political power, though the sources do not mention this as a possible motivation.

There were twenty-seven Sufis whose immigration to Bijapur during Ibrahim II's reign can be confirmed by reference to the relevant biographical sources. Table 2 lists these Sufis by order

TABLE 2

MIGRATION OF SUFIS IN THE REIGN OF IBRAHIM II (1580-1627)

Name	*Death Date*	*Place(s) of Origin*	*Source**
QADIRI ORDER			
'Abd al-Latif La-ubali, Shah	1640	Baghdad—Kurnool	10:9, 44
'Abd al-Razzaq Qadiri, Shah	1640	Baghdad—E. Africa	12:16 f
'Abd Allah 'Aidarus, Shah	1631-32	Arabia—Ahmadnagar	4:126-28
Abu'l-Hasan Qadiri, Shah	1635	Bidar	12:30 f., 36
Hamīd Qadiri, Shaikh	1603	Sindh—Bidar	1:63-65
Muntajab al-Din Qadiri, Shaikh	1670	Gujarat—Bidar	1:62a
Mustafa Qadiri, Shah	1659	Bidar	1:124
Nur Allah Qadiri, Shah	1656-57	Bidar	2:61a
Qasim Qadiri, Shah	1622	Bidar	1:108, 112
SHATTARI ORDER			
'Abd al-Jalil Buzurg	1590-1	Multan—Gujarat	4:497
'Abd al-Rahman, Saiyid (son of Shah Ruh Allah)	1618	Broach	3:148

[84] Yazdani, *Bidar*, pp. 13 f.

TABLE 2 *(continued)*

Name	*Death Date*	*Place(s) of Origin*	*Source**
ʿAbd Allah, Qazi	?	Gujarat	1:225
Amir Saiyid Shah Muhammad	c. 1640	Gujarat—Burhanpur	9:326b-327a
Hashim Pir ʿAlawi, Shah	1646	Ahmedabad	13:56b, 1:132 f., 1:149b
Murtaza Qadiri, Shah	1613	Ahmedabad	1:113
Nur al-Din Safawi, Shah	1625-26	Iran	1:102
Sibghat Allah, Shah	1606	Broach—Ahmedabad	9:330b, 1:79
CHISHTI ORDER			
Asghar Husaini, Shah	1611	Gulbarga	1:61
Bahr al-Din, Qazi	c. 1600	Madras	14:15 f.
Hashim Khudawand Hadi, Saiyid	1705	Bukhara	11:988
Hidayat Allah Husaini, Shah	1609	Gulbarga	1:61 f.
Khudanama, Shah Miranji	1675	Golconda	8:532, 7:1522
Khush Dahan, Shaikh Mahmud	1617	Bidar	15:27, 1:176
OTHER			
ʿAbd al-Rahman Muttaqi	1668	Ahmedabad (order unknown)	1:225
ʿAlam Allah Muhaddis, Shaikh	1616	N. India (ʿAidarusi order)	1:212-15
Nizam Narnuli, Shaikh	?	N. India (order unknown)	1:103 f.
Taʿzim Turk, Saiyid Muhammad	?	Iran (order unknown)	1:179

* 1—*Rauzat al-Auliya*, copy A
2—Ibid., copy B
3—Ibid., Urdu edition
4—*Tazkira-yi ʿAuliya*, I
5—Ibid., II
6—*Waqiʿat*, III
7—*Mishkat*, copy A
8—Ibid., copy B
9—*Gulzar-i Abrar*
10—*Latayif al-Latif*
11—*Makhzan al-Ansab*
12—*Sahifat*, Urdu edition
13—*Tuhfa az Kamtarin*
14—*Man Lagan*, introduction
15—*Sukh Anjan*, introduction

and indicates their point of origin.[85] From this table it can be seen that the majority of Sufis belonging to the Qadiri order came from Bidar, a major Qadiri center in the late fifteenth century. The table also indicates that even in the seventeenth century the Qadiri order was still nurtured by steady infusions of newcomers from Arabia and Baghdad. Sufis of the Shattari *silsila* came almost exclusively from Gujarat, especially the cities of Ahmedabad and Broach. The only Sufi to come to Bijapur in the reign of ʿAli I, Shaikh Shams al-Din Zinda Dil, was a Shattari ultimately from Shiraz, migrating thence to Ahmedabad and Bijapur.[86] And the only Shattari to come directly from Iran to Bijapur, Shah Nur al-Din Safawi, bears the name of the order of Ismaʿil Safawi, founder of the Safawi dynasty of Iran. Both cases suggest the Shattari order's connections with Iran, which might in turn explain the origin of the bitter anti-Shiʿism exhibited by some Shattari Sufis of Bijapur.

Early Chishti Sufis of Shahpur Hillock

While the histories of the two urban orders of Bijapur, the Qadiri and Shattari orders, closely paralleled the history of the city itself, the same cannot be said of the Chishti order. Throughout the sixteenth and seventeenth centuries—even during the Shiʿa phase of the kingdom's history—there thrived just outside the city an important tradition of Chishti Sufism. This tradition was centered on a single family of Sufis, perhaps the most famous of Bijapur: the family of Shah Miranji Shams al-ʿUshshaq (d. 1499). Although Qadiri and Shattari Sufis generally settled within the outer wall when they arrived in Bijapur, Shah Miranji and his descendants lived on a hill approximately one mile to the northwest of the outer wall. This hill is known popularly as Shahpur

[85] This is a minimum list, for there were doubtless other Sufis who for one reason or another failed to be recorded in the biographies of Sufis (*tazkirat*) on which this table is based. Still, the extent of Sufi immigration in Ibrahim II's reign is proportionally much higher than that of any other ʿAdil Shahi monarch. See Table 1.

[86] *Gulzar-i Abrar fi Sair al-Akhyar*, comp. by Muhammad Ghausi bin Husain bin Musa Shattari. Persian MS (Hyderabad: Andhra Pradesh State Archives, Oriental Manuscripts Library, no. 258), fol. 205a-b. Hereafter referred to as *Gulzar-i Abrar*. Shams al-Din lived as a recluse outside the city and died at the beginning of Ibrahim II's reign, in 1582-83.

Hillock; among the Chishti Sufis and their followers who lived there it was called Manauwarpur, "City of Light."[87] The physical separation of Shahpur Hillock from the city of Bijapur had important implications with respect to Chishti relations with the court and the religious establishment. In both Delhi and Gulbarga the Chishti tradition had died largely by becoming too closely involved in the affairs of the court. In Bijapur this was not to happen, partly because of this physical separation, and partly also because of the nature of the heterodox teachings that became identified with the Sufis of Shahpur Hillock. For two hundred years, the duration of ʿAdil Shahi rule, the Chishtis remained aloof from the affairs of the court and socially and doctrinally apart from the *ʿulama* of the city.

The source material available for reconstructing the life and work of Shah Miranji and his successors at Shahpur Hillock is unique in that we have so many writings composed by the Sufis themselves. In addition to their mystical and popular literature, to be discussed in chapter six below, we find various other types of writing—elegies, letters, autobiographies, etc.—which cast light on their careers. Apart from material composed by the leading mystics themselves, we also have a most important narrative poem concerning the lives of Bijapur's Chishti Sufis written in Dakhni by a certain Muʿazzam Bijapuri, a *murid* of Shah Miranji's grandson, Amin al-Din Aʿla. This poem, entitled *Shajarat al-Atqiya*, was nearly contemporary with the events it describes, as its author lived in the middle and late seventeenth century.[88] Finally, there are the general hagiographies already encountered in this study—the *Rauzat al-Auliya*, the *Tazkirat al-Qadiri*, the *Mishkat-i Nubuwat*, etc.—which include entries for Chishti as well as for non-Chishti Sufis.

Although none of the biographical or other accounts indicates Shah Miranji's place of origin, the Sufi himself wrote an autobiography that, if authentic, casts some light on the matter. The *Khud-niwisht wa Nasl-nama*, or "Autobiography and Genealogy," is a short Persian manuscript preserved in Hyderabad pur-

[87] Burhan al-Din Janam, *Marsiyat-i Hazrat Burhan al-Din Janam.* Dakhni MS (Hyderabad: copy in the possession of Professor M. Akbaruddin Siddiqi), couplet no. 34. See Figure 10.

[88] *Shajarat al-Atqiya*, comp. Muʿazzam Bijapuri. Dakhni MS (Hyderabad: Salar Jung Museum, Urdu MSS, Tasawwuf & Akhlaq, no. 131).

porting to be written in Shah Miranji's own hand.[89] In this manuscript it is stated that Shah Miranji was born in Mecca and that his father, Haji Sharif Dawam al-Din, belonged to the Chaghatai clan.[90] If he was a Chaghatai Turk, Shah Miranji's father might well have come from Central Asia or Khurasan on a pilgrimage to Mecca, married there, and fathered Shah Miranji. This interpretation would accord with the Chishti order's original association with the Khurasan region, for it was founded near Herat. Moreover few Chishti Sufis in India were known to have had purely Arab origins, as most were affiliated in some way with the Khurasan region.

According to the narrative poem *Shajarat al-Atqiya*, Shah Miranji as a young man traveled from Mecca to Medina and remained there for twelve years studying and meditating at the Prophet's tomb. While there, he is said to have had a dream in which the Prophet Muhammad appeared before him and instructed him to go to India, where near Bijapur he would find a "city of light" (Munauwarpur, or Shahpur) and there meet a certain Shah Kamal.[91] This aspect of the narrative may be seen as a touch of hagiographic embroidery intended to lend a degree of legitimacy to the entire Sufi tradition that stemmed from Shah Miranji. It may also be seen as an indication that the compiler of the *Shajarat*, Muhammad Mu'azzam, was aware of the moribund state of the Chishti tradition in mid-fifteenth-century India and accordingly inserted the story of Miranji and his command from the Prophet by way of providing a rejuvenating note into the history of the order. It can also be noted that the story of Miranji and his dream adds further support to the likelihood that he had migrated to India and was not born there. For it was recorded that in this dream Miranji complained to the Prophet that he did not know any of the languages of India, to which the Prophet replied that this was no problem and that he would learn them in due course.[92]

Shah Kamal, whom Miranji was instructed to meet in Bijapur, served as the link connecting Shah Miranji with the Chishti tradi-

[89] Miranji Shams al-'Ushshaq, *Khud-niwisht wa Nasl-nama*. Persian MS (Hyderabad: Idara-e-Adabiyat-e-Urdu, no. 863).

[90] Ibid., fol. 21a.

[91] *Shajarat al-Atqiya*, pp. 19 f.

[92] Miranji Shams al-'Ushshaq, *Khud-niwisht*, fol. 21a-b.

tion that had flourished in India for several centuries. We have noted above that the liberal and literary aspects of Chishti Sufism carried from Delhi to Gulbarga by Saiyid Muhammad Husaini Bandanawaz Gisudaraz had ended in Gulbarga when Gisudaraz himself became a landed notable under Bahmani patronage. Although most of his descendants functioned chiefly as landed caretakers of the venerable Sufi's tomb, a literary and prolific line of his spiritual successors was nonetheless maintained in Bijapur for many generations after his death. One of his immediate successors in Gulbarga was a certain Jamal al-Din Maghribi (d. 1423-24), whose biography is not known and who left no known writings. One of Jamal al-Din's *murids*, in turn, was Kamal al-Din Biabani (d. 1462-63), the same "Shah Kamal" whom Miranji was to meet on the hillock outside Bijapur. After migrating to Bijapur toward the end of the fifteenth century, Kamal al-Din met Shah Miranji, who had just arrived from Medina about the same time, instructed him in the secrets of the Chishti path, and passed to him the Chishti *khilafat*.[93] Then, records the *Shajarat al-Atqiya*, Kamal al-Din Biabani wandered into the forests and disappeared while Shah Miranji remained to illuminate Shahpur Hillock, or Manauwarpur, "City of Light."[94]

In this way the Chishti successorship was passed from Gulbarga to Bijapur just before the emergence of that city as the 'Adil Shahi capital. When Miranji Shams al-'Ushshaq died in 1499 the Chishti *khilafat* then passed to his son Burhan al-Din Janam (d. 1597), who was the most prolific and profound writer among the Sufis of Bijapur. Thus, throughout the sixteenth century, while the 'Adil Shahi kingdom was ruled by Shi'as and the city of Bijapur remained virtually empty of Sufis, two persons—Shah Miranji and his more famous son Burhan al-Din Janam—kept Chishti Sufism alive at Shahpur Hillock. By the time that Sultan Ibrahim II assumed the 'Adil Shahi throne in 1590 Burhan al-Din

93 *Rauzat*, copy A, p. 171; *Shajarat al-Atqiya*, pp. 21 f.; *Tazkirat al-Qadiri*, fol. 66a.

94 *Shajarat al-Atqiya*, p. 22. Nothing now remains of Shah Miranji's original *khanaqah* on Shahpur Hillock, and only a small gravestone marks his burial place there. The fame of the hill now rests more with his son and grandson, Burhan al-Din Janam and Amin al-Din A'la—especially the latter. Indeed, today Shahpur Hillock is locally known as the "Amin Dargah." Large tombs over the graves of both Burhan al-Din Janam and Amin al-Din now dominate the hill, as can be seen in Figures 10 and 11.

Janam was already established as one of the great Muslim mystics of the Deccan, with many devotees from diverse parts of the Indian subcontinent studying in his *khanaqah* on Shahpur Hillock.

Summary

Two sets of factors brought about the migration of Sufis to Bijapur in the 'Adil Shahi period: those pulling them to Bijapur, and those pushing them away from older centers. The growth of Bijapur as an important Islamic center was doubtless important in attracting to the city urban-oriented Sufis, as well as other Muslims having cultivated skills. The kingdom's change from a Shi'a to a Sunni state in 1583 was also a factor, for Qadiri Sufis were as attached to Sunni orthodoxy as Shattari Sufis were opposed to Shi'ism. "Push" factors also played a part in the migration of Sufis to Bijapur. Disturbances in late sixteenth century Gujarat, and to a lesser extent in Bidar of the same period, drove some Sufis to seek new homes. The doctrinal and especially the historical enmity between Shi'ism and Sufism seems to have operated in driving other Sufis from Safawi Iran, and Shattari Sufis carried with them to Bijapur a special hostility toward Shi'ism. Bijapur's Chishtis, on the other hand, were not concerned with sectarian disputes between Shi'a and Sunni Muslims. Nor did they perceive their fortunes in Bijapur linked in any way with the prosperity of the capital city. These considerations would seem to explain their continued existence at Shahpur Hillock even in the kingdom's Shi'a period.

Finally, one can note an important difference between the Chishti and non-Chishti patterns of settlement in Bijapur. Followers of the Chishti path generally came to Bijapur to study with Burhan al-Din Janam (and later with his son Amin al-Din A'la) at a single, well-established hospice on Shahpur Hillock. Individual Qadiri or Shattari Sufis, on the other hand, tended not to gravitate toward any such single center when they came to Bijapur, but more typically founded their own separate *khanaqahs*. The Chishti pattern of settlement thus produced a clustering of many individuals around a single center outside the city walls, while the Qadiri and Shattari pattern created a host of lesser *khanaqahs* within the walls.

two

REFORMERS AND WRITERS

Chapter Four

HISTORICAL SETTING: THE HEIGHT OF BIJAPUR UNDER SULTANS 'ALI 'ADIL SHAH I AND IBRAHIM 'ADIL SHAH II

PHYSICAL GROWTH UNDER SULTAN 'ALI I (1558-1580)

Robust, energetic, and militant, Sultan 'Ali I (1558-80) firmly established 'Adil Shahi hegemony over the Bijapur plateau.[1] It was under his rule that the government's military power and civil bureaucracy expanded most appreciably, that commerce rose, that diplomatic relations were established with foreign powers, and that the city grew to the proportions of a major metropolitan center. Immediately upon assuming the throne, 'Ali I allied himself with Vijayanagar, the large Hindu empire to the south, for the purpose of seizing from Ahmadnagar the Sholapur and Naldrug hill forts, thus securing his northern frontiers. This was followed shortly afterwards by a diplomatic volte-face leading to one of the major events in the political history of the Deccan. Sultan 'Ali 'Adil Shah I now forged a tripartite alliance with Ahmadnagar and Golconda, and together the league of the three principal Deccan sultanates overthrew the Vijayanagar Empire in 1565.[2]

[1] See Figure 7. This portrait of 'Ali I conveys his essentially martial character. A Portuguese Jesuit who met him in 1561 wrote, "He goes about accompanied by many soldiers and when we go to the palace so many are the meetings with crowds of people that Lisbon's Rua Nova does not have the advantage in the matter" (Correia-Afonso, "Bijapur Four Centuries Ago," p. 87).

[2] This battle is commonly known as the Battle of Talikota because it was in that town, located 45 miles southeast of Bijapur, that the armies of Bijapur, Golconda, and Ahmadnagar met before waging war against Vijayanagar. The battle was actually fought just south of the Krishna River near its confluence with the Malprabha River. See H. K. Sherwani, "The Site of the So-Called Battle of Talikota," *Journal of the Pakistan Historical Society*, 5 (1957), pp. 151-57.

The benefits accruing to Bijapur as a result of Vijayanagar's defeat were immense. The entire Raichur Doab, or the region between the Krishna and Tungabhadra rivers long disputed by the governments of Vijayanagar and Bijapur, fell permanently into 'Adil Shahi administration. Rich in iron deposits, diamond mines, and deep black soils, this area became Bijapur's basis of economic power throughout the remainder of its history.[3] During the twelve years following the Battle of Talikota, from 1565 to 1576, 'Ali I focused his efforts on consolidating both the Doab and the newly acquired southwestern region of the kingdom around Dharwar. In both regions the Kannada *nayaks*, or local chieftains formerly loyal to the rajas of Vijayanagar, were either replaced when possible by nobles of 'Ali I's own choice, or they were reduced to tributary status.[4] Thus between 1558 and 1576 the Kingdom of Bijapur, which from its inception in 1490 had maintained only a tenuous hold over a strip of the central Bijapur plateau, nearly doubled its territory.[5] In 1570 'Ali I even attempted

[3] See P. M. Joshi, "The Raichur Doab in Deccan History—A Reinterpretation of a Struggle," *Journal of Indian History*, 36 (1958), pp. 379-96.

[4] See Firishta, *Tarikh-i Firishta*, II, pp. 42-45. (Briggs's translation, III, pp. 81-85); *Basatin*, pp. 127 f. From Dharwar 'Ali I and his prime minister, Mustafa Khan Ardistani, moved further south in repeated campaigns during the early 1570s and reduced such hill forts as Bankapur, Chandragutti, and Karur. These are located in the present-day southern Dharwar District and northwestern Shimoga District. 'Ali I left his prime minister in Chandragutti to regulate the region (Firishta, *Tarikh-i Firishta*, II, p. 45. [Briggs's translation, III, p. 85]). It appears, however, that even this close supervision could not guarantee absolute control over the newly conquered portion of Karnataka, and that *jagirs* were probably distributed to 'Ali I's lieutenants only in areas accessible to the Bijapur forces. In less accessible regions local *nayaks* could not be easily dislodged. For example, an inscription in Lakshmeshwar, located 40 miles southeast of Dharwar, indicates that a local *nayak* had "received" from 'Ali I a number of villages that the *nayak* in turn handed over to his own underlings for administration. (*South Indian Inscriptions*, XX, subtitled *Bombay-Karnatak Inscriptions*, IV [Delhi: Manager of Publications, 1964], pp. 316 f.) In this case the indigenous administration from the *nayak* down to the cultivators doubtless remained intact, though presumably some percentage of the land revenue was sent as tribute to Mustafa Khan's headquarters in Chandragutti.

[5] The area in Karnataka added to Bijapur after the Battle of Talikota stretched approximately 100 miles wide and 250 miles long—that is, from the Malprabha and Krishna rivers, which had been the former southern frontier with Vijayanagar, to a point 100 miles south of these rivers, and from the Konkan Coast 250 miles east to the confluence of the Krishna and Tungabhadra rivers.

to recover the port of Goa, lost to the Portuguese in 1510, but was rebuffed in this attempt.[6]

The addition to 'Adil Shahi administration of these new areas had immediate effects on the growth of the kingdom's military and bureaucratic orginization. The vast increase in assigned lands and crown lands necessitated, for one thing, the formation of a regular standing army to keep under control the new nobility that emerged with this expansion.[7] The level of 'Ali I's military forces at 80,000 cavalry and 735 elephants,[8] which was not significantly surpassed even by his successors, more than doubled that of his nearest predecessor on the 'Adil Shahi throne.[9] Just as important was the establishment of a large and rationally organized civil bureaucracy at Bijapur, for which purpose 'Ali I appointed as his prime minister (*pishwa* or *wakil*) the very able Afzal Khan Shirazi. Called the kingdom's first administrator, Shirazi introduced a rational system of departments—chief military command, revenue, internal security, chamberlain, treasury, etc.—that existed apart from the personalities whom he delegated to head them.[10] Both 'Ali I's comprehensive administrative system and his increased military force might thus be seen as attempts by the central government to retain control over a large number of nobles, or *jagirdars*, whose power and lands (*jagirs*) had increased considerably as a result of the conquest of Vijayanagar.

We do not hear that the religious establishment under 'Ali I was organized to the same degree as were the military and civil establishments. The sultan was, after all, primarily a soldier and administrator. It was not until the reigns of 'Ali I's Sunni successors that the presence of a powerful *'ulama* concerned with enforcing Islamic orthodoxy in the administration of justice became clearly visible. 'Ali I did, however, leave one monument that was to cast

[6] P. M. Joshi, "Relations between the Adilshahi Kingdom of Bijapur and the Portuguese at Goa during the Sixteenth Century," *New Indian Antiquary*, 2 (1939-40), p. 366.

[7] I. A. Ghauri, "Organization of the Army under the Sultanates of the Deccan," *Journal of the Pakistan Historical Society*, 14 (July 1966), pp. 151 f.

[8] *Basatin*, p. 151.

[9] For a comparison of the military capacities of the various 'Adil Shahi monarchs, see Ghauri, "Organization of the Army," pp. 161 f.

[10] *Basatin*, pp. 130 f.; *Tazkirat al-Muluk*, fol. 67a. A good discussion of the subject can be found in I. A. Ghauri, "Central Structure of the Kingdom of Bijapur," *Islamic Culture*, 44 (January 1970), pp. 19-26.

a long shadow of influence over both the orthodox leaders of Islam in Bijapur and numerous Sufis. This was the Jami' Mosque, which was constructed in 1578 and remains today one of the most imposing and magnificent structures in the Deccan.[11] As we shall see, it was to become the physical embodiment of Islamic orthodoxy in the capital city.

If the victory at Talikota contributed to the growth of Bijapur, scarcely less important in this respect was the construction of Bijapur's outer wall, which 'Ali I completed in 1565-67 just after the battle with Vijayanagar. Prior to its construction, the city had lain exposed to the flat plateau with only a small citadel, built by the kingdom's first ruler, at its center. Stretching just over a quarter of a mile in diameter and surrounded by a moat, this citadel afforded little protection to any of the city's population other than its garrisoned troops.[12] But the construction of an outer wall nearly two miles in diameter rendered far greater security than ever before to the city as a whole. Undoubtedly it also contributed to the further centralization of 'Adil Shahi power, for it was the completion of this wall, recorded Zubairi in the *Basatin al-Salatin*, that prompted numerous nobles to move from outside to within the city where they built lofty palaces of their own.[13]

All of this building activity—the wall itself, palaces for the nobility, aquaducts, the Jami' Mosque, the Gagan Mahal or the royal palace within the citadel[14]—caused an appreciable influx at Bijapur of thousands of artisans, masons, stonecutters, and others constituting an urban proletariat.[15] Indeed, the swelling of the population within the walls reached such a state that already in 'Ali I's reign clusters of suburbs began appearing beyond

[11] *Basatin*, pp. 113, 151. See Figure 5. This mosque, occupying an area 450 feet by 270 feet, replaced as the city's leading mosque the much smaller Jami' Mosque built by Sultan Ibrahim I only twenty-six years earlier. Construction of the second mosque, which is four to five times the size of its predecessor, reflects the growth of Bijapur's urban Muslim population in the late sixteenth century.

[12] See Figure 4.

[13] *Basatin*, p. 112.

[14] Politically the most important of Bijapur's palaces, the Gagan Mahal was to the royal establishment what the Jami' Mosque was to the religious establishment. It is pictured in Figure 4, having the immense arch.

[15] *Basatin*, pp. 111 f.

4. Citadel, showing moat and Gagan Mahal

the outer wall. The most important such suburb, Shahpur, sprang up by the western wall of the city. Populated primarily by artisans, Shahpur became important as a great commercial emporium, especially for textile goods.[16]

The growth of the city reflected the commercial prosperity of the entire kingdom. Cotton grown in the interior, especially in the Raichur Doab and the Dharwar region, was sent to the Konkan Coast where it was woven into calicoes and muslins and then exported to points all around the Arabian Sea.[17] It was from 'Ali I's reign, too, that one hundred and eighty sailing vessels

[16] Ibid., p. 113; *Tazkirat al-Muluk*, fol. 66b.

[17] Joshi, "Notes on the Textile Industry," pp. 262-64. The Portuguese controlled only Goa along the Konkan Coast. Bijapur's principal ports were to the north of Goa: Vengurla, Rajapur, Dabhol, and Chaul.

plied the coasts from Gujarat to Bengal in service of the ʿAdil Shahi government and that diplomatic contact was established with the three great Muslim monarchs of the age: the Ottoman Sultan Sulaiman, the Safawi Shah Tahmasp, and the Mughal Emperor Akbar.[18] Thus by the end of ʿAli I's reign in 1580 the Kingdom of Bijapur may be said to have established a *Dar al-Islam* in fact as well as in name, as the umbrella of ʿAdil Shahi authority

5. Jamiʿ Mosque, constructed 1578

[18] *Basatin*, p. 136.

cast a shadow of peace and security over the Bijapur plateau. The city of Bijapur had become one of the major Islamic urban centers of the subcontinent.

Cultural Syncretism under Sultan Ibrahim II (1580-1627)

In terms of the maturity of its forms of cultural expression and the syncretism of its Hindu and Muslim components, the Kingdom of Bijapur reached its height during the reign of Sultan Ibrahim II (1580-1627). It was only after the kingdom's political consolidation, achieved by Sultan 'Ali I, and in the climate of the peace and prosperity that followed that consolidation, that such maturity and syncretism were able to evolve. Understanding this eclectic culture is important in interpreting the many Sufis who flourished at this time; for just as some were attracted by it and contributed to it, others rebelled against it.

The city itself had become by the early seventeenth century one of the most flourishing urban centers of India. In 1561, at the beginning of 'Ali I's reign, a visiting Jesuit had remarked that most of the people lived in old and torn tents and that not more than ten houses were worthwhile. But the visitor conceded that the city was still larger than Goa and that its Muslims were "as numerous as insects."[19] By 1604, on the other hand, the Mughal ambassador Asad Beg could marvel at the size and beauty of the city:

> All around the gates of my residence were lofty buildings with houses and porticos; the situation was very healthy and airy. It lies in an open space in the city. Its northern portico is to the east of a *bazar* of great extent, as much as thirty yards wide and about two *kos* [four miles] long. Before each shop was a beautiful green tree, and the whole *bazar* was extremely clean and pure. It was filled with rare goods, such as are not seen or heard of in any other town. There were shops of cloth-sellers, jewellers, armourers, vintners, bakers, fish mongers, and cooks. . . . In short the whole *bazar* was filled with wine and beauty, dancers, perfumers, jewels of all sorts, palaces, and viands. In one street were a thousand bands of people drinking, and

[19] Correia-Afonso, "Bijapur Four Centuries Ago," p. 86.

dancers, lovers, and pleasure seekers assembled; none quarreled or disputed with another, and this state of things was perpetual. Perhaps no place in the wide world could present a more wonderful spectacle to the eye of the traveller.[20]

The early seventeenth century also saw the peak growth of the city's population, estimates of which range from 500,000[21] to one million persons.[22]

The reign of Ibrahim II saw significant changes in the social composition of the kingdom's ruling class. The emergence of the Deccanis as the dominant ruling group can be traced to 1583 when Ibrahim's fourth regent, Dilawar Khan Habashi, replaced Shi'ism with orthodox Sunnism as the state religion. Thereafter enlistment of Foreigners was discontinued, although in North India Iranians and Arabs continued to be absorbed by the Mughal government. The effect was to give the sultanate a more indigenous character than ever before, as its ruling class was now composed of Dakhni-speaking Muslims who had been living for generations among the Kannadiga and Maharashtrian peoples. And as the Deccanis replaced the Foreigners in the Muslim nobility, Bijapur's civil and military bureaucracies became increasingly staffed by Marathas, who formed the large and dominant warrior caste among the Maharashtrian people. The power of those Maratha families that entered the Bijapur royal service was based on their status as hereditary *desais*, or district revenue officials, in the northwestern Marathi-speaking sector of the kingdom.[23] Maharashtrian Brahmins first appeared in Bijapur's civil bureaucracy, specifically the revenue department, during the reign of Ibrahim I (1534-58), the first anti-Foreigner sultan.[24] Meadows Taylor has suggested that whenever the Deccanis had the political opportunity, as they did under Ibrahim I, they deliberately employed Marathas and Maharashtrian Brahmins as a check against

[20] Asad Beg, "Wikaya-i Asad Beg," trans. by B. W. Chapman, in Elliot and Dowson, *The History of India*, VI, pp. 163 f.

[21] C. D. Deshpande, *Western India*, p. 111.

[22] Meadows Taylor and James Fergusson, *Architecture at Beejapoor* (London: J. Murray, 1866), p. 57.

[23] For an account of the rise of Maratha families within the Bijapur government, see James Grant Duff, *History of the Mahrattas*, ed. by J. P. Guha (2 vols.; New Delhi: Associated Publishing House, 1971), I, pp. 41-43.

[24] Firishta, *Tarikh-i Firishta*, II, p. 27. (Briggs's translation, III, p. 48.)

the power of the Foreigner class, especially the Iranians.[25] Under Ibrahim II, the kingdom's next anti-Foreigner sultan, the pattern was repeated and an even greater number of Maharashtrian Brahmins were permitted to replace the Iranian revenue officials then being phased out.

An impressive degree of Hindu-Muslim syncretism, resulting in part from these social changes, can be seen in the linguistic facets of seventeenth-century Bijapuri culture. Ironically, even though the number of Iranian administrators dwindled in the reign of Ibrahim II, it is clear that their Maharashtrian successors borrowed and assimilated a great deal of the Persian language, as is reflected in the revenue documents that survive from that period. The language used in these documents, which Professor G. H. Khare has called Perso-Marathi,[26] was described by Mark Wilks as "exclusively in the Mahratta character, and in a strange mixture of the Persian and Mahratta languages, which shews how intimately the forms and technical terms of the conquerers had been received into the language of business."[27] A linguistic analysis of the influence of Persian on seventeenth-century Marathi has revealed that nearly forty percent of the words used by the upper classes of the Marathi-speaking population were Persian.[28] Even today the Persian content in everyday Marathi has been estimated at ten percent, which Professor P. M. Joshi has judged to be the most important of the kingdom's legacies.[29]

Another aspect of linguistic syncretism in this period was the spread and rise to literary status of Dakhni, the vernacular tongue of Bijapur's Deccani class. Dakhni developed in a similar way as did its close relative, North Indian Urdu. It is generally agreed that the early Muslim invasions of the Punjab (from 1027) fused

[25] Taylor and Fergusson, *Architecture at Beejapoor*, p. 39. Sultan Ibrahim II in particular seems to have preferred employment of Marathas to Iranians in matters of state service (I. A. Ghauri, "The Political Institutions of Bijapur, 1536-1686, and Golconda, 1518-1636," Dissertation, University of London, 1961, p. 60).

[26] See Khare, "The Archives of the Deshmukh Family of Sholapur," *Indian History Congress, Proceedings*, 16 (1953), pp. 273 f.

[27] Wilks, *Historical Sketches of the South of India* (2 vols., 2nd edn.; Madras: Higginbotham and Co., 1869), 1, p. 47 fn.

[28] V. K. Rajwade, *Aitihasik Prastavana*, pp. 382 f. cited in Joshi, "The Kingdom of Bijapur," p. 280.

[29] Joshi, "Kingdom of Bijapur," pp. 281 f.

Persian with its heavy Arabic content with Old Punjabi, and that this "Lahore Urdu" then fused with the Delhi dialect, Khari Boli, when Muslim armies eventually settled in Delhi (from 1193). While the product of this second fusion, early Delhi Urdu, then continued to develop into modern Urdu in the North under the Delhi Sultanate and the Mughal Empire, its earlier form, which had been brought to the Deccan by the northern invaders and settlers who founded the Bahmani Kingdom, developed separately. Cut off from North India under the Bahmani and successor sultanates, this early Delhi Urdu developed its own regional peculiarities to the same extent that its speakers, the Deccanis, came to acquire a regional identity distinct from that of North Indian Muslims.[30]

Although the syntax of Dakhni remained the same as that of North Indian Urdu, and though Dakhni was also written in the Perso-Arabic script, its content differed from Urdu in at least three respects. First, it retained much of the Old Punjabi that diminished in the later Urdu of North India, causing one writer to remark that it is easier today for a Punjabi speaker than for an Urdu speaker to read and scan Dakhni poetry.[31] Second, Dakhni more than North Indian Urdu absorbed a large Sanskrit vocabulary, probably brought in with loan words from Telugu and Kannada, which both have large amounts of Sanskrit.[32] Third, Dakhni tended to use much less Arabic and Persian vocabulary than North Indian Urdu, and the spelling of those Persian or Arabic words it did retain was often distorted to match local pronunciation patterns.[33] In short, Dakhni speakers paid scant regard in their speech to the paramount language of Islam (Arabic) or the language of Bijapur's Foreigner class (Persian). The very name of the language indicates its ties with the region.[34]

[30] See T. Grahame Bailey, *A History of Urdu Literature* (London: Oxford University Press, 1932), pp. 6 f.; Muhammad Sadiq, *A History of Urdu Literature* (London: Oxford University Press, 1964), p. 43; S. K. Chatterji, *Indo-Aryan and Hindi* (2nd edn.; Calcutta: Firma K. L. Mukhopadhyay, 1960; reprinted 1969), pp. 204-6.

[31] Sadiq, *Urdu Literature*, p. 43.

[32] See Sharma, *Dakani Zaban*, p. 32.

[33] Rafi'a Sultana, *Urdu Nasr ka Aghaz aur Irtiqa* (Hyderabad: Majlis-i Tahqiqat-i Urdu, n.d.), p. 250; Sadiq, *Urdu Literature*, p. 46.

[34] Wrote Muhammad Sadiq, "Whether we accept the theory that Dakkani was Urdu transplanted in the Deccan, or that it was a new language born

Unlike Persian, Dakhni was not exclusively an elitist language in Bijapur, even though it was, as the language of the Deccanis, the language of the ruling class since the time of Ibrahim II. But the Deccani class included both elite and non-elite groups: descendants of the original Turkish settlers, of Arab traders, of Abyssinians, and converts to Islam. The last group, usually emerging from among the lower castes, probably acquired increasing amounts of Dakhni as part of the process of their Islamic acculturation.[35] In all probability Dakhni was also known to those indigenous elements that had not already become Muslim in any formal sense but were urban or had regular contact with the cities and were thereby integrated with Bijapur's Deccani-dominated markets or armies. The process probably paralleled the North Indian case, in which widening groups of Hindus had, since the eleventh century, become absorbed in the Muslim "camp"—i.e., the armies and markets—and thereby acquired a great deal of the foreigners' tongue. In sum, Dakhni was the only vernacular language in the sultanate spoken by Hindus and Muslims alike, though its area of influence seems to have been confined to urban centers, particularly the capital.

While both syncretic languages, Perso-Marathi and Dakhni, flourished in Bijapur under Sultan Ibrahim II, the Persian language seems to have declined to the same extent that the Foreigner class was eclipsed by the Deccanis. To be sure, Persian continued to be employed by court poets and historians, but the example of Ibrahim II himself, who as sultan set the cultural tone of the kingdom, rather dramatically indicates the change that had taken place by the first quarter of the seventeenth century. Although

---

of the impact of Urdu on old Dakkani, it is arguable that once left to itself it must have undergone a process of independent development. It must have dug its roots into the native soil and borrowed freely from Marathi, Tamil, Telugu, and other local languages. In fact the cultural and geographical contacts with the neighboring countries must have made such importations inevitable" (Sadiq, *Urdu Literature*, p. 43).

[35] See Appendix III, which illustrates the extent of Urdu spoken by various groups of Muslim converts surveyed in 1884. Some spoke no Urdu, some spoke a mixture of Kannada and Urdu, or Marathi and Urdu, or all three, and still others claimed to be native Urdu speakers. Such a spectrum of various degrees of linguistic integration among different groups of Muslim converts has probably been typical for this part of the Deccan since Bahmani times, as it still is today.

he had a thorough command of Marathi and Dakhni, the sultan had only an imperfect grasp of Persian, a fact noted with apparent surprise by the Mughal ambassador Asad Beg.[36]

Hindu-Muslim syncretism in early seventeenth century Bijapur was also reflected in the arts. A number of art historians have noted the extensive Hindu influence that pervaded the miniature painting and wall painting that flourished in that period.[37] One of them has pointed to the excessive gilding and the style of furniture and dress pictured in Bijapuri miniatures, reflecting the influence of the Vijayanagar artistic tradition.[38] Another has cited the representation of musical *ragas* in Bijapuri miniatures,[39] and a third has pointed to the treatment of women, who are

[36] P. M. Joshi, "Asad Beg's Mission to Bijapur, 1603-1604," in S. N. Sen, ed., *Professor D. V. Potdar Commemoration Volume* (Poona: D. K. Sathe, 1950), p. 191.

[37] See Moti Chandra, "Portraits of Ibrahim Adil Shah II," *Marg*, 5, No. 1 (1955), p. 26; Basil Gray, "Deccani Paintings: The School of Bijapur," *Burlington Magazine*, 73 (August 1938), p. 74; Hermann Goetz, "The Fall of Vijayanagar and the Nationalization of Muslim Art in the Dakhan," *Journal of Indian History*, 19 (1940), p. 254; Karl Khandalavala, "Five Miniatures in the Collection of Sir Cowasji Jehangir, Bart., Bombay," *Marg*, 5, No. 2 (1951), p. 26. For illustrated examples of the Bijapur school of painting and a discussion of the illustrations by three art historians, see S. C. Welch et al., "Deccani Kalams," *Marg*, 16, No. 2 (1963), pp. 29-39. A discussion of the distinguishing features of the Bijapur school may be found in Chandra, "Portraits," pp. 25 f. Other surveys of the Bijapur school are found in Gray, "Deccani Paintings"; Goetz, "Fall of Vijayanagar," pp. 249-55; R. Skelton, "Documents for the Study of Painting at Bijapur in the Late Sixteenth and Early Seventeenth Centuries," *Arts Asiatiques*, 5 (1958), pp. 97-125; Douglas Barrett, "Painting at Bijapur," in R. Pinder-Wilson, ed., *Paintings from Islamic Lands* (Oxford: Bruno Cassirer, 1969), pp. 142-59; and Edwin Binney 3rd, *Indian Miniature Painting*, vol. 1: *The Mughal and Deccani Schools* (Portland, Ore.: Portland Art Museum, 1973), pp. 136-71.

[38] Goetz, "Fall of Vijayanagar," p. 254.

[39] Khandalavala, "Five Miniatures," p. 27. Pictorial representation of Indian *ragas*, argued Khandalavala, occurred in Bijapur before anywhere else in India. It is almost certain, he added, that this kind of work "was entrusted by Ibrahim II to some Hindu artists in his atelier and not to the Persian or Turkish artists whom he had also gathered around him. The Hindu artists would be more at home in dealing with the 'pictorial motifs' of the *Ragas* and *Raginis* than the foreigners. The mixed style of the *Ragmala* miniatures indicates that they are the work of Hindu artists who have combined the Vijayanagar style with Persian and Turkish elements."

pictured in the South Indian fashion.[40] Of all the arts, however, architecture most vividly reflected this syncretism. Prior to the seventeenth century, the builders of Bijapur had slavishly copied architectural models of the Middle East. The great Jami' Mosque, constructed by 'Ali I in 1578, is a fairly close representation of the contemporary Iranian model.[41] But all of this changed under Ibrahim II. During his reign the Persian or Turkish characteristics of Bijapur's architecture, wrote the art historian Hermann Goetz, "gave way to another sculptural conception, a petrified representation of exuberant biological life, so characteristic for the genuine Hindu spirit. Walls dissolve into bundles of pillars, degenerate arches, cornices, etc. Suffocated by masses of ornaments, pillars become lotus stems, domes big bulbs, spires lotus buds, cupula-drums lotus crowns, and so on."[42] This "biological" aspect of Bijapur's composite architecture is nowhere more evident than in Ibrahim II's own mausoleum, in which such lotus stems, bulbs, and buds are all exquisitely merged with the regular pillars, domes, and spires of an Islamic mausoleum.[43]

How can one explain the extraordinary cultural syncreticism achieved in early seventeenth century Bijapur?—a movement having such a strong Hindu current that Hermann Goetz has called it a "revolution in Dakhani civilization."[44] One explanation lies in the kingdom's increasing isolation from Safawi Iran, whose model of Persian culture had inspired Bijapur's Shi'a monarchs of the sixteenth century and continued to inspire the Mughal Emperors for the next several centuries. Portuguese naval power in the sixteenth century effectively blocked the sea routes between the Konkan Coast and the Persian Gulf, thereby cutting off the easy contact with the Middle East that Deccan sultanates had formerly enjoyed. Moreover, the growing power of the Mughal Empire and the hostility it began to exhibit toward the Deccan kingdoms in Akbar's reign (1556-1605) had the effect of sealing

[40] Chandra, "Portraits," pp. 25 f. Specifically, they wear the Deccani sari and bodice and have a pointed nose, small mouth, eye corners extended to the ears, and double chin.

[41] See Figure 5.

[42] Goetz, "Fall of Vijayanagar," p. 250.

[43] See Figure 6.

[44] Goetz, "Fall of Vijayanagar," p. 251.

6. Ibrahim Rauza, tomb of Sultan Ibrahim 'Adil Shah II

off Bijapur's land routes to Iran. The political consequence of this isolation was the declining fortunes of Bijapur's Foreigner class, of which the Iranians had always constituted the largest and most important element. At the same time, Bijapur's isolation from Safawi Iran diminished the influence of the Persian cultural model in its many aspects—language, art, dress, etc.—compelling the sultanate's Deccani population to turn to indigenous cultural forms for inspiration.

Another explanation for the profound Hindu element in Bijapur's composite culture of the early seventeenth century has been advanced by Hermann Goetz. Citing the thousands of Hindu musicians, artisans, dancing girls, and literati who participated in the movement, Goetz concluded that the destruction of the gigantic capital of Vijayanagar between 1565 and 1567 caused a significant portion of its population to emigrate to Bijapur, either as prisoners of war or as refugees.[45] If Goetz is correct that some Vijayanagar artistic traditions survived in Bijapur in this way, then it is likely that those craftsmen and musicians who migrated to the 'Adil Shahi capital were Kannadiga and Telugu Hindus. The Bijapur court of Ibrahim II's age can therefore be seen as absorbing Hindus on two levels. While Maharashtrians were given control over the revenue structure of the kingdom, Kannadigas and Telugus excelled in the fields of art, architecture, and music. In this way the two major indigenous cultural traditions of the Bijapur plateau came to assert for themselves a share in the composite culture of medieval Bijapur, while at the same time adapting in various degrees to the Islamic or Middle Eastern models sustained by the Deccani Muslims.

A third explanation of the syncretism discussed above is found in the sultan's own liberal inclinations and the patronage that he fostered. The accord that Ibrahim II sought to achieve with the kingdom's non-Muslim population was in some ways a function of his cultivation of knowledge, music, the arts, and above all his personal religious eclecticism which, from the standpoint of Islamic orthodoxy, bordered on heresy. In the year 1603-4 he changed the name of the capital city from *Vijayapur*, Sanskrit for "City of Victory" (of which "Bijapur" is but a variant), to *Vidyapur*, Sanskrit for "City of Learning."[46] Although the name did not stick, it illustrates the sultan's inclination for intellectual rather than military affairs. His court attracted, besides Sufis, a great number of poets, historians, architects, artists, and musicians. Among these the most famous include the historians Muhammad Qasim Firishta and Rafi' al-Din Shirazi, the architects Malik Sandal and Shahnawaz Khan, the artist Farrukh Husain, and the poets

[45] Ibid., p. 252. Goetz argues that the reason this Hindu influence did not surface until the seventeenth century, though Vijayanagar had fallen in 1565, was that it took a generation for bitter memories of the Battle of Talikota to subside and for the Hindu immigrants to cease being considered strangers (ibid., p. 255).

[46] *Tazkirat al-Muluk*, fol. 101a.

Maulana Malik Qumi and Nur al-Din Muhammad Zuhuri. Of these the most eminent were Firishta (d. 1623), author of the authoritative history of India, *Gulshan-i Ibrahimi* (or *Tarikh-i Firishta*), and Zuhuri (d. 1615), the sultan's celebrated poet laureate and author of the lyrical *Saqinama*.[47]

Ibrahim II attracted such talent mainly because he himself was widely recognized in his own time as an outstanding poet and musician. This was not mere sycophancy, for he actually did compose one of the landmarks of Dakhni literature, the *Kitab-i Nauras*, a collection of songs and commentary on the nine sentiments (*rasa*) of Hindu aesthetics.[48] Although the sultan's grasp of Persian was imperfect, his knowledge of Sanskrit was considerable as judged by the extent of Sanskrit vocabulary in this Dakhni work.[49] His reputation as a man of extraordinary scholarship has even been preserved in the popular epithet *Jagat Guru*, or "Teacher of the World."[50] Ibrahim II was also an accomplished musician and an avid music-lover, a fact noted by the Mughal ambassador Asad Beg[51] and even the Mughal Emperor Jahangir.[52] His book *Kitab-i Nauras* dwelt to a considerable extent on the subject of Indian *ragas*, and miniatures of the sultan frequently pictured him with musical instruments.[53] He even

47 For further discussion of Zuhuri and his work, see M. A. Ghani, *A History of Persian Language and Literature at the Mughal Court* (2 vols.; Allahabad: Indian Press, 1930. Republished Westmead, England: Gregg International Publishers Ltd., 1972), II, pp. 181-219.

48 Discussions of this work can be found in B. G. Gayani, "Kitab-i Nauras," *Islamic Culture*, 19 (1945), pp. 140-52, and Nazir Ahmad, ed., *Kitab-i Nauras* (Lucknow: 1955). The latter work includes a transcription and Urdu translation of the *Kitab-i Nauras*.

49 Gayani, "Kitab-i Nauras," p. 146.

50 *Basatin*, pp. 279 f.

51 Joshi, "Asad Beg's Mission," p. 193.

52 Jahangir, *Tuzuk-i-Jahangiri*, I, p. 272.

53 One of these miniatures depicts the sultan holding a pair of castanets. This miniature, painted in 1610 and preserved in the British Museum, is reproduced in Skelton, "Documents," p. 117. In another miniature reproduced in ibid., p. 99, Sultan Ibrahim II is shown seated before a collection of drums. For a discussion of the latter painting see G. Yazdani, "Two Miniatures From Bijapur," *Islamic Culture*, 9 (April 1935), pp. 212-16. There exist more known portraits of Ibrahim II than of any other 'Adil Shahi sultan. Besides the one reproduced in this study as Figure 8, many others similarly reveal the sultan's refined and sometimes dreamy character. Robert Skelton has identified and located sixteen portraits of Ibrahim II in his "Documents," pp. 124 f.

instituted a national holiday, *'Id-i Nauras*, which was a great music festival in which thousands of Hindu musicians participated.[54]

More than any other sultan of Bijapur, Ibrahim II acquired a reputation for benevolence and tolerance toward all his subjects.[55] His conviction that devotion to the arts rises above communal partisanship was reflected in the following verse from his *Kitab-i Nauras*:

> There are different languages;
> But there is one emotional appeal,
> Be he a Brahmin [Hindu] or a Turk [Muslim].
> He is only fortunate on whom
> The Goddess of learning [Saraswati] smiles.
> O Ibrahim, the world only seeks knowledge—
> Serve and meditate upon with steadfast heart
> The power of words.[56]

In 1614 the sultan issued a special order insuring the right of pilgrims to perform rituals to the Hindu deity Khanderao or Mallari at Naldrug, in the northern sector of the kingdom. The annual fair associated with this deity, which had been discontinued by previous 'Adil Shahi governments, was with this order reinstated.[57] In 1618-19 he granted some land endowments for the upkeep of a Hindu temple at Chinchwad, near Poona.[58] And although he ceased employing Foreigners, who were generally

[54] *Basatin*, pp. 250-52.

[55] Wrote the French traveler François Pyrard in 1604, "He is an amiable and peaceable prince—no tyrant, but a friend of all foreigners, and of all neighbors that are at peace with him." (François Pyrard, *The Voyage of François Pyrard of Laval to the East Indies*, trans. by Albert Gray [2 vols. from 3; London: Hakluyt Society, 1887-90; reprinted, New York: Burt Franklin, n.d.], II, p. 134.) A copper coin struck in Ibrahim II's reign referred to the sultan in the Sanskrit epithet *abla bali*, "friend of the weak." (Mohammad Isma'il, "The Epithet Used on Copper Coins by Ibrahim 'Adil Shah II of Bijapur," *Journal of the Asiatic Society of Bengal*, NS 18, No. 9, [1922], Numismatic Supplement, pp. 37 f.)

[56] Chandra, "Portraits," p. 24. Chandra's translation. See also Gayani, "Kitab-i Nauras," p. 147.

[57] Khare, "Archives of the Deshmukh Family of Sholapur," p. 275. This is a *qaul* (revenue contract) of 10 Shaban, A.H. 1023, sent to the revenue officials of Sholapur.

[58] D. V. Apte, "Shivakalin Adilshahi," *Bharata Itihasa Sanshodhaka Mandal*, II (Poona, 1922), p. 21; D. V. Potdar, "Sri Moraya Dev Sansthan Chinchwad Sambandhi Kahin Junat Assal Kagad," in ibid., pp. 52 f.

Shi'as, his toleration extended to Shi'as as a religious sect as it did to other religious groups.[59] Christians, too, benefited from the sultan's religious toleration, as he was the first sovereign of Bijapur to allow Portuguese Jesuits to establish mission churches in various parts of the kingdom.[60]

There is considerable evidence that Ibrahim II's posture vis-à-vis Hindu beliefs went even beyond toleration. The very purpose of his writing his *Kitab-i Nauras*, so recorded his poet laureate Zuhuri, was to relay to the Muslims of Bijapur the theory of Hindu aesthetics and iconography with which he himself had already become so infatuated.[61] Moreover the book opens not with the traditional Muslim invocation, the *bism Allah*, but with a hymn of praise to the deity Ganapati, whose name is generally invoked at the commencement of Hindu literary works.[62] Lord Siva, his consort Parvati, and Bhairava are also given prominent attention throughout the *Kitab-i Nauras*.[63] The sultan's greatest praise, however, was reserved for the deity Saraswati, who is the goddess of eloquence, wisdom, and learning, the mother of poetry, the patroness of arts and of music, and the revealer of the Sanskrit language.[64] Signs of Ibrahim II's attraction to this deity even spilled over into the revenue bureaucracy, for we find that official government documents, written in the Perso-Marathi

[59] Firishta recorded the sultan's amusement, not anger, on hearing that a number of Sunnis had become Shi'as just before his coronation in anticipation of the new monarch's declaration in favor of Shi'ism. "He smiled at the sudden conversion of the Soony nobility," wrote Firishta, "and would frequently rally them upon it, calling them political Sheeas." Firishta, *Tarikh-i Firishta*, II, p. 66. (Briggs's translation, III, p. 103.)

[60] Taylor and Fergusson, *Architecture at Beejapoor*, pp. 47 f. These mission churches, still extant at the time that Meadows Taylor wrote (1866), were established at Chitapur (20 miles southeast of Gulbarga) where converts were weavers and distillers; at Raichur, where converts were potters; at Mudgal (75 miles southeast of Bijapur), the largest mission, where the three hundred converts were weavers and shepherds; and at a village between Raichur and Mudgal, where converts were cultivators. All these missions possessed, as late as 1866, *farmans* of both Ibrahim II and his successor, Muhammad, granting them either lands, collections of grain, or percentages of local customs or excise taxes.

[61] See Chandra, "Portraits," p. 23.

[62] Gayani, "Kitab-i Nauras," p. 143.

[63] For examples, see Nazir Ahmad, *Kitab-i Nauras*, pp. 11-13.

[64] Alain Danielou, *Hindu Polytheism* (London: Routledge & Kegan Paul, 1964), p. 260.

language mentioned above, sometimes began with an invocation to her: "*aj puja shrin Sarasvati.*"[65] The historian Zubairi recorded in his *Basatin al-Salatin* that it was the sultan's association with his musicians, who themselves were devotees of Saraswati as the goddess of music, that attracted Ibrahim II to this deity.[66] And in his biography of Bijapur's Sufis Zubairi wrote that the sultan regularly joined these musicians in their worship at the Saraswati Temple in Bijapur.[67] Another hagiographic source even went so far as to assert that he had an image of Saraswati installed in the royal palace for his personal worship.[68]

The sultan's religious eclecticism was thus unmistakable. The explanation for this, however, is less clear. According to the art historian Moti Chandra, the *Kitab-i Nauras* "reveals a mystic tinge in the character of Ibrahim and he often begins speaking in the language of the Nathpanthic saints who wandered all over the Deccan in the sixteenth century preaching the mystic yearning of the soul of God and who cared little for the outward forms of religion. It is possible that Ibrahim came into contact with them."[69] Another possibility is that as a Deccani Muslim Ibrahim II was bent upon dismantling the "foreign" aspects of the Bijapur

[65] A. R. Kulkarni, "Social Relations in the Maratha Country in the Medieval Period," *Indian History Congress, Proceedings*, 32nd session (Jabalpur, 1970), p. 234.

[66] *Basatin*, pp. 275 f.

[67] *Rauzat al-Auliya'-i Bijapur*, comp. by Muhammad Ibrahim Zubairi. Persian MS (copy B, Hyderabad: State Archives of Andhra Pradesh, Oriental Manuscripts Library, no. 196), fol. 23a. Hereafter cited as *Rauzat*, copy B.

[68] *Sahifat*, Urdu edn., p. 31. Given the sultan's inclination toward learning and music, his devotion to this deity is not surprising. More intriguing is his attraction to the other deities mentioned in the *Kitab-i Nauras*, all of whom are related to Siva: Parvati, who is Siva's consort; Ganapati, or Ganesh, who is Siva's son; and Bhairava, who is one of Siva's inferior manifestations (Gayani, "Kitab-i Nauras," pp. 145 f.). This suggests the influence on the sultan of the dominant Hindu sect in the Bijapur region, the Lingayats or Virasaivites, for whom Siva is the supreme deity. There is at least one miniature that portrays the sultan wearing dark beads, which have been suggested to represent *radraksha* berries, the ornaments of Saivite devotees (Skelton, "Documents," p. 105). And in this context, his epithet "Jagat Guru" is significant, for the term also refers to the highest-status leaders among the Lingayat population (McCormack, "Lingayats as a Sect," p. 63).

[69] Chandra, "Portraits," p. 25.

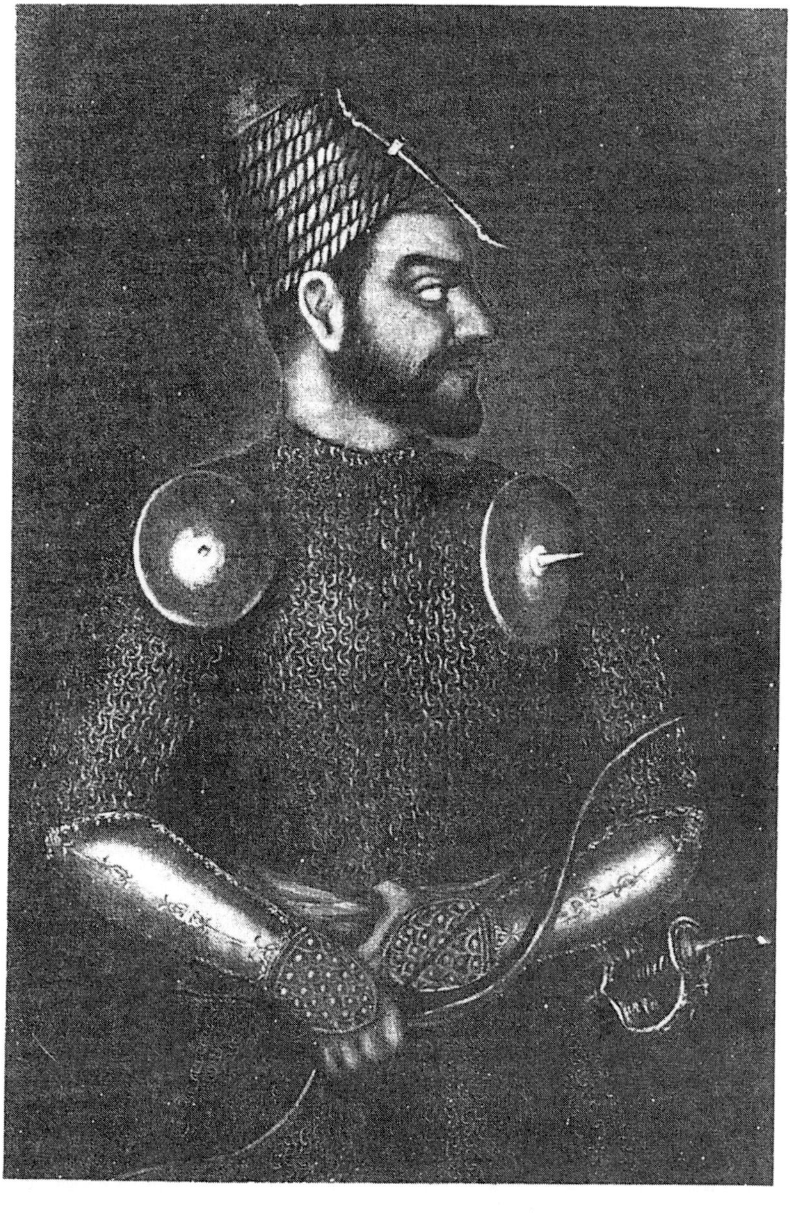

7. Sultan ʿAli ʿAdil Shah I (1558-80)

8. Sultan Ibrahim 'Adil Shah II (1580-1627)

court as represented by his Shi'a predecessors, and that emphasis upon the indigenous, non-Muslim culture of Bijapur was one way in which these efforts were expressed. Yet another possibility is that the sultan aspired to some sort of religious as well as political leadership along the lines of the *Din-i Ilahi* promulgated by his Mughal contemporary, Akbar. Chandra has suggested that in assuming the epithet *Jagat Guru* the sultan might have been imitating Akbar in view of the latter's claim to have been a *guru* to his followers.[70] Because of the diplomatic contact that existed between the two sovereigns, we can assume that Ibrahim II was aware of Akbar's own religious eclecticism. But as yet there is no firm evidence that Ibrahim II formed a syncretic religious sect of his own, much less that he was consciously following Akbar's example in this respect.

The critical question here is where this extreme liberalism placed the sultan in terms of orthodox Islam. How far could the monarch of an Islamic sultanate exhibit his respect for or even devotion to Hindu deities without provoking the wrath of the defenders of Islamic orthodoxy? Nominally and officially, of course, he was a Sunni Muslim like other Decannis, and he retained the Sunni *khutba* installed during his minority by the Abyssinian regent Dilawar Khan. Moreover, however eclectic his religious beliefs were during his lifetime, he apparently wished to be remembered by posterity as a good Muslim. Inscribed in various places on his mausoleum are Arabic couplets from the Koran extolling the piety and right-conduct of Abraham, father of Isaac. The following verse, for example, is inscribed on the pediment over the mausoleum's western doorway, the most important doorway since it faces Mecca:

> No; Abraham in truth was not a Jew
> neither a Christian; but he was a Muslim
> and one pure of faith; certainly he was never
> of the idolaters.[71]

[70] Ibid.

[71] Nazim, "Bijapur Inscriptions," p. 38. Four other such verses inscribed on the mausoleum can be found in ibid., pp. 38 f. The English translation of the verse quoted above is that of A. J. Arberry, trans., *The Koran Interpreted* (New York: Macmillan Co., 1970), Sura 3, verse 60, p. 83.

This play on words—"Abraham" in Arabic is "Ibrahim"—is seen by the historian Zubairi as the sultan's way of answering charges of heresy pressed on him by the upholders of Islamic orthodoxy at Bijapur.[72] Unfortunately, we have no further information on these charges, nor on the role played by the *'ulama* during Ibrahim II's reign. We do, however, know the reactions of some of the kingdom's Sufis to the sultan's religious eclecticism. These we shall consider in the following chapter.

Summary

If Sultan 'Ali I had transformed the struggling principality he inherited into the dominant power of the Deccan plateau, and the city of Bijapur into one of the major urban centers of India, his successor Ibrahim II presided over a remarkable flourishing of Hindu-Muslim syncretism in the kingdom. The extensive Dakhni literature produced in his reign, the fusion of Hindu and Muslim architectural styles, the rise of a Persianized class of Maharashtrian Brahmins in the central revenue administration, and the leadership of a sultan more devoted to the goddess Saraswati than to the glories of military conquest—all of these developments represent a degree of cultural accommodation seldom witnessed in Indian history. Hundreds of literati, artisans, and merchants, as well as Sufis, migrated to Bijapur in this period and participated in its unique culture.

Yet ironically, the very liberalism and devotion to aesthetics that attracted these men to Ibrahim II's court also drove some of them to struggle against it and to attempt to reform it of what they considered its un-Islamic ways. We may agree with Hermann Goetz's assessment of this extraordinary reign when he writes, "No doubt, a certain tendency towards a religious and cultural syncretism was then in the air, and also Ibrahim's greater contemporary Akbar dabbled in experiments of a new age, a new civilization, a new religion; no doubt, also Ibrahim's infatuation in the charms of his accomplished dancers may have had some say in the matter as the moral laxity of Bijapur in his reign aroused the indignation of leading men of Islam."[73] Like many

[72] *Basatin*, p. 277.

[73] Goetz, "Fall of Vijayanagar," p. 250.

other rulers of pre-modern Indo-Muslim states, Sultan Ibrahim II was unable to find lasting compromises between the dictates of Islamic Law and the realities of governing a predominantly Hindu society. As a result, as was the case with Akbar, whatever syncretism he was able to evolve in the early seventeenth century was paid for by a reaction to it in the middle or latter part of that century. Even during the sultan's lifetime, as Goetz noted, there were "leading men of Islam" whose indignation was aroused by Ibrahim II's syncretic tendencies. What is little appreciated is that these leading men of Islam included a most significant section of Bijapur's Sufis.

Chapter Five

SUFIS AS REFORMERS

The many Sufis who inhabited Bijapur during the reigns of Ibrahim II (1580-1627) and Muhammad (1627-56) may be divided into two broad categories. One consisted of Deccan-born Sufis of the Chishti order who were affiliated with the *khanaqah* of Shah Miranji Shams al-'Ushshaq on Shahpur Hillock. These Sufis, representing a relatively established tradition that had persisted even through the kingdom's Shi'a period, focused their energies on writing literature both for their fellow mystics and for non-elite elements of the population. Living beyond the city walls, they exhibited a distinct preference for withdrawal from urban society and urban institutions, particularly the 'Adil Shahi court. Another category of Sufis, for the most part Qadiris and Shattaris who had migrated to Bijapur from outside the Deccan, produced almost no literature at all, directing their energies mainly toward reforming the court of what they considered its un-Islamic tendencies. As city-dwellers, these Sufis were usually well integrated with the institutions of urban Islam.

The rustic Literati and the urban Reformist thus represented two Sufi responses to the Muslim city in its Hindu environment. The one reached directly toward the lower-class population, both Muslim and non-Muslims; the other employed his prestige and influence for reforming the court. The two types also formed Sufi counterparts to the old social dichotomy among Bijapur's Muslims: the Literati were the Deccanis, and the Reformists were the Foreigners, though with more of an Arab than an Iranian orientation.

Reformist Sufis in Relation to the Court

In view of the remarkable degree of Hindu-Muslim syncretism that had taken place during the reign of Ibrahim II, and especially in view of the sultan's personal religious eclecticism, it is not surprising that some kind of reactionary reform movement might appear at this time. But there is no record that such a movement emerged within the ranks of the *'ulama*, the class of Muslim clerics that collectively upheld Islamic law in the state.[1] Rather, the initiative for reform seems to have come from a number of Sufis, most of them newly arrived in Bijapur, of the Qadiri and Shattari orders. This phase of Bijapur's history roughly paralleled what Aziz Ahmad has called the "Naqshbandi reaction" with reference to Mughal India after Akbar—that is, an orthodox reaction, led by Sufis, to the monarch's religious experimentation.[2] In Bijapur this reaction took three distinct forms: one was by Sufis aggressively thrusting themselves on the court in the role of puritanical traditionalists; another was by their passively allowing the court to seek their council and influence; and a third was by affecting a posture of ostentatious disdain for the court, a maneuver that genuinely attracted more than one sultan to a Sufi.

Shah Abu'l-Hasan Qadiri (d. 1635), one of the outstanding representatives of orthodox Sufism in seventeenth-century Bijapur, was a reformist of the first variety. As was typical among Sufis of a more legalist and conformist type, Shah Abu'l-Hasan's spiritual and familial ancestry was closely linked with Bidar and the Arab Middle East, as indicated in Chart 1.[3] Abu'l-Hasan's grandfather had migrated from Baghdad to Bidar toward the end of the Bahmani period, by which time Bidar had become a major Qadiri center. Abu'l-Hasan's father, Badr al-Din Habib Allah, established his own Qadiri *khanaqah* in Bidar and appointed his eldest son, Abu'l-Hasan, his successor (*sajjada-nishin*) at the hospice.[4] Local disturbances in Bidar, however, compelled Abu'l-

[1] This does not necessarily mean that the *'ulama* were silent throughout Ibrahim II's reign; it only means that no records survive indicating their activities in that period. This contrasts with the reigns of Sultan Muhammad and his successors, when this class figured more prominently.

[2] Aziz Ahmad, *Studies in Islamic Culture*, pp. 182-90.

[3] This is an abbreviated genealogy. A more complete genealogy of Bijapur's Qadiri Sufis can be found in Appendix I of this study. The unbroken lines indicate familial or blood descent; the broken lines indicate spiritual descent, or the passing of the *khilafat*. It will be noted that these two lines remained somewhat distinct at this stage in the development of the order, in contrast to the case of subsequent generations for whom spiritual descent automatically accompanied familial descent.

[4] *Sahifat*, Urdu edn., p. 28.

CHART 1

ANCESTRY OF SHAH ABU'L-HASAN QADIRI

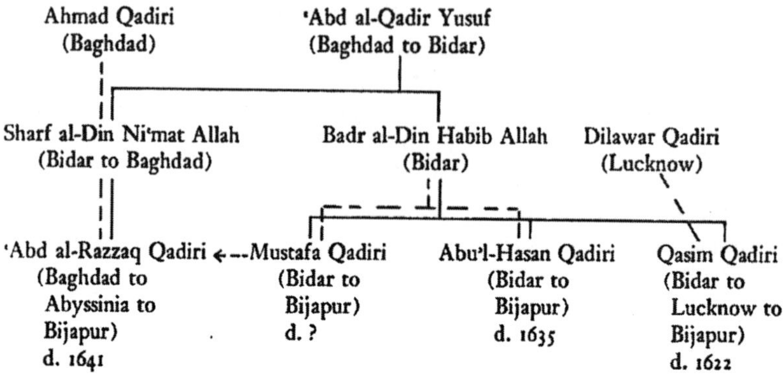

NOTE: Unbroken lines indicate family lineage; broken lines indicate spiritual lineage.

Hasan and his younger brother to move to Bijapur in 1580, the first year of Sultan Ibrahim II's reign. As he remained in Bijapur until his death in 1635, Abu'l-Hasan's life thus spanned the entire reign of Ibrahim II and the first seven years of Sultan Muhammad's reign.

Unlike many Sufis for whom standard histories or discourses (*malfuzat*) may be used to supplement and cross-check the hagiographic traditions, there exist only hagiographic sources for the study of Abu'l-Hasan, as is true for Bijapur's Qadiri Sufis generally. This limits our capacity to understand such Sufis since hagiographies customarily measure a Sufi's actions in terms of his spiritual power (*barakat*) as manifested in specific miracles (*karamat*). The only comprehensive biography of Bijapur's Qadiri Sufis is the *Sahifat-i Ahl-i Huda*, a biographical collection (*tazkira*) written in 1796-97 by a Qadiri descendant and based on notes collected by Abu'l-Hasan's grandson in 1684-85. One must recognize, therefore, a gap of fifty years between Abu'l-Hasan's life and the first written record of it, plus the possibility of further embellishments that may have been added by the final compiler in 1796-97. Despite these shortcomings, however, the *Sahifat*, like any hagiography, can be utilized as a valuable historical source if one ignores questions of the veracity of the miracles in this literature and concentrates on the intent behind them.

The biography of Abu'l-Hasan Qadiri in the *Sahifat*, though shrouded in an aura of the Sufi's powerful *barakat*, reveals a great deal of information about the Sufi's relations not only with Sultan Ibrahim II, but also with yogis:

> In the time of Sultan Ibrahim *jagat guru* there was a certain yogi in whom the sultan had great faith and who frequently kept the sultan's company. It is said that the reason for this lies in the following event. It happened that the sultan's beloved daughter suddenly died, leaving the sultan grief-stricken. On hearing this, the yogi came and offered to revive his daughter if the image of the goddess Saraswati and the girl's body were brought to the room. This was done, and the yogi, himself an accomplished musician, then began to sing. Before he had finished half the *raga* the girl's body began to quiver, and by the time he had finished the girl was totally restored to life. . . . The king and all the court thereafter accorded immense belief in the power of this yogi. And from that day the image of Saraswati was brought into the royal palace, where the sultan began to do *puja* before the image after the fashion of the Hindus.[5]

Apart from the yogi's resuscitation of the sultan's daughter tnere is little up to this point that contradicts what is known from a variety of trustworthy sources concerning Ibrahim II's personal attachment to the goddess Saraswati, to music, and to Hindu musicians at his court. What is unique about the hagiographical tradition is that it interprets Ibrahim II's religious experimentation as the undesirable result of a yogi's craft—a circumstance which the biography sees Shah Abu'l-Hasan as destined to rectify. "The people made it known to him," records another hagiographic source, "that despite his [Abu'l-Hasan's] presence in the city, the King of Islam was keeping company with an infidel."[6] Continues the *Sahifat-i Ahl-i Huda*:

> After Abu'l-Hasan arrived in Bijapur the people told him of these events and requested that he make his presence felt, that

[5] Ibid., p. 31.

[6] *Mishkat*, copy B, fol. 493b.

> it was not suitable that the king keep company with a yogi. He asked them if they wanted the sultan's belief to be diverted from the yogi to himself, and they replied "yes." So Abu'l-Hasan drew a portrait of himself on an earthen vessel and gave it to one of his followers with instructions to show it to the sultan the next time the latter would be on his way to see the yogi. This was done, and on seeing the picture, the sultan proceeded toward Abu'l-Hasan's *khanaqah* instead of to the yogi's.
>
> There, the Sufi counseled the king in this way: "Oh Sultan, today your heart has inclined toward seeking God. . . . The sunshine of Truth is shining on your soul. . . . Do not neglect the will of God, but seek His help. In sleep, wakefulness, presence, or absence, always remember Him. Strip from your heart the idols of greed and desire, and you will be happy in longing for His love and free from the fetters of both worlds."[7]

Thereupon, concludes the passage, Ibrahim II repented of his former ways, kissed the feet of Abu'l-Hasan, and eventually even became his *murid*. As for the yogi, Abu'l-Hasan is said to have passed a miracle—converting rain to milk and ghee—which so astounded the Hindu that he fell to the Sufi's feet and forthwith accepted Islam, later changing his name from Rukmang Pandit to Rukn al-Din.[8]

The above narrative may be seen as an allegory which, when shorn of its miraculous embellishments, leaves us with a few essential ideas. First, it is clear that Abu'l-Hasan was believed, at least by his immediate successors, to have pursuaded Sultan Ibrahim II to adopt a course of strict Muslim orthodoxy. Precisely how this influence may have been manifested is not clear. While it is doubtful that the sultan ever formally became his *murid*,[9] it is likely that the Sufi functioned as one of the sultan's religious guides, a practice common among most sultans of the age. Second, it is significant that the narrative makes such a point of Abu'l-Hasan's spiritual superiority over the yogi, suggesting a basic position of rivalry between Hindu and Muslim spiritualists.

[7] *Sahifat*, Urdu edn., pp. 31 f.

[8] Ibid., p. 33.

[9] In Ibrahim II's *Kitab-i Nauras* there is no praise of any Qadiri Sufi, though there is of the Chishti Sufi Bandānawaz Gisudaraz (d. 1422) of Gulbarga. See Gayani, "Kitab-i Nauras," pp. 146 f.

In terms of reformist zeal, Abu'l-Hasan Qadiri was surpassed by Shah Sibghat Allah (d. 1606), a Shattari Sufi whose life vividly illustrates the extent to which some Sufis exerted pressure on the 'Adil Shahi court. Born in the Gujarati seaport of Broach, Shah Sibghat Allah journeyed to the provincial capital of Ahmedabad where he enrolled in the spiritual following of the famous Shattari Sufi Shah Wajih al-Din 'Alawi, from whom he eventually received a *khilafat*.[10] His spiritual and familial ancestry is indicated in Chart 2.[11] Around the year 1590 Shah Sibghat Allah left his

CHART 2

ANCESTRY OF SHAH SIBGHAT ALLAH

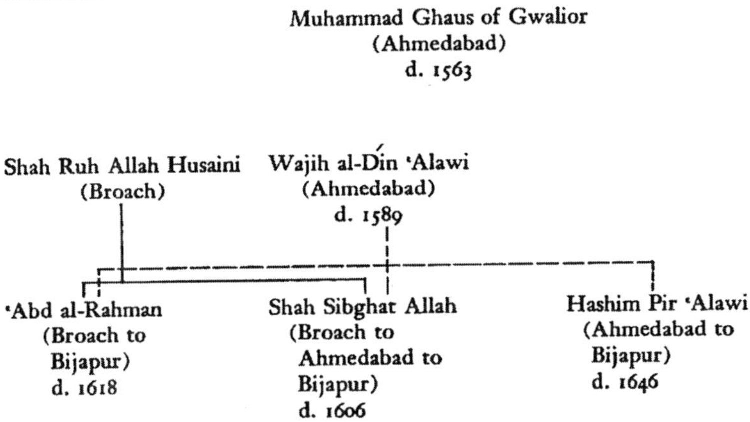

NOTE: Unbroken lines indicate family lineage; broken lines indicate spiritual lineage.

pir and made a pilgrimage to Mecca.[12] However, the political chaos that gripped Gujarat between 1583 and 1592 as a result of local resistance to the newly installed Mughal authority probably dissuaded the Sufi from returning to Ahmedabad on completion of the *hajj*. For in 1591 he sailed back to his native Broach, whence

10 *Mishkat*, copy A, fol. 72a; *Gulzar-i Abrar*, fol. 330a.

11 A more complete genealogy of Shah Sibghat Allah can be found in Appendix I of this study.

12 *Ma'asir al-Kiram*, comp. by Ghulam 'Ali Azad Bilgrami. Persian lithograph (2 vols.; Agra: Mufid-i 'Am, 1910), II, p. 40.

he traveled eastward to Malwa and Khandesh, then southward through Ahmadnagar and finally to Bijapur.[13]

The timing of his arrival in Bijapur, which by the Muslim calendar was A.H. 1000, is particularly significant since it coincided with the first millennium of Islam. Throughout the Muslim world the first millennium had long been awaited, both with dread that it might spell the end of the world and with expectations that it might usher in a Mahdi, a reformer and purifier of Islam. Hence, the possible millennial significance of Shah Sibghat Allah's arrival in Bijapur should not be forgotten when interpreting the events that followed his arrival.

The sources regarding Shah Sibghat Allah's brief but stormy five-year stay in Bijapur are considerably more extensive than those regarding Abu'l-Hasan Qadiri.[14] Ibrahim Zubairi, the historian and hagiographer of Bijapur, speculated in both his *Basatin al-Salatin* and his *Rauzat al-Auliya* that Shah Sibghat Allah's coming to Bijapur was specifically motivated by a desire to set Ibrahim II back on the path of strict Islam.[15] Writing from sources no longer extant, Zubairi recorded in both works the following exchange between the zealous Sufi and Sultan Ibrahim II:

> In the year A.H. 1000 he arrived in Bijapur. After a while it became known to him that the king had become enamoured to

[13] *Gulzar-i Abrar*, fol. 330b.

[14] As for the hagiographic traditions concerning Shah Sibghat Allah, there are two copies each of the *Mishkat al-Nubuwat* and the *Rauzat al-Auliya*, both comprehensive and reliable biographical hagiographies compiled in 1805-6 and 1825-26 respectively. The *Ma'asir al-Kiram*, a *tazkira* mainly of North Indian Sufis compiled in 1766-67, is also useful. The best *tazkira* source is the standard biography of the entire Shattari order, the *Gulzar-i Abrar*, compiled around 1613 or just seven years after Shah Sibghat Allah's death. Even this is surpassed, however, by nonbiographical traditions contemporary with the Sufi. Shah Sibghat Allah is one of the few Sufis of Bijapur of whom there exists a *malfuzat*, or the discourses of the *pir* as recorded by a *murid*. The *Malfuzat-i Shah Sibghat Allah*, compiled by his leading *khalifa* Habib Allah 'Abd al-Fattah, was composed in 1606, the year of the Sufi's death. Like other *malfuzats* used in this study, this manuscript provides first-hand observations of the Sufi's actions as well as his remembered conversations and sayings, which together make it an indispensable source.

[15] *Basatin*, p. 277; *Rauzat*, copy B, fol. 23b. Communication between Gujarat and Bijapur in the sixteenth and seventeenth centuries was sufficiently regular to render possible the Sufi's hearing about Ibrahim II while in Ahmedabad.

> Hindu singing and playing and had cultivated deviate skills. Seized by the command to do what is right, Shah Sibghat Allah told the sultan, "Take up the road of repentence and the true faith, clean your heart of false beliefs, and be a believer in the One." The sultan replied that he was only trying to improve his voice . . . but Shah Sibghat Allah retorted that good intentions were not sufficient and that he would have to refrain from these kinds of dangers altogether.[16]

Although there is no evidence that Ibrahim II ever did renounce his infatuation with Indian music, the likelihood that such an encounter actually did take place is suggested by other, even more zealous actions of the Sufi. Shah Sibghat Allah publicly attacked not only the monarch's personal religion, but more pointedly the kingdom's Shi'a population. Of all of Bijapur's Sufis, in fact, Shah Sibghat Allah was the most vociferous in attacking Shi'as and Shi'a tenets. A collection of his proverbs and sayings (*Malfuzat-i Shah Sibghat Allah*) compiled in the year of his death by a disciple of his successor frequently alludes to the Sufi's anti-Shi'a sentiment. It is remarked, for example, that a certain Shi'a teacher of Bijapur named Hasan Najafi was so terrified on merely hearing Sibghat Allah's name that "he broke into trembling just as the Devil trembles at the name of 'Umar."[17] Sibghat Allah's anti-Shi'a convictions probably originated in the polarized sectarian climate that characterized Gujarat in the latter half of the sixteenth century. The Bohras of Gujarat, a large community that had originally been exclusively Shi'a (of the Isma'ili variety), had split in the early fifteenth century into a large Sunni wing that enjoyed royal support, and a smaller wing that remained "orthodox" Shi'as. This split had been aggravated by a series of Sunni Bohra missionary movements, among the most fiery of which was that led by Maulana Muhammad Tahir in the 1570s. Maulana Tahir, wrote S. C. Misra, "learnt his tenets at Mecca and after his return, imbued with purist zeal, undertook the reform of his fellow Bohras. So vehement was his fervour against the heterodox sects that he is said to have made a vow that 'until the blackness of Shi'ism had been cleansed from the hearts of his tribe, he

[16] *Basatin*, pp. 276 f.; *Rauzat*, copy B, fol. 23b.

[17] *Malfuzat-i Shah Sibghat Allah*, comp. by Habib Allah 'Abd al-Fattah. Persian MS (Hyderabad: Asafiyah Library, Tasawwuf no. 1420), fol. 202.

would not bind his turban on his head.' "[18] Immediately upon his conquest of Gujarat in 1573 Akbar and his newly appointed governor supported the Maulana as he "embarked upon a rectification campaign in which he 'abolished many of the customs of his tribe.' "[19] This ferment lasted at least until 1578 when the Maulana was assassinated, and we know that Shah Sibghat Allah was living in Ahmedabad until around 1590 when he embarked on his own *hajj*.

It is not clear whether Shah Sibghat Allah's own anti-Shi'a sentiments were directly influenced by the fanatical campaigns of Maulana Tahir, whether they stemmed from the pro-Sunni position inherent in the teachings of the Shattari order, or whether they resulted, like the Maulana's own convictions, from his pilgrimage to Mecca. What is clear, however, is that the Sufi's anti-Shi'a sentiments were not at all welcome in Bijapur. For the kingdom then ruled by Sultan Ibrahim II had already had a bloody history of Shi'a-Sunni enmity that was still far from resolved. The Shi'a nobility, though recently eased out of its dominant position in Bijapur's political life, still formed a powerful segment of the kingdom's ruling structure—too powerful, as events proved, to submit to the venomous condemnation publicly cast upon it by Shah Sibghat Allah. Standing before the congregation in the city's great Jami' Mosque one Friday, Sibghat Allah announced that it was no longer possible to offer prayers in Bijapur as long as the sultan followed his worldly pursuits. He then declared that the selling of wine must be prohibited, as should the practice of prostitution, and that Shi'as should be barred from all positions of power in the kingdom.[20]

[18] S. C. Misra, *Muslim Communities of Gujarat* (Bombay: Asia Publishing House, 1964), p. 24.

[19] Ibid.

[20] *Mishkat*, copy A, fol. 72b. Ira Lapidus has noted similar instances of puritanical zeal displayed by Sufis of fourteenth-century Damascus. Some Sufis, he wrote, "represented the passionately puritanical strand of Islamic religious feeling and their personal wars on vice were an embarrassment to the more patient ulama. Sufi sheikhs and their followers often attacked the wine shops to spill out the forbidden beverages, and equally vigorously condemned the use of hashish. Emirs were not exempt from such assaults. These raids sometimes led to a good deal of trouble as people defended their activities and popular factions supporting and opposing the Sufis came to blows. In 1357 a group of Sufis broke up the wine and hashish

Shah Sibghat Allah's puritanical exhortations, directed especially at the Shi'as, were not confined to words alone. In 1596, the fifth and final year of his stay in Bijapur, Shah Sibghat Allah converted his fanatical zeal to actions that resulted in his own expulsion from the kingdom. The episode in question occurred around sundown on the second of Muharram, A.H. 1005, which in that year fell in the middle of the hot monsoon season (26 August 1596), when tempers would have been short. The Shi'as of Bijapur were noisily preparing for the celebration of *'Ashura*, the festival of public wailing, which commemorates the martyrdom of Imam Husain. As a clamorous procession of five hundred Shi'as approached Shah Sibghat Allah's *khanaqah*, the Sufi sent one of his followers out to destroy the Shi'a symbol being carried at the head of the procession. This was done, touching off a bloody riot between the Shi'as and a number of Sibghat Allah's *murids*. When Sultan Ibrahim II heard of this he immediately placed the Sufi under house arrest by locking him inside his *khanaqah* and stationing twenty guards outside. Meanwhile, the *murids* who had been wounded in their encounter with the Shi'as came to rescue their *pir*. This was to no avail, however, as the Sufi was not released until after the *'Ashura* celebrations were over.[21]

The above account, written by one of Shah Sibghat Allah's contemporaries and a possible participant in the struggle, makes intelligible what other sources have mentioned concerning the Sufi's somewhat abrupt departure from Bijapur.[22] The *Mishkat-i*

---

parlors in Damascus, but the falconers and dog handlers who profited from the business fought them, counterattacked their mosque, seized some of the Sufis, and paraded their prisoners about in the city for interfering with their business. Respectable opinion put a stop to this, but similar episodes often recurred" (Lapidus, *Muslim Cities*, p. 106).

21 *Malfuzat-i Shah Sibghat Allah*, fols. 4b-5a.

22 The details of Shah Sibghat Allah's anti-Shi'a behavior illustrate an interesting historiographical point. The *Malfuzat-i Shah Sibghat Allah*, written in the year of the Sufi's death (1606), gives full details of his enmity with the Shi'as and the conflict it produced. On the other hand the original and therefore the oldest copy of the *Mishkat-i Nubuwat*, compiled in 1804-5 and based in part on the *Malfuzat*, mentions the Sufi's anti-Shi'a speech but nothing of the street conflict. And a later copy of the same work (copy date unknown) omitted all reference whatsoever to Shah Sibghat Allah's anti-Shi'a behavior, even changing the word *rafaza* (Arabic

Nubuwat records that the Shi'a nobles held a special meeting with the sultan and remonstrated that the piety of Shah Sibghat Allah notwithstanding, the glory of the kingdom might be better served if he were absent. Accordingly, they then suggested that the time had perhaps arrived that Shah Sibghat Allah make the holy pilgrimage to Mecca.[23] The sultan accepted this council, and despite the fact that Sibghat Allah had just performed the *hajj* only five years earlier, the court provided him with a generous allowance of 3,000 *huns* for making a second pilgrimage.[24] The court's decision on this matter was relayed to the Sufi by one of his *murids*, 'Abd al-Qadir Chashnigir, who had attended the royal meeting. 'Abd al-Qadir arrived at the *khanaqah* to find his *pir* performing the evening prayers. But on hearing the court's decision Shah Sibghat Allah made such haste to submit his farewells to the sultan that he did not even change his clothes before going to court. He left the city the next morning, stopping only in the suburb of Shahpur to distribute the entirety of his travel allowance, and then continued on to Arabia, never again to return to Bijapur.[25] He died ten years later in Medina, where he was buried.

Despite his ignominious departure, Shah Sibghat Allah had in fact developed close relations with the court of which he became so critical. In 1594-95 he had prayed for the sultan during a minor internal revolt.[26] During one of Akbar's invasions of the Deccan members of the nobility and *'ulama* approached the Sufi seeking his blessings.[27] On a more mundane level, Sibghat Allah even developed a close friendship with the kingdom's treasurer and occasionally wrote letters to the court recommending friends for government employment.[28] But though the Sufi's reputation as a

---

plural of *rafiz*, "rejector," or "a group of Shi'a") in the original to *rauza* ("garden" or "tomb"). This suggests a deliberate attempt by later compilers and copyists, for motives known only to themselves, to tone down and finally to delete the anti-Shi'a nature of Shah Sibghat Allah's activities in Bijapur.

[23] *Mishkat*, copy A, fols. 72b-73a.

[24] *Malfuzat-i Shah Sibghat Allah*, fol. 26a.

[25] *Mishkat*, copy A, fol. 73a.

[26] *Malfuzat-i Shah Sibghat Allah*, fol. 27b. This was the unsuccessful rebellion of 'Ain al-Mulk. See Firishta, *Tarikh-i Firishta*, II, pp. 74-77. (Briggs's translation, III, pp. 108-12.)

[27] *Malfuzat-i Shah Sibghat Allah*, fol. 35b.

[28] Ibid., fols. 5b, 26a.

living saint enabled him to operate at a high level in the court, his zeal for Islamic orthodoxy would not be tolerated when it threatened to reopen the deep wounds of Shi'a-Sunni animosity in Bijapur, wounds that had been only partially healed by Ibrahim II's liberal policies.

Although Abu'l-Hasan Qadiri and Shah Sibghat Allah thus exhibited a posture of aggressive puritanism vis-à-vis the court, a more passive role was assumed by Shah Hashim 'Alawi (d. 1646), popularly remembered as Hashim Gujarati, or simply Hashim Pir.[29] Like Shah Sibghat Allah, Hashim Pir was a Gujarati Sufi of the Shattari order and had received his *khilafat* from Shah Wajih al-Din 'Alawi at Ahmedabad, as seen in Chart 3.[30] But beyond common origins in Gujarat and a similar spiritual ancestry, comparison between Shah Sibghat Allah and Hashim Pir ends. For Hashim Pir shared none of Shah Sibghat Allah's abrasive aggressiveness on matters of Islamic orthodoxy. His more liberal outlook made him, in fact, one of the only Sufis of Bijapur to establish close contacts at once with the court and with commoners. For the moment we are concerned with his relationship to Bijapur's political and religious establishments.

Hashim Pir was born in 1576-77 in the family of a wealthy judge of Ahmedabad, Qazi Burhan al-Din, whose holdings included a village in *in'am* worth Rs. 4,000.[31] At a very early point in his life Hashim became a *murid* of the famous Shattari mystic Wajih al-Din 'Alawi. But Wajih al-Din died when Hashim was

[29] Hashim Pir 'Alawi, whose portrait is reproduced in Figure 9 in this study, is one of the favorite Sufis of Bijapur, both among his immediate *murids* and biographers as well as among present-day devotees. The sources on him therefore range from valuable *malfuzats* written by his closest followers to lithographed panegyrics recently compiled by devotees attached to his *dargah*. He is the only Bijapuri Sufi of whom there exist two *malfuzats*: one is the *Ganj-i Asrar*, which one of his *murids* began to compile twelve years after the Sufi's death. Another of his *murids* wrote the *Maqsud al-Murad* (date unknown). In addition to these primary sources, there is a *tazkira* of Hashim Pir and several generations of his descendants: the *Tuhfa az Kamtarin* (date unknown) preserved in the Hashim *dargah* at Bijapur. The more general *tazkiras* of Bijapuri and Deccani Sufis also devote considerable space to Hashim Pir, though the two *malfuzats* mentioned above remain by far the most reliable sources for studying the Sufi.

[30] A complete genealogy of Hashim Pir can be found in Appendix I of this study.

[31] *Maqsud al-Murad*, comp. by Shah Murad bin Saiyid Jalal. Persian MS (Hyderabad: Asafiyah Library, Tasawwuf no. 335), p. 8.

CHART 3

ANCESTRY OF SHAH HASHIM PIR 'ALAWI

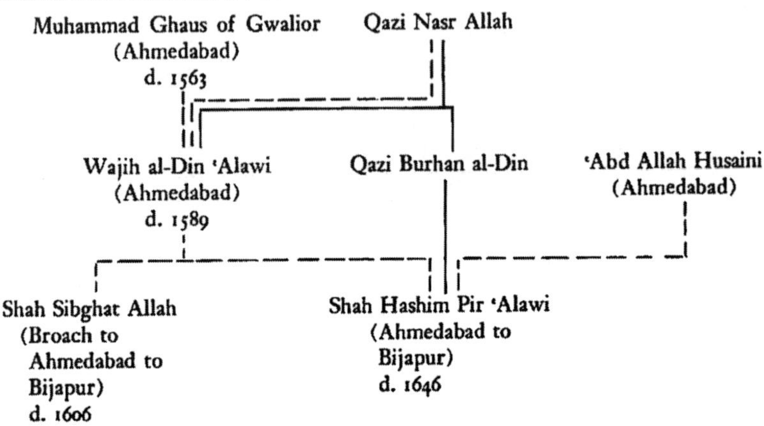

NOTE: Unbroken lines indicate family lineage; broken lines indicate spiritual lineage.

only fourteen years of age, and thereafter the boy fell under the spiritual discipleship of one of Wajih al-Din's older *murids*, Shah 'Abd Allah Husaini.[32] From this time Hashim, in the best of earlier Shattari traditions, seems to have become increasingly ascetic. When his father died in 1605-6 he gave away the family fortune including the village in *in'am*,[33] and at some time after that he left Ahmedabad, inexplicably, for Bijapur.

We hear nothing of Hashim Pir's activities in Bijapur until the end of Ibrahim II's reign, when events following a pilgrimage to Mecca brought him into close contact with the court. He was returning from the *hajj* in 1626-27 when the ship he was traveling on was captured off the Konkan Coast by the Portuguese, who interned the ship's cargo and passengers in Goa.[34] When this news reached the Bijapur court the aging Ibrahim II wrote a number

[32] *Rauzat*, copy A, pp. 132 f.

[33] *Maqsud al-Murad*, p. 7; *Ganj-i Asrar*, comp. by Shah Na'im Allah. Persian MS (Hyderabad: Salar Jung Museum, Tasawwuf no. 134), fol. 2a-b.

[34] *Basatin*, p. 331. Zubairi did not give his source in relating this episode. The earliest corroborating source known to me, and possibly one of Zubairi's own sources, is one of the *malfuzats* of Hashim Pir, the *Ganj-i Asrar*, written thirty-nine years after the event in question. See *Ganj-i Asrar*, fol. 101b.

of letters to the Portuguese governor of Goa requesting the release of Hashim Pir and the other prisoners.[35] Although Ibrahim II's motives for this intervention were not recorded, it is likely that the sultan wished to show his support for a man already widely venerated as a living saint in the capital city. Whatever the cause of Ibrahim II's intervention, his efforts were successful, and Hashim Pir was soon allowed to return to the capital.

Although we do not know what Hashim's relations with the court had been before this episode, it is clear that they became quite close after it. When Ibrahim II died the following year (1627), Muhammad 'Adil Shah continued the tradition of maintaining close links with the Sufi. Zubairi wrote that both Ibrahim II and Muhammad had a great deal of belief in Hashim's spiritual power and that Muhammad declared him to be superior to all other Sufis of Bijapur, even depending on Hashim's council on important matters of state.[36] One oft-related tradition that can be traced to Sultan Muhammad's time relates that when Muhammad fell seriously ill in 1646 Hashim Pir gave the sultan ten years of his life in return for the favor extended to the Sufi twenty years earlier by Ibrahim II.[37] Hashim thus died in 1646, and Muhammad in 1656. Whether or not Muhammad 'Adil Shah believed that his life had been prolonged in this way, the sultan's deep attachment to the Sufi is suggested by his having constructed his own huge mausoleum, the famous Gol Gumbad, directly behind Hashim Pir's *dargah* in the extreme eastern end of the city.

What were the reasons for the close contacts between Hashim Pir and Muhammad 'Adil Shah? One cause doubtless lies in Ibrahim II's intervention in securing Hashim's release from the Portuguese, an event that to some extent must have ingratiated the Sufi to the court. A more profound cause has its roots in the immense popularity that Hashim enjoyed throughout his long life in Bijapur. One of his *khalifas* wrote that Hashim had enlisted 5,500 affiliates into the outer circle of his following at Bijapur.[38] The basis of his popularity was suggested by another of his *khalifas*:

[35] *Basatin*, pp. 331 f.
[36] *Rauzat*, copy A, p. 133.
[37] *Ganj-i Asrar*, fol. 101b; *Basatin*, p. 330; *Rauzat*, copy A, p. 149a.
[38] *Ganj-i Asrar*, fol. 57b.

9. Shah Hashim Pir ʿAlawi (d. 1646)

> Every day a great number of men would come to that guide [Hashim] declaring that their poverty and unfortunate state had caused them to come to his service in want of relief. He would ask them if they wanted employment as domestic servants. Some said they would work for such-and-such a noble; others said they would work for anybody who would look after their welfare. And he [Hashim Pir] would express his willingness to write them letters of recommendation for employment. . . . And in every possible way he would take their pleas and stories to the king, the *wazir*, or to whomever was necessary for the task.[39]

Even after allowing for the *malfuzat*-writer's possible exaggeration on this point, the tenor of this passage clearly reveals a Sufi functioning in a broker's role between the court and unemployed commoners of the lower classes. Hashim Pir's support of the court, symbolized by his allowing the sultan to visit his *khanaqah*, can thus be seen as a mutually advantageous contract between the court and the Sufi. What the monarch gained in having Hashim's support was a deepening of his authority among commoners already spiritually affiliated with the Sufi. What Hashim gained was access to nobles through whom he could improve the material welfare of his many followers.

Hashim Pir ʿAlawi thus emerges an entirely different sort of reformer than Abu'l-Hasan Qadiri or Shah Sibghat Allah. Fired by puritanical zeal, the latter two seized the initiative in forging links with an institution they hoped to reform and purify of any un-Islamic influences. In the case of Hashim Pir it was the court that seems to have taken the initiative in gaining the Sufi's support. And while Shah Sibghat Allah's idea of reform was narrow and legalistic, Hashim Pir's idea seems to have been much broader and more socially ameliorative. He was perhaps the only Sufi of Bijapur to employ his good favor with the court for truly constructive social ends.

Most Qadiri and Shattari Sufis, living too close to the center of political power altogether to escape its magnetic field, either attempted to reform the court or yielded to its patronage. There were others, however, who for one reason or another stoutly resisted courtly favors and courtly visitations, living as urban

[39] *Maqsud al-Murad*, p. 84.

recluses (*gosha-nishin*). Since the courts of both Ibrahim II and Muhammad actively solicited the patronage of well-known Sufis, it would have been difficult for reclusive Sufis to resist court intervention when their *khanaqahs* were situated within only a half mile of the royal palace. It is perhaps for this reason that the few examples of this type exhibited a certain ostentatious disdain, and times open hostility, for the court. This differed from the aloofness of many Chishti Sufis who, living outside the city, were in a better position simply to ignore the court altogether.

Both of Abu'l-Hasan's younger brothers were urban recluses.[40] Shah Mustafa Qadiri (dates unknown) had accompanied Abu'l-Hasan when the latter migrated from Bidar to Bijapur. Living alone, he frequently refused audience to members of the nobility, and it is said that on one occasion he expelled from his *khanaqah* none other than Sultan Ibrahim II, who had come to see him.[41] The theme of a soliciting sultan being rebuffed by a reclusive Sufi finds more flamboyant expression in the biographies of Shah Qasim Qadiri (d. 1622), the youngest of the three brothers and the last to arrive in Bijapur. The *Sahifat-i Ahl-i Huda* records that Sultan Ibrahim II, desiring to meet Qasim Qadiri, was told that despite the Sufi's reclusive habits he could be found on Fridays in the great Jami' Mosque.

> On Friday Sultan Ibrahim arrived at the Jami' Mosque in all his majestic grandeur and decked in his jeweled crown. After prayers the sultan moved toward Shah Qasim who, however, made no notice of the sultan. After Ibrahim's departure, Shah Qasim asked who that snake-charmer was. Shah Hashim Pir, who happened to be there then, replied that he was the monarch of the kingdom, Sultan Ibrahim.[42]

Perhaps because he conformed to the model of the early Arab ascetic Sufis, the reclusive Sufi as an ideal type was highly venerated by Sufis and sultans alike. Apart from Mustafa and Qasim Qadiri, however, there were few Sufis of Bijapur who ever actually became recluses or adopted the sort of ostentatious disdain for the court that would cause them to call a sultan a snake-

[40] Abbreviated lineages of Abu'l-Hasan Qadiri's two brothers, Mustafa Qadiri and Qasim Qadiri, have been included in Chart 1.

[41] *Rauzat*, copy A, pp. 124 f.; *Sahifat*, Urdu edn., pp. 23 f.

[42] *Sahifat*, Urdu edn., p. 41.

charmer. As later Qadiri and Shattari Sufis became bound to court charity—and these even included the immediate descendants of Mustafa and Qasim Qadiri—this type vanished from the scene altogether.

Reformist Sufis in Relation to Sunni Islam

In terms of attending the community prayers, making the pilgrimage to Mecca, obeying the *shari'at*, and fulfilling all of the other formal aspects of the Islamic faith, the orthodoxy of the urban-dwelling Qadiri and Shattari Sufis considered in this chapter was undeniable. This is all the more true insofar as Islamic orthodoxy has traditionally been defined more in terms of conformity of practice than conformity of belief. We see this orthodoxy expressed in several ways. Opposition to Shi'ism, most violently expressed by Shah Sibghat Allah, was common among urban Qadiri and Shattari Sufis generally. The ill feeling between Arab Sufis and the Shi'a nobility residing in the city can be seen in the minor crisis that followed the death of a certain Arab migrant named Abu Bakr ba'l-Faqih (dates unknown). It happened that the Sufi's *khanaqah* was located in the Shi'a quarter of the city, and the Shi'as objected to the burial of the Sufi in their quarter. But the Sunni *wazir* 'Abd al-Muhammad intervened and, over Shi'a protests, had the Sufi buried near the *khanaqah*.[43] Besides opposing Shi'ism, these Sufis generally opposed the expression of spiritual ecstasy in forms such as dancing (*raqs*) or participating in musical sessions (*sama'*). Shah Sibghat Allah expelled from his *khanaqah* a *murid* who had collapsed in the ecstasy induced by *sama'*.[44] Abu'l-Hasan Qadiri, the only Reformist Sufi to write any books in Dakhni, summed up the orthodox Sufi position in this respect by declaring, "Mankind is defined thus—first comes knowledge (*'ilm*), then exhilaration (*hal*)."[45]

But more than their merely being orthodox Muslims, the Sufis examined in this chapter may be said to have represented the very model of "pure" Arab Islam in early seventeenth century Bijapur. In this role they were not entirely without precedent.

[43] *Rauzat*, copy A, p. 194.

[44] *Malfuzat-i Shah Sibghat Allah*, fol. 33b.

[45] Abu'l-Hasan Qadiri, *Sukh Anjan*, ed. by Saiyida Ja'far. Dakhni lithograph (Hyderabad: Lutf al-Daula Research Institute, 1968), p. 151, lines 7-8.

Colonies of Arab merchants had for centuries been settled along the harbors of the Konkan Coast and had, to some extent, retained their Arab culture. "In these mosques and monasteries," wrote one authority,

> where the sons and daughters of Arab sailors in particular and Muslims in general studied, and where Arab Khatibs and Shafi'i Jurists imparted education, it is obvious that there might have been no medium of instruction other than Arabic and no syllabus except Tafsir, Hadith, and Fiqh whose medium of study is nothing but Arabic. Learning of the Qur'an by heart might also have been one of the curricular activities in those mosque-schools, and that is why Ibn Battuta found that almost all women of Hanawar were Hafizat or memorizers of the Qur'an.[46]

In Sultan Muhammad's reign groups of reciters of the Koran (*huffaz*) would come from the Konkan settlements to the capital city each year during the month of Ramazan to sing in the city's mosques.[47] In this way these Arabs continued to exert an influence on the city's cultural life. Then too, scattered throughout the 'Adil Shahi period one meets with individual Arab scholars who resided in Bijapur. A certain Zain al-Din bin 'Ali al-Ma'bari (d. 1522) was a noted scholar who wrote Arabic works on nearly every branch of Islamic learning including the Traditions (*hadis*), Jurisprudence (*fiqh*), and mystical poetry.[48] Another Bijapur resident was his grandson, Zain al-Din bin 'Abd al-'Aziz al-Ma'bari (d. 1583), who wrote an important chronicle of Portuguese-Arab relations on the Malabar Coast and dedicated it to Sultan 'Ali 'Adil Shah I.[49] We also hear of an Arab poet named Hasan bin 'Ali al-Shadqam (d. 1636) who emigrated from Arabia as a youth and became attached to the Bijapur court.[50]

But apart from these scattered individuals and the Konkani reciters, the real torch-bearers of Arab Islam in Bijapur were

[46] M. A. Muid Khan, *The Arabian Poets of Golconda* (Bombay: University of Bombay, 1963), p. 5.

[47] *Basatin*, p. 337.

[48] Annemarie Schimmel, *Islamic Literatures of India* (Wiesbaden: Otto Harrassowitz, 1973), pp. 4 f.

[49] Ibid., p. 5.

[50] M. G. Zubaid Ahmad, *The Contribution of Indo-Pakistan to Arabic Literature* (Lahore: Sh. Muhammad Ashraf, 1968), p. xlvii.

Sufis such as Abu'l-Hasan Qadiri and Shah Sibghat Allah. It is true that Bijapur's sea links with the Middle East had been fragile, as was illustrated by the capture of Hashim Pir 'Alawi by the Portuguese, and that this served to isolate the kingdom from the rest of *Dar al-Islam*. We have also noted that it was this very isolation that had in part contributed to the formation of the kingdom's unique and syncretic culture, which had evolved under the aegis of Sultan Ibrahim II. Accordingly, Sufis migrating to Bijapur during Ibrahim II's reign came mainly from within India, especially from Bidar and Gujarat, and not directly from the Arab Middle East (see Table 2). But in Sultan Muhammad's reign (1627-56) we find a different situation. The Portuguese control over the Arabian Sea traffic had by this time diminished, and sitting on the 'Adil Shahi throne was a monarch more conscious of his role as an Islamic ruler than as an Indian king. It is perhaps for these reasons that in Sultan Muhammad's reign the majority of foreign Sufis came directly from the Arab Middle East, as seen in Table 3.

TABLE 3

MIGRATION OF SUFIS TO BIJAPUR IN THE REIGN OF MUHAMMAD (1627-56)

Name	*Death Date*	*Origin*	*Order*	*Source**
'Abd al-Latif Qadiri, Shah	1671	Bidar	Qadiri	6:404, 1:182
'Abd al-Samad Kan'ani	1650	Egypt	Qadiri	1:68-70
Isma'il Qadiri bin Hasan	?	Baghdad	Qadiri	8:491b
Na'im Allah, Shah	1693-94	Burhanpur	Shattari	5:1072
Abu Bakr ba'l-Faqih	?	Arabia	?	1:193
Ahmad Nazir, Saiyid	?	Arabia	?	1:197
Ja'far Saqqaf, Saiyid	1647	Arabia	?	1:188-90
Siraj al-Din Junaidi III	?	Gulbarga	?	1:179
Zain Muqbil, Saiyid	1718	Arabia	?	1:197
Zubairi, Qazi Ibrahim	1683	Gujarat	Suhurawardi	1:220-2

* Source numbers are keyed to those used in Table 2.

Unlike those Sufis of Bijapur who had been born and raised in India and were hence several generations removed from the

Middle East, Sufis arriving directly from Arabia or Iraq tended to retain Arab habits and customs while in Bijapur. Writing in Arabic, conducting initiation ceremonies in Arabic, making frequent pilgrimages to Mecca, and sending gifts of money back to the holy shrines of Arabia were all widely practiced by Reformist Sufis. Shah Sibghat Allah built a mosque in the city—"Masjid-i Ibrahimpur"—and personally supervised its construction.[51] He also wrote three works in Arabic[52] and was particularly renowned for his Commentary (*tafsir*) on the Koran.[53] The Arab influence of some of these Sufis was exerted in other ways, too. One migrant even brought his Arab *murids* with him to Bijapur. Of Hazrat Abu Bakr ba'l-Faqih it was recorded by Zubairi: "In the time of Sultan Muhammad ʿAdil Shah he turned his attention from Hadramaut to this country. He came accompanied by a great number of Arabs who attended his *khanaqah* and who had attained the utmost degree of devoutness, virtue, and piety. He was a leader of the people and had acquired interior knowledge, for he was among the great Arab Saiyids."[54] We are not told how Abu Bakr interacted with Bijapur's indigenous population, but the biographical notice clearly portrays him and his *murids* as exemplary models of Islamic behavior in Bijapur.

Some narratives point to the Sufis' desire to impart to the court certain symbols of Arab culture as well as orthodox Islam. This is indicated in the *Tazkira-yi Auliya's* account of the life of Shaikh ʿAbd Allah ʿAidarus (d. 1631-32), a Sufi of the eminent ʿAidarus family of Yemen. Before leaving Arabia Shaikh ʿAbd Allah journeyed to Mecca and Medina where he was inducted into a number of *tariqas* including the Qadiri, the Shadhili, and the Suhurawardi orders. In the year 1616-17 he left Arabia for India, sailing to Gujarat. In Ahmedabad he was warmly received by his uncle, Muhyi al-Din ʿAbd al-Qadir al-ʿAidarus (fl. 1622) who, son of the family's first emigrant to India, had become established in Gujarat as a distinguished Sufi and an eminent author of about a score of books.[55] After taking spiritual blessings from his uncle,

[51] *Rauzat*, copy A, p. 78.

[52] *Tarjama-yi Rauzat al-Auliya'-i Bijapur* (trans. Shah Saif Allah) Urdu lith. (Raichur: Sibghat Allahi Press, A.H. 1315), p. 61.

[53] *Malfuzat-i Shah Sibghat Allah*, fol. 30a.

[54] *Rauzat*, copy A, p. 193.

[55] Zubaid Ahmad, *Contribution*, p. 175.

Shaikh ʻAbd Allah continued from Ahmedabad to the Deccan and lived for a while in Ahmadnagar under the patronage of that kingdom's *wazir*, Malik Ambar. However, because of deteriorating conditions in Ahmadnagar at that time, the shaikh was compelled to leave for Bijapur, probably in the early 1620s. There, he encountered Sultan Ibrahim II in the final years of the great sultan's reign. After their initial meeting, records the *Tazkira*,

> He induced the king to wear Arab clothes, which accordingly, the king did most of the time. . . . Ibrahim ʻAdil Shah had been a Shiʻa, while the Shaikh associated with the Sunni sect. But the Shaikh brought the Sultan over to the Sunni community, making the latter a man of integrity and reverence. The Shaikh then propagated the Holy Law of Muhammad in Bijapur.[56]

Although the compiler of the *Tazkira-yi Auliya* did not indicate his sources for this narrative, it is interesting to compare it with the account of a near-contemporary Arab biographer, Muhammad al-Amin al-Muhibbi (d. 1699), who chronicled the lives of seventeenth-century scholars and Sufis of many parts of the Muslim world in his *Khulasat al-Asar*. Both accounts agree on the essential events dealing with Shaikh ʻAbd Allah's journeys to Mecca, Medina, Ahmedabad, and Ahmadnagar. In Bijapur, however, and with respect to the Sufi's relationship with Sultan Ibrahim II, the account of Muhibbi differs slightly from that of the *Tazkira*. Muhibbi recorded that a certain ʻAli bin ʻAlawi, whose name does not figure in any other hagiographic or historical source, had placed a curse on the sultan causing him to bear a permanent wound on his buttocks that prevented him from either sitting or lying down. Even the most experienced physicians of Bijapur could not cure the monarch. Finding the sultan in this state when he arrived in Bijapur, Shaikh ʻAbd Allah ʻAidarus is said to have ordered him to sit down, and from that moment the sultan was miraculously healed. On account of this manifestation of his spiritual power, Shaikh ʻAbd Allah was made an adviser to the sultan. Moreover, recorded Muhibbi, the shaikh converted the sultan from Shiʻism to Sunni Islam.[57]

56 *Tazkira-yi Auliya*, 1, pp. 127 f.

57 Cited in F. Wustenfeld, "Die Cufiten in Sud Arabien im XI (XVII) Jahrhundert," *K. Gesellschaft der Wissenschaften*, Gottingen. Abhandlungen, 30, No. 1 (1883), pp. 39 f.

The Indian and Arab biographers of Shaikh ʿAbd Allah ʿAidarus thus agree on several points respecting the Sufi's life. Though the story of ʿAbd Allah's healing the sultan was omitted in the *Tazkira*, and though the story of the Sufi's persuading the sultan to wear Arab clothes was omitted by Muhibbi, both accounts agree on the Sufi's role in converting the sultan from Shiʿism to Sunni Islam. In point of fact, however, we know that Ibrahim II had never been a Shiʿa. The historian Firishta, who resided at Ibrahim II's court, affirmed that the sultan had been educated as a Hanafi Sunni, noting that the sultan even ordered the confinement of criers who in 1590 read the *khutba* in the Shiʿa form.[58] Therefore, it is again necessary to place both accounts in the context of their purpose, which was to emphasize the Sufi's role in championing the cause of Islamic orthodoxy in Bijapur, even if this meant portraying the sultan as less orthodox than we know him to have been.

The Indian and Arab accounts also agree on ʿAbd Allah's love of his native country and his dedication to Arab culture. We are told that he intended to build in his native Hadramaut a large library with parks, but that the money and books he had collected and sent to Arabia for this purpose got lost at sea.[59] ʿAbd Allah thus emerges a non-Deccani to the end. Although he remained in Bijapur until Sultan Ibrahim II's death in 1627 and though he remained in India until his own death in Daulatabad several years later, the shaikh's sympathies and values never took root in Indian soil. It is doubtful that he ever learned Dakhni or Persian, though we have no specific information on this point. For unlike Shah Sibghat Allah or Shah Abu'l-Hasan Qadiri, ʿAbd Allah was native to Arabia, and it did not require the experience of a *hajj* to acquaint him with Arab Islam and fire him with a zeal to promote Islamic orthodoxy in Bijapur.

Unfortunately there is little information on the relations of the Reformist Sufis with Bijapur's *ʿulama*, though what little evidence we do have points to the likelihood that the two groups were reasonably well integrated. We know, for example, that many of these Sufis had their sons and successors educated by Saiyid ʿAli Muhammad, who was the Chief Judge (*qazi al-quzat*) under

[58] Firishta, *Tarikh-i Firishta*, II, p. 66. (Briggs's translation, III, p. 103.)
[59] Wustenfeld, "Die Cufiten," p. 40; *Tazkira-yi Auliya*, I, p. 128.

Sultans Ibrahim II and Muhammad.[60] Among his students were Shah Burhan al-Din 'Alawi (d. 1674), Hashim Pir 'Alawi's grandson and successor to his *khanaqah*; Saiyid Muhammad Mudarris (d. 1674), Shah Sibghat Allah's nephew; Qazi Ibrahim Zubairi (d. 1683), a Suhurawardi Sufi from Gujarat; and the successors of 'Abd al-Razzaq Qadiri (d. 1641), who was a migrant from Baghdad having spiritual and blood ties with the family of Abu'l-Hasan Qadiri. Study under the kingdom's Chief Judge could not have failed to bring at least one section of Bijapur's Sufis within the social and doctrinal orbit of the *'ulama*.

The only Reformist Sufi about whose relations with the *'ulama* there is much specific information is Hashim Pir 'Alawi. Shah Murad, one of his *murids*, recorded a significant exchange that took place in one of Bijapur's mosques between his *pir* and an *'alim* (singular of *'ulama*). This debate centered around Hashim Pir's practice of giving *bai'at*, which was the compact binding a *murid* to a *pir*. The *'alim* asked Hashim Pir whence he derived his authority to do this, since such a practice was mentioned neither in the books of Islamic Jurisprudence (*fiqh*), in the Traditions of the Prophet (*hadis*), nor in the Commentaries of the Koran (*tafsir*).[61] Hashim Pir replied by attacking the value of Islamic jurisprudence for knowing God, saying, "You are the sort that believes all religion lies in jurisprudence. In fact, jurisprudence tells us little beyond how to keep our bodies clean."[62] Shifting the discussion to the giving of *bai'at*, Hashim then argued that in fact there were precedents of *bai'at*-giving in the Traditions and that the Prophet Muhammad himself had made such compacts with his companions.[63] Hashim further argued that the idea of an intermediary between man and God, which is the philosophical basis of the *bai'at* compact, was also precedented in early Islamic history. Even the Prophet, asserted Hashim, required some sort of intermediary—the messenger-angel Gabriel.[64]

As retold by one of Hashim's *murids*, this argument is understandably biased on Hashim Pir's side. But the encounter is significant first because it brings out one of the major doctrinal issues dividing even orthodox Sufis from the *'ulama*, namely, the Sufi's claim to an intermediate status between his *murid* and God.

[60] *Rauzat*, copy A, p. 203.

[61] *Maqsud al-Murad*, p. 122.

[62] Ibid., p. 123.

[63] Ibid., pp. 123 f.

[64] Ibid., p. 126.

Second, the encounter shows how the *'alim* was able to draw the Sufi into arguing doctrinal questions on the *'alim's* terms. Although Hashim had begun by denying the value of Islamic jurisprudence for finding God, he eventually quoted passages from the Traditions to justify his use of the *bai'at*. The very use of precedents in earlier Islamic traditions underscores Hashim Pir's fundamentally orthodox orientation.

In the other *malfuzat* of Hashim Pir 'Alawi, the *Ganj-i Asrar*, there is another reference to Hashim's relations with the *'ulama*. Here, the Sufi made the analogy that an *'alim* is to the Sufi what the cultivator is to the oil-presser. As the oil-presser would have no job without first securing the raw grain brought to him by the cultivator, so also the Sufi would have no means of attaining esoteric knowledge (*ma'rifat*) without first mastering the exoteric knowledge (*'ilm*) of the *'ulama*.[65] On the one hand, the analogy reflects the Sufi's dependence upon the *'ulama*. On the other hand, it implies the Sufi's superiority by suggesting that his knowledge is more highly refined than the *'ilm* of the *'ulama*. Yet the important thing is that Hashim Pir, unlike unorthodox Sufis, did see a complementary relationship between Sufis and the *'ulama*. Furthermore, said Hashim, the Sufi must learn all aspects of "exterior" knowledge (*'ilm*) so as not to be disgraced in the presence of the *'ulama*.[66]

Although there did exist some doctrinal differences between Reformist Sufis and the *'ulama*, and although—if the case of Hashim Pir is typical—these Sufis apparently kept a guarded distance from the *'ulama*, their integration both with Islamic orthodoxy and with its class of upholders was far more complete than that of any other type of Sufi under review in this study. Indeed, in point of commitment to orthodoxy, the zealous puritanism of Shah Sibghat Allah even surpassed the conservatism of the *'ulama*, who if anything must have been embarrassed by the Sufi's fanaticism. On the other hand the more liberal position of a Sufi like Hashim Pir 'Alawi—who in his characteristic manner sanctioned the use of *sama'* and *raqs* in achieving ecstasy but defended it by quoting the *shari'at*[67]—stood just barely within the pale of orthodoxy.

[65] *Ganj-i Asrar*, fol. 96a-b.

[66] Ibid., fol. 96b.

[67] *Maqsud al-Murad*, pp. 101 f.; *Ganj-i Asrar*, fol. 46a.

Reformist Sufis in Relation to the Non-Muslim Population

Aziz Ahmad has asserted that Indian Sufis generally had to accommodate themselves with Islamic orthodoxy "because of the challenge and the risk of disintegration into Hindu mysticism."[68] Although this statement would not apply to many other Sufis examined in this study—in fact it is flatly contradicted by some of them—it does apply to Reformist Sufis with their urban and doctrinally orthodox orientation. In his *Sukh Anjan* Abu'l-Hasan Qadiri expressed the need of clinging to Islamic orthodoxy in order to avoid slipping into Hindu religious beliefs and practices:

> You should read as quickly as possible, Oh Muslim,
> And you must be a believer.
> If not, the Devil will drop the sacred thread
> Around your neck in a minute,
> And drag you with him wherever he goes
> Until he makes you as he is.[69]

Fixing their attention mainly on the orthodoxy of the court, Reformist Sufis regarded Bijapur's non-Muslim population with attitudes ranging from indifference to hostility. Towards Brahmins, Hindu ascetics, and yogis, their attitude was often hostile. This hostility is often portrayed in the hagiographies as a rivalry between a Sufi and a yogi over spiritual superiority, as manifested in the performance of miraculous deeds, or *karamat*. We have noted above how Shah Abu'l-Hasan Qadiri is said to have outperformed a yogi in the arena of miracle-making and that the latter acknowledged the Sufi's spiritual superiority by accepting Islam. The same kind of tradition exists concerning a certain Hindu ascetic (*bairagi*) and Shah ʿAbd al-Latif La-ubali (d. 1640), a Qadiri Sufi who had migrated from Baghdad to Kurnool in the period of Ibrahim II.[70] A variation on this theme is related of Shah Musa Qadiri (d. 1670), a son of ʿAbd al-Latif and a *murid* of Shah Sibghat Allah's nephew. When he first arrived at Bijapur from Kurnool, Shah Musa stayed outside the city walls in a Hindu *math* (hut or monastery) inhabited by a group of *gusains*,

[68] Aziz Ahmad, *Studies in Islamic Culture*, p. 131.
[69] Abu'l-Hasan Qadiri, *Sukh Anjan*, p. 157, lines 15-18; p. 158, lines 1-2.
[70] See *Mishkat*, copy A, fols. 123a-124a.

or mendicants. This was a *math* where Muslims had never before ventured, and Shah Musa was expelled by the *gusains* shortly after his arrival there. Later, however, he was reaccepted in the *math*. He eventually engaged the *gusains* in a "spiritual struggle" from which he emerged victorious, whereupon the Hindus abandoned the *math* and Shah Musa converted the structure into his *khanaqah*.[71]

Toward the masses of non-elite Kannadiga and Maharashtrian non-Muslims, on the other hand, the Reformist Sufis seem to have been, at best, indifferent. Hindu commoners, seldom even mentioned in the sources, were evidently dismissed as infidels destined beyond hope to damnation. These Sufis indicated no interest in converting non-Muslims to Islam.[72]

Summary

The Sufis considered in this chapter may be considered the "Foreigners" of Bijapur's spiritual elite. Most of them arrived in the reigns of Ibrahim II and Muhammad either from other Islamic centers within India or, increasingly, directly from the Arab Middle East. As non-Deccanis they did not participate in the movement toward Hindu-Muslim syncretism in Bijapur presided over by Sultan Ibrahim II. To the contrary, many of them, shunning use of the Dakhni language and avoiding social contact with the Hindu population, actively set for themselves the goal of Arabizing the court. Indeed, the shift toward a more strict interpretation of Islam by the court of Muhammad, in contrast to that of Ibrahim II, probably resulted in part from the influence exerted by these urbanized defenders of orthodoxy.

Despite their relatively complete integration with the *'ulama*, Reformist Sufis nevertheless maintained their identity as Sufis, at least so far as institutional aspects are concerned. They all had

[71] *Latayif al-Latif*, comp. by 'Ali Musawi al-Qadiri. Persian MS (Hyderabad: Asafiyah Library, Tasawwuf no. 681), pp. 60-78.

[72] A significant exception to this statement is the case of Shah Hashim Pir 'Alawi, who developed important contacts with various non-elite Muslim and non-Muslim groups in Bijapur. Since Hashim Pir was perhaps the only Bijapuri Sufi to develop close contacts with both the court and the general population, his case demands consideration in several places in this study. For a discussion of his relations with Hindus, see below, chapter six.

received a *khilafat* from some other *pir*—usually outside of Bijapur since most of them were first-generation migrants—and they all passed their *khilafat* on to new followers. Within the city walls they built their own *khanaqahs*, which served both as centers for transmitting the *tariqa* or "Way" to their *murids*, and places for receiving scholars, nobles, and even sultans. Their successors, however, generally did not found independent daughter *khanaqahs* as they themselves had done, for the distinguishing characteristic of Reformist Sufis was their court patronage. This, as we shall see, was to lend to their *khanaqahs* a certain illustriousness that after their death became transferred to their tombs. Institutions of the *khanaqah* were thereby swiftly replaced by a completely new set of institutions—those of the *dargah*, or the tomb. It is an irony of the Reformist Sufis that in spite of their efforts to reform Islam in Bijapur, the great tombs that were constructed over their graves eventually became objects of the very sort of popular, syncretic devotionalism which they themselves would have scorned.

Chapter Six

SUFIS AS LITERATI

Even before orthodox Sufis of the Qadiri and Shattari orders had established themselves in Bijapur there flourished an important tradition of Indian Sufism just beyond the city walls on Shahpur Hillock. This was the Chishti line descended by spiritual and familial lineage from Shah Miranji Shams al-'Ushshaq (d. 1499). Operating independently from the court and espousing its own distinctive school of mystical thought, these Sufis of all those considered in this study most closely approached the quietistic and mystical ideal of Sufism as outlined by such writers as A. J. Arberry,[1] R. C. Zaehner,[2] or J. S. Trimingham. The latter writer, for example, understands Sufism as "those tendencies in Islam which aim at direct communion between God and man," and the Sufi as "anyone who believes that it is possible to have direct experience of God and who is prepared to go out of his way to put himself in a state whereby he may be enabled to do this."[3]

Little in the lives of those Sufis heretofore considered indicates that they went out of their way to achieve such a state. Warrior Sufis were too occupied in military struggles to develop the speculative aspect of Sufism, and the Reformist Sufis, by championing the cause of orthodoxy within the Muslim establishment in Bijapur, too frequently divorced themselves from the free-thinking and free-living styles associated with Sufism as understood by writers like Trimingham. Both of these types should be understood as Sufis in a strictly institutional rather than a mystical sense. The Chishtis of Shahpur Hillock, by contrast, conformed to both senses of the term. Furthermore, many of them recorded their experiences and teachings in a body of prose and poetry works directed to either their own disciples or the non-Sufi pub-

1 See Arberry, *Sufism*, pp. 11-14.

2 See R. C. Zaehner, *Hindu and Muslim Mysticism* (London: Athlone Press, 1960), pp. 5 f.

3 Trimingham, *Sufi Orders*, p. 1.

lic. It is this that differentiates them from all other Sufis of Bijapur and on account of which they may be termed the Literati. They are significant for (a) their role in the development of Dakhni and Urdu literature, (b) their formulation and dissemination of Sufi doctrine, and (c) their role in the diffusion of popular Islam in the Deccan.

Linguistic and Literary Contributions of the Literati

The most important exponents of Chishti doctrine in Bijapur were Shah Miranji Shams al-ʿUshshaq (d. 1499), his son Shah Burhan al-Din Janam (d. 1597), and the latter's *khalifa*, Shaikh Mahmud Khush Dahan (d. 1617).[4] Although many lesser Sufis were associated with Shah Miranji's *khanaqah* on Shahpur Hillock, these three stand out in terms of the extent of writings that have survived today. An abbreviated table showing the spiritual and familial relations of these Sufis is found in Chart 4.[5]

The coming of Shah Miranji Shams al-ʿUshshaq to Bijapur revived in the Deccan the moribund Chishti tradition that had lingered on in Gulbarga after the death of Gisudaraz. One sign of this revival was Shah Miranji's resumption of the practice of mystical writing, which in the Deccan had lapsed since the time of Gisudaraz. Although the earliest work of a Bijapuri Sufi might well be traced to Miranji's own *pir*, Kamal al-Din Biabani,[6] it is Shah Miranji who is remembered as the first important Sufi writer

[4] Longevity seems to have been a family trait for Shah Miranji and his descendants. Miranji himself was 94 when he died in 1499. His son Burhan al-Din Janam was already eighteen years of age in that year, so he must have been around 120 when he died in 1597. And Burhan al-Din's son Amin al-Din Aʿla would have been 78 when he died in 1675, since we know that he was born in the year of his father's death. See M. Akbaruddin Siddiqi, "The Dakani Inscription on the Amin Dargah in Bijapur," *Epigraphia Indica. Arabic and Persian Supplement* (1968), pp. 79-81.

[5] A complete genealogy of the Chishti order can be found in Appendix I.

[6] This is the *Chahar Shahadat*, a poetic treatise that is published in Hashim ʿAli, ed., *Maghz-i Marghub & Chahar Shahadat of Meeranji Shamsulushshaq* (Hyderabad: Urdu Academy, 1966). The editor himself attributes the work to Shah Miranji, but Professor Akbaruddin Siddiqi has brought to this writer's attention evidence that it was more likely the work of Kamal al-Din Biabani. Kamal's name appears in the third and last lines of the work, and the language of the work is slightly more archaic than that of Shah Miranji's *Maghz-i Marghub*.

CHART 4

ANCESTRY OF PROMINENT BIJAPURI CHISHTIS

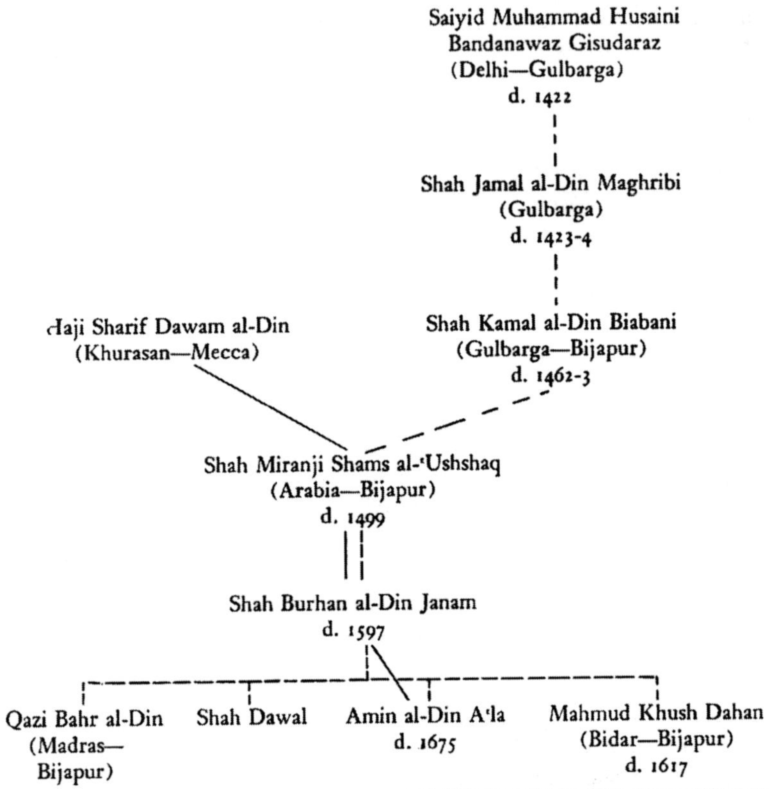

NOTE: Unbroken lines indicate familial lineage; broken lines indicate spiritual lineage.

of Bijapur. More than that, Shah Miranji and his successors did not write exclusively in Persian, as did most literate Sufis of India preceding him, but rather established the Dakhni language as a recognized medium of Sufi literature. We have noted earlier that Dakhni, the vernacular dialect of early Urdu spoken by Muslims of the Deccani class and by Hindus integrated into Bijapur's urban nexus, was distinguished by several characteristics: a retention of much of the Old Punjabi vocabulary carried down by fourteenth-century migrants from the Lahore region, an absorption of Sanskrit vocabulary borrowed from the Telugu and Kannada of its Deccan environment, and a lesser dependence upon Arabo-Persian vocabulary and spellings than obtained in North Indian Urdu.

These traits are perhaps best reflected in the mystical prose and poetry of Shah Burhan al-Din Janam, Shah Miranji's son and immediate successor to the Shahpur Hillock *khanaqah*. The historical linguist S. K. Chatterji has compared Burhan al-Din's "Hindi" with that of Kabir, noting that it "has the vocabulary and metre of Hindu Hindi, although it is written in the Perso-Arabic script."[7] Chatterji then expands on the theme of the Dakhni dialect's resemblance to Punjabi, basing his remarks upon Burhan al-Din's own description of his language:

> Shah Burhan's language has some distinct Panjabi affinities, and it is noteworthy that he calls it *Guj(a)ri*, as contrasted with *Bhaka* = *Bhakha*, i.e., any Western Hindi vernacular, including Braj-Bhakha. This name Gujri gives an indication of the origin and affinity of this dialect. Evidently the Gujars of the Panjab, who have given their name to Gujrat and Gujranwala, towns in the Panjab . . . had come in good numbers with the North Indian armies, and they maintained their name and their dialect in the Deccan for some time. . . . This Gujri speech of Shah Burhan is not Gujarati at all: it is a form of the -a dialect-group of Western Hindi and Panjabi, and is a Panjab dialect to start with. . . . The Deccan Urdu of Hindi literary tradition thus started in the fifteenth century with what may be called a sister form of Hindusthani; and this tradition continued to have quite a flourishing life, until it merged into that of Northern Hindusthani or Urdu, after paving the way for the latter.[8]

The timing of the literary development of Dakhni is also noteworthy. Insofar as Dakhni achieved literary expression several hundred years before North Indians gave regular literary status to Urdu,[9] the achievement of the early Sufis of Shahpur Hillock really represents a milestone in the literary history of India.

[7] Chatterji, *Indo-Aryan and Hindi*, pp. 205 f.

[8] Ibid., p. 206.

[9] Bailey, *History of Urdu Literature*, pp. 14 f.

10. Shahpur Hillock from the east

In North India it was not until the eighteenth century that Urdu-speakers overcame the literary tyranny of Persian and began composing in their own vernacular. In Bijapur, on the other hand, such inhibitions did not obtain among Deccani Muslims, who had become much more estranged from Persian culture than had their North Indian counterparts.

There were several reasons that the descendants of Shah Miranji Shams al-'Ushshaq used Dakhni as a literary medium. First, as the vernacular language of Deccani Muslims, it was their mother tongue. The same feeling of cultural distinctiveness that had led the earliest Deccani migrants to revolt against the North and establish the independent Bahmani Kingdom seems to have had its literary counterpart in the appearance of Dakhni compositions. Second, some Chishtis of Bijapur were strongly motivated to

11. *Dargah* of Shah Amin al-Din Aʿla

preach and teach, and Dakhni was evidently the only vernacular of Bijapur with which both Muslims and Hindus—at least those integrated with the city—were familiar. As the language of the army and the bazaar, Dakhni could reach more people than could the elitist Persian language. Of course, the use of Marathi or Kannada would have reached many more than even Dakhni. But Dakhni had the advantage of being written in the Perso-Arabic script, which would permit, when necessary, the easy importation of Islamic vocabulary.

Although the authentic writings of Shah Miranji himself were composed in Dakhni,[10] those of his descendants who lived in the sixteenth and seventeenth centuries were written either in Dakhni or in Persian. His son Burhan al-Din Janam, who was the most prolific of all Sufis of Shahpur Hillock and composed over a dozen works, invariably used Dakhni for his verse and either Dakhni or Persian for his prose. Similarly Mahmud Bahri (d. 1717-18), a much later Chishti of the same tradition, composed his verse in Dakhni but his prose in Persian. And Burhan al-Din's *khalifa*, Shaikh Mahmud Khush Dahan, wrote only prose, which was in Persian. It seems to have been the nature of the Sufis' audience that determined their choice of language. We find that verse was generally conveyed in Dakhni and prose in Persian, and that the Dakhni works were thematically addressed to wider, commoner audiences while the Persian writings dealt more exclusively with mysticism proper and were generally intended for use by the author's fellow Sufis. This clearly points to the oral value of verse in the medieval Deccan. As Annemarie Schimmel has observed with reference to Sufism and Indian poetry generally, "Since for many centuries poetry was practically the only vehicle for influencing the illiterate masses—who have had and still have an incredibly good memory for verse—the importance of these [Sufi] poems can not be overrated. Poetry was the daily bread for millions of people who formed their Weltbild according to the picture presented to them by the poets."[11]

[10] These would include two lyrical poems, *Khush-nama* and *Khush Naghz*, and one expository poem, *Maghz-i Marghub*—all of which have been published in Hashim 'Ali, ed., *Maghz-i Marghub*. Several prose works in both Persian and Dakhni have been attributed to Shah Miranji, but it is doubtful that they are authentic. See Hashim 'Ali, ed., Introduction to *Maghz-i Marghub*, pp. 38-41.

[11] Annemarie Schimmel, "The Influence of Sufism on Indo-Muslim

The level of abstraction of a particular work likewise determined the language used. The Dakhni language was well suited for conveying local symbols and familiar imagery of the Deccan. For the exposition of more theoretical problems or abstract concepts, on the other hand, Persian was generally preferred. The Dakhni of the fifteenth and sixteenth centuries apparently had not absorbed enough technical vocabulary to convey the abstractions that some writers such as Burhan al-Din Janam and Mahmud Khush Dahan wished to convey. An example of this is found in the case of two prose works by Burhan al-Din, *Irshad-nama* and *Kalimat al-Haqayiq*, both highly technical expositions of Chishti Sufism. The first of these, the *Irshad-nama*, was composed in 1582-83 in a highly Sanskritized form of Dakhni. Some time later Burhan al-Din wrote another work, the *Kalimat al-Haqayiq*, which recapitulated the earlier work in content but differed vastly in language, as it lapsed frequently into Persian. With reference to these particular works Professor M. Akbaruddin Siddiqi has suggested that since the Dakhni language alone could not convey the work's highly technical vocabulary, Burhan al-Din had to resort to one of India's two classical languages, Sanskrit or Persian. Failing to make himself understood in the Sanskritic *Irshad-nama*, Burhan al-Din was probably requested by his *murids* to render it in more comprehensible form, the result being the Persianized (but not entirely Persian) *Kalimat al-Haqayiq*.[12] A parallel situation occurred with Mahmud Bahri, who was asked by his disciples to translate his Sanskritized Dakhni poem *Man Lagan* into Persian, which he did in his *'Arus-i 'Irfan*.[13]

There were, in other words, two literary levels upon which the Chishti Sufis of Shahpur Hillock operated—the Dakhni level, usually verse, and intended for wider, non-Sufi audiences; and the Persian level, usually prose, and intended for fellow initiates. While it may not be fair to speak of these simplistically as "high" and "low" traditions, it is significant that the Sufis themselves were aware of the lower status of Dakhni as compared with

---

Poetry," in Joseph P. Strelka (ed.), *Anagogic Qualities of Literature* (University Park, Pa.: Pennsylvania State University Press, 1971), p. 202.

[12] M. Akbaruddin Siddiqi, private interview held at his home in Hyderabad, 10 December 1970.

[13] Hafiz Sayed, ed., *Kulliyat-i Bahri* (Lucknow: Nawal Kishor, A.H. 1339), p. 50.

Persian and that both Shah Miranji Shams al-ʿUshshaq and Burhan al-Din Janam felt constrained to apologize for using the former, which they called "Hindi." Yet, argued Burhan al-Din in his *Irshad-nama*, "There is nothing the matter with speaking Hindi,/ Open your eyes to the meaning in the treasure."[14] As the earliest writers of Dakhni, the Sufis of Bijapur must therefore be credited with contributing to the respectability and standardization of an evolving vernacular language. After them, court poets and even monarchs—we have noted that Sultan Ibrahim II's *Kitab-i Nauras* was a Dakhni work—employed Dakhni in their secular writings.[15] The pattern by which Sufis gave Dakhni literary respectability has been well stated by Professor Schimmel, who wrote that Sufis

> wanted to explain the mysteries of divine love and divine grace to the people who flocked around them and who understood neither Arabic, the language of the Qur'an and of the lawyer divines, nor Persian, the language of poetry and historiography. Thus the mystical leaders had to recur to the vernacular, even if they sometimes thought it necessary to start their book with an excuse for using the popular idiom. . . . They composed little songs for their followers, songs which condensed their teachings and which might also be used in musical assemblies. Then would follow the composition of small treatises in the vernacular, mostly rhymed so that they were easy to memorize, and eventually larger books, like *mathnawis* and, later, prose works. Thus the language was prepared for adapting itself to higher poetry of non-mystical content. That is how we should see the development of early Dakhni Urdu literature and the other regional languages.[16]

On the other hand, Sufis did not hesitate to continue employing the older, more-familiar medium of Persian when addressing

[14] Quoted in Abdul Haq, *Urdu ki Ibtidai Nashv-o-nama men Sufiya-i Kiram ka Kam* (Delhi: Anjuman-i Taraqqi-yi Urdu, 1939), p. 50. See also Abdul Haq, *Qadim Urdu* (Karachi: Anjuman-i Taraqqi-yi Urdu, 1961), pp. 19, 37.

[15] For a list of Dakhni poets of Bijapur with a short discussion of their lives and literature, see Nasir al-Din Hashimi, *Dakan men Urdu* (6th edn.; Lucknow: Nasim Book Depot, 1963), pp. 185-269. See also Muhiuddin Zore, *Dakan Adab ki Tarikh*, 1350-1750 (Karachi: Urdu Akadami-yi Sindh, 1960), pp. 32-59, and Jamil Jalibi, *Tarikh-i Adab-i Urdu*, vol. i, *Aghaz se 1750 tak* (Lahore: Majlis-i Taraqqi-yi Adab, 1975), pp. 181-377, passim.

[16] Schimmel, "Influence of Sufism," p. 196.

themselves or when the expression of mystical abstractions taxed Dakhni beyond its capacities.

In the remainder of this chapter we shall examine in more detail both literary traditions of the Chishti Sufis—first their mystical literature, with regard to the evolution of Sufi doctrine at Bijapur; and second their folk literature, with regard to the means by which that doctrine was conveyed to the non-Sufi population and the possible role it played in the expansion of Islam in the Deccan.

The Literati and Their Mystical Literature

If Shah Miranji Shams al-'Ushshaq can be considered the reviver of Chishti Sufism in the Deccan, Shah Burhan al-Din Janam and Shaikh Mahmud Khush Dahan were its major propounders. Little, however, is known of their lives. The *Shajarat al-Atqiya* records only that at age fifteen Burhan al-Din became a *murid* of his father, Shah Miranji, and that shortly thereafter he left Shahpur Hillock on a journey that lasted three years.[17] Although it is not known where he went, the experience probably brought him into contact with Hindu *sannyasis* and philosophers, judging from the considerable amount of Sanskrit vocabulary and Hindu thought that pervaded his work. Upon his return to Bijapur Burhan al-Din became the successor to his father's *khanaqah* where he established an inner circle of at least nine trusted disciples and a much larger circle of devotees who would come to Shahpur Hillock for his blessings. Even the hagiographical account of Bijapur's Qadiri Sufis affirmed that many people of both high and low social standing would bow in Burhan al-Din's presence.[18] He died in the middle of Sultan Ibrahim II's reign, in 1597.[19]

Shaikh Mahmud Khush Dahan (d. 1617) had very different origins. A nephew of Abu'l-Hasan Qadiri and a native of Bidar, Shaikh Mahmud was brought up with deep roots in the Qadiri order. He had even become Abu'l-Hasan's *murid* before the latter left Bidar for Bijapur. Shaikh Mahmud also left Bidar for Bijapur, probably following Abu'l-Hasan, but soon thereafter abandoned the spiritual direction of his Qadiri *pir*, who as we have seen became involved with the affairs of Ibrahim II's court. Attracted

[17] *Shajarat al-Atqiya*, pp. 23 f.
[18] *Tazkirat al-Qadiri*, fol. 67a.
[19] Siddiqi, "Dakani Inscription," p. 80.

to Chishti Sufism as taught at Shahpur Hillock, Shaikh Mahmud fell under the spiritual influence of Burhan al-Din Janam and was enrolled in the Chishti order as one of Burhan al-Din's most trusted followers.[20] A man of extraordinary learning and liberal outlook, Shaikh Mahmud in fact became his *pir's* chief heir as propounder of Chishti doctrine at Shahpur Hillock. His "conversion" from the Qadiri to the Chishti order perhaps illustrates the limited extent to which free-thinking Sufis could move within the orthodox confines of the Qadiri order, and the magnetic effect the Chishtis had in attracting such individuals to their fold.

The essence of the doctrine taught by Bijapur's Chishti Sufis was that there exists between Man and God a hidden, spiritual Path (*rah*) along which the seeker (*talib*) or traveler (*salik*) journeys on his life's quest to reach the Divine. Two conditions were required of the prospective traveler: one was that he be a Muslim or become a Muslim,[21] and the other that he entrust himself to the guidance of a learned *pir* who would lead him from one stage to the next.[22] Their system of four stages (*maqamat*) through which the traveler passed, as well as their basic ontological perspective, differed little in substance from the systems already fully developed in the older Sufi traditions of the Middle East and North India.[23] But as these stages formed

[20] *Rauzat*, copy A, p. 176.

[21] Since obedience to the *shari'at* is the first stage of a Chishti's journey, being a self-confessed Muslim was implicit for one's progress. In the same way, a Sufi who formally rejected Islam forfeited his right to continue on the Path. Burhan al-Din Janam wrote,

> He who renounces Islam (*murtadd*)
> Turns away from the soul of Truth;
> He will not understand the Path of the Sufis
> And will trod the path of negligence

(Burhan al-Din Janam, *Manfa'at al-Iman*. Dakhni MS [Hyderabad: Copy in the possession of M. Akbaruddin Siddiqi], lines 108-9).

[22] This injunction is commonly found in most Sufi orders. "If you do not follow the *murshid's* advice," wrote Burhan al-Din Janam, "you will talk of worldly and fruitless affairs, as aimlessly as the wandering bee" (Burhan al-Din Janam, *Manfa'at al-Iman*, line 111).

[23] Among the classic studies on the development of Sufi thought are R. A. Nicholson, *Mystics of Islam*; R. A. Nicholson, *Studies in Islamic Mysticism* (Cambridge: University Press, 1921; reprinted 1967); Arberry, *Sufism*; and Louis Massignon, *Essai sur les Origines du Lexique Technique de la Mystique Musulmane* (Paris: J. Vrin, 1968). The powerful undercurrent of

the basis of their outlook on life and religion, which in turn affected their relations with both Muslims and non-Muslims, they are vital to understand. The first stage was the *Shari'at*, or the stage of the Law, in which the traveler acquired the outward or exoteric knowledge (*'ilm*) of the canons of Islam. The second was *Tariqat*, or the stage of the Way, in which the first esoteric secrets and practices of the order were imparted to the traveler. The third was the *Haqiqat*, or the stage of Truth, in which the traveler was rewarded for his efforts by "seeing" God. And the fourth was the *Ma'rifat*, or the stage of esoteric Knowledge, in which the traveler realized the divine within himself. Through these four stages the Sufi could be guided and assisted by his *pir*. But there was yet another stage beyond these four called by Bijapur's Chishtis the *maqam-i qurb* ("place of nearness"), to which no *pir* could assist his *murid*. Only through the grace of God could a traveler attain *maqam-i qurb* which was, indeed, the goal of all Chishti Sufis.

The earliest statement of these stages by a Bijapuri Sufi was succinctly expressed in a verse of Shah Miranji Shams al-'Ushshaq:

> One who hears (*Shari'at*), does (*Tariqat*);
> One who does, sees (*Haqiqat*);
> And one who sees, enjoys (*Ma'rifat*).
> At this place, if God is kind, what good fortune comes.[24]

These themes were more fully developed and systematized by Burhan al-Din Janam and Mahmud Khush Dahan. In his *Ma'rifat al-Suluk*, which has been described as the summary work of all Bijapuri Chishti teachings and a book upon which scores of later treatises were based,[25] Shaikh Mahmud Khush Dahan presented

---

monistic pantheism in the doctrine of Bijapuri Chishtis finds its most forceful antecedent in the philosophy of Ibn 'Arabi (d. 1240), the Spanish-Arab mystic. For a discussion of his philosophy see A. E. Affifi, *The Mystical Philosophy of Muhyd Din-Ibnul 'Arabi* (Lahore: S. M. Ashraf, 1964). The system of stages expounded by Bijapur's Chishtis was borrowed, with slight modifications, from Delhi's Chishtis of the thirteenth and fourteenth centuries, especially Mu'in al-Din Chishti and Bakhtiyar Kaki.

[24] Miranji Shams al-'Ushshaq, *Maghz-i Marghub*, in Hashim 'Ali, ed., *Maghz-i Marghub & Chahar Shahadat*, p. 82, lines 3-4.

[25] Sakhawat Mirza, "Shaikh Mahmud Chishti al-Mulaqqab ba Khush Dahan Bijapuri," *Urdu-nama* (January-March 1962), p. 71.

the system in tabular form, of which an abbreviated version is found in Table 4.[26] It can be seen from this table that a certain

TABLE 4

THE CHISHTI PATH ACCORDING TO SHAIKH MAHMUD KHUSH DAHAN

	Stage (*rah*)	Exercise (*zikr*)	Abode (*manzil*)	Degree (*martaba*)
I	*Shari'at* Law	*Zikr-i Jali* with the voice	*Nasut* Humanity	*Nafs* Soul
II	*Tariqat* Way	*Zikr-i Qalbi* with the heart	*Malakut* Celestial Realm	*Dil* Heart
III	*Haqiqat* Truth	*Zikr-i Ruhi* with the soul	*Jabarut* Heaven	*Ruh* Spirit
IV	*Ma'rifat* Knowledge	*Zikr-i Sirri* secret *zikr*	*Lahut* Divinity	*Nur* Light
. . .	. . .	. . .	. . .	. . .
goal:	*Tauhid* Divine Unity	*Zikr-i Khafi* hidden *zikr*	*Maqam-i Qurb* Place of Nearness	*Zat* Essence

form of spiritual exercise (*zikr*) accompanied each stage, as did also a certain abode (*manzil*) within which the traveler existed, and a certain degree (*martaba*) of God's manifestation upon which his concentration was fixed. Of these the *zikrs* were particularly important, for it was normally through them that Sufis passed their teachings to both *murids* and the lay public. Literally meaning "remembrance," the *zikr* represented the specialized practices that could enable the traveler to attain higher stages on his spiritual journey. Because of the power that was believed to be released by performing a *zikr*, novices were forbidden to use them except under permission of their *pir*.

The first *zikr*, the *zikr-i jali*, consisted of phrases, verses, or simply names of God which the *murid* was instructed to repeat out loud. This *zikr*, which was used in the *Shari'at* stage, was the easiest form of spiritual exercise to perform since one's attention could more readily be concentrated on concrete perceptions—in

[26] Mahmud Khush Dahan, *Ma'rifat al-Suluk*. Persian lithograph (Lucknow: Nawal Kishor, 1898), p. 64. Also in Persian MS (Hyderabad: Salar Jung Museum, Tasawwuf no. 185), p. 27.

this case the sound of one's own voice—than on abstractions or mental images characteristic of higher *zikrs*. Wrote Burhan al-Din Janam,

> Recite God's name out loud
> So that you can reach *manzil-i nasut*.
> You should recite *zikr-i jali*
> Such that each limb participates.[27]
> . . . .
> We should move our tongues by saying the name of God
> So that each word falls upon our ears.[28]

In the second stage, *Tariqat*, the aim of the traveler was to begin, if only for fleeting moments, to lose his sense of self. Like the first *zikr*, the exercise for this stage, *zikr-i qalbi*, involved repetition of God's names in prescribed forms—but with the difference that the recitation was done in the heart and not vocally.

> *Zikr-i qalbi* is done under the breath, not out loud.
> We heard *zikr-i jali* with our ears.
> Now keep your mind away from the sense organs,
> And lose your selfness.
> We should keep our hearts on this *zikr* only briefly—
> For as long as a diver jumps in water and comes out again.[29]

In the third stage, *Haqiqat*, the traveler for the first time caught a glimpse of God. This was accomplished through performance of the *zikr-i ruhi*, a more difficult *zikr* than the first two since it carried the process of internalizing the *zikr* one step further. Instead of concentrating on the repetition of words, spoken or thought, the traveler now focused on mere symbols or mental images which would guide him in rapture toward the sight of God.

> This meditation should be like the lotus seeing the sun,
> Or the Greek partridge seeing the moonlight.

[27] Burhan al-Din Janam, *Wasiyat al-Hadi*. Dakhni MS (Hyderabad: Salar Jung Museum, Urdu MSS, Tasawwuf & Akhlaq no. 54), fol. 7a-b.
[28] Burhan al-Din Janam, *Basharat al-Zikr*, Dakhni MS (Hyderabad. Salar Jung Museum, Urdu MSS, Tasawwuf & Akhlaq no. 9), fol. 8a.
[29] Ibid., fol. 8b.

Many *sadhus* meditate in this way,
As if one is constantly imagining a treasure.
God has hinted that he is near our vein,
And also in our heart, invisibly;
In meditation we see God invisibly;
The eyes of the heart can see Him.
The traveler will see God in this meditation
As if He were in a house surrounding him.[30]

In the *zikr-i sirri*, which accompanied the fourth stage, *Ma'rifat*, the traveler again concentrated upon images rather than words. But his aim was different. Now, full of love and with no thought of self, he approached the deity he had only seen in the previous stage. The image of the moth and the candle poignantly conveys this idea of self-sacrifice:

This is *zikr-i sirri*,
By which we see that God is without properties.
It is at this juncture that love of God
Overwhelms our heart, body, and spirit.
When the candle burns, the moth comes and gives his life.
He does not reflect on whether he will come to harm or not.
He gives his heart to that most beautiful form of light
And forgets his own self completely.[31]

The goal of the Chishti was to transcend all of these four stages and attain *maqam-i qurb*, the "place of nearness" for which the *zikr-i khafi* was appropriate. But because this stage was ineffable, description of the *zikr* or of the stage itself was exceedingly difficult:

We call *khafi* that place where
Neither man is mortal, nor anything else.
We cannot say a word from our mouth in that place;
He who has reached it sees nothing, though he has eyes.

[30] Ibid., fols. 8b-9a. Some of Burhan al-Din's references in this passage deserve notice. The reference in the third line to God's being nearer to man than his own jugular vein is from the Koran (50:15) and is one of the most frequently quoted verses among Sufis. Yet immediately before drawing from the Koran, Burhan al-Din alluded approvingly to Hindu *sadhus*. He evidently had respect for those pious Hindus who had renounced the world, but not for the austere, and to him bizarre, practices of the yogis.

[31] Ibid., fol. 9b.

We cannot say anything about that place,
  Yet it is unbearable for us to keep silent.
It seems as if we exist no more, but again shall be alive,
  That we see something, but are unable to mention it.[32]

What was the Sufi's relationship to God in this stage? It is clear from the above account of the four stages that the general purpose of each stage was to diminish, by degrees, the fundamental separation of Man and God that characterizes the transcendental aspect of Koranic theology. As each stage brought the traveler closer to God, the ultimate stage would logically seem to unite the two. Herein lay the most important theological issue dividing orthodox from unorthodox Chishtis of Bijapur. Unorthodox Chishtis, whom we shall examine more closely in chapter nine, interpreted *maqam-i qurb* as the actual union of Man and God, stressing the idea of *fana*, or the passing away of the individual self in God.[33] Orthodox Chishtis, on the other hand, interpreted *maqam-i qurb* as "nearness to God," stressing the idea of *baqa*, or the eternal and blissful dwelling in God's company. Their orthodoxy lay in maintaining a separation, however slight, between humanity and divinity.

The Literati generally upheld this latter, orthodox position. True, on occasion Burhan al-Din edged toward the heretical notion of union with God in several statements about *maqam-i qurb*:

The worshiper and the worshiped are now the same,
  And there is no place for dualism.[34]

. . . .

As soon as camphor is set to fire it disappears;
  So also is the case of your spirit.[35]

But he never explicitly resolved the logical problem of what happened to the subject-object aspect of the *zikr* (involving a clearly demarcated worshiper and worshiped) if and when Man and God

32 Ibid.

33 This radical tradition, which can be traced back to Bayazid Bistami (d. 875) and Mansur al-Hallaj (d. 922) of Khurasan and Baghdad respectively, was represented in Bijapur by a number of descendants of the Chishti Literati—in particular Burhan al-Din Janam's son Amin al-Din A'la (d. 1675). See below, chapter nine.

34 Burhan al-Din Janam, *Wasiyat al-Hadi*, fol. 10a.

35 Burhan al-Din Janam, *Basharat al-Zikr*, fol. 10a.

achieved identity.[36] And in the last analysis he came down on the side of orthodoxy concerning the Man-God relationship. "On this we must be sure," he wrote, "that if we say that Man is God we are wrong. For God is ancient and without change, while Man has change. God is face-less. If He had any shape He would also be a man, and nothing else."[37]

Although these Sufis did not declare the absolute identity of Man and God in the state of *maqam-i qurb*, they did see God as a personal deity actively involved in furthering the *murid's* spiritual progress while at the same time being the loving object of the Sufi's adoration and devotion. Shaikh Mahmud Khush Dahan expressed this most eloquently when he described the changing nature of God and God's relation to the traveler as perceived by the latter in the four stages of the Path. God is described in the first stage as the Master (*sahib*), in the second as the Father (*pidar*), in the third as the Beloved (*mahbub*), and in the fourth as the Lover, or Friend (*muhibb*).[38] The relationship achieved in the final stage, God as Lover or Friend, finds a parallel in the *bhakti* ideal of a personal deity actively concerned with his devotees, characteristic of both the Lingayat and Vithoba traditions of the Deccan. On occasion, Bijapuri Chishtis drew directly from the *bhakti* tradition to illustrate their doctrines. Burhan al-Din, for example, borrowed from the lore of Krishna in his discussion of the importance of asceticism:

> Although Kanhiya [Krishna] was surrounded by sixteen thousand Gopis, yet he was a celibate from his youth (Bal Bramachari). That is the way to true wisdom.[39]

[36] In his *Wasiyat al-Hadi* (fol. 10b) Burhan al-Din wrote:

> Let me know how one can find *zikr-i khafi*
> [involving both worshiper and worshiped]
> When "myself" and "yourself" have been lost in mingling—
> This is difficult to understand.
> We can only say that the Unity of Being is like
> The condition in which *zikr-i khafi* is said.
> This is suitable for him who can understand.

[37] Burhan al-Din Janam, *Kalimat al-Haqayiq*, edited by M. Akbaruddin Siddiqi (Hyderabad: Idara-e-Adabiyat-e-Urdu, 1961), p. 57.

[38] Mahmud Khush Dahan, *Ma'rifat al-Suluk*, lithograph edn., p. 39; MS copy, p. 134.

[39] Burhan al-Din Janam, "*Suk-Sahela* of Shah Burhan-uddin Janam," ed. and trans. by Mohammad Hafīz Syed, *Allahabad University Studies*, 6, pt. 1 (1930), p. 507.

And he frequently used Sanskrit nomenclature in expressing Sufi concepts, such as his designation of God as *Shuddha Brahma* (Pure Being) or the phenomenal world as *Maya*.[40]

While Burhan al-Din went far in incorporating aspects of Hindu cosmology and nomenclature into his own theosophy, and while many parallels can be found between Sufi devotionalism and *bhakti* thought,[41] it would be dangerous from this to generalize about the relations between Sufis and Hindu *bhaktas*, and much less between Sufis and Hindus as a whole. For one thing, the central ideas expressed by these Sufis remained thoroughly within the framework of the Islamic mystical tradition, and such Hindu influences as those cited above seem to have been selectively borrowed only when they could serve as supporting buttresses for this framework. There is certainly nothing syncretic about one religious system borrowing the vocabulary of another religious system if the latter is used only to support the former. For another thing, literary interaction and social interaction are two very different and separate matters. Borrowing names or illustrations from non-Muslim devotional or philosophical traditions, as Burhan al-Din did, tells us little if anything about how Sufis interacted with non-Muslims. The reality seems to have been that Sufis could on occasion readily accept or incorporate abstract aspects of Hindu philosophy and religion, while reacting quite differently to specific Hindu groups. Burhan al-Din himself could accept the abstraction of unbelief in Islam with an almost indifferent air: "Regard unbelief and Islam as the same thing, / For both are from the court of that Record-keeper."[42] Yet his thoughts on specific Hindu groups such as the yogis were, as we shall note below, another matter altogether.

To understand how any Sufis of Bijapur interacted with the non-Muslim population it is necessary to distinguish between the elite and non-elite non-Muslims of the region. On the one hand were those accorded high status because of their function as carriers of Indic culture. The social and political elites of this hierarchy included Brahmins among Maharashtrian and Kan-

[40] Ibid., p. 508.

[41] See Charles White, "Sufism in Medieval Hindi Literature," *History of Religions*, 5 (Summer 1965), pp. 114-32.

[42] Burhan al-Din Janam, *Makhzan-i Salikin*, Persian MS (Hyderabad: Asafiyah Library, Tasawwuf no. 197), p. 141.

nadiga Hindus, and the Jangams among the Lingayats. Yogis among both the Maharashtrian and Kannadiga peoples constituted a religious elite of their own. Although they wielded no political or economic power and comprised only a fraction of the non-Muslim population in medieval Bijapur, yogis were apparently highly conspicuous to Muslim and European observers, judging from the frequent references to them that one finds in all forms of literature. Set apart from these elite elements were the non-elite Hindus who had neither social power nor ritual status. These probably included, for the most part, Kunbi agriculturalists among both Kannadigas and Maharashtrians, a number of specialized artisan castes in Bijapur's urban centers, and untouchables such as the Mahars.

Concerning the non-Muslim social and political elites—the Maharashtrian Brahmins and the Kannadiga Jangams—the Literati were silent. But vis-à-vis the one group that could be called an exclusively religious elite, the yogis, the Sufis of Shahpur Hillock were openly hostile, judging from the writings of Burhan al-Din Janam who was the chief Chishti spokesman throughout the sixteenth century. Following are some of his criticisms of the yogis and their practices:

> They offer their worship for mere outward show, and the ill-refutation of the people of the world cleaves to their body. Out of hope and fear they could not discern the unique being, and thus their hearts remain uninfluenced. Such devotees are liable to forget the word (of wisdom) in the same manner as the colour of a moth vanishes quickly. . . .
>
> The Hatha-Yogis perform their yogic exercises by immersing their bodies or by drawing water to their bodies and inhaling air as easily as serpents swallow moths, and thus desire to get spiritual insight. In that temple where there is no lamp of gayana [knowledge], how is the darkness to be removed?
>
> They have long pleated tufts of hair on their heads and keep their nails as long as a bear's. They wear earrings made of skin in their ears, and some turn their tongues back into their throats. . . . They breathe in and out while repeating the name of God with a rosary in their hands. It is all an idle talk if the rosary of the mind is not turned in one's hands. It is equally fruitless to sit in a posture the whole night by conquering one's sleep.

> Or else, roaming about in the jungles of various countries, they live upon herbs and grass. They masquerade as ascetics and celibates, and thus they commit fraud upon the public and go about asking for alms holding their ascetic rod and exposing their naked bodies to the public gaze.
>
> Without understanding the difference between true and false, pure or impure, they are (keen on) cleansing their bodies. They have not removed the impurity of their hearts, yet they rise to take baths a hundred times. They are (like) fish which live perpetually in water, and yet they do not cease to stink.
>
> They occasion themselves to live in darkness and in sequestered spots, sitting in meditation like cranes. Or they assume the samodhic as if they were guillotined, just like an insect which dwells in its nest.[43]

This passage reveals almost as much of the Sufis' self-image as of their harsh attitudes toward yogis, and thus illustrates a real confrontation of life-styles among Bijapur's spiritual practitioners. Where the yogis are perceived as ostentatious and hypocritical in their religious practices, Burhan al-Din would apparently see Sufis as reclusive and sincere. Where the yogis are perceived as socially offensive ("exposing their naked bodies to the public gaze"), he would apparently see Sufis as conforming more closely to the mores of Bijapuri urban society.[44]

The passage also refutes the belief, occasionally expressed by scholars of medieval Indian society, that there existed some sort of accommodation between Sufis and yogis. Burhan al-Din Janam clearly found it easier to compare yogis to serpents, bears, fish, cranes, bats, or insects, than to understand the meaning behind their exercises or physical self-discipline. The reason for this lies not in the fundamental differences between Islam and Hinduism, but in the radically different meanings that Sufis and yogis attached to the human body in relation to their respective spiritual disciplines. Almost all of Burhan al-Din's arguments concentrated on what to him were the ludicrous physical exercises to which

[43] Burhan al-Din Janam, "Suk-Sahela," pp. 503 f. Translated by Mohammad Hafiz Syed.

[44] The irony of this was that an unorthodox wing of Burhan al-Din Janam's own spiritual descendants were, within only several generations of his death, to adopt for themselves the same ostentatiousness and social offensiveness, sometimes in imitation of the yogis.

yogis subjected their bodies. Indeed, the whole point of the Chishti Path was to shed the traveler of concern for his mortal shell and to train his soul for meeting God. The yogis, on the other hand, regarded their bodies as the universe in microcosm, and accordingly attached cosmic significance to their physical self-discipline.[45]

The Literati and Their Popular Literature[46]

Written for the edification of fellow Sufis, the mystical literature examined above does not seem to have circulated among the lower elements of Bijapur's population, nor was it intended to. Moreover the Persian language, in which most of this literature was written, certainly was not a vernacular among the non-elite Hindu or Muslim population. Indeed Shaikh Mahmud Khush Dahan once stressed the elitist nature of the innermost circle of a *pir*'s followers and the necessity of keeping their esoteric knowledge to themselves.[47] Pursuing this theme, one distinguished scholar of Persian language and culture, Professor A. K. Lambton, has argued that Sufis felt a certain distrust of the common man, as evidenced by their separation of the initiated from the non-initiated in their proceedings.[48]

On the other hand a number of writers on medieval Indian society have taken a position opposite that of Professor Lambton. They have argued that it was the Sufis who reached out to the non-elites and in fact provided a link between Hindus and Muslims in medieval India, to some extent mitigating the harshness of the Muslim military conquest of the subcontinent.[49] Many writers

[45] For a discussion of this topic, see A. K. Banerjea, *Philosophy of Gorakhnath* (Gorakhpur: Mahant Dig Vijai Nath Trust, 1961), chaps. 12-15.

[46] This section, along with part of the following section on the Literati and the Expansion of Islam, has been published by me in slightly different form as "Sufi Folk Literature and the Expansion of Indian Islam," *History of Religions*, 14 (November 1974), pp. 117-27.

[47] Mahmud Khush Dahan, *Ma'rifat al-Suluk*. Lithograph edn., p. 79; MS copy, pp. 46 f., 55a.

[48] Ann K. S. Lambton, "Free Thinking and Individual Freedom," in *Islam in the Modern World*, ed. by Syed Ali Ahsan (Dacca: Abu Jafar Shamsuddin, 1964), p. 82.

[49] See Abdul Haq, *Qadim Urdu*, p. 39; M. L. Roy Choudhury, "Background of Sufism in Indian Environment," *Journal of the Greater Indian*

have advanced the argument somewhat further by identifying the Sufis as important agents in the conversion to Islam of a large segment of India's Hindu population, especially Hindus of lower castes.[50] But what is lacking in this literature is a satisfactory explanation of how such conversions might have taken place, of how an essentially esoteric mystical tradition might have filtered down to commoners in some sort of comprehensible and appealing form. It would be difficult to imagine, for example, how depressed and illiterate Hindu castes such as the cotton cleaners or the barbers of seventeenth-century Bijapur could have been attracted to an abstract system of stages and *zikrs* as expounded by Sufis like Shaikh Mahmud Khush Dahan. One likely reason for the failure to explain the attraction of Hindu non-elites to Sufis has been the tendency among many scholars of Sufism to concentrate almost exclusively on the mystical literature, as opposed to the folk literature, as representing the sum and substance of the Sufi movement. A great scholar in the field, R. A. Nicholson, has already noted that "Sufism is at once the religious philosophy and the popular religion of Islam."[51] Yet the link between the two has not been clearly established, at least as far as concerns Indian Islam.

Society, 2 (1944), pp. 39 f.; H. K. Sherwani, "Cultural Synthesis in Medieval India," *Journal of Indian History*, 41 (April 1963), pp. 256 f.; Tara Chand, *Society and State in the Mughal Period* (Delhi: Ministry of Information & Broadcasting, 1961; reprinted 1965), pp. 96-100; Yusuf Husain Khan, "Sufism in India," *Islamic Culture*, 30 (1956), p. 252; M. Yasin, *A Social History of Islamic India, 1605-1748* (Lucknow: Upper India Publishing House, 1958), p. 51.

50 See Arnold, *Preaching of Islam*, pp. 270 f.; Aziz Ahmad, *Studies in Islamic Culture*, pp. 83 f.; A. B. M. Habibullah, *The Foundation of Muslim Rule in India* (2nd edn.; Allahabad: Central Book Depot, 1967), pp. 305 f.; Mujeeb, *Indian Muslims*, p. 22; Nizami, *Studies*, p. 92; M. G. Panse, "Religion and Politics in the Early Mediaeval Deccan," *Journal of Indian History*, 45, pt. 3 (Dec. 1967), p. 684; I. H. Qureshi, "Relations between the Hindus and the Muslims in the Subcontinent of India and Pakistan," *Civilisations*, 5 (1955), p. 47; Fazlur Rahman, *Islam* (London: Weidenfeld and Nicolson, 1966), p. 155; A. Rashid, *Society and Culture in Medieval India* (Calcutta: Firma K. L. Mukhopadhyay, 1969), pp. 192 f.; A. L. Srivastava, *Medieval Indian Culture* (Agra: Shiva Lal Agarwala & Co., 1964), p. 78; Murray T. Titus, *Islam in India and Pakistan* (Calcutta: Y. M. C. A. Publishing House, 1959), pp. 48 f.

51 Nicholson, *Studies*, p. 65.

It is my opinion that such a link was supplied, at least in Bijapur, by the folk literature composed by Sufis. Consisting of a number of short poems in the vernacular idiom, Dakhni, this literature employed indigenous themes and imagery for the propagation not of complex mystical doctrines of the sort described above, but of a simpler level of Sufi and also of Islamic precepts. Written mainly in the seventeenth and eighteenth centuries by Bijapuri Chishtis or their descendants scattered elsewhere in the Deccan, this literature has been preserved in the oral tradition of Dakhni-speaking villagers throughout the Deccan plateau. It has been suggested that until the twentieth century, when radio and cinema took its place, folk poetry of Sufi origin has occupied a dominant position in the folk culture of Deccan villages.[52] What, then, was the nature of this literature, to whom did it appeal, and what was its relation to Islam or to Sufism?

The bulk of the folk poetry written by Sufis was sung by village women as they did various household chores. The most common types included the *chakki-nama*, so called because it was sung while grinding food grains at the grindstone or *chakki*, and the *charkha-nama*, sung while spinning thread at the spinning wheel, or *charkha*. Other types of such folk poetry included the *lori-nama* or lullaby, the *shadi-nama* or wedding song, the *suhagan-nama* or married-woman's song, and the *suhaila* or eulogistic song.[53] It is evident that most of these poetic forms appealed especially, and probably exclusively, to women. For in the villages of the Deccan it was the women who for centuries spun the cotton into thread, ground the *juwar* into meal, and rocked the children to sleep. Each of these activities involved a steady moving of the hands, which the singing of songs composed in a regular meter could easily assist. This is especially true for the *chakki-nama* and the *charkha-nama*, the most widespread forms of Dakhni folk poetry, both of which involved the turning of a wheel by hand. Such village poetry appealed to women not only because it accompanied the household chores that they in particular performed, but also because its content was permeated with imagery especially meaningful to them. Female love and

[52] Zinat Sajida, "Dakani Git," *Majallai Osmania. Deccani Adab Number*, No. 65 (1963-4), p. 217.

[53] Saiyida Ja'far, Introduction to Abu'l-Hasan Qadiri, *Sukh Anjan*, pp. 60 f.

its manifestations were typical themes in this literature, and metaphors frequently drew on the two worlds of a young bride: the parental home she had left (*maika*) and her new father-in-law's home (*susral*).[54]

The few studies that have been made of Dakhni folk literature trace it to the efforts of Sufis to expand their teachings among the unlettered folk of the Deccan plateau.[55] This is no doubt true as far as the written tradition of this folk poetry is concerned. But it does not mean that Sufis originated the idea of singing songs while grinding *juwar* or while spinning thread. Some sort of folk poetry relating to work at the spinning wheel or the grindstone undoubtedy existed in the Marathi and Kannada oral traditions long before Islam penetrated the Deccan plateau and is probably as old as the ubiquitous grindstone and spinning wheel themselves.[56] What Sufis did was to adapt the simplest elements of Sufi doctrine to the already existing vehicles of folk poetry and to substitute vernacular Dakhni for vernacular Marathi or Kannada.[57] Since the Sufism injected into this literature carried with it the essentials of Islam, the Sufis' use of this vehicle may be said to represent a major development in the cultural history of the Deccan.

Sufi folk literature can be found today in both written and oral traditions. Despite the intrusion of modern media in the villages, folk poetry relating to household chores is still sung, though apparently less so today than formerly. In the written tra-

[54] See Rafi'a Sultana, *Urdu Nasr*, p. 250.

[55] Zinat Sajida, "Dakani Git," pp. 217 f.; Rafi'a Sultana, *Urdu Nasr*, pp. 247 f.; Saiyida Ja'far, Introduction to Abu'l-Hasan Qadiri, *Sukh Anjan*, pp. 60 f.; Annemarie Schimmel, "Influence of Sufism," p. 196.

[56] The Marathi poems that village women of Maharashtra sing today while grinding meal are functionally identical to the *chakki-namas* of the Sufis. Significantly they too, like the Sufis' *chakki-namas*, serve a devotional purpose, the object of their devotion being the deity Vithoba at Pandharpur. See Deleury, *Cult of Vithoba*, p. 6.

[57] So far as this writer is aware, Bijapuri Sufis used Dakhni in all their popular literature. It is possible, however, that an exhaustive search of Deccan villages might turn up folk poetry written by Sufis in the Kannada, Marathi, or Telugu language. The *qazi* of Kolhar, a town on the Krishna River directly south of Bijapur, said that he had some *chakki-namas* in the Dakhni language but transliterated into the Kannada script (Akbar Khan, private interview at the Hashim *dargah*, Bijapur, on 10 July 1970).

dition, *chakki-namas* and *charkha-namas* have appeared in various cheap lithograph editions that can still be found in the Deccan countryside. There also exist manuscript versions of this poetry, of which some dozen, preserved in collections in Bijapur and Hyderabad, have come to my attention. These manuscripts indicate that most of the folk poetry discussed here originated with Bijapuri Sufis of the Chishti order.

All twelve of these manuscripts, most of which are *chakki-namas*, are undated copies of poetry which, judging from the style of Dakhni used, can be ascribed to the seventeenth or early eighteenth century. One *chakki-nama* is attributed to Amin al-Din A'la (d. 1675),[58] son of Burhan al-Din Janam and a Sufi of notably heterodox tendencies. But this *chakki-nama* cannot be authentic since it refers to events that occurred after Amin al-Din's death. Its style and content, however, clearly prove it to be the work of a Sufi, and probably a Sufi of Bijapur since the scribe was himself a resident of that city.[59] Another *chakki-nama* closes with the name of Shah Hashim Khudawand Hadi (d. 1704-5),[60] one of Amin al-Din's *khalifas* at Bijapur, and both internal and external evidence would support its authenticity. A third *chakki-nama* was written by a certain Faruqi,[61] a *murid* of another of Amin al-Din A'la's followers and hence most likely affiliated with Shahpur Hillock.[62] Two other *chakki-namas* in manuscript form are of more recent origin. One of them, catalogued as that of a certain Ghausi,[63] has recently been ascribed to a Bijapuri Sufi named Fi'l-Hal Qadiri (dates unknown).[64] The other is of a certain Shah Kamal,[65] or Shah Kamal al-Din (d. 1809-10), a Chishti from Belgaum who eventually settled in what is now Chittoor District and wrote the *chakki-nama* at his wife's request.[66] There is also

[58] Hyderabad: Salar Jung Museum, Urdu MSS, Tasawwuf & Akhlaq no. 36.

[59] Ibid., fol. 6a.

[60] Hyderabad: Idara-e-Adabiyat-e-Urdu, no. 93B, fols. 126b-128a.

[61] Hyderabad: Idara-e-Adabiyat-e-Urdu, no. 657, fols. 1b-2b.

[62] See Muhiuddin Zore, *Tazkirah-e-Makhtutat* (5 vols.; Hyderabad: Idara-e-Adabiyat-e-Urdu, 1957), III, p. 282.

[63] Hyderabad: Salar Jung Museum, Urdu MSS, Tasawwuf & Akhlaq no. 37, fols. 1a-3a.

[64] Saiyida Ja'far, Introduction to Abu'l-Hasan Qadiri, *Sukh Anjan*, p. 62.

[65] Hyderabad: Salar Jung Museum, Urdu MSS, Pand & Nasayih no. 4.

[66] Sakhawat Mirza, "Saiyid Shah Kamal al-Din," *Urdu* (April 1939), pp. 263-65; Zore, *Tazkirah-e-Makhtutat*, III, p. 207.

a manuscript copy of a *suhagan-nama*,[67] a married-woman's song, written by Shah Raju (d. 1681 or 1685), a Bijapuri Chishti who later migrated to Golconda.[68] There are two copies of a *suhaila* composed by Shah 'Ali Pir Husaini, grandson of Shah Amin al-Din A'la and *sajjada-nishin* of the Shahpur Hillock shrine in the early eighteenth century. This work, sung by women accompanying themselves on drums, is at once a devotional eulogy of the Prophet and also a popular song (*git*) concerning weddings and the nature of married women's life.[69] A manuscript copy of a *charkha-nama* is attributed to a certain Salar,[70] but his place of origin is not known. Two other *chakki-namas* are attributed to the most famous Muslim saint of the Deccan plateau, Saiyid Muhammad Husaini Bandanawaz Gisudaraz (d. 1422).[71] These, however, are of doubtful authenticity, first because they are signed "Bandanawaz," an epithet that the Sufi himself never used,[72] and second because he lived a century and a half before the first authentic *chakki-namas* began appearing, putting any such work of his in gross chronological isolation.

Certain conclusions emerge from this discussion. In the first place, there is no doubt that all of the above manuscripts, even those whose authorship is most dubious, are the work of Sufis. Devotion to God and respect for one's *pir* are their constant themes. Second, most of these manuscripts originated in Bijapur and are the work either of resident Chishtis of Shahpur Hillock or of lay members of the order who had studied there and then migrated elsewhere in the Deccan. Third, this popular literature was not the work of the mystical writers of Bijapur—Shah Miranji Shams al-'Ushshaq, Shah Burhan al-Din Janam, or Shaikh Mahmud Khush Dahan—but of their immediate spiritual descend-

[67] Hyderabad: Salar Jung Museum, Urdu MSS, Pand & Nasayih no. 144, fols. 1a-5a.

[68] *Tazkira-yi Auliya*, I, pp. 337-41.

[69] Both copies, one complete and the other defective, were copied by *murids* of Shah 'Ali and are preserved in the library of the Amin Dargah in Bijapur. See M. Akbaruddin Siddiqi, *Bujhte Chiragh: Dakani Adab par Masamin ka Majmu'a* (Hyderabad: National Fine Printing Press, 1975), pp. 56-58.

[70] Hyderabad: Salar Jung Museum, Urdu MSS, Tasawwuf & Akhlaq no. 35.

[71] Hyderabad: Idara-e-Adabiyat-e-Urdu, no. 120B; Salar Jung Museum, Urdu MSS, Tasawwuf & Akhlaq no. 37.

[72] Nasir al-Din Hashimi, "Khwaja Bandanawaz ki Urdu Sha'iri," *Hindustan* (October 1934), p. 447.

ants who lived in the second half of the seventeenth and early eighteenth centuries. But despite their separation in time by a generation or more, the mystical and popular writers were linked by close familial and doctrinal ties. In his *Kalimat al-Haqayiq* Burhan al-Din Janam alluded to the central symbol of the *chakki-nama*, the grindstone, in the same way that popular writers alluded to it:

> In the case of the *chakki*, some other power is required—somebody's hand must be applied to move the wheel. There are many people who use the *chakki*, yet only the power hidden in the hand actually turns the wheel. That hand is *'arif al-wujud* ["knower of existence," i.e., God], and those who see that the power is in the hand are witnesses of the light; thereby they witness the essence, which is God.[73]

If one analyzes the content of the *chakki-nama* or the *charkha-nama*, three interwoven themes can be found: (1) an ontological link established between God, and Prophet Muhammad, one's own *pir*, and the reciter herself; (2) the use of the grindstone or the spinning wheel, or the mechanical parts thereof, to illustrate the above; and (3) the use of the mystics' *zikr* to accompany and even to regulate the various phases of the women's work.

In the following *chakki-nama* of Shah Hashim Khudawand Hadi (d. 1704-5) the first theme, the ontological link between God, the Prophet, the *pir*, and the woman at the grindstone, is clearly stated. In this passage are also explicated in simplified form the essential elements of the Chishti theory of Creation and of God's relation to the material world, a theory traceable to a famous Sufi tradition attributing to God the words "I was a hidden treasure, and I wanted to be known, so I created the world":

> First was God's name,
> And then His qualities.
> In my mind I keep the name,
> And with each breath
>   [refrain]: Say *la ilaha* [There is no god]
>   Dwell in *illa'l-lah* [But God]
> God Himself from the hidden treasure
> Has created the whole world artistically.

[73] Burhan al-Din Janam, *Kalimat al-Haqayiq*, p. 53.

He has created it with His own power—
  [refrain]
God Himself came out from the hidden treasure
And showed Himself in the guise of the Prophet.
  [refrain]
In the presence of God, the Prophet is chief
Whose teachings have given us support in both worlds.
  [refrain]
The Prophet's *khalifa* is ʿAli, who is dear to Him,
And whose disciples are our *pirs*.
  [refrain]
Allah, Muhammad, and ʿAli
Are our leaders whom we trust most
And obey as slaves.
  [refrain]
Our *pir* has taken our hands in his;
He has given us connections whole-heartedly.
May he keep this connection forever.
  [refrain][74]

The theology here is as simple as the language. The devotee is not asked to master either the exoteric knowledge of the theologian or the fine points of the Sufi's esoteric knowledge, but only to feel comfort in God's unity and majesty.

These simple Islamic precepts were reinforced by parallels and metaphors drawn between them and the various parts of the grindstone or spinning wheel at which the woman was working. "As the *chakki* turns, so we find God," concludes the above poem; "it shows its life in turning as we do in breathing."[75] Again, in the following *chakki-nama* the parts of the grindstone and the tasks of the woman are both woven together with the simplest of Islamic precepts:

See that our body is also a *chakki*,
And be careful in grinding.
The devil is my *saukan* [one of several wives]
  Which prevents me from working and tires me.
    Ya *bism Allah*, hu hu Allah.

[74] Hashim Khudawand Hadi, *Chakki-nama ʿIrfan*. Dakhni MS (Hyderabad: Idara-e-Adabiyat-e-Urdu, no. 93B), fols. 126b-127b.

[75] Ibid., fol. 128a.

The *chakki's* handle resembles *alif*, which means Allah;
And the axle is Muhammad, and is fixed there.
In this way the truth-seeker sees the relationship.
Ya *bism Allah*, hu hu Allah.
We put the grains in the *chakki*,
To which our hands are witnesses.
The *chakki* of the body is in order
When you follow the *shari'at*.
Ya *bism Allah*, hu hu Allah.
The name of Allah comes from *alif*.
Know that *pirs* and *murshids* can lead our lives.
Grind the flour and then sift it—
Ya *bism Allah*, hu hu Allah.

. . . .

Grind the flour and make stuffed *puri*;
Put in it heavenly fruits and sugar,
The seven qualities of God must be taken in the body
As the seven ingredients fill the *puri*, oh sister.
Ya *bism Allah*, hu hu Allah.[76]

Similar analogies are found in the *charkha-nama*:

Imagine that your body is a spinning wheel, oh sister.
We should get rid of our negligence
And give up worldly differences, oh sister.

. . . .

The tongue is the unspun thread for the message of God;
The tongue is the rim of the spinning wheel.
Bring out the thread of breath and show it, oh sister.
Both of these memories should be in our throat:
God has given us the ability to turn our hand,
And it is that which moves the wheel, oh sister.
Faith must be for you what the drive-rope is for the wheel.
Perhaps you know of the two wheels connected by the rope;
Then you will know how the wheel turns, oh sister.[77]

A third feature of this literature is its incorporation of the Sufi *zikrs*. We have noted that for practicing mystics the *zikrs*

[76] Khwaja Bandanawaz Gisudaraz, *Chakki-nama*. Dakhni MS (Hyderabad: Idara-e-Adabiyat-e-Urdu, no. 120B).

[77] Salar, *Charkha-nama*. Dakhni MS (Hyderabad: Salar Jung Museum, Tasawwuf & Akhlaq no. 35).

had a specialized use, certain ones being associated with certain stages on the traveler's Path toward God. In the popular literature, however, the *zikrs* were largely divested of their mystical content and became more devotional. Although the various *zikrs* were still differentiated, they did not correspond to the stages of the Path as they did for the mystics, but to different functions being performed at the grindstone or the spinning wheel. Furthermore, all of the *zikrs* in this literature seem to be of a similar type —repetition of the names of God out loud—which in the mystical tradition would correspond only to the first *zikr*, the *zikr-i jali*. The following extract from a *charkha-nama* illustrates these points:

> As you take the cotton, you should do *zikr-i jali*.
> As you separate the cotton, you should do *zikr-i qalbi*,
> And as you spool the thread you should do *zikr-i ʻaini*.
> *Zikr* should be uttered from the stomach through the chest,
> And threaded through the throat.
> The threads of breath should be counted one by one, oh sister.
> Up to twenty-four thousand.
> Do this day and night,
> And offer it to your *pir* as a gift.[78]

The above passage perhaps best epitomizes the union of the high and low Sufi traditions of which Nicholson wrote, of Islam's religious philosophy and its popular religion. In it are found the main components of the Sufis' esoteric practice, merged with and adapted to a popular literary idiom that would be repeated in many households each time cotton thread was spun. The result was quite comparable to the non-Muslim *bhakti* poetry of the contemporary Deccan—the Kannada *vachanas* of the Lingayats or the Marathi *abhangs* of the poet-saints of Pandharpur—in its use of a vernacular medium, its special appeal to women, and its devotional character. And its popularity was undoubtedly aided by the rhythmic similarity that existed between repeating a *zikr* and turning a wheel, each activity serving as a metronome for the other. The remaining question regarding this literature is its possible role in the expansion of Islam in Bijapur.

[78] Ibid.

The Literati and the Expansion of Islam

In his lucid essay, *Islam Observed*, Clifford Geertz has identified what has probably been the key social and historical role that Sufism has played in the history of Islam, namely, the reconciliation of formal Islam with the various non-Muslim beliefs and practices that are found throughout the Muslim world. Sufism, wrote Geertz,

> has been less a definite standpoint in Islam . . . than a diffuse expression of that necessity . . . for a world religion to come to terms with a variety of mentalities, a multiplicity of local forms of faith, and yet maintain the essence of its own identity. Despite the otherworldly ideas and activities so often associated with it, Sufism, as an historical reality, consists of a series of different and even contradictory experiments, most of them occurring between the ninth and nineteenth centuries, in bringing orthodox Islam (itself no seamless unity) into effective relationship with the world, rendering it accessible to its adherents and its adherents accessible to it.[79]

There were at least three agents through which Sufism in Bijapur manifested this mediating capacity: (1) the initiation ceremony of the Sufis themselves; (2) the tombs under which these Sufis, later canonized as saints, were buried; and (3) the folk literature written by their immediate successors.

The earliest mechanism by which Bijapur's Sufis mediated Islam to non-Muslims was the institution of the initiation procedure, known as the *bai'at* ceremony, by which lay persons were inducted into a Sufi's spiritual following. The most important Sufis of Bijapur having large *khanaqahs* generally had two or three circles of followers attached to them. First was an inner circle of *murids* who had pledged themselves to undertake spiritual studies and disciplines under the direction of a *pir*; they were formally initiated by the *pir* into the *silsila* as heirs to a spiritual path that stretched back to the founder of the order. This inner circle of *murids* is to be distinguished from the still smaller circle of *khalifas*, who were given not only the spiritual

[79] Geertz, *Islam Observed*, p. 48.

instruction of the *murids* but also the right to succeed the *pir* in his capacity of initiating other *murids*. Then there was also an outer circle of lay persons, usually of lower classes and castes, who had not taken any formal pledge of spiritual discipleship but who were attracted to the spiritual power of the *pir* and accordingly venerated him, attending such public functions of the *khanaqah* as prayers and feasts. This outer circle may be termed the affiliates. Although a *pir*'s outer circle of affiliates was generally composed of an undifferentiated group of lower class non-Muslims as well as Muslims, his inner group of *murids*, or adepts, consisted exclusively of Muslims. We have noted that one of the preconditions for undertaking the Chishti path was being or becoming a Muslim. While most *murids* were probably born Muslims, there is ample evidence in both the Chishti and Shattari traditions that non-Muslims of Bijapur were converted to Islam at the time of their initiation into the orders as *murids*. Burhan al-Din Janam hinted at this when he wrote,

> If you have the patience I will tell you what *zikr-i jali* is.
> The follower, whatever his religion, will become purified
> If he understands this.[80]

By saying "whatever his religion," Burhan al-Din opens to non-Muslims the door leading to the Chishti path. Yet to "become purified" in this context certainly means becoming Muslim since the *zikr-i jali* is the spiritual exercise corresponding to the first stage of the Chishti path (*Shari'at*), which enjoins the *murid* to master and obey the Islamic Law.

Another instance of a non-Muslim being converted to Islam during induction to the Chishti order is found in the narrative poem *Shajarat al-Atqiya*. The relevant passage concerns the relations between Burhan al-Din's son, Amin al-Din A'la (d. 1675) and a certain Hindu *sannyasi*. This account, written by one of Amin al-Din's *murids*, records that the *sannyasi* presented a philosophers' stone to Amin al-Din after having just demonstrated the stone's gold-producing qualities. But Amin al-Din merely threw the stone into Shahpur tank, a large reservoir that was in those times located near his *khanaqah* on Shahpur Hillock. Distraught, the *sannyasi* wept for his lost philosophers' stone, but Amin al-Din only smiled and said,

[80] Burhan al-Din Janam, *Basharat al-Zikr*, fol. 8a.

"Go in the water and find the stone,
 And if you find it take it."
The *sannyasi* went there and discovered that
 Many philosophers' stones were in the water.
Thereupon he became a believer in Amin
 And having said the *kalima*, he became his *murid*.[81]

The last line clearly indicates that reciting the *kalima*, or the Muslim confession of faith, was prerequisite to becoming Amin al-Din's *murid*. It is implied that the *sannyasi's* taking *bai'at* from Amin al-Din immediately followed his reciting the *kalima*, as if both were part of the same ceremony.

The most persuasive evidence that the initiation process into the inner circle was used also for making Muslims is found in the literature on Shah Hashim Pir 'Alawi (d. 1646), the Shattari Sufi discussed in the preceding chapter. An examination of Shah Hashim's initiation or *bai'at* ceremony illustrates the point. A prospective *murid* would face Mecca while holding Hashim Pir's hand. He would then recite the Islamic confession of faith and several prescribed verses from the Koran, followed by a pledge of spiritual loyalty to Hashim Pir, who would remain his mediator with God.[82] Most significantly, one of the phrases used in this ceremony specifically referred to the initiate's having left the non-Muslim community by joining Hashim Pir's following. This phrase was recited either in Persian or in Dakhni:

Bizar shudam az kufr wa kafiri
Dar amadam dar din-i Musulmani[83]

[I have become wearied of unbelief and infidelity,
and have entered the religion of the Muslims].

Shah Hashim Pir's *khanaqah* was perhaps the only Sufi center in Bijapur, apart from that of Shah Miranji and his successors on Shahpur Hillock, that had an observable impact on the non-Muslim population of the seventeenth century. Besides initiating non-Muslims into his inner circle of adepts, Shah Hashim gave blessings to 5,500 affiliates in his lifetime, which gives us some idea of the numerical extent of his outer circle.[84] And, as was the

81 *Shajarat al-Atqiya*, pp. 29 f.
82 *Maqsud al-Murad*, pp. 129 f.
83 Ibid., p. 129.
84 *Ganj-i Asrar*, fol. 57b.

case with the Sufi popular literature, women were also integrated into the *khanaqah* life of Hashim Pir ʿAlawi. One of Hashim's *murids* noted that women were allowed to enter even the inner circle of the Sufi's followers as *murids*.[85] This suggests that the female-oriented folk Islam that later developed around the *dargahs* of Sufis like Hashim Pir had its origins in the circles of living Sufis.

As a mechanism mediating Islam to non-Muslims, then, the *baiʿat* ceremony was both formal and instant. To recite the *kalima* sincerely and before a *pir* was a ceremony as decisive as it was simple. But while this mechanism undoubtedly served to introduce some members of the non-Muslim community to Islam, there are only a few references to it in the primary sources. Moreover, some of these references can be suspected of hagiographic hyperbole when they involve the conversion of Brahmins, *sannyasis*, yogis, or other members of the religious elite among non-Muslims. One is therefore compelled to suspect that the *baiʿat* ceremony was probably the least significant mechanism, from the standpoint of the numbers converted, by which Sufism mediated Islam to non-Muslims. It should be added, too, that the Chishti Literati of Shahpur Hillock were not the only Sufis of Bijapur to use the *baiʿat* ceremony in this fashion, as Shah Hashim Pir ʿAlawi, a Shattari, also made Muslim converts while initiating *murids*.

A second, and far more lasting, Sufi mechanism mediating Islam to Bijapur's non-Muslim population was the institution of the *dargahs* that grew up on, or near, the *khanaqahs* of famous Sufis. Built by the government, by wealthy nobles, or by *murids*, these tombs derived their importance in Indo-Muslim history from being the carriers of the *barakat* of the Sufis buried beneath them. The Sufis would in this way pass into popular tradition canonized as saints. As a magnet attracts iron filings by an unseen force, so also did these *dargahs* attract people by the spiritual power that had been transmitted from the buried saint to his tomb. Above all, these *dargahs* represented the physical embodiment of Sufism in its third and final stage of development, the *ta'ifa* stage. Their date of construction provides perhaps the best single indicator of the passing from the *tariqa* phase to the *ta'ifa* phase in Bijapur as

[85] *Maqsud al-Murad*, p. 129.

elsewhere, for it was the *dargahs* that became the focus of the popular devotionalism that, above all else, characterized that phase. Most of the important Sufi tombs of Bijapur were built in the late seventeenth century. The principal *dargah* of Shahpur Hillock and hence the focus of Bijapur's Chishti order in its *ta'ifa* phase is the tomb of Burhan al-Din Janam's heterodox son, Amin al-Din A'la (d. 1675), which was completed in 1677-78.[86]

In this third phase of Sufism a saint's *barakat* was transmitted not only to the physical site of his burial, the *dargah*, but also to his family descendants, or *pirzadas* (*pirzada*: "born of a *pir*"). These individuals, who maintained the *dargahs* and managed their social functions, came to occupy positions of great social status among the illiterate and superstitious common folk of the Deccan. True, the *pirzadas* styled themselves "*pirs*" and continued to induct *murids* into an inner circle, but with the passing of time and generations they seem to have become increasingly concerned with exploiting the *dargah's* and their own influence as possessors of *barakat* than with teaching mystical discipline. Indeed, all available evidence indicates that from the late seventeenth century a sizable non-elite constituency clustered around famous *pirzadas*, believing in their miraculous powers (*karamat*) and their ability to intercede with God, taking blessings from them while offering simple gifts to them, lighting candles at the *dargahs* of departed saints, and participating in the festivals at these *dargahs*, the most important one being the *'urs* festival commemorating the saint's death date (*'urs*: "marriage" with God).[87] This was India's folk Islam in its most dynamic form.

Who formed this constituency and what explains their attraction to the *dargahs*? Women played by far the dominant role in all aspects of *dargah* life, just as Sufi folk poetry, which may legitimately be called the litany of Bijapur's folk Islam, appealed primarily to women. As Trimingham has observed with reference to *ta'ifa* Sufism generally, "The dualism between male and female religion was brought out on Fridays when the men went off to the *Jami'* [mosque] to display their communal solidarity by participation in ritual prayer, whilst the women were at the saint's

[86] Siddiqi, "The Dakani Inscription," p. 83.

[87] The best contemporary description of this phenomenon is Abbé Carré's 1673 account of an *'urs* festival at the *dargah* of Muhammad Husaini Bandanawaz Gisudaraz in Gulbarga. See below, pp. 228-30.

tomb or graveyard making their offerings, petitionings, or communings with the spirit of the tomb."[88] In effect, then, folk Islam in Bijapur as elsewhere seems to have been a female-oriented Islam: what the mosque, the mulla, and the Koran were for men, the *dargah*, the *pirzada*, and the *chakki-nama* were for women.

Their motivation for participating in the *dargah's* various functions seems to have been primarily votive in nature. Flowers, coins, or prayers would be offered up to the spirit of the *pir* buried at a particular *dargah* in the belief that the latter would redress some specific grievance or provide some specific fortune that had become associated with that *dargah*. This votive aspect of the *dargahs* is, of course, very much in keeping with indigenous traditions with respect to Hindu shrines and pilgrimages and underscores the *dargah's* capacity to mediate between Islam and local religious systems.[89] But whatever the special vows that became associated with individual *dargahs*, they were all generally associated with fertility. Indeed, the belief that visits to *dargahs* would in some measure enhance a woman's fertility is an obvious reason for their continuing popularity among rural women of the Deccan today.

Women originally attracted to the *pirs* and *pirzadas* of the seventeenth century were probably of the same social origins as those presently participating in the social life of the *dargahs*, e.g., Maharashtrian and Kannadiga women of the Kunbi agriculturalist castes. One could speculate that non-elite women living on the fringes of Hindu society would have gravitated toward *pirs* and their tombs as places of religious refuge from any number of worldly concerns. These women would certainly have included widows of most castes, for organized Hindu society has

88 Trimingham, *Sufi Orders*, p. 232.

89 With reference to Hindu, Buddhist, and Jain pilgrimages, Agehananda Bharati has written that "*vrata*, 'vows', are often highly specific and they usually require a visit to one place only. It is the place where a deity specializes, as it were, in repairing damage, or balancing some need of the pilgrim who seeks remedy. The formulation of the *vrata* (vow), most generally put, is something like this: 'If I gain x or overcome y or accomplish z, I shall make a pilgrimage to A'; or, 'Because I have *not* gained x, etc., I shall make a pilgrimage to A in order to gain it, for A is known to specialize in granting x.' " (A. Bharati, "Pilgrimage Sites and Indian Civilization," in Joseph W. Elder, ed., *Chapters in Indian Civilization* [2 vols., Dubuque, Ia.: Kendall/Hunt Publishing Co., 1970], I, p. 94.)

little room for such individuals. Then, too, one could expect that barren women of various castes would have been attracted to the *dargahs* because of the latter's association with fertility. What all such women probably shared in common was an eclectic religious attitude on account of which they would have perceived no great theological or social wall separating Islam and Hinduism. For them, the *dargahs* formed only several facets of an already diffuse and syncretic religious life, and fulfillment of a vow made this year at a Sufi's *dargah* might inspire as much belief in the efficacy of the Islamic deity as a similar fulfillment inspired belief in a Hindu deity the year before.

The folk literature examined above was the third Sufi mechanism mediating Islam to non-Muslims of Bijapur. The role that this literature has played in this capacity, though impossible to measure with precision, seems to have been related to the *dargah*-centered devotionalism characteristic of Sufism in its *ta'ifa* form. The authors of this folk poetry, as we have seen, were not themselves mystics or theoreticians like Burhan al-Din Janam, but were either spiritual descendants of the mystics or the latter's familial descendants, or *pirzadas*. As noted above, these individuals had much less hesitation than the mystics in allowing themselves to become objects of popular veneration among Bijapur's lower classes. Indeed, one important reason that they wrote this literature, apart from their general desire to expand their teachings among a constituency of commoners, seems to have been to secure for themselves the role of mediator between God and the people who used the literature. Typical is this closing line of a *charkha-nama*:

> You are the maid-servant in your dervish's house.
> Say Allah and the Prophet's name on every breath.[90]

This passage, like many others found in the *chakki-namas* and *charkha-namas*, indicates that the relationship between the reciter of the poem and the *pir* was intended to be one of utter spiritual dependence. It is probable that such was in reality the case given the *pirzadas*' high status derived from the *barakat* they inherited from their saintly predecessor.

But regardless of the authors' possible motives for writing this literature, its effect in terms of the expansion of Islam among

[90] Salar, *Charka-nama*.

Bijapur's lower classes was probably profound, though gradual. The pervasive influence of women in the life of the *dargahs* provides perhaps the most important clue in tracing this effect. Judging from the content of the folk literature it seems likely that the women who had come into contact with the folk traditions of the *dargahs* transmitted this tradition to the children living in their households by constantly repeating the poetry. Children would be rocked to sleep at night or day by lullabies (*lori-nama*) that had originated in the *dargahs*; they would hear *chakki-namas* or *charkha-namas* recited daily in their own households each time grain was ground or thread was spun. Hence, just as one's first language is frequently termed one's "mother tongue" because of the predominant role of the mother in transmitting language, so also the mother—or indeed any household woman in the proximity of children—has doubtless been instrumental in the transmission of religious practices and attitudes at rural levels. So it was through this medium that Sufi folk literature entered rural households and gradually gained an established place amidst the eclectic religious life of the rural Deccan.

The above argument is that both the vehicle of folk literature originally penned by successors to Bijapuri Sufis and the institution of the *dargah* have assimilated into the world of folk Islam various non-elite and predominantly female elements of the Deccan rural population from the seventeenth century to the present. However, this process should not be construed as "conversion" to Islam, nor should the Sufis themselves be considered as Muslim "missionaries," though both terms have frequently been used in the general context of Sufis and the expansion of Islam. The main problem is that both terms carry connotations of a nineteenth- and twentieth-century Christian movement in India, a context in which "missionary" denoted a self-conscious propagator of the Christian faith and "conversion" a self-conscious turning around in religious conviction. But the evidence concerning Bijapur's Sufis would not permit calling any of them missionaries in this sense. They made no conscious effort to gain non-Muslim followers, though it is true that many lower-caste non-Muslims were attracted to the *pirs*' and *pirzadas*' supposed supernatural power and entered, by gradual degrees, their outer and inner circles. Both the Literati's folk literature and the various *bai'at* ceremonies discussed above aimed primarily at committing their followers to a *pir*; the diffusion of Islamic precepts seems in the final analysis to have been a by-product of these efforts.

Similarly, "conversion" in the sense of a self-conscious, sudden and total change of belief is an inadequate term to describe the process by which non-Muslims of Bijapur became attracted to certain Sufis, their folk literature, or later, their *dargahs*. There are today several Muslim groups in Bijapur District whose ancestors are claimed to have been converted to Islam by one or another medieval Sufi.[91] But ethnographic evidence indicates that these same groups, far from having been suddenly "converted" to Islam at any single time, have been and still are undergoing a gradual process of Islamic acculturation—reflected in dress, food, speech, etc.—which is not only gradual but uneven from one group to another.[92] While it is true that some Sufis seem to have initiated such a process by attracting non-Muslims to both their outer and inner circles, what they left behind them, namely their folk literature and their tombs, have deepened and continued an on-going process of Islamic acculturation among non-elites of Bijapuri society.

Summary

From the beginning of the ʿAdil Shahi dynasty in the early sixteenth century through the end of the dynasty in the late seventeenth century, and even beyond, a continuous tradition of Chishti Sufism was maintained on Shahpur Hillock at the *khanaqah* of its founder, Shah Miranji Shams al-ʿUshshaq. Its independence from the court, aided by a physical separation of several miles, contributed to the longevity of a distinctive literary tradition begun by Shah Miranji and upheld by his spiritual and familial descendants. By contrast, most of the Reformist Sufis,

[91] According to an oral tradition collected in 1884 the Momins, or Weavers, the largest group of Muslim converts in Bijapur District, were converted in part by the persuasion of Hashim Pir ʿAlawi (*Gazetteer of Bombay Presidency. Bijapur District* [Bombay: 1884], 23, p. 299).

[92] An ethnographic survey of Bijapur District conducted for the 1884 *Bombay Gazetteer* illustrates this point. The survey showed twenty-one Muslim "castes" of Hindu origin, all in various stages of Islamic acculturation as measured by variables such as purity of Urdu speech, practice of circumcision, diet, attachment to Hindu deities and festivals, etc. See below, Appendix III.

being more closely integrated with the court and the *'ulama*, tended to appear only in the early seventeenth century in response to specific political events then taking place in the capital city.

While the Literati played a leading role in propagating and giving respectability to written Dakhni, the vernacular of the Deccani class, their achievements in the religious history of the Deccan were probably more significant. Here the distinction between their mystical literature and their popular literature is crucial. In the field of mystical literature the Persian writings of Burhan al-Din Janam and Mahmud Khush Dahan compare with those of any of their North Indian contemporaries in point of erudition, even if they lacked originality. It was in the field of their popular literature, however, that successors of the great Chishti mystics made a truly original and important contribution to Deccan history. By blending the simplest tenets of Islam and the terminology of the Sufi tradition with the imagery of an existing literary form, they were able to reach non-elite commoners that their spiritual ancestors had apparently never tried to reach. It is true that their motives for writing this literature may have been somewhat self-serving in that they aimed, among other things, to fix the readers' spiritual loyalty to themselves. And it is also true that this literature seems to have become important only when the Sufism of the great *dargahs* had replaced that of the true mystics. Nonetheless, it was through the agency of this popular literature, more so than through the actions of mystics in their initiation ceremonies, that non-Muslims, particularly women and children, were introduced into the wider circles of Sufi *dargahs*. This literature thus contributed to the gradual acculturation of many commoners to a variety of folk Islam more oriented around tombs than mosques, an on-going process still plainly visible on the Bijapur plateau today.

three

SUFIS OF THE LATE 'ADIL SHAHI PERIOD

Chapter Seven

HISTORICAL SETTING: THE DECLINE OF BIJAPUR FROM 1646 TO 1686

From about the middle of Sultan Muhammad 'Adil Shah's reign to the dynasty's collapse, a period of about forty years, the Kingdom of Bijapur underwent a steady decline in all aspects of its life. Most visible to the historian are the political aspects of this decline, in particular the rise of an independent Maratha power within the kingdom's northwestern districts and the repeated invasions by armies of the Mughal Empire, which finally defeated and annexed the kingdom in 1686. One also finds in this period ample evidence of weak monarchal leadership, overblown luxury at court, and administrative inefficiency—all of which are observable symptoms of many declining monarchies. But the decline of Bijapur was not only political in nature; it was also economic, military, social, and cultural. Moreover, Sufis were by no means immune to this general malaise. Inextricably enmeshed with a decaying social order, they revealed in their writings and their actions not only the structural changes taking place within their own organizations, but also the tensions that the entire Islamic social order was experiencing as it faced its ebbing fortunes.

There has been little sociological research on the kinds of responses that various segments of a society evoke when the political structure arching over that society undergoes severe decline. Research conducted for the present study, however, suggested that as the kingdom declined certain pressures were placed on elite groups only partially integrated with or peripheral to the political system's ruling establishment. Such groups, which included bankers, guild leaders, members of the rural gentry, and heterodox leaders of the state religion, shared in common a situation of having only part of their wealth and social status linked to the changing fortunes of the state. As long as the state remained stable such partial integration was politically tolerable. But as soon as it became evident to the ruling institution that the political fabric was beginning to shred apart, pressures were exerted to gather to its cause the loyalty of such partially integrated elite groups and to tidy up, as it were, the loose edges of the political fabric. Such pressures to bring about the social and ideological integration of elite groups eventually resulted in a bifurcation, and ultimately a polarization, of such groups into two general camps: one that enthusiastically supported the ruling establishment, and one that vehemently rejected it.

It is not argued here that the Sufis of Bijapur were behaving according to any universal or predictable sociological pattern with respect to the development described above, for there were several factors involved in this development that were unique to them and their historical environment. First, perhaps more so than most social elites of Bijapur, Sufis held a particularly ambiguous position with respect to the kingdom's ruling establishment. On the one hand they shared the religion that legitimized the ruling institution and which in many respects separated that institution from the ruled. On the other hand they had inherited a well-established tradition of distrust for institutional Islam and its political supporters. These factors generated a tension between Sufis and the ruling establishment that could never be fully resolved and that left their integration with that establishment at best only partial. Second, Bijapur was an Islamic state, and in theory such a state was merely the political expression of the Muslim community of believers, the *umma*. Leaders of such states accordingly had a special tendency to view social unity and ideological solidarity as necessary preconditions for political stability, and correspondingly to reject social pluralism as politically unhealthy. As Muslims, therefore, Sufis were capable of contributing to the social solidarity, and thereby the political stability, of the kingdom.

As long as the political order in which they lived was stable, Sufis along with other partially integrated Muslim groups were not unduly pressured to manifest this solidarity. We have noted in earlier chapters how some Sufis took it upon themselves to reform the court of what they considered its un-Islamic tendencies while others pursued their own spiritual and social lives unhindered by court pressures. But as soon as the political decline of the kingdom became evident, the court began to question the culturally syncretic ideology upon which the kingdom at its height had been based and sought signs of political loyalty and religious orthodoxy from among all segments of the Muslim community. This most definitely included Sufis. However, in response to the changed political circumstances that accompanied Bijapur's political decline, Sufis were by no means of a single voice. The radically different, and in some respects opposite, types of Sufis that appeared in the middle and late seventeenth century are subjects to be examined in later chapters of this study. Our first task, since the evolution of these types of Sufis was so closely related to the evolution of Bijapur's cultural and political history, is to examine the various dimensions and possible causes of the kingdom's decline.

Political Aspects of the Decline of Bijapur

The Kingdom of Bijapur reached its height of political fortunes in the 1630s and 1640s, during the reign of Sultan Muhammad 'Adil Shah (1627-56). It was in this period that the kingdom launched its most ambitious scheme of conquest. The Mughal-Bijapuri treaty of 1636, which guaranteed the common frontier of the two parties and thereby secured Bijapur from pressure from the north, freed the sultan to extend his suzerainty southward over the Karnatak principalities formerly dependent upon the Vijayanagar Empire. By the mid-1640s most of these principalities had been subdued by Bijapur's armies, and it is probable that in that decade the kingdom gained more in booty from the Karnatak campaigns than it cost to conduct the expeditions.

But the glory of claiming sovereignty over an area stretching from the Arabian Sea to the Bay of Bengal was short-lived, as the economic and political signs of overextension soon became apparent. In 1648 Bijapuri arms captured Jinji, the wealthy hill-fortress located in present-day South Arcot about thirty-five miles northwest of Pondicherry. This single conquest yielded to the government forty million *huns* of gold bullion, all loaded on a caravan of eighty-nine elephants and forwarded to the capital.[1]

[1] *Basatin*, pp. 328 f.; G. S. D. Sardesai, *New History of the Marathas* (3 vols.; Bombay: Phoenix Publications, 1957), 1, p. 84. The *hun*, the standard gold currency of Bijapur, averaged about fifty grains in weight. For details of Sultan Muhammad's Karnatak conquests see H. K. Sherwani

But only six years later the sultan debased the gold *hun*, the kingdom's standard of exchange, by about seventeen percent and ordered that anyone who refused to accept the devalued coin would have his property confiscated.[2] This action strongly suggests that the treasury's gold supply had already become seriously depleted.

A political consequence of the court's preoccupation with the wars in the South was the loss of control over the kingdom's older districts in Maharashtra. Shivaji, a son of the kingdom's Maratha general Shahji Bhonsle, was beginning to emerge in Sultan Muhammad's reign as the leader of a movement to establish an independent Maratha power in the Western Ghats. Busily occupied in the Karnatak wars, Shahji had lost contact with and effective control over his own *jagir*, or land holding, in the extreme northwest corner of the kingdom. He had also lost control over his son Shivaji, who was using the Poona *jagir* as a power base for his own political movement. Finally, in 1646 the young Maratha chieftain seized control of his father's *jagir* in Poona. According to 'Adil Shahi usage, as also with Mughal usage, the term "*jagir*" designated an area of land whose revenues were assigned to a noble, or *jagirdar*, who agreed to use such revenues to support military contingents that he would lead in service of the sultan. Shivaji's seizure of his father's *jagir* therefore did not deprive the government of the land revenues coming from the *jagir* since such revenues had already been alienated to Shahji, who was the official *jagirdar*; and in any event Shahji and his considerable Maratha cavalry were still fighting for the 'Adil Shahi government in the Karnatak. Thus, the nature of the system that permitted Shivaji's rise to power was such that the court's loss of control over land—any land—did not matter so long as it could still exact the loyalty and military contingents from the *jagirdar* who claimed that land as his *jagir*. As Grant Duff wrote with reference to Shivaji's seizure of various Maratha *jagirs*, "All these acquisitions were made without stir or bloodshed; the government districts [i.e., crown districts, not *jagirs*] were not molested, Mohammad Adil Shah was building palaces and mauso-

and P. M. Joshi (eds.), *History of Medieval Deccan, 1295-1724* (2 vols.; Hyderabad: Government of Andhra Pradesh, 1973), I, pp. 359-68.

[2] Khare, "Archives of the Deshmukh Family of Sholapur," p. 275.

leums, or intent on acquisitions in the Carnatic; and the irregularities in the jagheer of Shahjee, if fully known, were not deemed of magnitude, whilst the jagheerdar himself was in the power of the king."[3]

A second portentous event of 1646 was that Sultan Muhammad fell seriously ill with a paralysis from which he never recovered during the remaining ten years of his life. In this period the day-to-day administration of the kingdom fell to his queen, Bibi Sahiba. Given the obviously central role played by the sultan in medieval Indo-Muslim polities, one would normally expect that a paralyzed monarch could only have a paralyzing influence on the state of which he is the crowned head. But although the prolonged illness of the sultan may have weakened the central authority somewhat, government nonetheless continued to flow out of the capital and not from semi-independent hill forts. And if the prolonged Karnatak wars had ceased being productive some time in the early 1650s, the immense booty hauled to the capital in the 1640s provided the court with considerable cash in gold bullion until the very end of the sultan's reign. So long as he did not cut off Bijapur's link with the seaports, which were vital both for importing Arabian horses and for exporting textile products, Shivaji posed no real threat to the kingdom.

But the death of Muhammad 'Adil Shah on 4 November 1656 served as a catalyst for a number of new forces that would hasten the political decline of the kingdom. Foremost among these was renewed pressure from Mughal armies. As the Mughal viceroy of the Deccan, Prince Aurangzeb had for some time sought an excuse to invade and annex both Bijapur and Golconda but had been restrained by his father, Shah Jahan. In early 1656, however, on slender pretext and with only grudging authorization from Delhi, Aurangzeb launched an invasion of Golconda. Just when victory lay within his grasp the viceroy received explicit orders from Shah Jahan, who had fallen under the influence of Golconda's agents in Delhi, to lift the siege and retire from Golconda. "With his greed of territory unsated and his heart sore against his father," wrote Sarkar, the bitter viceroy left Golconda and its extensive wealth behind him.[4]

3 Grant Duff, *History of the Mahrattas*, I, p. 69.

4 Jadunath Sarkar, *History of Aurangzib* (5 vols.; Calcutta: S. C. Sarkar and Sons, 1925-30), I, p. 217.

It was at this juncture that Muhammad 'Adil Shah died. Within only a week of his body's interment Mughal officers were already drawing up plans for the annexation of Bijapur. On 10 November 1656 Prince Aurangzeb rushed a request to Shah Jahan for permission to invade, arguing that Muhammad's heir, 'Ali II, was not a legitimate son of the deceased sultan but only a stranger of obscure origin brought up in the royal harem and that the 'Adil Shahi line had therefore legally ended. Now under the influence of Mir Jumla, a renegade noble from Golconda who, like Aurangzeb, favored Bijapur's annexation, Shah Jahan sanctioned his son's request. In early 1657 a Mughal army of 20,000 crossed the frontier and seized the two vital forts guarding Bijapur's northeastern frontier, Bidar and Kaliani. Exposed now to Mughal aggression, the kingdom might well have collapsed at this time had it not been for the sudden illness of Shah Jahan, which caused Aurangzeb hastily to patch up a treaty with Bijapur and repair to Delhi.

Although the kingdom was spared conquest by Mughal arms, Aurangzeb's decisive victories in the northeastern quarter had hastened the dissolution of Bijapur's flagging authority in the Karnatak as well as in the Western Ghats. With the kingdom's leading generals called up to fend off Mughal armies, *zamindars* of the entire trans-Tungabhadra region swiftly moved to recover their former lands. Furthermore Shahji Bhonsle defied the new sultan's orders to help resist the Mughals and remained on his Bangalore "*jagir*," now virtually an independent state dominated by a Maratha military aristocracy. Meanwhile his son Shivaji challenged the young sultan's authority even more audaciously than before. Seeing that Aurangzeb's invasion was throwing the government into chaos, Shivaji burst through the Western Ghats and seized Kalian, a Bijapur crown district on the northern Konkan seacoast. This was Shivaji's first such appropriation, and it provoked the government's firm determination to capture and bring to submission the young Maratha chief.[5] To accomplish

[5] Bijapur's total loss of control over the Karnatak and its most powerful noble, Shahji, is reflected in the royal correspondence of the period. In 1648, the previous time that Shivaji had provoked the central government, the young Maratha's famous father had been arrested in the Karnatak and brought in chains to the capital. Ten years later, when Shivaji committed an even more audacious act, Shahji was merely assured that he would

this task one of the ablest generals of the realm, Afzal Khan, was sent out from the capital in September 1659 at the head of 10,000 cavalry.

The episode that followed, the personal confrontation of Shivaji and Afzal Khan at Pratapgarh where the Maratha rebel slew the Bijapuri general, has been popularly heralded as the beginning of the Maratha revolt against Muslim rule. But the drama of that notorious encounter has overshadowed an event of perhaps far greater significance for the future of Bijapur, as well as for that of the Marathas. This was the wanton destruction and desecration of Hindu temples indulged in by the Bijapuri general while en route to meet Shivaji in the Western Ghats. The zigzag route Afzal Khan chose to follow between Bijapur and the Ghats suggests his determination to desecrate temples of particular importance to Maharashtrian Hindus. Instead of traveling from the capital directly northwest toward Poona, where Shivaji was believed to be hiding, Afzal Khan went north by northeast to Tuljapur. In this town is located a great shrine to the goddess Bhavani, or Parvati, to which Shivaji's family had always made an annual pilgrimage.[6] After desecrating the Tuljapur temple, Afzal Khan's forces moved toward a temple of even greater pan-Maharashtrian importance—the temple of Vithoba at Pandharpur.

We have noted in chapter one that since the thirteenth century the temple of Vithoba at Pandharpur had been one of the chief centers of Hindu devotionalism in the entire Deccan as well as the focus of a specifically Maharashtrian *bhakti* movement. From the thirteenth century onward this movement attained immense popularity among lower-caste Maharashtrian Hindus, and from the seventeenth century or earlier this popularity had been en-

---

not be blamed. In point of fact, the writ of Bijapur had vanished in the Karnatak. The *farman* from 'Ali II to Shahji (26 May 1658) reads: "At this time it has been reported to His Majesty that owing to the disloyalty and audacity of Shivaji Bhonsle you are alarmed lest his faults should be laid on your head. Be it known to this loyal subject that the improper conduct and acts of Shivaji are evident to His Majesty. Therefore, the faults of Shivaji will not be laid upon you, but his offences are being imputed to him only." (Quoted in Jadunath Sarkar, *House of Shivaji* [3rd edn., Calcutta: M. C. Sarkar, 1955], p. 84.)

[6] C. A. Kincaid and D. B. Parasnis, *A History of the Maratha People* (New Delhi: S. Chand and Co., 1968), pp. 152, 158.

hanced by the institution of the annual pilgrimages to Pandharpur undertaken by the millions of Vithoba *bhaktas*. Converging on the city from the major centers of Maharashtrian culture—Poona, Nasik, Nagpur, Kolhapur—great lines of pilgrims annually made the long march to Pandharpur singing the songs and spiritual messages of the great poet-saints of the city as they went.[7] Prior to 1659 Muslim sultans seem to have been aware of the importance of the temple of Vithoba and the great cult that had grown up around it. In the early seventeenth century Pandharpur had even experienced a period of revival, and at that time the great temple was rebuilt.[8] When in 1636 the city was transferred from Ahmadnagar's to Bijapur's administration it continued to enjoy a prosperous, if uneventful life.

But Afzal Khan, determined to vent his wrath on Shivaji, changed all of this. With the apparent aim of frightening Shivaji's supporters, he took his 10,000 cavalry to Pandharpur and desecrated the temple, destroying all the Hindu images he could find. And although the actual image of Vithoba was spared destruction by mindful temple priests who had removed and hidden it before Afzal Khan's arrival, the Bijapuri general's deeds in Pandharpur were not soon forgotten.[9] There is no evidence indicating whether

[7] Deleury, *Cult of Vithoba*, pp. 86-88.

[8] Ibid., p. 45.

[9] The most authoritative sources for the episodes of Afzal Khan in Tuljapur and Pandharpur are three Marathi chronicles or *bakhars*: the Sabhasad *bakhar*, the Chitnis *bakhar*, and the Sivadigvijaya *bakhar*. Of these the Sabhasad *bakhar* is the most reliable since its author was contemporary with Shivaji. This chronicle is explicit in stating that Afzal Khan smashed the Tuljapur deity, adding that having left Tuljapur the army advanced to Pandharpur and through the Bhima valley, "committing sacrilege on the gods" along the way. The much later Chitnis *bakhar* states that at Tuljapur the officiating priests managed to remove the actual image of the deity to a place of safety. Although the same is said to have happened at Pandharpur, the chronicle relates that the Bijapuri general "molested the people of that place." According to the Sivadigvijaya *bakhar*, written probably sometime in the nineteenth century, vigilant temple priests saved the images of the deities of both places by removing them before the army's arrival, though the head priest at Pandharpur wrote a letter to Shivaji pleading that Afzal Khan had "oppressed in various manners the Hindus, Brahmanas and cows of Tuljapur and Pandharpur." See Surendranath Sen (ed. and trans.), *Siva Chhatrapati*: volume 1 of *Extracts and Documents Relating to Maratha History* (Calcutta: University of Calcutta, 1920), pp. 9-10, 183, 188-89.

Afzal Khan acted under government orders in carrying out the desecration of this temple. Yet it is doubtful that the court was unaware of his activities while on this campaign. The Bijapur government certainly knew of the vindictiveness and callous cruelty of the man sent to capture Shivaji—a man who five years earlier had threatened to have village officials cut to pieces and squeezed in a mill for failing to perform their duties.[10] Since there is no record of the court having censured Afzal Khan for his desecration of the Vithoba temple, one must conclude that the government at least gave these activities its tacit approval.

Whatever may have been the court's motive in this affair, one must appreciate the overwhelming political significance of Afzal Khan's activities in Tuljapur and Pandharpur, for it is doubtful that any act committed by a Bijapuri officer could have alienated more people in a single stroke. Among the Marathi-speaking half of Bijapur's population even the name of Shivaji was not in 1659 as well known nor as intensely revered as was the Vithoba shrine. Stories of Afzal Khan's fanaticism swiftly spread throughout Maharashtra, as did tales of Shivaji's slaying of the Bijapuri general one month later.[11] Following these two events, Shivaji's troops poured out of the mountain passes and onto the broad plains west of the capital, seized the hill fort of Panhala just north of Kolhapur, and even appeared at the gates of the capital. By 1662 a thoroughly independent Maratha kingdom, dominating the entire western quarter of the Kingdom of Bijapur and possessing a rationalized administrative apparatus with a decidedly Hindu orientation, had been established under Shivaji. In that same year the Bijapur government found it necessary to enter in a treaty relationship with the Maratha leader and recognize his de facto control over this area.

These events did not, however, lead immediately to the wholesale abandonment of 'Adil Shahi service by the many Maharashtrians who had staffed Bijapur's military and revenue administrations. Although as yet we have no figures on the desertion of Marathas from Bijapur's to Shivaji's service, we do know that

[10] See Khare, "Archives of the Deshmukh Family of Sholapur," p. 275.

[11] For a discussion of the meeting between Shivaji and Afzal Khan during which the Maratha leader killed the Bijapuri general, see Jadunath Sarkar, *Shivaji and His Times* (5th edn.; Calcutta: M. C. Sarkar & Sons, Ltd., 1952), pp. 63-74.

some Maratha *jagirdars* remained loyal to the kingdom even after Shivaji's movement was well established. In 1665 when the kingdom had to fend off the combined forces of Shivaji and the Mughals, Bijapur's Maratha cavalry was still conspicuous and, noted Grant Duff, "fought with uncommon spirit on this service."[12] The same was true for the Maharashtrians in the revenue administration. Even as late as Sultan Sikandar's reign (1672-86) one finds revenue *farmans* addressed to the hereditary class of Maharashtrian *desais*, indicating their retention of lower-level positions in both the Kannada-speaking sector of the kingdom and in the Marathi-speaking sector not under Shivaji's administration. But in areas that did fall to Shivaji's control the transfer from ʿAdil Shahi administration was greatly facilitated by a thoroughly Maharashtrian-dominated local infrastructure long confirmed in its position.[13] And the growing power of Shivaji's kingdom always provided an attractive alternative to all Maharashtrians willing to sacrifice family tradition and a modicum of security for loyalty to ethnic sentiment.

A clear indication of the kingdom's waning political authority by Sultan ʿAli II's reign was the desertion of much of his nobility, and particularly the Muslim nobility, beginning from about the mid-seventeenth century. "I am trying my utmost," wrote Prince Aurangzeb while preparing for the Mughal invasion of 1657, "to win the Bijapur army over, for then the chiefs of that country will join us of their own accord."[14] To this end the viceroy lent Rs. 20,000 to the governor of Ahmadnagar with instructions to bribe into Mughal service as many ʿAdil Shahi officers as possible and to offer Rs. 2,000 to every noble accompanied by a hundred

[12] Grant Duff, *History of the Mahrattas*, I, p. 113.

[13] In his study of Bijapur's local administration, Hiroshi Fukazawa concluded: "There is no doubt that the great rise, the rapid expansion, and then quick consolidation of Shivaji's power resulting in the establishment of a solid Hindu kingdom was made institutionally possible only by the positive support and active participation of a large number of those Hindus who had trained themselves in the administrative routines under the Muslim rule. Accordingly we may say that the administrative foundation for the rise of the Marathas was already prepared in the Adilshahi Sultanate" (Hiroshi Fukazawa, "A Study of the Local Administration of Adilshahi Sultanate [A.D. 1489-1686]," *Hitotsubashi Journal of Economics*, 3 [June 1963], p. 113).

[14] Quoted in Sarkar, *Aurangzib*, I, p. 235.

men.[15] Maintained throughout the period 1656-86, this policy proved eminently successful in achieving its immediate political objective. As is indicated in Table 5, a sizable number of 'Adil

TABLE 5

BIJAPURI NOBLES DESERTING TO MUGHAL SERVICE, 1658-1683

Name	*Group**	*Mughal Rank*	*Source†*
Mulla Ahmad Nawayat	Arab	6,000/6,000	S. 100; A. 176
S. Latif, Sarfaraz Khan	Deccani	6,000/6,000	A. 218
Fath Jang Khan Miana	Afghan	6,000/5,000	A. 219
S. Ahmad s/o S. Makhdum, Sharza Khan Bijapuri	Abyssinian	6,000/—	S. 98-9; A. 177
Ikhlas Khan, Abu'l-Muhammad	Afghan	5,000/4,000	S. 96; A. 179
Randaula Khan Ghazi	Abyssinian	4,000/4,000	G. 31b; A. 180
Ghalib Khan	Deccani	4,000/4,000	A. 180
Da'ud Khan	Afghan	4,000/—	G. 31b; A. 182
'Abd al-Rahman Bijapuri, Sharza Khan	Abyssinian	3,500/2,000	G. 31b; A. 183
Abu Muhammad g/s of Ibrahim 'Adil Shah	Deccani	3,000/2,000	A. 186
Hakīm Shamsa	Deccani	3,000/1,000	A. 236
Mana Ji Bhonsle	Maratha	2,500/1,500	G. 32a; A. 189
Mulla Yayia	Arab	2,000/1,500	S. 100; A. 192
S. 'Ali s/o Afzal Khan	Afghan	2,000/1,500	A. 193
Asad Allah b. Mulla Ahmad	Arab	2,000/1,200	A. 244
Sharza Rao Kawa	Maratha	1,500/900	G. 32a; A. 200
Salabat Deccani	Abyssinian	1,500/700	G. 32a; A. 201
Raji s/o Afzal Khan	Afghan	1,500/700	A. 201
Jalal Afghan	Afghan	1,500/800	A. 201
Yusuf Khan	Deccani	1,500/600	G. 31b; A. 202
Mir Abu'l-Hasan	——	1,000/200	A. 213

* The term "Deccani" in this table designates those nobles born in the Deccan. Although Abyssinians were ethnically differentiated from these Deccanis since they originated as African slaves, politically they behaved as one class, opposing in the sixteenth century the Iranian Foreigners, and in the seventeenth century the Afghan Foreigners.

† S—Sarkar, *House of Shivaji.*

G—*Guldasta-yi Bijapur*, comp. by Mir Ahmad 'Ali Khan. Urdu MS, Andhra Pradesh State Archives, Oriental Manuscripts Library, no. 852.

A—M. Athar Ali, *The Mughal Nobility under Aurangzeb* (Bombay: Asia Publishing House, 1970).

[15] Ibid.

Shahi nobles were seduced into Mughal service between 1658 and 1683, some at the highest levels of the Mughal ranking system.

One reason for the success of Aurangzeb's policy lay in the bitter factionalism that plagued the nobility immediately upon Sultan Muhammad's death and the Mughal invasion of 1657. What made this factionalism especially sinister was its alignment along ethnic lines. Although Sultan Ibrahim II had halted the importation of Iranian officers, resulting in the dominance of the Deccani class during his and Muhammad's reigns, by the period of 'Ali II (1657-72) a powerful new group of Foreigners had appeared to challenge Deccani supremacy. These were Afghans, most of them renegades from Mughal service such as the powerful family of Buhlul Khan Miana.[16] Opposing the Afghan faction were the Abyssinians, who had emerged by the 1660s as the most powerful element of the Deccani class.[17] Throughout the sixteen stormy years of 'Ali II's reign these two parties became increasingly polarized, and toward the end of that period the sultan's *wazir* even proposed partition of the kingdom as the only solution for problems caused by its fractured nobility and threatened frontiers.[18]

The most vivid sign of Bijapur's political decline is seen in the diminishing number of cavalry it could muster between 1656 and 1686. Bhimsen, a Mughal officer writing in 1700, estimated the armed strength of the kingdom under Muhammad 'Adil Shah at 120,000 cavalry, under 'Ali II at 80,000, and at the fall of the dynasty a mere 2,000.[19] Aurangzeb's policy of seducing 'Adil Shahi nobles thus had the effect not only of contributing to Bijapur's factional splits but also of physically stripping away a large part of its armed forces. Assuming that deserting nobles brought with them their own men and horses, the Bijapuri cavalry lost to the Mughals in the period 1658-83 must have been considerable.[20]

[16] Sarkar, *House of Shivaji*, pp. 95-98.

[17] In 1676 Dr. John Fryer, a surgeon based in Bombay with the English East India Company, noted that Abyssinian slaves "only in this nation [Bijapur] arrive to great Preferments, being the Frizled Wooly-pated Blacks" (John Fryer, *A New Account of East India and Persia*, ed. by W. Crooke [3 vols.; London: Hakluyt Society, 1909-15], II, p. 53).

[18] *Basatin*, p. 436.

[19] Cited in Sarkar, *Aurangzib*, IV, p. 155 fn.

[20] The right-hand column under "Mughal Rank" in Table 5 represents the *sawar* or number of cavalry a noble in Mughal service was in theory

A decline of monarchal leadership also marked the period after Sultan Muhammad's death. A youth of eighteen years when he ascended the throne, ʿAli II showed initial signs of energy during the first several years of his reign, moving personally from one end of the shrinking kingdom to the other putting out fires of rebellion. From around 1666, however, he seems to have abandoned all efforts to check the forces that were driving the kingdom to ruin and sought relief in the harem and the wine goblet. Yet his excessive indulgence in the pleasures of this world only hastened his progress toward the next; by the age of thirty-five he had drunk himself to death.[21]

The death of ʿAli II aggravated the process of the devolution of power away from a monarchal center to a variety of peripheral points. ʿAli II's son and heir, Sikandar, was only a four-year-old child when he became Bijapur's ninth and last monarch, thus placing the administration of the kingdom in the hands of successive regents whose primary loyalty adhered not to the state but to their ethnic group. After three years of domination by an Abyssinian regent (Khauwas Khan, 1672-75), the regency was usurped by an Afghan (ʿAbd al-Karim Buhlul Khan II, 1675-77), who murdered his predecessor.[22] After two years of Afghan rule the regency swung back to Abyssinian control under Sidi Masʿud (1677-83), but only with the aid of Golconda's arms and finances. By this time both city and kingdom had plunged into horrific chaos: Afghan and Abyssinian armies ravaged the countryside in civil war while inside the city the Hindu bandit Chintu Jamna and his henchmen extorted money from the population.[23] Finally, on 21 November 1683, Sidi Masʿud resigned from the regency in disgust and despair, retiring to his fort at Adoni where he

---

required to maintain. The number of cavalry he actually maintained, however, was in Aurangzeb's reign considerably less than these figures indicate.

[21] *Basatin*, p. 434.

[22] Dr. Fryer described reports of the Afghan usurpation only a year after it occurred. ʿAbd al-Karim Buhlul Khan, he wrote, invited Khauwas Khan to a feast to which the latter, "suspecting least when nothing was pretended but Friendship, came with a slender Retinue, and taking of his Cups freely, fell dead drunk into the merciless Snare of his Enemy, who surprizing his Followers with 12,000 brave *Patans*, made way into the Royal Castle, where the young King became a Prey, the *Caun* first a Prisoner, and then a Sacrifice to the Lust of the Usurper" (Fryer, *East India and Persia*, II, p. 54).

[23] *Basatin*, p. 463.

hoped to carve out his own principality.[24] At this point any remnant of centralized government at Bijapur effectively ceased to exist, and three years later the rotted hulk of the 'Adil Shahi dynasty was, after a protracted siege, delivered up to Aurangzeb.[25]

Analysis of the Decline of Bijapur

What happened to Bijapur in the period under discussion was essentially a snapping of the key social and political ties that had held the polity together: ties between the sultan and the intermediate nobility (*jagirdars* on *jagirs*, and bureaucrats on crown lands), and ties between the *desais* and the sultan.

From the end of Sultan Muhammad's reign (1627-56) Muslim nobles in 'Adil Shahi service increasingly accepted Mughal inducements to abandon their service to the Bijapur crown, taking with them their considerable retinue and horses as they went. By the time of Sultan Sikandar's reign (1672-86) the nobility's allegiance to central authority was so weak as to render royal authority a mere shadow of what it had been under 'Ali I or Ibrahim II. Indeed, the bitter civil wars that raged between the Afghan and Abyssinian factions in the 1670s and 1680s prompted one or another group to appeal to foreign powers—the Mughals, Golconda, and even Shivaji—for intervention. In 1676 Dr. John Fryer, a surgeon based in Bombay with the English East India Company, made the following assessment of the kingdom's position when the Afghans controlled the regency:

> And this is the sum of the present Tumults of this Kingdom, which at this juncture of time, in the face of a mighty Host of the *Mogols*, and the frequent Incursions of *Seva Gi* from the Mountains on the other side, beside the Civil Mutinies and Dissentions within, to prevent ill consequences, calls for a skilful Pilot; for it never since the primary defection of [Yusuf 'Adil Khan] was in such danger.[26]

[24] Sarkar, *Aurangzib*, iv, p. 367.

[25] For narrative details of the political decline of the kingdom, see ibid., iv, chaps. 42 and 45, and Sherwani and Joshi, *History of Medieval Deccan*, i, pp. 371-94.

[26] Fryer, *East India and Persia*, ii, p. 54.

But no pilot was to emerge. Sultan Sikandar 'Adil Shah was just a boy to whom the nobility refused even nominal respect. As Dr. Fryer went on to point out, the nobles "are obliged by Fealty to follow his Command, as their shewing themselves at *Visiapour* in course to pay their Respects demonstrates; which yet of late they have done but remisely, making a Salam at Four or Five Course [1 *kos* = 2 miles] distance, and then accompanied in an Hostile manner, as if coming to Besiege the City, more than to perform their Duty."[27]

The breaking of the ties between the sultan and the nobles, aggravated by ethnic factionalism and Aurangzeb's diplomacy, hurt the kingdom mainly in its ability to field effective cavalry units. But this was a purely military problem. In terms of the court's ties with the common people the desertion of the nobility was far less significant than the severing of the vital political linkages which bound district revenue officers, the *desais*, to the sultan. A basic feature of Bijapur's administrative system had been the direct linkages between the sultan and the *desais*, unmediated by any *jagirdars* or bureaucrats. The sultan provided the *desai* with political legitimacy by identifying him as the court's representative among the people of his *pargana*. The sultan also provided for the *desai's* welfare by giving him grants in tax-free lands (*in'am*), usually amounting to several villages in the *desai's* own district. In return for these the *desai* supervised the collection of local taxes and saw to it that they were remitted to the central government. In addition, he was to provide for the defense of his district and settle disputes within the area.[28] But most germane to this discussion, the *desai* was expected to provide an important check against the *jagirdars* or bureaucrats who were theoretically his superiors in the official hierarchy. In his study of Bijapur's local administration Hiroshi Fukazawa has noted that the *desai's* first duty was "to maintain his loyalty to the Sultan. As a part of this duty he was ordered by the Sultan to obey his local Bureaucrats, either Havaldar or fief-holder, so long as they were also faithful to their master. Accordingly, when the local Bureaucrats deviated from the principle of loyalty, it was a duty of the Desai to the Sultan to subdue the rebellions."[29]

[27] Ibid., p. 53.

[28] Fukazawa, "Local Administration," pp. 51-55, *passim.*

[29] Ibid., pp. 48 f.

In all the reigns of Bijapur's sultans prior to Sikandar's the Maharashtrian *desais* of the kingdom had demonstrated steadfast loyalty to the center, even during the rise of Shivaji and the establishment of an independent Maratha kingdom within Bijapur's borders. Whenever local disturbances arose royal *farmans* were sent to the *pargana's desai*, who had been given both the power and the responsibility to bring refractory elements to justice, even when these included the nobles above him. But in Sikandar's reign many *desais* themselves began asserting their independence of the sultan, seizing crown villages and refusing to remit land revenue to the central administration. In a *farman* of 1675 the court admonished the *desai* of a Karnatak *pargana* for seizing several villages but expressed no power to prevent the action:

> It is now made known in the court of exalted dignity that you have refractorily assumed to yourself the *mauza* [village] of Fatahpur and the villages of the said *samt* [sub-district]. When the said *samt* has been granted for the maintenance of the . . . sons of the late Khan Muhammad, what right have you to yourself, with a desire to cause disturbance, the *mauza* of Fatahpur and the villages of the said *samt*?[30]

Such land grabs were not confined to villages granted to Muslim heirs. A *farman* of the same year addressed to a certain Baswant Rao Haryanhali reads as follows:

> Know that as the Miras [hereditary proprietorship] of Diskat and other mirases of the *samt* of Kotal have [been] held from the ancestors of Lingan Gonda, the son of Hanmant Gonda, (therefore) they have now been conferred on the said Lingan Gonda by his glorious Majesty. It is now made manifest to the august court that you have unjustly seized the *mauzas* of Hulal and Hogali and the Diskat and other Mirasagis. What right have you to do this?[31]

Given the important pivotal position occupied by the *desais*, linked as they were both with the village representatives below them and the regional nobility above them, their direct ties with

[30] Walter Elliot Collection. Farmans (London: India Office Library, European MSS, no. F. 50), Farman no. 31, fol. 46b. Elliot's translation.
[31] Ibid., Farman no. 32, fol. 48a. Elliot's translation.

the sultan were absolutely essential for the continued functioning of the kingdom's political system. These links seem to have been stronger than those between the nobility and the sultan, as suggested by the fact that Hindu *desais* rose in rebellion against the sultan's authority relatively late in the kingdom's history, whereas many of the Muslim *jagirdars* in whose *parganas* they functioned had been selling out to the Mughals as early as the 1650s. Hence, when the ties between the *desais* and the sultan began to loosen, there remained little sociopolitical cement to hold the kingdom together.

Coinciding with the political decline of the kingdom was an effort on the part of the court and its clerical auxiliaries to entrench themselves in Islamic orthodoxy. Under Sultan Ibrahim II the high tide of communal accommodation had been reached. From 1627, however, beginning with the accession of Sultan Muhammad 'Adil Shah (1627-56), the ruling element among Bijapur's Deccani Muslims began moving away from the communal accommodation that had marked the first quarter of the seventeenth century. This movement most likely represented the gradual but definite reaction to Ibrahim II's liberalism and was reflected in official policies of Muslim entrenchment and anti-Hindu partisanship.

The class primarily responsible for promoting the cause of Islamic orthodoxy in the government was the *'ulama*. Between the years 1638 and 1649 Bijapuri armies made a series of thrusts deep into the politically fragmented Karnatak—the remnants of the Vijayanagar Empire—and brought most of the area from the Tungabhadra to the Kaveri rivers into tributary status.[32] It

[32] On Bijapur's Karnatak campaigns, see Sarkar, *House of Shivaji*, ch. 4; S. Krishnaswami Aiyangar, "The Rise of the Mahratta Power in the South," *Journal of Indian History*, 9 (1930), pp. 173-217; C. S. Srinivasachari, "A Great Maratha Service to South India in the Pre-Shivaji Epoch," in S. R. Tikekar, ed., *Sardesai Commemorative Volume* (Bombay: Keshav Bhikaji Dhawale, 1938), pp. 73-79. Sarkar relies mainly on the contemporary chronicle *Muhammad-nama*, compiled by Muhammad Zuhur bin Zuhuri Persian MS (Patiala: Punjab State Archives, no. M/727). An abridged translation of this chronicle can be found in Bhagwat D. Verma, "History in Muhammad Nama," in *Shivaji-Nibandhavali*, II (Poona: Shri Shivacaritrakaryalaya, 1930), pp. 73-134. Because of his dependence on this source, Sarkar tends to view the expeditions from the viewpoint of the Bijapur government. On the other hand, Krishnaswami, relying on the records of

has been estimated that as much as a fifth of the wealth derived from these conquests was spent in support of Bijapur's religious establishment, from the Chief Judge (*sadr al-sudur*) down to the thousands of local preachers (*khatibs*), expounders of Islamic Law (*muftis*), and judges (*qazis*) who were appointed to posts all over the kingdom.[33] From the reign of Muhammad ʿAdil Shah an orthodox Muslim establishment was to become increasingly visible in Bijapur, and it was to play an increasingly important role in the shaping of government policies. The very emergence of a class whose collective interest lay in upholding Islamic orthodoxy helped spell the end of the court's brief flirtation with Hindu-Muslim syncretism.

Government regulations pursuant to Muslim retrenchment first appeared in Sultan Muhammad's reign.[34] The Karnatak wars of 1638-49 not only expanded Bijapur's political influence in South India; the addition of vast, new territories to administer precipitated considerable governmental reorganization, of which the most important instrument was Sultan Muhammad's *Dastur al-ʿAmal*, or government regulations.[35] Having as its political

---

European trading companies, stresses the internal dissensions among the successor principalities of Vijayanagar as creating a political low-pressure area that drew Bijapur's armies into the Karnatak. Srinivasachari mainly discusses the Maratha role in Bijapur's Karnatak wars, especially that of Shahji Bhonsle. A list of Bijapur's tribute states in the Karnatak, together with their annual tribute paid during Muhammad's reign, can be found in the *Basatin*, pp. 346-47.

33 Saiyid ʿAli Bilgrami, *Tarikh-i Dakan* (3 vols.; Agra: Mufid-i ʿAm, 1897-1903), III, p. 541.

34 To be sure, some elements of Ibrahim II's liberal policies carried over into his successor's reign. Sultan Muhammad continued to let Portuguese Jesuits operate their mission churches in the Karnatak, and in 1655 he even let them reside at his court (see H. Heras, "Some Unknown Dealings between Bijapur and Goa," *Indian Historical Records Commission, Proceedings*, 8 [1925], p. 131). And in 1652 he issued *farmans* protecting individuals, Hindu and Muslim, against state confiscation of their goods if they died without sons (Muhammad Nazim, "An Inscription From Dabol," *Epigraphia Indo-Moslemica* [1933-34], p. 9; and Nazim, "Bijapur Inscriptions," p. 81). But the former regulation concerned foreigners, not subjects of the crown, and the latter measure seems to have aimed primarily at protecting one small and powerful guild, Hindu jewelers, and does not necessarily reflect the sultan's religious benevolence toward Hindus in general.

35 The *Dastur al-ʿAmal* of Muhammad ʿAdil Shah can be found in the *Basatin*, pp. 348-60. A translation of parts of it has been published by K. K.

object the promulgation of regulations for absorbing the tribute states of the Karnatak into the kingdom's *jagirdari* system,[36] the *Dastur al-'Amal* also laid down specific guidelines regulating Hindu-Muslim relations. The thrust of these regulations, the likes of which had never before appeared in Bijapur, was to separate the Hindus and Muslims as distinct and unequal communities. *Khatibs*, or local preachers, were instructed to see that the Muslim population living in the vicinity of their mosques attend the Friday prayers. They were likewise instructed to preach a strict interpretation of Islam in order to prevent Hindu influences from creeping into their faith.[37] At the same time, Muslims were enjoined not to celebrate Holi, Divali, Desarah, and other Hindu festivals.[38] In fact, Muhammad imposed special taxes on the celebration of these festivals, at which time the government took sheep, ghee, and rice in specified amounts according to the wealth of particular villages.[39]

Reviving a device used by Sultan 'Ali I in the Karnatak campaigns of the 1570s, Sultan Muhammad styled himself a *mujahid* (wager of *jihad*) and *ghazi* (religious fighter) in the Karnatak campaigns of 1638-49.[40] It is true that the cry of *jihad* frequently meant little more than a general call to arms to those Indo-Muslim rulers who invoked it. In fact, there is no evidence that Muhammad actually engaged in any overt acts of anti-Hindu fanaticism such as temple-desecration. Nonetheless, the anti-

---

Basu, "The Dasturu'l-amal of the Bijapur Court," *Indian Historical Records Commission, Proceedings*, 17 (1941), pp. 123-29.

[36] See especially *Basatin*, pp. 349 and 356. Essentially, the former, indigenous nobility was to be pensioned off, while Muslim nobles (usually generals) were to become *jagirdars*, and the local revenue administration was to be handed over to Hindus. Details were also given regarding the appointment of new fort commanders and *jagirdars*, the review of *jagirdars* in court, the branding procedures for their horses, and the means by which their land was to be measured and its assessment calculated.

[37] *Basatin*, p. 350.

[38] Ibid.

[39] Elliot Collection, Farman no. 9, fol. 12b. The four Hindu festivals mentioned in this *farman* are "Divali, Desarah, Yelmasi, and Karhunavi." The first two are popular festivals celebrated all over India. "Yelmasi" is probably "yallama," a festival celebrated among the Kannadiga peoples. "Karhunavi" is not identifiable.

[40] *Basatin*, pp. 316 f.

Hindu sentiment with which the word *jihad* is charged entirely opposed the spirit of communal accommodation that had characterized Ibrahim II's reign, and must have weakened the bonds of loyalty among groups only partly integrated into Bijapur's political system.[41]

Further evidence of Sultan Muhammad's anti-Hindu sympathies can be seen in his taxation policies. Reference was made above to his imposition of taxes on the celebration of Hindu festivals. The *farman* relating to that order was dated 28 October 1640. Another kind of discriminatory tax of this period is indicated in a 1647 *farman* issued to the revenue officials of *pargana* Sholapur, located to the north of the capital. This *farman* refers to the "Ganachari" tax, which was levied exclusively on the district's Lingayat population and made payable to the government a portion of the fees that Lingayats paid to their priests for performing marriages. It is not known when this tax was originally imposed, but the function of the 1647 *farman* was to replace it with a new tax called the "Khanakhushi."[42] This tax was based on the incomes of Lingayat households according to the following schedule:[43]

[41] Some Maratha historians have vastly overstated this point. G. S. Sardesai contended that if Muhammad 'Adil Shah "had not resumed the old practice of desecrating Hindu temples and plundering their wealth, it is probable that Shivaji would not have undertaken to found an independent Maratha Kingdom" (Sardesai, *New History*, I, p. 37). This argument suffers on several grounds. In the first place there is no evidence that Sultan Muhammad desecrated any temples either in Maharashtra or in Karnataka; Sardesai apparently confused the sultan's declaration of *jihad* with actual temple-destruction. In the second place, it was the Kannadigas, not the Maharashtrians, who lay in the path of Muhammad's southward campaigns. It would seem unwarranted to identify events in Karnataka as precipitating Shivaji's movement in Maharashtra. This is particularly so insofar as Bijapur's Karnatak expeditions were in many ways Maratha expeditions, staffed by Maratha cavalry and administrators, in which Shivaji's own father played a prominent part. Maharashtrians were allowed substantial administrative and military power in Muhammad's government, and throughout his reign the temples of Maharashtra remained unmolested. It was not until the reign of his successor 'Ali II that the government became anti-Maharashtrian, that Afzal Khan was sent out to seize Shivaji, and that the great temple of Vithoba at Pandharpur was desecrated.

[42] Khare, "Archives of the Deshmukh Family of Sholapur," p. 274.

[43] A. R. Kulkarni, *Maharashtra in the Age of Shivaji* (Poona: R. J. Deshmukh Deshmukh & Co., 1969), p. 123. A *chawal* is a Marathi monetary

First-class Lingayat house	3 chawals
Second-class Lingayat house	2 "
Third-class Lingayat house	1½ "
Fourth-class Lingayat house	1 chawal

Although we cannot be certain that the imposition of this tax represented a change for the worse without knowing the rates of the tax it superseded, it is clear that the "Khanakhushi" tax represented a form of *jizya*, or poll-tax on non-Muslims. Yet it was a peculiar sort of *jizya*—Khare called it a "miniature" *jizya*—since it was imposed only on the Lingayat portion of the non-Muslim population.

Surviving revenue records do not indicate whether a kingdom-wide *jizya* tax was collected in Muhammad's reign or in the reign of any other 'Adil Shahi monarch. However, we do know that Sultan Muhammad imposed such a tax in the *Dastur al-'Amal* as a matter of policy. That document, promulgated by Sultan Muhammad, levied the *jizya* on an all-kingdom basis at the following rates:[44]

Wealthy Hindus without dependents	full *jizya*
Wealthy Hindus with dependents	half *jizya*
Poor Hindus with a job and income	quarter *jizya*
Converts to Islam, invalids, and youths	no *jizya*

It will be recalled that the *Dastur al-'Amal* was only an administrative manual defining the broad outlines of government policy; it was not a revenue document stating what the government in reality assessed on its population. In the tax schedules sent to local collectors stating those taxes that the government actually expected to collect we find no mention of a kingdom-wide *jizya* apart from the "miniature" *jizya* mentioned above.[45] Nonetheless,

unit equal in value to one-eighth of a rupee (H. H. Wilson, comp., *A Glossary of Judicial and Revenue Terms . . . of British India* [2nd edn.; Delhi: Munshiram Manoharlal, 1968], p. 107).

[44] *Basatin*, p. 355. The full *jizya* was to be paid in silver in units of one *tola* and 4 4/5 *gunj* per month. These were jewelers' terms, a *tola* being equal in weight to about 179 2/3 troy grains, and a *gunj* to about 2 1/4 troy grains. See Wilson, *Glossary*, pp. 190, 524.

[45] Some of the most complete surviving lists of Bijapur's assessed *sa'ir* taxes—taxes other than land revenue—are included in *farmans* of Sultan Muhammad's reign. Of these, Farman no. 9 of the Elliot Collection, issued

Sultan Muhammad's imposition of the *jizya*, like his declaration of *jihad* in the Karnatak wars, can be interpreted as a symbolic expression of the partisan mood forming within the ruling Muslim elite.

What this discussion suggests is that while on one level there is evidence of an orthodox reaction to Ibrahim II's liberal policies, governmental measures to purify Islam of Hindu accretions or to discriminate against non-Muslims were checked in Sultan Muhammad's reign by a countervailing force. This force was the entrenched power of Maharashtrians throughout the government's revenue branch. By accompanying Maratha armies serving in Bijapur's various Karnatak campaigns in the 1640s many Maharashtrians, both Marathas and Brahmins, had become established as local revenue officials in the tribute states of southern Karnataka, just as they were already established in the Marathi- and Kannada-speaking portions of Bijapur proper.[46] It was these Maharashtrian elites upon whom the kingdom's small Muslim ruling class had to rely in order to realize the collection of land revenue and provide for the administration of justice at the local level. It therefore seems that owing only to the most pragmatic considerations did Muhammad's government refrain from enforcing discriminatory measures such as the collection of the *jizya* tax.

In Sultan 'Ali II's reign, however, the government indulged in overt acts of anti-Hindu fanaticism that in Muhammad's reign had only simmered beneath the surface. This new development was most violently exhibited in the vengeful iconoclasm of Afzal

---

28 October 1640, is the most thorough, listing no less than twenty-two separate taxes covering a broad range of services and goods transactions (Elliot Collection, Farman no. 9, fols. 12b-13b). This schedule makes no mention of the *jizya* tax. Nor is such a tax mentioned in H. Fukazawa's intensive study of 'Adil Shahi local administration. (See Fukazawa, "Local Administration," pp. 50-5.)

[46] "It was at this time," wrote Mark Wilks, "that a swarm of Mahratta bramins was first introduced into the south for the purpose of establishing, under the direction of Shahjee, a new system of revenue administration; and of suppressing not only the universal anarchy which then prevailed, but with it most of the traces of the former order of things. Among other innovations, the offices and Mahratta names of Deshpondee, Deshmook, Koolkurnee, together with the Persian designations of Canoongoe, Serishtadar, and numberless other novelties, were then introduced" (Wilks, *Historical Sketches*, I, p. 45).

Khan, and in particular his desecration of the temple of Vithoba at Pandharpur. But it was also evidenced in contemporary documents suggesting a constrictive attitude adopted by the government, an attempt to pull together and unite the Muslim community while keeping non-Muslims at arm's length. In a *farman* of 10 October 1658 defining the functions of the police chief and the *qazi* of rural communities, 'Ali II ordered a *qazi* to see that all Muslims residing in the town of his jurisdiction attend the five daily prayers and pray for the eternal strength of the government.[47] And in 1663, while campaigning in the Karnatak (southern Dharwar District), the sultan imposed the hated *jizya* on Hindus, Lingayats, and other non-Muslim communities by including it in the annual tribute that petty *zamindars* were to pay the central government.[48] By the end of 'Ali II's reign, when many of these same Karnatak holdings were throwing off allegiance to the 'Adil Shahi crown, communal riots between Muslims and non-Muslims sometimes merged with antigovernment revolts.[49]

How can one explain the government's move toward the strident Muslim orthodoxy that characterized the late 'Adil Shahi period? It is possible that the sultans of Bijapur beginning with Muhammad and continuing through his successors felt a political necessity of maintaining a facade of thorough-going conformity to Islamic Law so as not to give Aurangzeb any further inducement or excuse to absorb the kingdom into the Mughal Empire. There may have been the attempt, in other words, to appear to exceed the Mughals in matters of religious orthodoxy. If, however, such a purely political consideration had any validity for the later sultans—and there is nothing in the original literature to sustain this conjecture—it certainly did not hold true for Sultan Ibrahim II, during whose liberal reign Mughal pressure was already felt in Bijapur.

An alternative explanation might focus on the historical coincidences of religious reform movements and political decline in Muslim states. Johannes Baljon has noted that one aspect of Muslim disapproval of the Hindu way of life is the movement to purify Islam of Hindu accretions. "As a rule," he wrote, "this starts at a time of *political* decline. This is typical of Islam. Muslims read God's favour and anger from historical events.

[47] *Waqi'at*, III, p. 397. [48] *Basatin*, p. 395. [49] See below, pp. 238f.

Islam at the height of power means divine approval of His community, whereas defeat and ruin point to heavenly wrath. In the latter case it is incumbent to make a critical analysis of the religious situation."[50] The fundamental premise here, grounded on the Islamic conception of God and man's role in the universe, is that history consists of a projection into this world of God's pleasure or wrath with His community. God frequently intervenes in the affairs of this world to demonstrate His power or to indicate His will. Political events such as revolutions or battles are consequently viewed as caused directly by the hand of God acting for some teleological end.

There can be little doubt that Bijapur's own ideologues were thoroughly imbued with this outlook; indeed, it is so fundamental to Islamic historiography and philosophy as hardly to warrant explication in works dealing with these subjects. As an example of an expression of this teleological interpretation of human history we may cite a passage from one of the final pages of the history of Sultan Ibrahim II's reign recorded by Bijapur's foremost historian, Muhammad Qasim Firishta. Referring to an unsuccessful revolt led by one of the kingdom's nobles, Firishta wrote:

> The great First Cause, who created the universe by his single word, in order to display the fullness of his power, at frequent periods effects revolutions surprising to the human intelligence, of which there could not be a greater proof than this victory, which was unexpected by all; as most of the nobility favoured Ismael, and the zamindars throughout the kingdom of Beejapoor were ripe for revolt.[51]

Given this view of God and history it follows that in a Muslim state, which is but the political expression of God's community, a period of peace and prosperity is prima facie evidence of God's satisfaction that His community is living in accordance with the *sharīʿat*. Conversely, a period of decline in the Muslim state would indicate evidence of God's wrath with the Muslim community. Since such wrath could only have been caused by the commu-

[50] Johannes M. S. Baljon, "Islam in Afghanistan," in A. J. Arberry (ed.), *Religions in the Middle East* (2 vols.; Cambridge: Cambridge University Press, 1969), II, p. 127. Emphasis Baljon's.

[51] Firishta, *Tarikh-i Firishta*, II, p. 77. (Briggs's translation, III, p. 112.)

nity's having strayed from the straight path, it follows that the proper antidote in such circumstances is a return to that path. This might account for the occurrence not only of Islamic reform movements during periods of political decline in Muslim states, but also of the negative aspect of such movements, which in India was manifested by anti-Hindu persecution. The latter phenomenon, of course, would only have the effect of worsening the original problem of political decline since a measure of Hindu-Muslim accommodation was necessary to keep in power a Muslim minority ruling over a Hindu majority.

The political decline of Bijapur and the court's attempt to find its moorings in Islamic orthodoxy—or its negative counterpart, to persecute the non-Muslim population—seem therefore to have been related phenomena. And, if Bijapur's *'ulama* and court functionaries believed that the record of human affairs represents but an unfolding of divine will, one could expect that the state's decline would have engendered a certain measure of anxiety within that segment of the society entrusted with the duty of upholding Islamic Law. Deviants from the Law would be sought out and brought to conformity. In all the kingdom there were no Muslims more vulnerable to a charge of deviance from Islamic Law than the Sufis.

Chapter Eight

SUFIS AS LANDED ELITES

During the latter half of the seventeenth century many of Bijapur's Sufis, irrespective of order, underwent the profound organizational and institutional changes that signaled the passing from what Trimingham termed Sufism's second, or *tariqa* phase, to its third, or *ta'ifa* phase. The physical structure that had served as the center for Abu'l-Hasan Qadiri, Hashim Pir 'Alawi, Miranji Shams al-'Ushshaq, and other first-generation migrants was the *khanaqah*. This was a rather humble hospice in which the *pir* instructed a fraternity of *khalifas* and *murids* in the Way (*tariqa*) of the order in which he himself had been taught. Although no physical description of Bijapur's *khanaqahs* has survived, we can surmise that they were simple dwellings reflecting the values of asceticism and poverty that most first-generation migrants espoused. In the late seventeenth century, however, the *khanaqahs* of many of the early Sufis were replaced by another structure that carried with it a completely new set of institutions—the *dargah*. This was the tomb of a departed *pir*, typically a structure about twenty feet in height having a square or octagonal base supporting a nearly spherical dome.[1] In a broader sense the *dargah* sometimes referred to the whole courtyard including most importantly the tomb, and also a small mosque and a graveyard of the *pir's* descendants. The *dargah* became the central unit of *ta'ifa* Sufism since the tomb was the physical heir to the spiritual power possessed by the Sufi buried there.

If the *dargah* was the physical heir to the Sufi's *barakat*, the human heirs to his spiritual power were his family descendants, or *pirzadas*. The process operating here, to use Max Weber's terms, was that the "charismatic authority" of the "charismatic leader," now that the leader had disappeared from the scene and

[1] See Figure 11, the *dargah* of Shah Amin al-Din A'la (d. 1675). This particular *dargah* was built by Amin al-Din's *murids* two years after the Sufi's death.

the problem of succession had to be faced, was being routinized or channeled on a regular basis to the leader's closest kin on the basis of heredity.[2] This process of "hereditary charisma" had the effect of legitimizing the authority of the *pirzadas*, and of endowing them with tremendous social prestige on the basis of their blood ties with an illustrious forefather now popularly accepted as a saint. Emphasis upon the efficacy of blood as the carrier of *barakat* also had the effect of reducing, and eventually of eliminating altogether, the importance of spiritual merit in the making of *murids*. In this final stage of Sufism's evolution *pirzadas* would freely make "*murids*" of any illiterate commoners willing to demonstrate their belief in the *barakat* of the *dargah* institution by rendering devotions to the spirit of the saint and by offering small gifts (*nazr*) to his descendants, the *pirzadas*. It was also at this time that magic and superstition crept into the popular devotionalism associated with the *dargahs*, as miracle-laden legends became attributed to the saints and specialized powers of many sorts became attributed to their tombs. While there may have been many *pirzadas* of a given saint, there was only one manager of the *dargah* who resided there and who presided over its various devotional and social activities. This was the *sajjada-nishin* ("one who sits at the prayer-carpet"). As the man primarily responsible for overseeing the festivities commemorating the birth date and death date of the *pir*, for maintaining the public kitchen at the *dargah*, and for leading the community prayers held within the *dargah's* compound, the *sajjada-nishin* occupied just as central a position in the *dargah* as the *pir* had had in the *khanaqah*.

We have noted in chapter five that in relation to the state some Sufis had functioned during the first half of the seventeenth century as spiritual preceptors for sultans. Both Ibrahim II and Muhammad, though differing from each other in other respects, solicited the council of such Sufis either by going to their *khanaqahs* or by receiving them in the royal palace much in the manner of special consultants or advisors to modern heads of state. In general, the ties between Sufis and the state remained informal at this time. From about the mid-seventeenth century, however, some Sufis or their *pirzadas* began entering into more formal relations with the government. One of the most significant devel-

[2] See Max Weber, *The Theory of Social and Economic Organization*, trans. by A. M. Henderson and Talcott Parsons (Glencoe, Ill.: The Free Press, 1947), pp. 363-73.

opments in the social history of the kingdom in its later period was the intrusion of state power in Sufi institutions by the conferral of permanent grants in land, called *in'ams*, on selected Sufis or *pirzadas*. Such grants brought the recipients, called *in'amdars* ("holders of an *in'am*"), into fundamentally new relationships with each other as well as with the state and the general population.

In order to illustrate these changes, and the role that *in'am* grants played in them, three representative families of the period will be examined in detail. The first of these, a nonlanded family, illustrates the institutional changes that were taking place in Sufi institutions irrespective of government influence of any kind. Then, following a more expanded discussion of the *in'am* grant and its implications for recipient Sufis, two landed families will be examined, one in Bijapur city and the other in nearby Gulbarga.

Aspects of Institutional Change—The Family of Muhammad Mudarris

Saiyid Muhammad Mudarris (d. 1675), whose immediate lineage is shown in Chart 5, was born and raised in Bijapur as the only

Chart 5

FAMILY OF SAIYID MUHAMMAD MUDARRIS

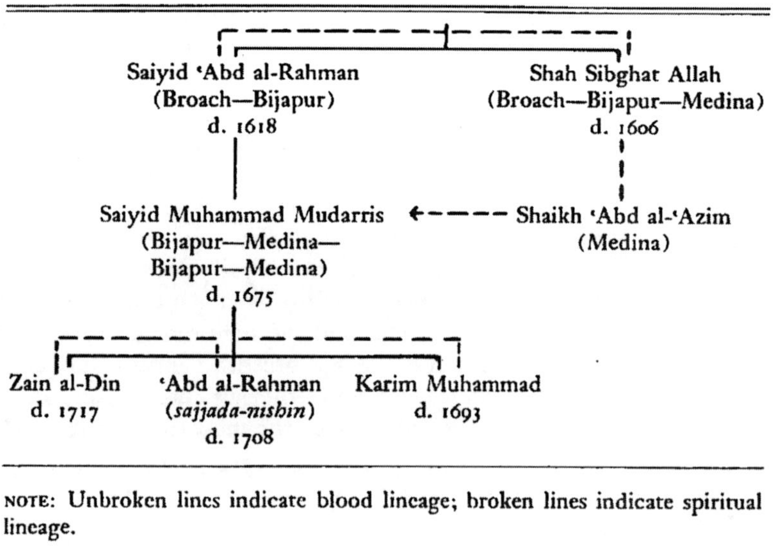

NOTE: Unbroken lines indicate blood lineage; broken lines indicate spiritual lineage.

son of 'Abd al-Rahman (d. 1618), brother of the puritanical reformist, Shah Sibghat Allah. During his first pilgrimage to Mecca, which he made in 1642-43, Mudarris received a Shattari *khilafat* from one of his uncle's followers. In the *Tajalliyat-i Rahmani*, a hagiographic account written by Mudarris's grandson who died in 1724-25, the following exchange is recorded. Just before he died in Medina in 1606, Shah Sibghat Allah intimated to his *khalifa*, Shaikh 'Abd al-'Azim: "My death date will be the birth date of my nephew, who will come to Mecca to perform the *hajj* and also to pay homage to me. Give him my frock, handkerchief, permission, and blessings, that many persons may profit from his grace and thereby gain sanctity. Be sure that his spiritual succession continues, for there will be none other in his epoch like him."[3] Accordingly, when Muhammad Mudarris arrived in Arabia 'Abd al-'Azim passed the *khilafat* to the pilgrim, so that Mudarris was now linked to Shah Sibghat Allah with spiritual as well as with family ties. After returning to Bijapur he established in the city his own *khanaqah*, which he maintained for thirty years with large numbers of followers coming to his fold, and nearly a hundred of them taking a *khilafat* from him. Then in 1672 he left for a second *hajj* to Mecca, pausing for a month outside of Bijapur to give *bai'at* to throngs of people who even followed the Sufi to the Konkan Coast as he proceeded on his holy journey. In Medina he died (1675) and was buried near the grave of his uncle, Shah Sibghat Allah.[4]

The above sketch portrays a Sufi whose life exemplified one of the best of Sufi traditions. "Mudarris" means "teacher," and the hagiographic accounts affirm that he was just that, a renowned scholar and teacher of Islamic Law and orthodox Sufism. Yet a closer examination of his career reveals a number of fundamental changes that were taking place in Sufi institutions. For example, his identification with one or another order became blurred when he was enrolled in multiple orders simultaneously. A biography of Qadiri Sufis records that Mudarris gave to Shah Musa Qadiri (d. 1670) his Shattari *khilafat* in return for which Musa gave

[3] *Mishkat*, copy A, fol. 77a-b; *Tajalliyat-i Rahmani*, comp. by Saiyid 'Ali Muhammad Husaini. Persian MS (Hyderabad: Salar Jung Museum, Tasawwuf no. 28), fol. 61a. This passage illustrates the importance of Mecca in the early seventeenth century, as doubtless it had been for centuries before, as a center for the diffusion of Sufism.

[4] *Rauzat*, copy A, pp. 205-8.

Mudarris his Qadiri *khilafat.*[5] The practice of exchanging *khilafats* suggests that meaningful distinctions between these two orders were evaporating in the late seventeenth century. Belonging to an order had formerly implied exclusive membership in an exclusive group with exclusive doctrines and practices. Now it signified little more than an additional title to one's name.[6] Furthermore, since Muhammad Mudarris belonged to both the Shattari and Qadiri orders simultaneously his followers were apt to identify with neither one in particular, but rather with the person of Muhammad Mudarris. And the replacement of a cult of the Way with a personality cult was one indication of the final stage in the evolution of institutional Sufism.

The use of heredity instead of merit as the principle of succession to the leadership of a *khanaqah* is also reflected in the case of Muhammad Mudarris. The question of who would succeed him as *sajjada-nishin* of his *khanaqah* came to a head around 1672 when the Sufi embarked on his second pilgrimage to Mecca, apparently with the intention of never returning to Bijapur. Before leaving, Mudarris offered the office to his eldest son, Saiyid Zain al-Din (d. 1717). But the latter refused it saying that he was not worthy of the position. Passing over his other two sons, Mudarris appointed his son-in-law as *sajjada-mishin.* One of his *murids* strongly protested this action, however, arguing that since the Sufi had three sons there was no reason to give the office to a son-in-law. Acquiescing in his *murid's* judgment, Muhammad Mudarris named as *sajjada-nishin* his second son, ʻAbd al-Rahman (d. 1708), and departed for Mecca.[7] This incident demonstrates that by the 1670s the principle of hereditary succession to a *khanaqah's* leadership had become widely accepted. An examination of the spiritual and familial lineages of Sufis belonging to the Qadiri order shows that beginning from the mid-seventeenth century not only the *sajjada-nishins* but also the *khalifas* were affiliated by close kinship ties as well as spiritual links.[8]

[5] *Latayif al-Latif*, p. 62.

[6] Abu'l-Hasan Qadiri II (d. 1719-20), grandson of Abu'l-Hasan Qadiri, mentioned a total of eleven orders in which he had received *baiʻat* and quite mistakenly traced them all to Arabia (Abu'l-Hasan Qadiri II, *Makhzan al-Salasil al-Hasaniya.* Arabic MS [Bijapur: Gachi Mahal], fols. 2a-3a).

[7] *Mishkat*, copy B, fol. 547a-b.

[8] See Appendix I.

In this same period *pirzadas*, the sons of famous Sufis, tended either to leave the *khanaqah* entirely or to convert the structure into a shrine built on the grave of their illustrious predecessor. Since Muhammad Mudarris died in Medina he, of course, left no tomb in Bijapur around which any *dargah* institution could develop. Only his *khanaqah* in Bijapur remained. This structure, however, must have deteriorated as a center of spiritual discipline when two of the three sons abandoned it altogether and the third exploited its renown to his own advantage. The eldest and youngest sons of Muhammad Mudarris accompanied their father on his pilgrimage to Mecca, while ʿAbd al-Rahman remained in Bijapur as the *sajjada-nishin*. On the Konkan Coast, as he was preparing to leave by ship for Mecca, Mudarris gave a *khilafat* to his youngest son, Karim Muhammad, and sent him back to Bijapur to preach. But when he arrived, Karim did not join his elder brother in the *khanaqah*. Rather, he professed no desire to belong to the orthodox Muslim establishment ("to be a *shaikh*"), with which living in a *khanaqah* had by then evidently become identified, and he spent the remainder of his life as a recluse.[9]

While still on the coast, Muhammad Mudarris likewise gave a *khilafat* to his first son, Zain al-Din, and sent him back to Bijapur to preach as he had done earlier with his youngest son. But Zain al-Din, who had already refused the successorship once before when it was offered to him, still showed no interest in the life of the *khanaqah*. A hagiographic tradition describes the encounter that took place back in Bijapur between Zain al-Din and his younger brother, who was the *sajjada-nishin*:

> One day Shah ʿAbd al-Rahman prepared a dinner table on which he placed his father's frock as the tablecloth. On another table he placed the cloak of a nobleman. He then invited his older brother to supper, advising the latter that either table was available to him. . . . Hazrat Zain al-Din chose the table with the nobleman's cloak, which he then wrapped around him. Wearing that garment, he went to meet the king of those times.[10]

[9] *Mishkat*, copy B, fol. 547b.
[10] *Mishkat*, copy B, fols. 547b-548a.

Of Muhammad Mudarris's three sons, two had abandoned the life of the *khanaqah* altogether, one of them preferring to live as a hermit and the other one apparently choosing to live as a courtier. In a word, sons were leaving the profession, though their motives were never explicitly stated. Meanwhile ʿAbd al-Rahman, as *sajjada-nishin* of his father's *khanaqah*, had evidently turned the job into a lucrative enterprise. It is recorded that he reaped so much money in gifts from his followers that he prayed from his "majestic *dargah*" that it be empty of money after his death.[11] When reviewing the landed Sufis who became wealthy from revenues defrayed to them by the government in *inʿam* grants, it is well to remember cases such as that of ʿAbd al-Rahman. The *inʿam* was not the only path to a Sufi's wealth. Having an illustrious ancestor in whose name one was the *sajjada-nishin* was itself sufficient for guaranteeing a steady income given directly and gratuitously by devotees.

In sum, many of the institutional changes that occurred among late seventeenth century Sufis were reflected in the lives of Muhammad Mudarris and the members of his family. The basis of succession passed from merit to blood, leadership passed from a *pir* to a *sajjada-nishin*, membership passed from a fraternal order to a family, the religious focus passed from the Way (*tariqa*) to the personality of the *pir*, and the overall appeal of the institution passed from an elite-oriented to a popular-oriented phenomenon. But two other institutional changes characteristic of late seventeenth century Sufis were absent in the case of Muhammad Mudarris and his family: the passing from the *khanaqah* to the *dargah* as the institution's central physical structure, and the acceptance of *inʿam* grants by *pirzadas*. There was no Mudarris *dargah* simply because the *pir* did not die in Bijapur, but in Medina. Nor did the state ever bestow grants in land to the family; for, as we shall see, the court was usually more interested in supporting a *dargah* than individuals. So in these respects the family of Muhammad Mudarris was somewhat exceptional. Among most urban Sufi families of late seventeenth century Bijapur the *dargah* and the *inʿam* were the characteristic institutions. The remainder of this chapter will concentrate on measuring the significance of both.

[11] *Rauzat*, copy A, p. 210.

State intervention in Sufi Institutions—The *In'am* Grant

In the course of the seventeenth century the Bijapur court's policy vis-à-vis Sufis passed from an informal patronage characterized by a monarch's visiting the tombs of departed Sufis or engaging the company of a few living mystics as spiritual counselors, to a formal patronage characterized by the court's granting rent-free lands to certain Sufis. In the first, informal stage, both Sultans Ibrahim II and Muhammad indulged in visiting *khanaqahs* of living Sufis. Sultan Muhammad in particular made frequent visits to the *khanaqahs* of Shah Hashim Pir 'Alawi and Abu'l-Hasan Qadiri and had a great deal of respect for both Sufis.[12] At the same time, these two sultans paid their devout respects to the most famous *dargah* of the Deccan, the tomb of Muhammad Husaini Bandanawaz Gisudaraz of Gulbarga. Ibrahim II sang praises to the *dargah* in his *Kitab-i Nauras*,[13] and in 1605-6 he gave one of his daughters in marriage to a family descendant of Gisudaraz.[14] On his part, Sultan Muhammad 'Adil Shah participated in at least two of the annual pilgrimages to Gulbarga—in 1638 and 1645-46—in celebration of the Sufi's death date (*'urs*).[15] And in 1640 the tomb was rebuilt and enlarged, probably under the sultan's orders.[16]

But it was also in Sultan Muhammad's reign that there was a perceptible change in the court's attitude toward Sufis, a change toward enjoining a select few of them into formal association with the state. The *Dastur al-'Amal*, the government regulations promulgated by Sultan Muhammad, specifically provided for the continuation of *in'ams* or pensions formerly made to *dargahs* of prominent Sufis, the granting of government aid to help finance the annual *'urs* celebrations at such *dargahs*, and the dispensation of state support in the form of land grants in *in'am* or pensions (*yaumiya*) to "people of God."[17] The pattern of land grants made to Sufis by the 'Adil Shahi government has been presented in Table 6, below.[18] It can be seen that prior to the promulgation

[12] *Sahifat*, Urdu edn., p. 114.

[13] See Gayani, "Kitab-i Nauras," p. 146.

[14] *Basatin*, p. 258.

[15] Zuhuri, *Muhammad-nama*, pp. 165, 259. According to Bhagwat D. Verma, the sultan also attended the *'urs* celebrations in the year 1647. See his "History in Muhammad Nama," pp. 96, 107, 120.

[16] Briggs, *Rise of the Mahomedan Power*, II, p. 240 fn.

[17] *Basatin*, pp. 350, 352.

[18] This table does not claim to be complete owing to the extent to which

TABLE 6

GRANTS MADE BY THE 'ADIL SHAHI COURT TO BIJAPURI SUFIS

Recipient	*Grant**	*Donor*	*Year*	*Source†*
'Abd al-Qadir s/o Mustafa Qadiri. Successor, Qasim Qadiri *dargah*	*Ma'ash* of several villages	Ibrahim II	—	S. 46
Hamīd Qadiri	*In'am* of nine royal gardens	Ibrahim II	—	R. 64
Habib Allah Sibghat Allahi	*In'am* of one village	Ibrahim II	—	M. S. 37a

* Symbols and terms used in this column: p.—*pargana*, or a locally administered district; m.—*mu'amala*, or a centrally administered district; s.—*samt* or a sub-district in both *parganas* and *mu'amalas*. *In'am* and *ma'ash* both refer to lands whose revenues were reserved for the maintenance of their holder. A *chawar* is a Marathi land measurement term equivalent to 120 *bighas*, and one *bigha* is approximately nine-tenths of an English acre (Wilson, *Glossary of Judicial and Revenue Terms*, pp. 85, 107). Hence a *chawar* is equivalent to roughly 109 acres.

† A. M.— Archeological Museum, Bijapur. 'Adil Shahi *farmans*
C.— Cousens, *Bijapur and Its Architectural Remains*
Ch.— Chaghatai, M. A., "'Adil Shahi Grants"
E. C.— Elliot Collection
G. M.— Gachi Mahal, Bijapur. *Farmans* in the possession of the *sajjadinishin* at the Qasim Qadiri *dargah*
K.— Khan, Yusuf Husain, *Farmans and Sanads*
L.— *Latayif al-Latif*
M.A.— *Makhzan al-Ansab*
M. N.— *Mishkat-i Nubuwat*, copies A and B
M. S.— *Malfuzat-i Shah Sibghat Allah*
R.— *Rauzat al-Auliya'-i Bijapur*, copy A
S.— *Sahifat-i Ahl-i Huda*, Urdu edn.
S. A.— State Archives, Andhra Pradesh. 'Adil Shahi *farmans* of the Khwaja Bandanawaz Collection
T.— *Tazkira-yi Auliya*, I
W.— *Waqi'at*, III

farmans and other references to *in'am* grants have been lost or scattered in the past three hundred years. The table is, however, as complete as possible to my knowledge, and certainly suggests the trends discussed in this chapter.

Table 6 (continued)

Recipient	*Grant**	*Donor*	*Year*	*Source*†
Qasr al-Din Mahmud Junaidi. Successor, Siraj al-Din *dargah* at Gulbarga	Refers to an earlier *in'am* granted to Siraj al-Din's descendants in p. Raibagh	Ibrahim II	1621-22	E. C. no. 3
Abu'l-Hasan Qadiri	A generous pension	Ibrahim II or Muhammad	—	T. 49
Ja'far Saqqaf	*Ma'ash* of one village (refused); and some cash (accepted)	Muhammad	—	R. 189 f.
'Abd al-Qadir s/o Mustafa Qadiri. Successor, Qasim Qadiri *dargah*	House opposite Gachi Mahal	Muhammad	—	S. 43
Pyar Muhammad. Attendant, Qasim Qadiri *dargah*	House at Qasim Qadiri *dargah*	Muhammad	—	S. 43
Isma'il Qadiri of Nilur	*In'am* of several villages	Muhammad	—	M. N(B)491b
Muhyi al-Din s/o Ahmad, Attendant, *dargah* of Qutb al-Aqtab	*In'am* of some lands and gardens to maintain mosque and kitchen	Muhammad	1636	C. 130
Abu Bakr s/o Shaikh Kuchik	*In'am* of 4 *chawars* and 77 *bighas* in p. Aland	Muhammad	1640	S. A. no. 8
Mustafa s/o Shaikh 'Ali. Successor to *dargah* of 'Ain al-Din Ganj al-'Ilm	*In'am* of one village in s. Tamba	Muhammad	1643	A. M. no. B43
Muhyi al-Din s/o Jamal al-Din Qadiri	Lands formerly granted to Muhyi al-Din s/o Ahmad, plus 27 *chawars*	Muhammad	1645	A. M. frame no. B73

Table 6 (*continued*)

Recipient	*Grant**	*Donor*	*Year*	*Source†*
Saiyid Safi Allah. *Murid* of Abu'l-Hasan Qadiri	*In'am* of one village: Mangoli	Muhammad	1656	G. M.; W. 390
'Abd al-Qadir s/o Hazrat Shah Badr al-Din Sharif al-Qadiri	*In'am* of 4 *chawars* in s. Chitgupa	Muhammad	1656	K. 6
Muhammad Abu Turab Mudarris. Teacher at *dargah* of Habib Allah Sibghat Allahi, Bijapur	Daily allowance of one *hun* (gold coin)	Muhammad	1656	Ch. 7 f.
Zain Muqbil	*Ma'ash* of several villages	'Ali II or Muhammad	—	R. 197
Muhammad Abu Turab Mudarris. Teacher at *dargah* of Habib Allah Sibghat Allahi, Bijapur.	*In'am* of 4½ *chawars* crown land	'Ali II	1658	Ch. 8
'Abd al-Latif s/o Musa Qadiri	*Jagir* offered and refused	'Ali II	—	M. N(A)157a
Asad Allah s/o Asad Allah bin Husain. Successor at *dargah* of Bandanawaz, Gulbarga	*In'ams* totaling 15 villages in northeastern districts of the kingdom	'Ali II	1659	S. A. nos. 16, 19-23
Asad Allah s/o Asad Allah bin Husain. Successor at *dargah* of Bandanawaz, Gulbarga	*In'am* of one village in p. Terdal	'Ali II	1661	S. A. no. 74
Mahmud and 'Ali, sons of Ahmad Qadiri, the successor of *dargah* of Miran Muhyi al-Din	*In'am* of one village in p. Raibagh	'Ali II	1661	E. C. no. 27

Table 6 (*continued*)

Recipient	*Grant**	*Donor*	*Year*	*Source*†
'Abd al-Latif. Attendant, Muhammad Qadiri *dargah* at Raibagh	*In'am* of 2 *chawars* in p. Raibagh	'Ali II	1662	E. C. no. 37
Shah Hazrat Qadiri	*In'am* of s. Ana Husur plus villages in m. Mudgal	'Ali II	1663	W. 403
Asad Allah s/o Asad Allah bin Husain. Successor, Bandanawaz *dargah*, Gulbarga	*In'am* of 10½ more villages, plus 25 *chawars* from 5 other villages	'Ali II	1663	S. A. no. 33
Husain s/o Asad Allah. New successor at Bandanawaz *dargah*	All *in'ams* previously granted to his father	'Ali II	1664	S. A. no. 38
Husain s/o Asad Allah. New successor at Bandanawaz *dargah*	House and some lands in Gulbarga	'Ali II	1665	S. A. no. 41
(name illegible, though addressed to a Sufi)	*In'am* of one village in s. Berur	'Ali II	1665	A. M. no. B64
Husain s/o Asad Allah. Successor, Bandanawaz *dargah*	*In'am* of 5½ more villages and 23 *chawars* in 7 other villages	'Ali II	1670	S. A. no. 46
Husain s/o Asad Allah. Successor, Bandanawaz *dargah*	*In'am* of 5½ more villages in m. Gulbarga and p. Nilanga	'Ali II	1670	S. A. nos. 47, 48
Muhammad Junaidi. Successor, 'Ain al-Din Ganj al-'Ilm *dargah*, Bijapur	*In'am* of one village in s. Tamba	'Ali II	1671-72	A. M. frame no. B46

Table 6 (continued)

Recipient	*Grant**	*Donor*	*Year*	*Source†*
Abu'l-Hasan Qadiri II	*Ma'ash* of one village: Kankal	'Ali II or Sikandar	—	R.124
Husain s/o Asad Allah Husaini. Successor at Bandanawaz *dargah*, Gulbarga	*In'am* of one village in p. Nilanga	Sikandar	1675	S. A. no. 52
Shams al-Din Qadiri and Isma'il Qadiri, sons of 'Abd al-Qadir	*In'am* of two villages in p. Sindhnur	Sikandar	1676	G. M.
Tahir La-ubali	House in Adoni	Sidi Mas'ud, regent for Sikandar	—	L. 152
The four sons of Tahir La-ubali: Husain, Zahid, 'Abd al-Qadir, Muhammad	*Jagirs of* one village to each son: Tamapur, Rangdhal, 'Ali Banda, Hogrur	Aurangzeb	—	L. 155 M.A. 158 f.
'Abd al-Latif s/o 'Abd Allah Qadiri	*Jagir* of one village, Kalkonta	Aurangzeb	—	L. 57
Shah Hazrat Qadiri	*Ma'ash* of several more villages	Aurangzeb	—	R. 184
Isma'il Qadiri s/o 'Abd al-Qadir	*Ma'ash* of one village in p. Sindhnur and 2 *chawars* in Bobleshwar	Aurangzeb	—	S. 64 f.
Mustafa Qadiri s/o Chand Muhammad	*Ma'ash* of one village: Manthal	Aurangzeb	—	R. 182 f.
Shams al-Din Saiyid Shah Husain al-Basri	*Jagir* of one village: Hosur	Aurangzeb	—	W. 354
Murtaza s/o Shams al-Din Qadiri	*In'am* of one village in p. Molvar	Aurangzeb	1705	G. M.

of the *Dastur al-'Amal*, that is prior to the reign of Sultan Muhammad, there were only occasional instances of Sufis receiving state support. In a *farman* of 1621-22 Sultan Ibrahim II made reference to an *in'am* that for many generations had been held by the descendants and successors of Shaikh Siraj al-Din Junaidi, a fourteenth-century Sufi of Gulbarga. Ibrahim II also gave a few villages in *in'am* to the sons or successors of Shah Qasim Qadiri and Shah Sibghat Allah. But during and after the reign of Sultan Muhammad one finds a significant increase in the number of *in'ams* granted to Sufis, especially to *pirzadas* attached to the *dargahs* of Qadiri *pirs*. While only four such grants are known to have been issued by Ibrahim II, eleven were issued in the reign of Muhammad, and fourteen in the reign of 'Ali II. The effect of the *Dastur al-'Amal* therefore seems to have been immediate in terms of formalizing a new relationship between the state and certain Sufis.

What was the cause of the profusion of *in'am* grants to Sufis between 1640 and 1670? The court's desire to create a measure of religious uniformity among the kingdom's Muslims probably played a part. For one thing, the process of reducing some Sufis to appendages of the state had the effect of absorbing into the ranks of the *'ulama* individuals who had inherited a tradition that deviated from strict orthodoxy, individuals who were at least potentially dangerous from a doctrinal standpoint. Notwithstanding the monumental efforts of the great twelfth-century theologian Abu Hamid al-Ghazali to reconcile Sufism with orthodox Sunni theology, Sufism's pantheistic and ecstatic elements had always placed Sufis under the suspicion of Islamic rulers who regarded the upholding of strict orthodoxy as one of their foremost duties. We have seen how Sultan Muhammad bin Tughluq, certainly one Indo-Muslim ruler whose thinking ran along these lines, attempted to harness to state service the Chishti Sufis of thirteenth-century Delhi by requiring them to engage in the propagation of Islam and even to wear the uniforms of government servants. Of course Muhammad bin Tughluq was a most eccentric sultan, and such extreme behavior was perhaps unique in the history of Indo-Muslim rulers as regards their relations with Sufis. But Muhammad bin Tughluq's attitude was not unique. The granting of land grants in the form of *in'am* was but a more subtle instrument for achieving the same end that the Tughluq sultan desired, for the Sufis of Bijapur were not the only recipients of *in'am* grants in the middle and late seventeenth century; many such grants were also given to various shaikhs, *qazis*, *muftis*, and other members of the *'ulama* class. Therefore, by listing Sufis alongside the *'ulama* in the revenue department's *in'am* registers, the government was, in effect, guiding the former into the socio-economic world of the latter for the apparent purpose of rendering a degree of uniformity and conservatism to the entire religious establishment. Irfan Habib characterized the *in'amdars* of the Mughal Empire as "a bastion of conservatism, because they had nothing except their orthodoxy to justify their claims on the State's bounty."[19] Every indication is that the same dynamic operated in Bijapur, that *in'am* grants tended to be given either to people whose religious conservatism was already beyond doubt, or to people whose religious conservatism the court wished to secure. For Muslims, at least, performance of religious orthodoxy seems to have been an implicit condition for the receipt of the state's bounty.

Another motive for granting *in'ams* to Sufis has more to do with the court's desire of securing their political loyalty *per se*. Unlike land assignments in *jagir*, which required the recipient to maintain military contingents in return for the right to administer *pargana* districts, the *in'am* represented a free gift from the central government. The land revenue of *in'am* districts, which usually consisted of an allotted number of acres in allotted villages, was permanently alienated from the government in favor of the *in'amdar*. Moreover, the *in'am* grant was perpetual, continuing throughout the lifetime of the grantee with no need for renewal, whereas *jagir* assignments lasted only with the pleasure of the sultan. The sole compensation owed by the *in'amdar* for perpetual state support—and this was crucial for Sufis, with their tradition of aloofness from worldly affairs—was to render unswerving loyalty to the government. In a *farman* of 1636 granting lands to the attendants of a *dargah* of a certain Qutb al-Aqtab, the government of Muhammad 'Adil Shah made quite clear what was expected in return for state support:

> In A.H. 1046 a petition was submitted in the Imperial Court . . . to this effect: that Jannat Makani [i.e., the former sultan] assigned some land and gardens as a subsistence to the servants

[19] Irfan Habib, *The Agrarian System of Mughal India* (Bombay: Asia Publishing House, 1963), p. 310.

> in charge of the shrine of Qutb-ul-Aqtab, the kindest of saints —may the most high God hallow his grave. The daily allowance of the refuge of saintly people—Shaikh Muhyu-d-din, son of Shaikh Ahmad—as well as the expenses of the mosque and *langarkhanah* [kitchen] were also defrayed out of the income of the above land. But after the death of Jannat Makani the above lands and gardens were taken away from their possession and consequently they are all in a sad plight, and the mosque and *langarkhanah* have fallen into decay. The Imperial Court now pitying their miserable state gives them back the above land and gardens, and *expects that they, living on the income of this state, will pray for the long life of the king.*[20]

The last line of this passage—that the government "expects that they, living on the income of this state, will pray for the long life of the king"—is a crucial passage in this document. Why would the court want the *pirzadas* to pray for the perpetuity of the government when this was absolutely all that was owed the court in return for direct and perpetual monetary support? The answer seems to lie in the immense political significance that the court attached to the *dargahs* as centers of popular devotion. The court realized that hundreds, even thousands, of common folk—Hindu as well as Muslim—thronged to these *dargahs*. The court knew that such people made regular devotions at the tombs on Thursdays, that they made regular pilgrimages from distant parts to attend the special festivals associated with the *dargahs*, and above all that these people shared immense belief in the spiritual powers of the managers and caretakers of the *dargahs*, namely the *sajjada-nishin* and other *pirzadas*. Hence, it is logical that by securing the loyalty of an elite group considered by the court to wield such influence among the lower population, the government hoped to deepen the roots of its own authority throughout the kingdom. For it was presumably in the *dargah's* mosque and among the *dargah's* devotees that the functionaries of the institution offered their prayers in support of the state. This explanation is further supported by the fact that it was not the lone Sufi or the recluse of the *khanaqah* that normally received *in'am* grants. Rather, the typical recipients were, like those mentioned in the

[20] Cousens, *Bijapur and Its Architectural Remains*, p. 130. Translated into English in Cousens. Emphasis mine.

passage quoted above, attendants and leaders of the kingdom's major *dargahs*. Although *in'am* grants were normally made out to individuals and not institutions, it seems really to have been the institution of the *dargah* that the government was interested in supporting.

A number of scholars have noted that the Mughal Emperors had similar motives with respect to land grants made to Sufis, or indeed to any elite group that enjoyed popular religious patronage. A collection of six Mughal grants to a certain Shaikh Hāfiz Muhammad Sa'id invariably closed with the phrase, "He should always assiduously pray for the perpetuity of the State."[21] Similar grants in land that the Mughal government made to non-Muslims indicate the court's interest in staying on the right side of any popular elite, regardless of religion. It has been observed that the enormous local influence wielded by the yogis of Jakhbar "must have been yet another consideration with the Mughals when they conferred these grants on this establishment, for by these gifts they were creating what could easily be called a vested interest."[22] Emperor Jahangir called the class of pious *in'amdars* in the Mughal Empire his "Army of Prayer" and was reported to have said that this army was as important for the empire as was the real army. Irfan Habib concluded from this statement that such a class constituted the empire's "natural apologists and propagandists."[23] Professor Abdur Rashid has also understood the securing of political loyalty as one of the Mughal court's primary motives for making land grants to Sufis and other groups.[24] Thus the 'Adil Shahi sultans were certainly not acting alone with respect to their *in'am* policy vis-à-vis Sufis or their *dargahs*.

The procedure of granting *in'ams* to Sufis seems to have been well established in the time of Sultan Muhammad. A petition for an *in'am* originated either with the potential recipient who sent his request to the central revenue ministry, or it originated in the revenue department itself and was recommended by its highest

[21] M. A. Chaghatai, "Grant of Land in Favour of Hāfiz Mohammad Sa'id," *Journal of the Pakistan Historical Society*, 10 (1962), pp. 25-37.

[22] B. N. Goswamy and J. S. Grewal, *The Mughals and the Yogis of Jakhbar* (Simla: Indian Institute of Advanced Study, 1967), pp. 15-16.

[23] Habib, *Agrarian System*, p. 310.

[24] Abdur Rashid, "*Madad-i-Ma'ash* Grants under the Mughals," *Journal of the Pakistan Historical Society*, 9 (1961), p. 101.

officials, the *wakil al-saltanat* (also called *amir-i jumla*), or the *mustaufi al-mulk*. All petitions had to be personally approved by the sultan, who would order a *farman* to be sent to the local revenue officers of the *pargana* in which the *in'am* lands were to be reserved. This *farman*, normally sent to the *desai* since he was the chief revenue officer of a district, would instruct the local officials to see that the revenues of a specified piece of land were reserved for the maintenance of a specified grantee. Although *in'am* grants were theoretically perpetual for the lifetime of the grantee, and many of them for his descendants as well, *in amdars* frequently requested assurance from the central government that the local revenue officials honor former *farmans* in their favor. The following *farman* of Sultan 'Ali II, dated 26 July 1662, illustrates the procedure followed by the court when reaffirming a grant made to a functionary of a *dargah* in Raibagh, a town located seventy miles west by southwest of Bijapur:

> To Ramji Chandras, Sar-Samt [*desai*] and Karkonan [clerks] of *pargana* Raibagh: . . . in the year 1062 Shaikh 'Abd al-Latif . . . who takes care of the rauza [*dargah*] of Saiyid Muhammad Qadiri . . . represented to our august court that
>
> 1 chawar of land in Dhurang Kari Kara Pati
> ¾ chawar of land in Dhurank Topla
> ¼ chawar of land in Dhurang Tapal Pati
>
> in the lands of Qasba [town] Sabaryal of the said *pargana* have been enjoyed and continued in Inam for the purpose of lighting and making 'urs at the glorious tomb and mosque built by the said (person) according to the deed of gift by Shahbaz Khan, the son of Daud Khan. Be pleased to issue a farman conferring it that it may be a powerful and permanent sanad [document]. . . .
>
> The said land shall be regarded as exempted from the (income) of the moqasai [service lands] of the said Qasba and continued to his heirs and sons after him.[25]

[25] Elliot Collection. Farman no. 37, fols. 54a, 55a. Elliot's translation. The year quoted in this *farman* follows the Shahur San calendar, which Bijapur's revenue officials used because it was solar and therefore geared to the harvests. In the mid-seventeenth century it lagged behind the lunar Muslim calendar by about ten years. The Hijri date of this *farman* was 9 Zi'l-Hijja 1072.

In'am lands were taken either from directly administered crown districts (*mu'amala* or *qal'a*) whose land revenues were collected for deposit in the central treasury, or, as in the above case, from locally administered districts (*pargana*) whose land revenues were collected for *jagirdars* to support the *jagirdars'* troops. In both instances it was the *desai* who was primarily responsible for executing the sultan's orders and for seeing that revenues derived from *in'am* lands went neither to the government nor to a *jagirdar*, but to the *in'amdar*.

Farmans issued in this manner reveal much about how *dargahs* were administered. A *farman* of 1640 instructed the *desai* of *pargana* Aland, a district to the immediate northwest of Gulbarga, to see that an *in'am* in favor of a certain Shaikh Abu Bakr be implemented in the following manner. First, he was to confirm Shaikh Abu Bakr with the supervision of the *dargah* of Shaikh Ladali Ansar, a saint who does not appear in the hagiographic literature but whose tomb was evidently located in *pargana* Aland. Second, he was to allocate four *chawars* and seventy-seven *bighas* of land yielding 225 *huns* to meet expenses for supervising the *dargah*, leading prayers there, and providing for the public kitchen (*langar-khana*). Third, he was to reserve from the above lands sixty cultivated *bighas* for expenses of the *'urs* celebrations, the feast of Kanduri, and grain for pigeons. Fourth, he was to allocate to Abu Bakr cash from eleven months of *sa'ir* taxes (taxes other than land revenue) of Aland town. And finally, he was to continue in the shaikh's favor an earlier grant of thirty *bighas* of orchard in the town of Aland.[26]

The above *farman* indicates that the operation and maintenance of a *dargah* was a well-organized affair thoroughly integrated with government interests and expenditures. It also graphically illustrates the paramount importance of land in the social and economic organization of medieval Bijapur and how the control of land could be converted to the control of people. For it was by means of the judicious allocation of the material resources yielded up through land revenue that the court could create elite groups of whomever it pleased. In the present instance we are concerned with how the court's use of *in'am* grants could affect

[26] Khwaja Bandanawaz Collection, 'Adil Shahi Farmans. Persian MS (Hyderabad: State Archives of Andhra Pradesh), Farman no. 8.

the Sufis. While most of the income derived from *in'am* lands was specifically allocated for maintaining the *dargahs* as public institutions, much of it undoubtedly served to supplement the income of those *pirzadas* who were already receiving money in gifts from their devotees. This twin source of income, in addition to the social status acquired by becoming an *in'amdar*, coincided with and possibly served to accelerate institutional changes among Bijapur's Sufis. This process can be best illustrated with reference to case studies of several landed families of Sufis living in late seventeenth century Bijapur.

The State and the Family of Shah Mustafa and Qasim Qadiri

Both Mustafa and Qasim Qadiri, brothers of the Reformist Sufi Abu'l-Hasan Qadiri, led reclusive lives in Bijapur and both haughtily refused audience with Sultan Ibrahim II. As much as any other Sufis of Bijapur, they lived the ideals of ascetic poverty and aloofness from worldly affairs—ideals that so many immigrant Sufis to Bijapur had brought with them. Yet the descendants of these brothers, whose spiritual and family genealogy is indicated in Chart 6, overturned these ideals and freely accepted grants

Chart 6

DESCENDANTS OF MUSTAFA AND QASIM QADIRI

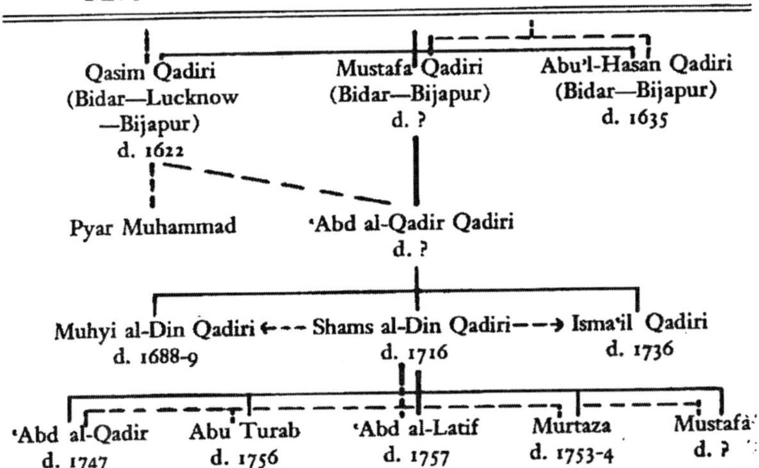

NOTE: Unbroken lines indicate familial lineage; broken lines indicate spiritual lineage.

from the 'Adil Shahi court. These actions appear to have had a profound impact on the descendants.

Shah Qasim Qadiri had a *khanaqah* in Bijapur but no sons, while his brother Mustafa had a son, 'Abd al-Qadir, but apparently no *khanaqah*. Consequently, it was 'Abd al-Qadir who became the successor to Shah Qasim's *khanaqah* when Qasim, his uncle, died in 1622. Yet it was also 'Abd al-Qadir who accepted the sort of royal favors that his father and uncle had refused. Approaching the *sajjada-nishin* after the death of his father, Shah Mustafa, Sultan Ibrahim II expressed regret that throughout Shah Mustafa's life the court had neglected the Sufi's welfare. The sultan accordingly offered to build a dome over Shah Mustafa's grave. In the best tradition of his father and uncle, 'Abd al-Qadir refused the offer.[27] This attitude, however, soon changed. The biography of Bijapur's Qadiri Sufis, the *Sahifat-i Ahl-i Huda*, records the following exchange between Sufi and sultan:

> In that same meeting Sultan Ibrahim fixed several villages in *ma'ash* [land grant, similar to an *in'am*] for the necessary expenditures of the Saiyid's followers. And most of the Sultanate's nobility contributed to this *ma'ash* from their own *jagirs* according to their capacities. Any further land grants he acquired were spent on his followers.[28]

After Sultan Ibrahim II's death Sultan Muhammad gave 'Abd al-Qadir a plot of land and a building which is known today as "Gachi Mahal" and is located adjacent to Qasim Qadiri's *dargah* near Bijapur's Jami' Mosque.[29] Towards the end of his life, however, 'Abd al-Qadir is said to have had second thoughts about the alliance with the state into which he had entered. Fearing that after his death his three sons would quarrel over the rights to the lands given him by the court, he burned all the *farmans* and other court documents in his possession, hoping in this way to restore the family to the landless and penniless state of his ancestors.[30]

But 'Abd al-Qadir's efforts notwithstanding, land managed to creep into the lives of at least two of his three sons. The present-day *sajjada-nishin* at the Qasim Qadiri *dargah* possesses a *farman* issued in 1676 by Sikandar 'Adil Shah donating an *in'am* of two

[27] *Sahifat*, Urdu edn., p. 46.
[28] *Sahifat*, MS copy, p. 92; Urdu edn., p. 46.
[29] *Sahifat*, Urdu edn., p. 43.
[30] Ibid., p. 47.

entire villages to 'Abd al-Qadir's two elder sons, Shams al-Din (d. 1716) and Isma'il (d. 1736).[31] According to the *Sahifat-i Ahl-i Huda*, on the other hand, the elder son and *sajjada-nishin* of the *dargah*, Saiyid Shams al-Din Qadiri, did not possess any *in'am* at the time of the Mughal conquest in 1686. When Aurangzeb queried Shams al-Din as to whether he owned any land, the Sufi replied that he had none and furthermore refused three offers of *in'am* grants made by the victorious Mughal Emperor.[32] The biography further states that Saiyid Shams al-Din, though he was the successor to the Qasim Qadiri *dargah* in Bijapur, migrated late in his life to the village of Gomarsi in *pargana* Sindhnur, located 100 miles southeast of Bijapur city near the Tungabhadra River.[33] Since this village was one of the very same villages that Sultan Sikandar in the above mentioned *farman* of 1676 had granted to Shams al-Din and his younger brother Isma'il, it is clear that the *sajjada-nishin* must have enjoyed at least partial possession of the Gomarsi *in'am* ever since Sikandar 'Adil Shah's reign.

But why does the *Sahifat-i Ahl-i Huda* have Shams al-Din deny to Aurangzeb his *in'am* holdings when an independent *farman* proves that the Sufi had held the land before the Mughal conquest? The answer probably lies in the tendency of most hagiographic accounts to depict Sufis as detached from worldly affairs despite their worldly activities; hence, the occasional flamboyant encounters between Sufi and sultan in which the former rejects the values of the latter. On the other hand, the same hagiographic accounts were frequently written by descendants and heirs of the very Sufis they describe. Compilers of Sufi biographies could hardly deny the presence of *in'ams* in their families when their own livelihoods often depended on them. Such was evidently the case with the account of Shams al-Din Qadiri in the *Sahifat-i*

[31] *Farman* of Sikandar 'Adil Shah, dated A.H. 12 Rajab 1087. Persian MS (Bijapur: Gachi Mahal). The town of Sindhnur is located 35 miles northwest of Adoni in the Tungabhadra valley. The two villages mentioned in the *farman* were Gomarsi and Madaldani. Gomarsi was said in the *Sahifat-i Ahl-i Huda* to lie just several miles from the town of Sindhnur (*Sahifat*, Urdu edn., p. 62). It is not, however, found on modern maps. "Madaldani" might be either the present village of Butaldinni, two miles north of Sindhnur town; or the village of Maldanni, six miles east of Sindhnur town.

[32] *Sahifat*, Urdu edn., p. 52.

[33] Ibid., p. 87.

Ahl-i Huda, a biography compiled in 1796-97 by one of the Sufi's great-grandsons and heirs, Saiyid Muhyi al-Din Qadiri (d. 1831-32). The compiler apparently wished to account for the existence of *in'ams* in Shams al-Din's family without maligning the sanctity of his own great-grandfather. To this end something of a villain was made of the Sufi's younger brother, Isma'il. According to this biography although Shams al-Din had refused any *in'am* from the emperor, Isma'il, from whom the compiler was not descended, accepted from Aurangzeb not only the two villages in *pargana* Sindhnur, but also two *chawars* in the village of Bobleshwar, located just fifteen miles southwest of Bijapur city. He is said to have done this, moreover, without the knowledge of his brother Shams al-Din, who had moved to Gomarsi. Then, after the death of Shams al-Din, whose five sons in Bijapur were entrusted to Isma'il's care, the *in'am* was transferred to the children.[34] By this account the piety and humility of Shams al-Din was scrupulously kept intact while the *in'am* was nonetheless injected into the family bloodstream.[35]

By the time of the generation succeeding Saiyid Shams al-Din, thirty years after the collapse of the dynasty, all of the immediate Sufi heirs to Qasim Qadiri's *dargah* had become full-time landholders retaining few vestiges of their inheritance from Islamic mysticism. The eldest of Shams al-Din's five sons, 'Abd al-Qadir (d. 1747), was born in Bijapur, received his *khilafat* from his father and later moved to the family estate in Gomarsi. There, he enjoyed a comfortable living derived from the village income, which even afforded him several maidservants and a harem.[36] As the eldest son, he evidently had inherited his father's *in'am* grant of Gomarsi village. However, owing to land disputes with other share-holders (*hissa-daran*) in Gomarsi—it is not stated whether these included his own brothers—'Abd al-Qadir left the village for Sira, in modern Tumkur District. Eventually, though, he was

[34] Ibid., pp. 64 f.

[35] Of all the Qadiri Sufis mentioned in the *Sahifat-i Ahl-i Huda*, Saiyid Shams al-Din Qadiri is accorded the most numerous and the most fanciful miracles. His title is rather unabashedly given as "The knower of God, the one who mixes with the Divine, the saint of God, the perceiver of God, the exemplar among perfect men, the way of the community and the faith, the best of monotheists, Hazrat Saiyid Shams al-Din Qadiri" (*Sahifat*, MS copy, p. 98).

[36] *Sahifat*, Urdu edn., pp. 67 f., 72.

persuaded by his brothers to return to Gomarsi, where he died.[37]

A similar pattern of *pirzadas* immersed in worldly concerns is found in the other sons of Saiyid Shams al-Din. His second son, Abu Turab (d. 1756), lived and died in Bijapur where he likewise enjoyed some lands in *in'am*.[38] His third son, 'Abd al-Latif (d. 1757), migrated from Bijapur to Gomarsi where he continued to live on a state pension.[39] His fourth son, Murtaza (d. 1754), initially accompanied his father from Bijapur to Gomarsi. But when Shams al-Din appointed him the *sajjada-nishin* of the Qasim Qadiri *dargah*, the position that Shams al-Din himself had held, the son returned to Bijapur.[40] Murtaza's integration with the city's orthodox establishment is indicated by the fact that after his return to Bijapur and installment as the chief manager of the Qasim *dargah*, he married the daughter of a prominent *sadr*, a chief officer in the judicial administration in the Mughal province of Bijapur. Later, after Bijapur had passed from Mughal control to that of the Nizam of Hyderabad (1724), Saiyid Murtaza Qadiri was given some lands in the city whose revenues were reserved for his personal use.[41]

From the time of Saiyid Shams al-Din Qadiri the family thus operated on two bases of influence. One of these was the *dargah* of Qasim Qadiri in Bijapur. Administered chiefly by the *sajjada-nishin* and his attendants, the tomb of the renowned ancestor gave the family of *pirzadas* their credibility and legitimacy among the *dargah's* many devotees.[42] The second base of the family's influence was the various *in'am* holdings both in the city and in villages, particularly the village of Gomarsi near the town of Sindhnur. Here, those members of the family other than the *sajjada-nishin* became firmly entrenched as a resident petty gentry. The extent to which their life-style as *in'amdars* had merged with

[37] Ibid., p. 68. [38] Ibid., p. 73. [39] Ibid., p. 77.

[40] Abu'l-Hasan Qadiri II, *Makhzan al-Ansab*, pp. 156 f.; *Sahifat*, Urdu edn., pp. 83, 87.

[41] *Sahifat*, Urdu edn., pp. 83 f., 87.

[42] Today the *dargah* is out of use, though a *sajjada-nishin* still lives in a nearby building. The *dargah's* discontinued use can be quickly ascertained by its lack of whitewash, which devotees are fond of coating on the "living" *dargahs* of Bijapur. But the Qasim Qadiri courtyard is nonetheless picturesque. On its western side is a mosque, on its northern side the tomb of Qasim Qadiri, and in the center are the graves of many of the family descendants discussed above.

that of the local Muslim nobility is graphically reflected in the tragic fate of Shams al-Din's fifth and youngest son, Saiyid Mustafa. In *pargana* Sindhnur, where Mustafa resided as did some of his brothers, the *desai* happened to be a Muslim. One day several Hindu pearl merchants, seeking to avenge a crime earlier committed by this *desai's* father against some of their caste-fellows, attacked and killed Mustafa on the mistaken belief that he was the *desai* they sought. The cause of the mistaken identity, records the *Sahifat-i Ahl-i Huda*, was the similarity between Saiyid Mustafa's lavish clothing and that of the intended victim.[43]

By the collapse of the dynasty in 1686, and continuing into the eighteenth century, two important developments had taken place within the family descended from Mustafa and Qasim Qadiri. First, the *dargah* and the *in'am* grants that supported it had emerged as the two central institutions of the family; and second, the *khanaqah*, in the sense of a hospice inhabited by practicing mystics, had vanished with the death of Shah Qasim himself. More precisely, in both a physical and an institutional sense the *khanaqah* of Shah Qasim Qadiri had at his death been replaced by the *dargah* that still stands today.

The State and the Family of Bandanawaz Gisudaraz[44]

The above interpretation of the family of Mustafa and Qasim Qadiri has been based primarily on the biography compiled by an early nineteenth century descendant of the Sufis he described. The shortcomings of hagiographical accounts in general and of the *Sahifat-i Ahl-i Huda* in particular have been mentioned above; and indeed, only a single but crucial *farman*—that of Sikandar 'Adil Shah to Isma'il and Shams al-Din Qadiri—can be brought to bear in verifying the biographer's account of the family's landed status. With the family of Saiyid Muhammad Husaini Bandanawaz Gisudaraz of Gulbarga, on the other hand, essentially the same process of institutional evolution can be documented with harder data. This includes a series of over twenty-five *farmans*

[43] *Sahifat*, Urdu edn., pp. 78 f. No date is given for this event. It evidently took place sometime in the early eighteenth century.

[44] This section has been published in slightly different form in my article "The Court and the Dargah in the Seventeenth Century Deccan," *Indian Economic and Social History Review*, 10 (March 1973), pp. 50-63.

in favor of the *sajjada-nishin* of the Bandanawaz *dargah* dispatched by the Bijapur court over the seventeen-year period, 1659-76. These *farmans* not only corroborate the case of Mustafa and Qasim Qadiri's successors in documenting the formation of a class of Sufi *in'amdars*; they also afford deeper insights into the relations between the *in'amdars* and the court.

Both the *dargah* of Bandanawaz Gisudaraz and the *in'am* grants supporting it had become hallowed institutions in the Deccan nearly from the moment of the famous saint's death in 1422. The Bahmani sultans granted the first *in'am* lands to Gisudaraz in the early fifteenth century and thereafter continued them in favor of the Sufi's family descendants. After the city of Gulbarga and its surrounding lands passed to Bijapur's control in the early sixteenth century the 'Adil Shahi court evidently honored these grants, for in 1609 the historian Firishta noted that "in the present day . . . most of the estates given by the former princes are still in possession of the Syud's descendants."[45]

The *dargah* of Bandanawaz Gisudaraz was originally constructed in the year of the Sufi's death and was enlarged in 1640. Praised by Sultan Ibrahim II and visited at least twice by Sultan Muhammad, this *dargah* had become by the mid-seventeenth century one of the great devotional centers of the Deccan, rivaled perhaps only by the temple of Vithoba at Pandharpur.[46] The most important annual event of the Bandanawaz *dargah*, as is true of any *dargah*, was the *'urs*, celebrated on the saint's death date. This being the biggest *dargah* of the kingdom, or even of the Deccan, the Bandanawaz *'urs* had been and still is a particularly celebrated institution. In early March 1673 Abbé Carré, a French agent then en route from Surat to Madras, traveled through Gulbarga around the time of the *'urs* celebration. His vivid description of this event merits quoting in full because its fine attention to detail accurately illustrates the sort of popular devotionalism that characterized Sufism in its third or *ta'ifa* phase in Bijapur.

[45] Firishta, *Tarikh-i Firishta*, I, p. 320. (Briggs's translation, II, p. 245.)

[46] Firishta, a contemporary witness to the widespread belief that commoners had in Gisudaraz and his tomb, wrote: "The people of the Deccan have such respect for the saint that a Deccany, on being once asked whom he considered the greatest personage, the Prophet Mahomed or the Syud, replied, with some surprise at the question, that although the Prophet was undoubtedly a great man, yet Syud Mahomed Geesoo-duraz was a far superior order of being" (ibid., Briggs's translation, II, pp. 245-46).

Indeed, it is the best contemporary description of popular Sufism that survives from Bijapur's medieval period. "After having marched all the morning while it was cool," wrote the Abbé,

> I was surprised to find the road [to Gulbarga] full of processions of fakirs and Hindus. . . . Most of the men had a sort of cradle on their heads, covered by little streamers of cock's feathers, bells, and the like. The women and children all carried sticks which they lifted in the air, for the wind to turn whirligigs on them, made of cloth in all sorts of colours. They also carried plates of copper, little pots, and a sort of caldron on which they beat as on our Basque drums. Others, who had shaved their heads, carried their hair on the end of sticks, as if it was a very precious possession. . . . Here [in the village of "Trapour"] were still more of the same sort of folk that I had met on the road. This led me to enquire of a local Hindu, who came to speak to me, what it all meant. "Why," he replied, "don't you know that these are holy families, who have come from a great distance to worship their saint called Mundun la Heb [Bandanawaz] whom they have at Calberga, a large village about two leagues from here. Every year there is a pilgrimage there by a great number of people such as you have seen. They are thus sanctified when they return home." "But," I said, "what is meant by all those instruments and streamers paraded by them?" "Those," he said, "are souvenirs of their pilgrimage, which they keep all their lives, and which they regard with much confidence and devotion in any afflictions or maladies that befall them. They put their children, when sick, into those little cradles you saw, and are quite content, whether the child lives or dies, because the cradle had been in the saint's house and had been sanctified by him. The little banners carried by the women are put on the head, or into the hands, of a woman in childbirth for her safe delivery. The copper pots and plates are for the food of anyone who is dangerously ill, and those who carry their hair on the end of sticks are, as you saw, quite young girls. They cut their hair, while virgins, to get it sanctified by the saint, and keep it carefully to show that they were very young at the time of this pilgrimage."[47]

[47] Abbé Carré, *The Travels of the Abbé Carré in India and the Near East, 1672 to 1674*, trans. by Lady Fawcett, ed. by Charles Fawcett (3 vols.; London: Hakluyt Society, 1947), II, pp. 323-25. Actually, the Abbé had

The "fakirs and Hindus" whom Abbé Carré had seen comprised the outer circle of devotees at the Bandanawaz *dargah*. That they represented the lower elements of both Muslim and Hindu society is suggested by the Abbé's astonishment at "the stupidity, coarseness and foolishment of these poor people," whose lives he judged as "the lowest and most infamous and unhappy in the world."[48]

The Abbé's account clearly shows the economic and religious importance that the Bandanawaz *dargah* possessed in the seventeenth century. The various "souvenirs" noted by Abbé Carré—streamers, bells, whirligigs, pots, plates, cradles—indicate that the celebrations were accompanied by great markets and fairs, which must have attracted considerable trade to Gulbarga. Similarly, the passage indicates the spiritual grip exerted by the *dargah* over the inestimable numbers of pilgrims and local devotees who participated in its functions. One sees this in various objects serving as talismans against sickness and in the special importance the pilgrimage represented in the lives of women and girls. The practice of a girl's having a lock of hair (*chonti*) consecrated in the name of a saint and later cut at the saint's *dargah* is a custom still current in various parts of India.[49] Hence, for both economic and religious reasons it is reasonable to assume that the leader of the Bandanawaz *dargah*, the *sajjada-nishin*, must have commanded a position of considerable influence in the kingdom at that time. For either or both of these reasons the 'Adil Shahi court deemed it politic to exercise its influence over the *dargah* and its *sajjada-nishin*, and extant *farmans* issued by the court between 1659 and 1676 illustrate how this took place.

The earliest surviving 'Adil Shahi communication regarding the Bandanawaz *dargah* is a *farman* issued early in 'Ali II's reign, in 1659, notifying the revenue officials of Gulbarga district to recog-

---

just missed the main festivities. The last and biggest day of the *'urs* celebrations, which corresponds to the actual date of the Sufi's death, is 16 Zi'l-Qa'da. In A.D. 1673 that date fell on the fifth of March. Since the passage quoted here was entered in the Abbé's journal on 9 March 1673 when en route to Gulbarga, he must have missed the peak festivities by four days and was evidently witnessing pilgrims leaving Gulbarga for their home villages.

[48] Ibid., II, p. 325.

[49] Ja'far Sharif, *Islam in India, or the Qanun-i-Islam: the Customs of the Musalmans of India*, trans. G. A. Herklots, ed. William Crooke (New Delhi: Oriental Books Reprint Corp., 1972), pp. 39 f., 135.

nize Shah Asad Allah Husaini as the rightful *sajjada-nishin* of the *dargah*.[50] Later that same year, on 12 October, the court issued three separate *farmans* to the *desais* and other revenue officials of districts Akalkot, Masarkal, and Raichur instructing them to release one village in each district for the *in'amdari* of Asad Allah Husaini.[51] A month later, on 9 November 1659, the court issued five more *farmans* to the revenue officials of districts Terdal, Masarkal, Raichur, Sagar, and Gulbarga directing the transfer of still more villages to the *sajjada-nishin*.[52] From each of the first four districts one village was reserved in *in'am*, while in Gulbarga district six and a half villages plus six and a half *chawars* from four other villages were placed in his favor.

In August 1660 another *farman* was sent to the officials of Gulbarga again confirming Shah Asad Allah as the legitimate *sajjada-nishin* at the Bandanawaz *dargah* and stating that "all the villages, gardens, *chawars*, houses, bazaars, etc., which are his shall continue with his children and grandchildren."[53] This royal assurance would seem redundant unless there had occurred a challenge to Asad Allah's authority at the *dargah*. The very next *farman* to Gulbarga, dated 26 February 1661, indicated that such was the case. A certain Shah Hazrat bin Shah Manjla had committed obstructions that the *sajjada-nishin* brought to the attention of the court, and which the court in turn brought to the attention of the Gulbarga revenue officials:

> But Shah Hazrat [bin Shah Manjla] does not desist from causing disturbances and will not allow the followers at the *dargah* to do service to Pir Dastgir [Asad Allah]. Insofar as the *in'ams*, the successorship, and the above-mentioned houses have already been apportioned by order of the *farmans*, what is the meaning that Shah Hazrat will not desist from causing disturbances and oppression, but rather extends the arm of appropriation?[54]

50 Khwaja Bandanawaz Collection, Farman no. 14.

51 Ibid., Farmans nos. 16, 19, 20.

52 Ibid., Farmans nos. 21, 22, 23, 24, 73. *In'ams* were taken from both directly administered districts (*mu'amala*) and locally administered districts (*pargana*). For example, Akalkot, Masarkal, and Terdal were *parganas*, while Raichur, Sagar, and Gulbarga were *mu'amalas* since they all had forts. In the context of *in'ams* however, the distinction is not pertinent, and both *mu'amalas* and *parganas* are here referred to simply as districts.

53 Ibid., Farman no. 27.

54 Ibid., Farman no. 30.

The court then ordered the Gulbarga officials thereafter to thwart any attempt by Shah Hazrat to interfere with the affairs of the *dargah*. It is evident that the court had already assumed for itself the role of protector of Shah Asad Allah and the Bandanawaz *dargah*.

In the next year a crisis developed within the *dargah's* leadership that prompted the court to intervene even more vigorously than before. A *farman* of 13 September 1662 explained that a certain Shah Buzurg had emerged claiming for himself the rightful successorship to the *dargah*, disputing the position of Shah Asad Allah. It is not certain what this man's family lineage was or on what basis he made his claim, but his assertion of successorship represented a far more fundamental threat to the *dargah* than interference with its functions. At issue here was a son's right to the spiritual succession of his father. The *farman* stated,

> The aforesaid case has been brought before the Chief Judge of the Faith [*ḥākim al-shar'*] of the Sultanate of Bijapur, as well as the high shaikhs and the great *'ulama*. . . .
>
> Therefore a satisfactory and peaceful solution for both [disputants] has been fixed. The successorship and management of the sacred *dargah* shall continue in the name of Shah Asad Allah, as it had been inherited by him from ancient times. And from the *in'ams* of the *dargah*, the villages of Nagarhal and Korampalli in the subdistrict of Chincholi, the village of Dhotarka Khurd in the subdistrict of Jasur, and the village of Hanchanal in the subdistrict of Nilogi, in Sagar district, shall be made over to Shah Buzurg.[55]

By transferring to Shah Buzurg several villages from the considerable *in'amdari* of the *dargah* the court apparently hoped to pacify the disputant while upholding Shah Asad Allah's rightful claim to the successorship.

What is most significant about this event is not how the court adjudicated the dispute, but that it was the court, not the *dargah*, which resolved it. Throughout the period 1659-76 the government with one hand gave the Bandanawaz *dargah* land grants while with the other hand it took away rights and functions that were specifically Sufi in nature. The most hallowed of these was

[55] Ibid., Farman no. 32.

the right of a *pir* to select his own spiritual followers, of whom the chief was the *sajjada-nishin*. Even though the *dargah* had replaced the *khanaqah* as the institutional basis of Bijapur's urban Sufis, and even though the office had become in practice hereditary, the *sajjada-nishin* remained in theory a spiritual successor and his selection remained in theory the prerogative of his predecessor. Economic dependence upon the court, however, had damaged this prerogative and undermined the spiritual nature of the office. Regardless of who claimed to be the legitimate successor at the Gulbarga shrine, only the court, as the 1662 case illustrates, was the final arbiter in the matter.

The court's intrusion in the *dargah's* affairs resulted not only from royal design, however, but probably also from the sheer mechanics of an administrative bureaucracy. In the event of an *in'amdar's* death, for example, local revenue officials would have to know in whose name to continue *in'am* payments. An original grant would have stated only that the *in'am* would continue in the hands of the *in'amdar's* descendants, without specifying those individuals by name. Only royal authorization would confirm the matter to the satisfaction of the local clerks. Hence, when Shah Asad Allah died and the issue of successorship again surfaced, the court on 10 March 1664 issued such authorization to its revenue clerks in Gulbarga: "Shah Asad Allah has died. Therefore his wish has been brought to [our] blessed memory, and in the way of royal kindness and kingly benevolence the successorship to the *dargah*, formerly held by the late Shah Asad Allah, has been bestowed upon his son, Shah Husain."[56] Now confirmed as the new *sajjada-nishin*, Shah Husain bin Asad Allah received all the villages in *in'am* formerly held by his father, plus some more subsequently granted in his own name in the Gulbarga region.[57] And in 1670 he was even allowed to establish his own Thursday bazaar at a town near Gulbarga and to keep the profits he derived from this enterprise.[58]

But the period of Shah Husain's successorship at the Bandanawaz *dargah* was not an auspicious one. In 1672 'Ali II died,

[56] Ibid., Farman no. 36.

[57] Ibid., Farman nos. 38, 41, 47, 48.

[58] Ibid., Farman no. 46. The name of the town was Sinur, which is not traceable on modern maps. It is possible that Sinur was the present village of Sidnur located eight miles south of Gulbarga, or possibly Sirnur, located twelve miles south of Gulbarga.

delivering the kingdom's leadership to quarreling regents and a factious nobility while the central administration seriously deteriorated. In 1677 Mughal armies, which had been hovering in the region for several decades, succeeded in wresting the city of Gulbarga from 'Adil Shahi control, thus severing all administrative connections between the *dargah* and the Bijapur court. The decade prior to the Mughal conquest of Gulbarga was as much a time of troubles for the Bandanawaz *dargah* as for the Bijapur court. Twice in this period Shah Hazrat bin Shah Manjla, the same man who in 1661 had committed obstructions at the *dargah*, asserted his own claim as successor to Shah Asad Allah.[59] In 1666 a certain Mir Muhammad Sarkhail had been appropriating for himself the cash flow from some of the *in'am* villages to the *dargah*.[60] Although both Shah Hazrat and Mir Muhammad were censured by the court, it is conjectural how effective Bijapur's *farmans* were when the central administration at this time was breaking down.

One of the clearest indications of the *dargah's* deteriorating affairs is found in a *farman* of 5 September 1672. This *farman* recorded that the *sajjada-nishin's* brother, Shah Akbar, had been murdered by a group of Hindus just outside Gulbarga. Shah Akbar, stated the *farman*, "was walking from Gulbarga to the village of Kirsavali, one of the *in'ams* of the *dargah*. On the road were gathered some revenue officials and other Hindus of the village of Sirasgi. According to Hindu custom they had brought out from their village an image of Kans [a foe of Krishna], which they were about to 'kill.' But this ritual was obstructed by Shah Akbar, who thereupon was murdered by the accursed Hindus."[61]

Not only were communal relations involving Gulbarga *in'amdars* deteriorating in this period, but these individuals were flaunting their high status to excessive degrees. Abbé Carré noted in 1673 that the most powerful of the "fakirs" of Gulbarga, "and those who are considered the wisest and most judicious in this country, are esteemed and worshipped to such an extent that they are allowed to commit the most dreadful acts in a household,

[59] Ibid., Farman nos. 49, 54. [60] Ibid., Farman no. 42.

[61] Ibid., Farman no. 51. The *farman* then awarded three villages in *in'am* to Shah Akbar's mother to support herself and the three wives of her slain son. No steps were taken, at least by the central government, to avenge Akbar's murder.

which is supposed to be sanctified thereby."[62] Twenty-two years later another European, John F. Gemelli Careri, traveled along the Konkan Coast and in parts of the Deccan plateau near Goa and also noticed the remarkable privileges accorded to the "fakirs." By "fakirs" Careri presumably referred to the same sort of *pirzadas* to whom his French contemporary, Abbé Carré, referred with respect to the functionaries of the Bandanawaz *dargah*. "The Gentils," wrote Careri, "pay so great a Respect to these Penitents, that they think themselves happy, who can Prostitute Daughters, Sisters, or Kins-women to their Leudness, which they believe lawful in them; and for this Reason there are so many Thousands of Vagabond *Fakirs* throughout *India*."[63] As for the later history of the *pirzadas* of the Bandanawaz shrine, an 1855 British gazetteer stated that the vices committed by these descendants eventually compelled the Nizam's government to expel them from Gulbarga and to appoint a government nominee to receive the *in'am* revenues.[64]

Landed Sufis in Relation to the Common Populace

In discussing the relations between the landed Sufis and the common population of Bijapur it is important to distinguish those groups that believed in the *barakat* of the *dargah* and the *pirzadas* from those non-Muslim groups that were in no way associated with these institutions of popular Sufism. With respect to the comments of Abbé Carré and Careri concerning "the most dreadful acts in a household" and the "leudness" of the *pirzadas*, it is evident that they were referring to the *pirzadas*' behavior not with respect to the unaffiliated non-Muslim population in general, but rather to the lower-class female constituency that formed the outer circle of devotees at the *dargahs*. It is also evident that the sort of behavior to which the European travelers referred represented the most extreme cases of abuse of the vast social prestige accorded to this group. A more usual manifestation of the *pirzadas*' prestige seems to have been the air of nobility that they had derived from their landed status. Of course this air of nobility

[62] Carré, *Travels of the Abbé Carré*, II, p. 325.

[63] Surendranath Sen, ed., *The Indian Travels of Thevenot and Careri* (New Delhi: National Archives of India, 1949), p. 258.

[64] *A Gazetteer of Southern India* (Madras: Pharoah and Co., 1855), p. 676.

was altogether incompatible with the stern standards of austerity and poverty espoused by the first-generation Sufi migrants in Bijapur, many of whom were the immediate predecessors of the people we are considering here. One must be very careful in assessing the role of the *in'am* as causing this phenomenon. Certainly the high social status of the *pirzadas* was already assured on the basis of the saintly *barakat* they had inherited by birth. Cases such as that of Muhammad Mudarris illustrate that the *in'am* grant was not crucial, or even necessary, for the progression of institutional Sufism from the *tariqa* to the *ta'ifa* stage. Nonetheless the receiving of *in'am* grants does seem to have enhanced the prestige enjoyed by *pirzadas* and, in a very direct way, to have accelerated an evolutionary process inherent in the history of Sufism.

The case of Shah Habib Allah Sibghat Allahi (d. 1632) perhaps illustrates how the status of being an *in'amdar* affected his esteem in the eyes of his devotees. It is significant that Shah Habib Allah was the leading *khalifa* of one of the most zealous and puritanical reformists in the history of Bijapur, Shah Sibghat Allah. But notwithstanding Shah Sibghat Allah's stern puritanism and his problems with the court, Habib Allah joined the ranks of the landed Sufis only shortly after the court had expelled Sibghat Allah to Arabia. When Habib Allah's *murids* objected to their *pir's* having accepted from Sultan Ibrahim II an *in'am* of a village worth 700 *huns* in land revenue, the Sufi gave in reply one of the few recorded justifications for such an action. By accepting the grant, he argued, cash that otherwise would only fill the central treasury could now be diverted to the people.[65] Commendable as this rationale would appear, it is doubtful that the lives of his followers were materially enhanced by his having accepted the grant. His discourses (*malfuzat*), recorded during his lifetime by his own son, reflect an image of a man who, seated upon his palanquin, appeared to be taking on the airs of a noble: "Five wandering faqirs, dressed in green, stood waiting at the head of the road with jugs of water in their hands. When they saw my palanquin they said to each other. 'This man is Habib Allah! This man is Habib Allah!' "[66]

[65] *Malfuzat-i Shah Sibghat Allah*, fol. 37a.
[66] Ibid., fol. 38a.

With reference to modern Gujarat it has recently been observed that the *pirzadas* as a class "lost the fervour of their predecessors and looked upon their followers more as a source of revenue than as a people to be guided in the Islamic way."[67] Although the same statement may legitimately be made with reference to the seventeenth-century *pirzadas* of Bijapur, one must put the issue in proper perspective. The passage quoted above concerning Shah Habib Allah suggests that from the perspective of the devotees at the *dargah* the landed *pirzadas* cannot be dismissed as a class of social parasites draining their monetary resources or those of the state. Even when they collected stipends like nobles, dressed like nobles, or were carried about in palanquins like nobles, their influence among the common population derived from something even more fundamental than land. Living in the luster of a fortunate ancestry, the landed Sufis, though perhaps ignorant of Sufism, filled a need in the spiritual lives of the common devotees who attended the *dargahs*. The latter, after all, went to a *dargah* for communication with a departed saint, and the physical structure standing over the grave of that saint gradually acquired a spiritual life of its own quite independent of the more worldly attendants who supervised it. In the devotees' eyes, then, there may have been no necessary contradiction between the sanctity of the building and the material prosperity of its *in'amdars*. Indeed, the devotees may have considered it appropriate that the spiritual power of a deceased saint be expressed in the material prosperity of his descendants.

If the landed Sufis' relations with their own devotees were naturally conditioned by the belief the latter had in the *dargahs*, relations with the non-Muslims unaffiliated with *dargahs* tended to be strained, and sometimes violent. In both of the cases examined above concerning the *pirzadas* at the Qasim Qadiri and Bandanawaz *dargahs*, relations with unaffiliated Hindus reached outright violence. We have seen that the youngest son of one *sajjada-nishin* was killed by Hindu merchants who mistook the Sufi for a Muslim noble, and that the brother of another *sajjada-nishin* was killed while interfering with a Hindu ritual near Gulbarga. These were not isolated examples. Sufis seem to have been participating in the various struggles that accompanied the

[67] Misra, *Muslim Communities in Gujarat*, p. 161.

general rise in the level of violence in late seventeenth century Bijapur. Careri, the Italian traveler who was in the Deccan plateau near Goa in 1695, wrote of their relations with *bairagis*, a class of Hindu mendicants and ascetics: "When the *Fakirs* meet with *Baraghis* (which is another sort of Penitents, differently habited, with their Hair and Beard shav'd) they Fight desperately."[68]

One of the most interesting developments of this period, representing in several senses a throwback to the Warrior Sufis of the early fourteenth century, was that landed Sufis both participated in the Hindu-Muslim conflicts that were then flaring up, and more significantly, personally gave such conflicts the sanction of holy war, or *jihad*. This had not happened for over three centuries in the Bijapur region, and it perhaps indicates the degree to which communal accord had broken down in the rural districts as the 'Adil Shahi state underwent its decline. In May 1662, the hottest month of the year and perhaps the most likely time for such events to occur, a communal riot broke out in Kurnool, a provincial outpost located 175 miles southeast of the capital city. A Muslim revenue officer, whose dispute with a Hindu had sparked the riot, went to the residence of his own *pir*, Shah 'Abd Allah La-ubali, with the aim of requesting the latter to mobilize the Muslims of Kurnool by declaring a general *jihad*. Although 'Abd Allah was not home at that time, his younger brother 'Isa La-ubali was present. The revenue officer thereupon asked the younger brother to oblige in this matter. Shah 'Isa not only complied with the request but joined the struggle himself and, on 6 May 1662, was killed.[69]

Nine years later a similar fate befell Shah 'Abd Allah La-ubali himself. The eldest son of a Qadiri *saiyid* who had migrated from Baghdad to Kurnool in the reign of Sultan Ibrahim II, Shah 'Abd Allah had received his *khilafat* both from Shaikh 'Ali, his father's only *khalifa*, and from the well-known Reformist Sufi Shah Abu'l-Hasan Qadiri.[70] With the latter he had marital as well as spiritual ties, for he was married to Abu'l-Hasan's daughter. Toward the end of March 1671 the Sufi was passing through Chitradurga, a town in a part of the Karnatak that was then revolting against 'Adil Shahi overlordship, located 75 miles south of the ruined city of Vijayanagar. There, the community of local

[68] Sen, *Indian Travels*, p. 258.

[69] *Latayif al-Latif*, pp. 196 f.

[70] Ibid., p. 45.

Muslims sought him out and, complaining that the Hindu chieftains (*nayak*) were persecuting them, begged that he help alleviate their condition. "The injunction of Islam is this," replied 'Abd Allah, "that one must anticipate the struggle before they do. I shall be a partner to your *jihad*." In the conflict that ensued 'Abd Allah, like his younger brother before him, was slain.[71]

Shah 'Isa La-ubali was possibly the first Bijapuri Sufi since the Warrior Sufis of the fourteenth century to have been slain at the hands of Hindus. More than that, the phenomenon of Sufis using their prestige to lead, or as was more likely the case, to legitimize a *jihad* spelled the ultimate breakdown of relations between landed Sufis and non-Muslims. There is no record of any landed or orthodox Sufi in the kingdom at this time urging the policy of "peace with all" (*suhl-i kull*), a slogan that many writers have attributed to Indian Sufis generally. On the contrary, what little evidence we have indicates that as Hindu-Muslim relations deteriorated in late seventeenth century Bijapur, such Sufis threw in their lot with the Muslim establishment. There is some indication, furthermore, that after conquering Bijapur in 1686 Aurangzeb gave his blessings to this development and in other ways contributed to widening the gap between landed Sufis and non-Muslims. When granting a *jagir* to a certain Shams al-Din al-Basri he ordered the Hindus of Raichur city to evacuate the area in which the Sufi was to live.[72] More significant still, by granting the descendants of Shah 'Abd Allah La-ubali a *jagir* in the Karnatak he was in a way consecrating a Sufi martyr slain by infidels only several years earlier.[73]

Finally, it might be noted that this antagonism between Hindus and landed *pirzadas* seems to have taken place outside the context of the *dargahs* with which many *pirzadas* were associated. For the great tombs of Sufi saints had taken root in Indian soil as sacred places immune from communal strife and remained vitally important in the lives of common folk, particularly village women. Thus the *chakki-namas* and the votive devotionalism that were associated with the *dargahs* of both the city and the countryside continued to work their effect of absorbing non-Muslims into the folk Islam of popular Sufism despite the flaring up of Hindu-

[71] Ibid., pp. 53 f.

[72] *Waqi'at*, III, p. 354.

[73] *Latayif al-Latif*, p. 57. The name of the *jagir* was Kalkonda, which has not been located on modern maps.

Muslim tensions in the late seventeenth century. Even though some of these conflicts involved the landed *pirzadas* themselves, they never seem to have involved the Hindu devotees of the *dargahs*.

Summary

Among urban Sufis of late seventeenth century Bijapur deep institutional changes were taking place. Their identity with one or another fraternal order began to vanish when the practice of multiple membership became widespread. This development, in turn, was an early indication of the replacement of the cult of the order by the cult of the personality. While this may have broadened the base of popular Sufism by culminating eventually in *pir*-worship, it did so at the expense of the various schools of Islamic mysticism that had theretofore enriched the intellectual aspect of Sufism. Moreover, heredity had thoroughly replaced merit as the criterion of selection for the leadership of *khanaqahs*, and later, of *dargahs*. Hereditary succession in turn contributed to the emergence of a class of sons of *pirs*, the *pirzadas*, whose fortunate ancestry enabled them to capitalize on the personality cults forming around their predecessors.

The most fundamental development of this period saw the replacement of the *khanaqah* by the *dargah* as the basic institution of late Sufism in Bijapur. The tomb of a saint served as a focal point both for the *pir*-worship of the common devotees and the sustenance of the *pirzada* class. When Hashim Pir 'Alawi died in 1646, for example, his sons and grandsons did not continue teaching in their predecessor's *khanaqah* but built a tomb over his grave. There, Hashim Pir's grandson Shah Burhan al-Din 'Alawi (d. 1674) established himself as the first *sajjada-nishin* of the Hashim *dargah* and, as his descendants would do after him, received the offerings in flowers or coins given by the devotees at the *dargah*.[74] The same thing was happening at the Qasim Qadiri *dargah*, the Habib Allah Sibghat Allahi *dargah*, the Hamīd Qadiri *dargah*, the 'Abd al-Razzaq *dargah*, and in Gulbarga at the Bandanawaz *dargah*, among others.

The case of Muhammad Mudarris and his three sons indicates

[74] *Ganj-i Asrar*, fol. 112b.

that some of these changes were intrinsic to the evolution of institutional Sufism and developed independent of state power or policy. On the other hand, the cases of the Qasim Qadiri and Bandanawaz families as examined above suggest that the land grant in *in'am* played an important part in accelerating some of these and other institutional changes. For example, the court's policy respecting the allocation of *in'am* grants clearly reveals its preference for supporting the large and socially important *dargah* as opposed to the lonely *khanaqah* of a Sufi and his small circle of adepts. For it was the tombs, not the hospices, that attracted the large crowds of common devotees and consequently fell within the court's sphere of political patronage. While it cannot be said that court interests as reflected in its *in'am* policies were alone responsible for the evolution from *tariqa* to *ta'ifa* Sufism, they certainly tended to entrench and to confirm the *dargah* as the Sufis' basic institutional unit.

A second effect of the *in'am* grant was that it served as the instrument by which the state could penetrate the internal affairs of a *dargah*. Not only were the *farmans* specific about how the money from *in'am* lands was to be spent; the court also assumed the right to decide the all-important question of succession to a *dargah's* leadership, as seen in the *farmans* concerning the Bandanawaz *dargah* in Gulbarga. Since land grants were given nominally to Sufis but implicitly to a *dargah*, the passing of the successorship to a *dargah* carried with spiritual succession the lands formerly granted by the court. And since matters of land inheritance could be settled only in court, the entire matter of spiritual succession was brought into the jurisdiction of the state. In this way the state arrogated to itself one of the bases of institutional Sufism—the right to choose one's own successor.

Finally, the issuance of *in'am* grants generally succeeded in realizing one of its primary aims, namely, the purchase of the political loyalty of their recipients. Part of the price of becoming an *in'amdar*, judging from the closing lines of many *farmans* granting land to Sufis, was to pray for the state and the sultan—presumably in the *dargah's* mosque and among the devotees. But when the state was in danger, as was frequently the case after 1657, the government occasionally received considerably more from its landed Sufis. The *Rauzat al-Auliya* relates a tradition that Saiyid Zain Muqbil (d. 1718), who had received an *in'am* of several villages from Sultan 'Ali II, was brought to court by the sultan to offer prayers for Bijapur during one of Shivaji's raids. This he did; in fact he did much more. In the Sufi context any form of gift given by a *pir* to a *murid* was called a *ta'wiz* and consisted of a written *zikr* for the *murid* to memorize. In the popular Sufism of the *dargahs*, however, the *ta'wiz* came to denote any kind of talisman or magical charm given by a *pir* to the common devotees. What Zain Muqbil gave to Sultan 'Ali II was a *ta'wiz* consisting of a piece of paper with a prayer written on it, which the sultan was instructed to attach over the muzzle of the city's cannon before firing at the Marathas.[75] This episode quite clearly illustrates the harnessing of degenerate Sufism to state interests. In the 1660s and 1670s the 'Adil Shahi government, quite likely because it perceived its own decline as resulting from a lack of Islamic orthodoxy in the kingdom, endeavored to rally around the standard of political loyalty and religious orthodoxy all key elements of the Muslim population, including especially the Sufis. To this end the land grant in *in'am* proved the decisive instrument in creating for the later sultans of Bijapur what the Mughal Emperor Jahangir called his "army of prayer."

In sum, the landed Sufis of Bijapur reflected the very decline of the state in which they lived. Attached by land grants to a state that was itself sinking, they jealously clung to their own vested interests, namely the land, while exhibiting little regard for compatible relations with non-Muslims unaffiliated with their *dargahs*. Although the conquest of Bijapur in 1686 ended the 'Adil Shahi monarchy, it did not spell the ruin of landed Sufis. Aurangzeb both renewed existing *in'am* grants and granted new ones.[76] Indeed, one could expect that among the first to tender their submission to the new Mughal regime were the landed *pirzadas*, for without government-bestowed *in'ams* there could be no *in'amdars*.

[75] *Rauzat*, copy A, p. 198.
[76] *Basatin*, pp. 567 f.

Chapter Nine

SUFIS AS DERVISHES

Not all Sufis of the late ʻAdil Shahi period joined the ranks of the kingdom's landed class. Nor were all attached to the flourishing *dargahs* of their predecessors. On the contrary, just as a number of the kingdom's Sufis were at this time absorbed into the urban establishment of the ruling orthodox Muslims, many others—the dervishes—adopted life styles in apparent defiance of that establishment. J. S. Trimingham has distinguished the term "dervish" from the more general term "Sufi" by stressing the former's emphasis upon practice as opposed to theory. "The *sufi* follows a mystical theory or doctrine," he wrote, "the *darwish* practices the mystical Way. Of course, one is a *darwish* and a *sufi* at the same time and there is no essential distinction in theory. . . . but in practice there is a disproportion of emphasis, some *sufis* being predominantly intellect or creative imagination, like Ibn ʻArabi, and others mainly dervishes, all feeling, emotion, and action."[1]

The word consistently used by contemporary and later biographers to describe the "dervishes" of seventeenth-century Bijapur was "*majzub*," a term that literally and most generally means someone "attracted" to God. In the context in which our sources used the term, however, it further denoted a person who had forsaken the path of strict Islamic orthodoxy in favor of a life of unrestrained spiritual ecstasy. The social implication of this usage was that the *majzub*, to the extent that he departed from the *shariʻat* in his "attraction" to God, risked disapprobation by the community of Muslims. We find this in large measure to have

[1] Trimingham, *Sufi Orders*, p. 264. The distinction between "Sufi" and "dervish" is clearer when the terms are used in European rather than in Islamic languages. In the Persian sources used in this study the two terms were often used synonymously. In these same sources the Arabic word *majzub* was used to denote what in European languages is now meant by "dervish," i.e., an individual who, following Trimingham's account, emphasizes feeling, emotion and action over intellect or creative imagination. It is in this sense that the term "Dervish Sufi" is used in this study.

been the case. The *majzubs* espoused doctrines that were often heretical from the orthodox standpoint, they indulged in practices like the use of wine and opium that emphatically dissociated themselves from the *'ulama*, and they generally identified with non-elite rather than elite groups of the society. In short, they represented a type of Sufi that was quite opposite the landed *in'amdar-pirzada*. Indeed, there is evidence that they consciously opted for a social role in explicit reaction to, and rejection of, the type of Sufis they stigmatized as "worldly."

Many Dervish Sufis of seventeenth-century Bijapur were linked by either spiritual or family ties to the Chishtis of Shahpur Hillock. Concerning two such Sufis in particular there is a good deal of information. One was Shah Amin al-Din A'la (d. 1675), the only son of Burhan al-Din Janam and, like his father, the *sajjada-nishin* of the *khanaqah* of Miranji Shams al-'Ushshaq on Shahpur Hillock. The other was Muhammad Mahmud Bahri (d. 1717-18), a son of one of Burhan al-Din's *murids* and a resident of a town seventy miles east of Bijapur. First, detailed attention will be given to the lives and teachings of these two non-urban Chishtis. Bijapur's non-literate dervishes, about whom only scattered information has survived, will then be considered.

Amin al-Din A'la and Doctrinal Radicalism

Shah Amin al-Din A'la put into practice the spiritual life of which his father, Burhan al-Din Janam, had written. Born in the year of his father's death, 1597, Amin al-Din was raised and taught on Shahpur Hillock by three of Burhan al-Din Janam's most prominent *khalifas*: Mahmud Khush Dahan, Saiyid Dawal, and Saiyid Khudawand Shah.[2] Little is known of his activities during the entire first half of the seventeenth century, though it is certain that he had no contact with the courts of Ibrahim II and Muhammad 'Adil Shah. One biographical account relates only that early in his life he submerged himself in reclusive meditation for twelve years.[3] Another records that he spent his childhood and boyhood brooding at his father's tomb until finally, one moonlit night, he emerged from his reflections to declare to some devotees that union with God was possible only through insensible rapture

[2] Siddiqi, "Dakani Inscription," p. 80; *Shajarat al-Atqiya*, p. 28, lines 2-3.

[3] *Tazkirat al-Qadiri*, fol. 68b.

(*bi-khudi*).[4] It was from this point, perhaps the middle 1600s, that a cult seems to have coalesced around Amin al-Din, for he became to his *murids* not only a *pir* to be venerated but a living object of worship.

The mystical doctrine taught by Amin al-Din was not presented as any systematized theory as was that of his father Burhan al-Din Janam or his principal teacher Mahmud Khush Dahan. As a *majzub*, Amin al-Din was inclined neither to speculative reasoning nor to composition; and although several Dakhni works have been attributed to him, it is more likely that such writings were written by his disciples who took down the words of the master while he lapsed into ecstatic moods.[5] Some of his teachings were non-conventional, such as his protest against the idea that the mosque was the exclusive house of God:

> Some great people say that prayers to God consist of constructing a mosque and praying in it. They would pray day and night to God in the house of God. [But] the first mosque is the whole creation; the body is the *mihrab* [a mosque's niche indicating the direction of prayer], and the heart is the spiritual light which, when filled and illuminated, prepares a man to offer prayers.[6]

Although the above sentiment perhaps reflected Amin al-Din's conscious alienation from urban Islam, it was far from heretical. Much more serious were his claims to have achieved union and identity with God. Herein lay the crucial difference between Amin al-Din and his father; indeed, it was the difference between the radical Sufism of the *majzubs* and the more moderate position

4 *Rauzat*, copy A, p. 173.

5 See bibliography for a partial list of these works. Some of the works listed, such as *Guftar-i Shah Amin* and *Ganj-i Makhfi*, are explicitly stated to be the work of disciples. The remainder vary so much in style that common authorship is unlikely, though their inspiration and subject matter are quite similar. Professor M. Akbaruddin Siddiqi has recently identified a certain Jan Muhammad Muharrami (d. 1682) as one of the most prominent *munshis* or scribes at Shahpur Hillock in the late seventeenth century. It appears that Muharrami, who was a *murid* and *khalifa* of Shah Amin al-Din A'la, wrote copies not only of Amin al-Din's essays, but also those of Burhan al-Din Janam, Miranji Shams al-'Ushshaq, and Muhammad Husaini Bandanawaz Gisudaraz. (See Siddiqi, *Bujhte Chiragh*, pp. 138-48.)

6 Amin al-Din A'la, *Risala-yi Tasawwuf*. Dakhni MS (Hyderabad: Salar Jung Museum, Urdu MSS, Tasawwuf & Akhlaq no. 60), fol. 21a.

of the Literati. As noted above, Burhan al-Din Janam maintained the position of orthodox Chishtis that in the stage of *maqam-i qurb* the Sufi can attain "nearness" to God but not union or identity with the Divine Being. With reference to his own arrival at the *maqam-i qurb* Amin al-Din said:

> When I saw that this is the place of God
> I saw that two names signify one thing.
> You should know and accept that in reality
> God and Man are one.
> The extremity [*siwat*] of Man is God,
> And the extremity of God is Man.
> There is only one place of both God and Man
> And they both have one sign.[7]

And in another essay he stated,

> At that time we will cease to recognize
> Human qualities in ourselves,
> As well as divine qualities in God.
> To single out divine qualities would be false,
> As also to single out human qualities.[8]

In the passage quoted above, Amin al-Din was speaking not of himself so much as of the general relationship between Man and God. Even more heretical were his own claims to divinity, or more accurately, to a share of God's divinity. This sentiment, which represents the logical culmination of a *majzub's* religious experience, was eloquently expressed in a first- and second-person essay attributed to him:

> You [i.e., God] were a witness on the day of creation
> And it is certain that my light was also a witness.
> As far as You wanted to reveal, You did so;
> And so was revealed the brightness of my light.
> The sun of my light has appeared brightly,
> And it has happened in our presence.

[7] Amin al-Din Aʿla, *Risala-yi Qurbiya.* Dakhni MS (Hyderabad: Salar Jung Museum, Urdu MSS, Tasawwuf & Akhlaq no. 99), fol. 70b, lines 7-10.

[8] Amin al-Din Aʿla, *Risala-yi Tasawwuf.* Dakhni MS (Hyderabad: Salar Jung Museum, Urdu MSS, Tasawwuf & Akhlaq no. 59), fol. 74a, lines 22-23.

You have made my light a mirror of Your own self,
And in that light have filled Your qualities
like a hidden treasure.
The qualities have been given to me,
Yet the praise is for You;
so how can I distinguish between You and myself?[9]

Both manuscript and epigraphic sources suggest that the followers of Amin al-Din believed in their *pir's* quasi-divine status. Evidently writing after Amin al-Din's death, one of his *murids* praised the Sufi's charismatic and quasi-divine qualities, even comparing him with the Mahdi (a spiritual personage who will appear on the last day and establish Islam over all unrighteous forces):

I myself have seen with my own eyes
That whoever met Amin benefited from him.
In the eleventh century [A.H.] he became our leader,
And is like a Mahdi for us.
Everyone believed that his disciples
Are able to reflect God.
The public all agreed that Amin was a *majzub*,
A *salik*, a friend of God.
For it is true that Amin has dissolved himself with God
And in truth has become immortal.[10]

Further evidence of the cult surrounding Amin al-Din is seen in an important inscription on the Sufi's mausoleum, built in 1677-78, just two years after his death. Professor M. Akbaruddin Siddiqi of Hyderabad has recently published a transcription and translation of this massive epigraph, which he suggests is the largest single inscription to be found on a Muslim tomb in all of India.[11] Over the doorway of the tomb are inscribed the Islamic credo, several Traditions of the Prophet, and the names of the twelve Imams. Flanking both sides of the tomb's doorway is inscribed a Dakhni *ghazal* of fifteen couplets extolling the saintly character of Amin al-Din and describing his closeness to

[9] Amin al-Din A'la, *Risala-yi Wujudiya*. Dakhni MS (Hyderabad: Salar Jung Museum, Urdu MSS, Tasawwuf & Akhlaq no. 102), fol. 4b, lines 6-10.

[10] *Shajarat al-Atqiya*, p. 35, lines 2-6.

[11] Siddiqi, "Dakani Inscription," p. 82. See Figure 11.

God.[12] On both sides of the doorway, interspersed between these couplets, are some short phrases enclosed in small circles. At a glance their function would appear to be purely decorative, serving only to fill the gaps between the verses of the Dakhni *ghazal*. But a close examination strongly suggests that they are appeals to Amin al-Din authored by one of the Sufi's disciples:

> O Amin! Help! (2)
>   O fulfiller of needs!
> O performer of miracles! (2)
>   O Amin! Help!
> A Shamsu'l-'Ushshaq [literally, "sun among the lovers"]!
>   O divine beloved!
>   O sun of [and?] the moon!
> O fulfiller of needs! (2)
>   O Amin! Help!
> O 'Ashiq-i-Shahbaz [literally, "lover-falcon"]!
>   O Amin! Help!
>   O secret of My secret!
> O light of My light!
>   O Amin! Help!
>   O secret of My secret!
> Allah sufficeth!
>   Allah, Muhammad, 'Ali!
>   Allah is the Healer!
> O Allah! (2)
>   Verily, I am Allah![13]

The last line in this inscription is of more than casual interest, for it was the utterance of essentially this phrase that led to the execution of the martyr-Sufi Mansur al-Hallaj in tenth-century Baghdad. Thenceforth the phrase became a watchword for heresy among Sufis. It is therefore significant that the phrase is given such prominent position in the inscription, appearing at the head of both sides of the doorway, and that its characters are larger than most others in the inscription. Furthermore, it hardly seems coincidental that the phrase is inscribed inside a drawing of a spherical dome resembling the Amin al-Din *dargah* itself. These

[12] Ibid., pp. 90-92.

[13] Ibid., pp. 88 f. This translation, made by Professor Siddiqi, is of the twenty-four Arabic phrases as they appear from bottom to top on the right-hand side of the doorway.

facts, plus the constant repetition of Amin al-Din's name and epithet in other lines would seem to associate the heretical phrase with the Sufi.[14] It was probably used by both the *pir* and followers when in states of extreme ecstasy.

The cult that coalesced around the figure of Amin al-Din A'la on Shahpur Hillock, consisting of at least a dozen *khalifas* and numerous *murids*,[15] was not only heretical from the standpoint of orthodox Islam, but was also accommodating toward the non-Muslim population. Muhammad Mu'azzam, one of these *khalifas*, related that "*lakhs*" (hundreds of thousands) of Hindus were attracted to Amin al-Din:

> On the same night he was in exhilaration
> Many followers became his *murids*.
> Hearing this, *lakhs* of Hindus
> Came and worshiped him.
> A *lakh* of people having sacred threads
> Also came before Amin presenting themselves as offerings.
> A *lakh* of Jangams also came to worship him
> And to ask him of their own existence,
> Saying, "I, I—who am I?
> Who is in Amin uttering these truths
> When he is exhilarated?"
> Having been asked about these secrets,
> Amin taught them as he had been taught.
> After they mastered these secrets
> *Lakhs* of infidels showed their gratitude [i.e., became Muslims][16]

14 The epithets "'Ashiq-i-Shahbaz" and "Baland-parwaz" both referred to Amin al-Din A'la and Bandanawaz Gisudaraz of Gulbarga (Siddiqi, "Dakani Inscription," p. 88, notes 3 and 4). Professor Siddiqi did not comment on any connection between the phrase discussed above and either Amin al-Din himself or the *dargah*, noting only that the line came from the Koran, 28:30 (ibid., p. 89, note 1).

15 I have identified fourteen *khalifas* of Amin al-Din A'la, including his only son and *sajjada-nishin*, Baba Shah. These appear in Appendix I. Professor Husaini Shāhid of Hyderabad, who has made an exhaustive study of Amin al-Din's life and thought, has listed a total of twenty-five *khalifas* in his "Shah Amin-uddin 'Ali A'la aur unke Khulafa," Dissertation, Osmania University, Hyderabad, 1966, p. 167. Unfortunately, the writer did not cite the sources in which he learned of these *khalifas*.

16 *Shajarat al-Atqiya*, p. 34, lines 8-13; p. 35, line 1.

After all due account is made for hagiographical exaggeration, the passage nonetheless indicates the Sufi's receptive attitude toward non-Muslims.

There seem to have been especially close ties between Shahpur Hillock and the Kannada-speaking Lingayat population of the region. This is suggested in the above passage by reference to the Jangams, the Lingayat priesthood. It is further suggested by the life and even the name of one of Amin al-Din's foremost *khalifas*, Qadir Linga. According to one tradition Qadir Linga was even permitted by the Lingayat community to wear their divine emblem, the *linga*, on his left foot. This purportedly occurred after he had miraculously recovered a number of *lingas* from a deep well and restored them to their Lingayat owners.[17] "They then declared their belief in him," concludes the hagiographic account, "and even to this day [1804-5] it is customary among their descendants to wear the *linga* on their left foot."[18] These passages accord with other evidence suggesting a symbiotic relationship between Sufis and Lingayats, and the possibility that Lingayats formed a significant component of the outer circle of devotees attached to seventeenth-century Shahpur Hillock.[19]

[17] *Tazkirat al-Qadiri*, fols. 70b-71a. [18] *Mishkat*, copy A, fol. 153a.

[19] Apart from the doctrinal similarities between the Lingayat faith and Islam, specific Lingayat socioreligious institutions compared remarkably with those of Sufis. The *math* and the *khanaqah* both functioned as centers for spiritual guidance, the distribution of food, and education, while both the *guru* and the *pir* initiated members into the spiritual fold and mediated between the devotee and the deity. To this day Lingayat Jangams preside over the *'urs* ceremony at the tomb of Shah Ahmad Wali in Bidar (Sherwani, *Bahmanis*, p. 195). And a social anthropologist has recently observed that at least one Lingayat ascetic (*virakta*) in recent times has been a Muslim who drew his followers from both Muslim and Lingayat groups (McCormack, "Lingayats," p. 64). Furthermore, today's devotees at the various Sufi *dargahs* in Bijapur are primarily Lingayats engaged in urban trades—carpenters, ironsmiths, tonga-drivers, etc. ('Abd al-Qadir, teacher in Urdu at the Government Teacher Training College, Bijapur; interview held in Bijapur, 27 October 1970). As yet it is not possible to state with certainty at what time Lingayats began frequenting Sufi *dargahs*. Indeed, the whole phenomenon of Lingayat devotionalism at Sufi *dargahs* holds promising avenues of investigation for researchers utilizing the techniques of gathering oral tradition. At any rate, the accounts quoted above concerning Amin al-Din A'la and Qadir Linga suggest that some Lingayats had become devotees of Sufis even before *dargahs* were constructed, during the lives of the Sufis in question.

As the guardians of Islamic orthodoxy in Bijapur, the *'ulama* could not, and did not, stand idly by as the cult of Amin al-Din showed these signs of syncretism and, worse still, heresy. While they differ in details, all hagiographical accounts of Amin al-Din's life mention the *'ulama's* decisive steps to check the Sufi's excesses. One of the most complete reports of the encounter that took place between Amin al-Din and the *'ulama*, and the most contemporary such account, is found in a biographical work entitled *Makhzan al-Amin*. Composed by the son of one of the Sufi's closest *khalifas*, Amin al-Din A'la II, this work was possibly written during the Sufi's own lifetime since the author died in 1690-1. The *Makhzan al-Amin* records that during the reign of Sultan 'Ali II (1656-72) one of the leaders of the city's *'ulama*, Saiyid Muhammad Bukhari (d. 1685-86), accused Amin al-Din of permitting *pir*-worship among his followers in conscious violation of the commandment that only God can be worshiped. A delegation of *'ulama* headed by Muhammad Bukhari then brought this accusation to Shahpur Hillock where they were received by the Sufi's son, Baba Shah. The latter went to the mosque attached to the *khanaqah* where he informed his father of the *'ulama's* arrival and the nature of their complaint. Replied Amin al-Din sarcastically, "And whom do *these* men worship? Very well, if they are coming, let them come."[20]

When Muhammad Bukhari and the delegation of *'ulama* arrived at the mosque, Amin al-Din had them all sit down and present their arguments in light of the Koran, the Traditions of the Prophet, and the Commentaries and opinions of earlier scholars. The discussion focused on the meaning of prostration (*sijda*), and whether or not the prostration performed by the followers of Amin al-Din before their *pir* constituted worship of Amin al-Din himself. After delving into the fine points of Islamic jurisprudence, the learned assembly eventually ruled in favor of the Sufi. It concluded that two types of prostration must be distinguished, the prostration of servitude (*sijda-yi bandagi*) and the prostration of respect (*sijda-yi ta'zim*). The first of these was reserved only for worship of God, while the second was lawfully suitable for any of five special relationships: the faithful to the Prophet, a *murid* to a *pir*, a citizen to a king, a child to a parent,

[20] Amin al-Din A'la II, *Makhzan al-Amin*. Persian MS (Hyderabad: Asafiyah Library, Tasawwuf no. 1722), p. 194.

and a slave to a master. Acquiescing in this decision, Muhammad Bukhari reported these events to Sultan 'Ali II, later confessing shame for ever having brought the accusations against Amin al-Din.[21]

Since the above account was recorded by one of Amin al-Din's own descendants, the resolution of the conflict in the Sufi's favor is perhaps understandable. On the other hand the *Tazkirat al-Qadiri*, an undated account of Bijapur Sufis written by a Qadiri compiler who generally viewed Chishtis as rivals, lends a different perspective to this event. According to this account the *'ulama* of the city brought the transgressions of Amin al-Din directly to the attention of the sultan, not the Sufi.[22] The sultan then summoned to court the disciples of the heterodox Sufi and admonished them to see that Amin al-Din participate in the orthodox prayers and follow the dictates of Islamic Law. Missing from this account is any reference to a meeting between Amin al-Din and the *'ulama*, much less a decision of the learned doctors of Islam in favor of the Sufi. On the contrary, by this account the court toughened its dealings with Amin al-Din and his cult by ordering all the city's shops to refuse goods to both the Sufi and his disciples.[23]

Other descriptions of the encounter between Amin al-Din and the *'ulama* likewise mention Muhammad Bukhari as the leader of the orthodox party, though they differ slightly in narrative details. Mentioning the encounter as a "tradition" (*naql*), Ibrahim Zubairi wrote:

21 Ibid., pp. 194-97.

22 *Tazkirat al-Qadiri*, fol. 69a. This source states that the sultan was Sikandar 'Adil Shah (1672-86). The *Makhzan al-Amin*, on the other hand, states that 'Ali II was the reigning monarch at the time of this confrontation. Since Amin al-Din died in 1675 and Sikandar came to the throne in 1672, it is possible that the event occurred during Sikandar's reign, though not likely. As Sikandar ascended the throne at the tender age of four, he would have been only seven years old when the Sufi died. During the three-year period 1672-75 it was the Abyssinian regent Khauwas Khan who actually ruled the kingdom; presumably, then, he would have been the person with whom Amin al-Din's followers came in contact, not Sikandar. Unfortunately, other hagiographic sources do not specify the monarch's name but refer only to the *padshah*. Since Khauwas Khan's title was *wakil* and not *padshah*, the balance of evidence would favor the *Makhzan al-Amin's* version—namely that the reigning monarch at the time of Amin al-Din's confrontation with the *'ulama* was 'Ali II (1656-72).

23 *Tazkirat al-Qadiri*, fol. 69a.

> Owing to the predominance of his exhilaration and the intensity of his senselessness, Amin al-Din paid no attention to the pillars of Islamic Law. And by abandoning existence and by persisting in his vigilance and his sight of God, he failed to observe the [obligatory] prayers. When Saiyid Muhammad Bukhari . . . heard of the Sufi's exhilaration and his ignoring the pillars of Islamic Law, he became seized by a will to protect the *shari'at* and a zeal to do what is commanded. So, in the company of several great men and prayer-leaders, Saiyid Muhammad verbally attacked the Sufi . . . [saying that] first he must obey the pillars and commands of the Law, turning his foot from the path of the [Sufi] Way.[24]

From this point Zubairi follows a version of the encounter that first appeared in the *Shajarat al-Atqiya*, a contemporary narrative poem composed by one of Amin al-Din's *murids*, Muhammad Mu'azzam Bijapuri. In this account Saiyid Muhammad was again portrayed as the champion of orthodoxy. But instead of going to Shahpur Hillock or to the sultan, Bukhari tried to persuade Amin al-Din to come to the Jami' Mosque for the regular prayers. Doing so would have symbolized the Sufi's submission to the city's *'ulama*. Amin al-Din accordingly refused to yield to this pressure and instead invited Muhammad Bukhari to Shahpur Hillock. The latter accepted, went to the hill, and was astonished to watch Amin al-Din spread out his prayer-carpet on the water of a nearby reservoir and proceed to offer his prayers in that fashion.[25] As far as concerns the *'ulama*, the episode abruptly ends at this juncture and nothing further is mentioned of Shaikh Muhammad Bukhari. Yet the theme that runs through this and the other biographical notices concerning this confrontation is clear: Amin al-Din A'la implacably refused to submit to the city's *'ulama* either by recanting his doctrine or by performing his prayers in the city's Jami' Mosque.

Shah Amin al-Din A'la's heterodox views and the cult that he attracted around him drew sharp opposition not only from the city's *'ulama*, but also, and far more significantly, from fellow Sufis of the Qadiri and Shattari orders. Among them was a certain Mir Muhammad Sadiq, a *murid* of 'Abd al-Latif Qadiri (d. 1671-

[24] *Rauzat*, copy A, pp. 174 f.

[25] *Shajarat al-Atqiya*, p. 30, lines 10-12; and p. 31, lines 1-5. *Rauzat*, copy A, p. 175.

72) and a contemporary of Amin al-Din. In his *Shams al-Haqayiq*, a Dakhni poem explaining orthodox Sufi terms, Mir Muhammad Sadiq leveled an attack on Amin al-Din in which the epithet "*majzub*" was clearly employed as a pejorative:

> Amin was absolutely a *majzub*,
>   And nobody can trod the path of belief with a *majzub*.
> Nor can the *majzub* guide anybody—
>   Madmen always seek madmen.
> Even though there have been many thorough *majzubs*,
>   No chain [of followers] has ever issued from them.
> *Majzubs* are like diamonds—
>   They cannot give or reflect light,
>   But keep it in themselves.[26]

An even more vicious attack on Amin al-Din is found in a letter among the papers belonging to the present *sajjada-nishin* of the Qasim Qadiri *dargah* in Bijapur. This letter was written during Amin al-Din's lifetime by a certain Karim Allah. Little is known of Karim Allah's identity, but the persons to whom he was writing as well as the content of the letter indicate that he was a landed Sufi, a resident of the city, and a member of either the Qadiri or the Shattari order, or both. One of his two addressees was the maternal nephew of one of the grandsons of the Shattari Sufi Hashim Pir 'Alawi. The other addressee, 'Abd al-Razzaq Qadiri, resided in the village of Gomarsi, which from 1676 would become an *in'am* for two grandsons of Shah Mustafa Qadiri. The letter, which is undated, further identifies its author as a *jagirdar* of the village of Salkonda (not located on modern maps). Since the content of the letter indicates that Karim Allah lived during the lifetime of Amin al-Din, who died in 1675, it is possible to conclude that the author was a late seventeenth century landed Sufi having close ties with *pirzadas* of prominent Qadiri and Shattari *pirs*. The most significant aspect of this letter is that it reflects the alarm with which urban Sufis viewed the expanding popularity of Amin al-Din. Karim Allah wrote, "Not only have all the inhabitants of Bijapur shown preference for Khwaja . . .

[26] Mir Muhammad Sadiq, *Shams al-Haqayiq*. Dakhni MS (Hyderabad: Salar Jung Museum, Urdu MSS, Tasawwuf & Akhlaq no. 136), fol. 11a-b. A second copy of this work is in the Gachi Mahal, Bijapur, in which the above passage appears on p. 19.

Amin, but all the people of the Deccan have placed their heads before his greatness and have become believers in him. It has come to this that even several ignorant Qadiri shaikhs have recently joined his following."[27] Karim Allah then fired several volleys of poetic invectives at Amin al-Din and his followers:

> The followers of Amin are all
>   disbelievers,
> For they all emphasize the body
>   as self-existent.
> Actually, they have no understanding
>   of self-existence—
> Nor of the meaning of possibility,
>   those asses.
> They say there are five elements
>   having twenty-five qualities,
> But no wise-man can accept this talk;
>   these five elements are only five devils.[28]

The tenor of these passages suggests that the hostility for Amin al-Din harbored by his Sufi detractors sprang from causes more profound than academic differences over the nature of the cosmos. Indeed, even that dispute had its wider implications, for Amin al-Din evidently borrowed his cosmology from a Hindu philosophical system, while that of orthodox Sufis originated in Middle Eastern thought.[29]

The hostility between Amin al-Din and his Sufi opponents reveals just how far apart the *in'amdar* and the *majzub*, the two Sufi types most characteristic of late seventeenth century Bijapur, had strayed from each other. While the one had become thoroughly absorbed into the social and religious world of the *'ulama*, the other had just as resolutely turned his back on that world

[27] Bijapur: Gachi Mahal. This letter of Karim Allah is inserted in the manuscript *Shams al-Haqayiq*, in Gachi Mahal.

[28] Ibid.

[29] Amin al-Din's teachings on this point probably originated in the *Vishnu Purana*, which posits five elements in the cosmos—earth, water, fire, wind, and ether. Orthodox Sufis, on the other hand, upheld the view grounded in Middle Eastern tradition, that only four elements made up the universe—earth, water, fire, and air. See H. H. Wilson, trans., *The Vishnu Purana* (Calcutta: Punthi Pustak, 1961), p. 17. For the cosmology of Mir Muhammad Sadiq, see his *Shams al-Haqayiq*, Gachi Mahal copy, pp. 33-36.

while adopting unorthodox doctrines and practices. This important theme can be further elucidated by examining the career of a late seventeenth century poet affiliated with Chishti Sufism, Muhammad Mahmud Bahri.

Mahmud Bahri of Gogi—Poet and Critic

There is no body of literature written by the *majzubs* of Bijapur, for while they might have been literate they certainly were not literary. This can probably be attributed to their rejection of the necessity, or even the possibility, of expressing their mystic experiences in writing. There are, however, some valuable works written about these Sufis by a poet who, though not himself a *majzub*, was sympathetic toward heterodox dervishes and recorded perceptive observations of their place in Bijapur's society both before and after the Mughal conquest of 1686.

Mahmud Bahri (d. 1717-18) was the son of Qazi Bahr al-Din, a migrant who had come to Bijapur from Madras in the reign of Sultan Ibrahim II and became attached to the spiritual following of Burhan al-Din Janam.[30] The father did not remain in the capital city, however, but moved to Gogi, a prominent town located about seventy miles east of the capital. It was in Gogi that young Mahmud Bahri grew up and lived throughout the reign of 'Ali II (1656-72). Only toward the end of the dynasty's history, in 1683-84 during Sultan Sikandar's reign, did Bahri move to Bijapur.[31] By this time the kingdom had reached an advanced stage of political dissolution. Bahri, in fact, was present throughout the fifteen-month Mughal siege of the capital. Shortly after the Mughal conquest he moved to Hyderabad, and in 1688-89 he finally returned to Gogi where he lived the remainder of his life.[32]

Bahri's Sufi affiliations were thoroughly Chishti. For a twenty-year period before moving from Gogi to Bijapur he studied under a certain Shah Baqar, who was his *pir*. While it is not known

[30] Muhammad Sakhawat Mirza, Introduction to Mahmud Bahri, *Man Lagan*, ed. by Muhammad Sakhawat Mirza (Karachi: Anjuman-i Taraqqi-yi Urdu, 1955), pp. 15 f.

[31] *Basatin*, pp. 546 f. Mahmud Bahri, *'Arus-i 'Irfan*. Persian MS (Hyderabad: Salar Jung Museum, Tasawwuf no. 114), fol. 28a.

[32] Bahri, *'Arus-i 'Irfan*, fols. 5b-6a.

whether Shah Baqar had any direct ties with Amin al-Din A'la, we do know that on several occasions he held discussions on the *Ma'rifat al-Suluk* of Mahmud Khush Dahan, indicating that ties must have existed between Shahpur Hillock and Gogi.[33] These ties are further suggested in Bahri's remark that he, Bahri, had read all the works of Burhan al-Din Janam and was familiar with the teachings of Amin al-Din A'la.[34] He spent the first half of his life engaged in worldly pursuits, though it is not specified what this entailed.[35] But during the last thirty years of his life, having returned to Gogi after living in Bijapur and Hyderabad for five years, Bahri adopted the life of the Sufi recluse, attached neither to *in'am*, nor *dargah*, nor *pir*.[36]

These two sides of his own life might explain the double roles he seems to have played as author. In some of his writings, in particular the *Bangab-nama*, Bahri internalized the moods and cadences of "intoxicated" Sufism and recorded perceptions as seen through the glazed eyes of the *majzub*. But in other, more "sober" writings Bahri seems to have adopted the role of social critic. Herein lies the significance of his long Dakhni poem *Man Lagan*, which the author later translated into Persian under the title *'Arus-i 'Irfan*.[37] Resembling Sa'di's *Gulistan* in form, this work consists of a series of short stories interspersed with didactic verses. Though unoriginal in its mystical content, the work is invaluable for its observations of Sufis contemporary with the political dissolution of the kingdom.

The style and inspiration of Bahri's lyric poetry drew heavily from the tradition of Sufi lyricism as developed and made universally famous by earlier Persian poets. This tradition has been traced to 'Abd Allah Ansari (d. 1088), whose fusion of Islamic devotionalism and Persian imagery served as the prototype for

[33] Sakhawat Mirza, Introduction to Bahri, *Man Lagan*, p. 16.

[34] Bahri, *'Arus-i 'Irfan*, fols. 44b, 46b. This further supports the probability that Amin al-Din himself wrote nothing. For Bahri, who died about forty years after Amin al-Din, would surely have mentioned any works of Amin al-Din, had the latter written them.

[35] In a short prose work entitled *Lashkar-nama* Bahri wrote that he was able to correspond with members of the nobility because he had mixed with them and knew their ways (Mahmud Bahri, *Lashkar-nama*, included in his *Majmu'a*. Persian MSS [Bijapur: Gachi Mahal]).

[36] Sakhawat Mirza, Introduction to Bahri, *Man Lagan*, pp. 18, 22 f.

[37] Bahri, *'Arus-i 'Irfan*, fol. 132a.

the lyric poetry of Sana'i, 'Attar, Rumi, Sa'di, Hāfiz, Jami, and others.[38] One of the salient features of this tradition was its use of wine imagery, which has been variously interpreted as referring literally to alcoholic intoxication, allegorically to spiritual intoxication, or to both simultaneously.[39] Of course any favorable reference to the use of wine in Islamic poetry was fraught with the danger of drawing the wrath of the orthodox. A. J. Arberry argued that austere Persian Sufis who made liberal use of such imagery, such at 'Attar, Rumi, or Jami, could have intended only a metaphorical meaning. Arberry further cited a list of technical terms which, along with their allegorical meanings, were compiled by a seventeenth-century Persian Sufi "to defend the mystical poets against their orthodox critics, and to clear them of charges based on too literal an interpretation of their technical vocabulary."[40]

In his most "intoxicated" poetry Mahmud Bahri went a step further than the Persian lyricists by substituting for wine an even more potent image—*bhang*, a narcotic prepared from the leaves of hemp (*cannabis sativa*), which was either eaten, smoked, or drunk. Furthermore, Bahri left little doubt that his reference to the use of *bhang* had literal as well as allegorical meanings.[41] Unlike wine, which was liberally imbibed in the Bijapur court despite its prohibition by Muslim law, *bhang* was identified exclusively with

[38] Arberry, *Sufism*, pp. 71-73.

[39] Ibid., pp. 115 f. See also A. J. Arberry, *Fifty Poems of Hafiz* (Cambridge: University Press, 1947), pp. 31 f.

[40] Arberry, *Sufism*, p. 113. Below are some of the images that pertain to wine, as mentioned by Arberry's source:

Wine (*sharab*): ecstatic experience due to the revelation of the True Beloved, destroying the foundations of reason.

Cup-bearer (*saqi*): Reality, as loving to manifest itself in every form that is revealed.

Cup (*jam*): the revelations of (Divine) Acts.

Pitcher (*sabu*), or Jar (*khum*): the revelations of (Divine) Names and Qualities.

Tavern (*kharabat*): Pure Unity (*wahdat*), undifferentiated and unqualified.

Tavern-haunter (*kharabati*): the true lover who is freed from the chains of discrimination, knowing that all acts, and the qualities of all things, are obliterated in Divine Acts and Qualities (ibid., p. 114).

[41] In one passage he even claimed to have written his *'Arus-i 'Irfan* while under the influence of *bhang* (Bahri, *'Arus-i 'Irfan*, fol. 39a).

the lower classes of the population.[42] Bijapur's Muslim establishment—the court, the *'ulama*, and orthodox Sufis—during the decline of the kingdom came to identify the drug with non-elites and nonconformists generally. Therefore Bahri's use of *bhang* instead of wine as the image of intoxication had important social implications.[43]

Mahmud Bahri's *Bangab-nama*, a Dakhni work consisting of a dozen "cups" (*jam*) each having a dozen couplets, was a poetic panegyric of *bhangab*, a greenish drink made by mixing powdered *bhang* with water or milk. To be sure, there was an allegorical aspect to Bahri's poem. At the beginning, for example, the author clearly referred to the Creation story in explaining the origin of *bhang*.[44] But later, Bahri shifted to a discussion of *bhangab* itself and its use in aiding the Sufi to achieve his goal of self-annihilation.[45] As Bahri became more explicit about the Sufi's use of *bhang*, the identification of the narcotic as a symbol of protest

[42] One is immediately reminded of the Bhangis, an untouchable caste found throughout India as sweepers and menials. Their name, as noted in Wilson's glossary, "is probably derived from Bhang, for the Bhangis are generally addicted to the use of intoxicating drugs and liquors" (Wilson, *Glossary*, p. 76). With reference to the medieval Deccan, there is the observation of a Dutch traveler who resided in Goa in the late sixteenth century: "[*Bhang*] is a seed like Hempe-seed, but somewhat smaller and not so white. . . . The Indians eate this seed or the leaves thereof being stamped, saying that it maketh a good appetite, but useth most to provoke lust; as it is commonly used and sold in the shops, it is mingled with some poulder of the leaves and the seede together. . . . The common women (or whores) use it when they meane to have a mans companie, (thereby) to be (lively and) merrie, and to set all care aside. . . . It causeth such as eate it, to reele and looke as if they were drunke, and halfe foolish, doing nothing but laugh and bee merrie, as long as it worketh in their bodies" (Linschoten, *Voyage*, II, p. 115 f.).

[43] For a full discussion of the social implications of narcotics and their use in Islamic civilization, see Franz Rosenthal, *The Herb: Hashish versus Medieval Muslim Society* (Leiden: E. J. Brill, 1971), pp. 131-62. It has been suggested by one writer that Mahmud Bahri's use of *bhang* as a poetic symbol derived from his contact with Shaivite devotees who used the drug. (See Mohammad Hafiz Syed, "Qazi Mahmud Bahri: A Mystic Poet of the 11th Century A.H., and his Poetical Works," *Allahabad University Studies*, 5 [1928], p. 471.) There is, however, no evidence either in Bahri's poetry itself or in external sources to support this hypothesis.

[44] See Mahmud Bahri, *Bangab-nama*, in M. Hafiz Syed, ed., *Kulliyat-i Bahri*, pp. 263, 264, lines 1, 4-8.

[45] Ibid., p. 269, line 7; p. 270, lines 1-3.

against orthodox Sufism and orthodox Islam likewise became clearer. At the end of the poem Bahri admonished,

> Drink your *bhangab* and be happy—
> Be a dervish and put your heart at peace.
> Lose all your life in drinking this exhilaration,
> And not in sewing shabby clothes.[46]

The contrast between the orthodox Sufis of the city and the unorthodox dervishes, or *majzubs*, was here made explicit. While Bahri identified *bhangab* with both the spiritual and physiological exhilaration of the dervish, he ridiculed conventional Sufis. The shabby clothes (*gudari*) referred to the *khirqa*, or the frock that a *pir* passed to his *khalifa* as a symbol of successorship. In attacking the sewing of *khirqas* Bahri was lodging a protest against the proliferation of *khalifas*, which was characteristic among most of the urban Sufis discussed in the previous chapter.

In a broader sense the use of *bhang* symbolized the intoxicated Sufi's disaffection with the established Muslim ruling class, jealous of its diminishing wealth and power. In one passage Bahri urged his readers,

> Throw your crown in the fire and burn it;
> Rub out your wealth and kingdom.
> Instead of an elegant cumberband, a loin-cloth is enough;
> Instead of a large purse, use a small one.[47]

Or, in another passage,

> *Bhang*-users have taken the cup in hand
> and urinated on the shield;
> They have thrown away the sword and kept the pestle.
> *Bhang*-users have discarded their clothes
> to make the *bhang*-cloth,
> Which means that all things suffice for this exhilaration.
> They understand nothing but *bhangab*,
> And are concerned with neither Islam nor unbelief.[48]

The last line suggests the exhilarated Sufi's alienation from organized religion in general, and in particular from the representatives

[46] Ibid., p. 282, lines 9-10.
[47] Ibid, p. 276, lines 4-5.
[48] Ibid., p. 280, lines 3-5.

of Islamic orthodoxy. This sentiment is also seen in Bahri's advocacy of music (*sama'*) as an inducement for a Sufi's ecstasy, a practice long condemned by the *'ulama*. The poet merely dismissed as "boys" those who disapproved of the practice.[49] And in other passages the author illustrated his readiness to employ Hindu nomenclature: he once referred to the intoxicated Sufi as a *sadhu*,[50] and to God as Hari Ram.[51] Elsewhere Bahri expounded his views on religious relativism. "God's knowledge has no limit," he wrote, "and in His infinite knowledge all the world is perceived. Consequently there is not just one path to Him. If some one were to say that nobody else could see that which he had seen, he goes too far. . . . In point of fact, anybody from any group can find [God] to the extent that his own knowledge will permit."[52] All of the above passages point to Bahri's opposition to a narrow or strident conception of Islam, though the author's specific targets were not mentioned.

The nature of Mahmud Bahri's conflict with Bijapur's orthodox Muslim establishment is more clearly seen in his *'Arus-i 'Irfan*. In this work the poet threw off the mask of the intoxicated Sufi writing in allegories and made open complaints about Bijapur's ruling class, which in his lyrical poetry had been veiled in metaphors. More important, he distinguished two definable kinds of Sufis in late seventeenth century Bijapur: those who had been absorbed into the ruling establishment, whom he condemned, and those who had pursued their own unrestrained life styles—the *majzubs*. For the first of these two groups, stigmatized by the author as "worldly" Sufis (*ahl-i dunya*), Bahri reserved his most bitter words. "The essence of Sufism," he wrote, "has been aban-

[49] Ibid., p. 278, lines 1, 4-6:

> Do not drink *bhangab* without music;
> If you are sick with no love (of God)
> you should not hear music.
>
> . . . .
>
> Some people say that music must not be allowed
> And that it drives away Islamic Law.
> But such people do not understand the time, conditions,
> And the rapture of those who use music.
> They are only boys who do not know rapture.

[50] Ibid., p. 272, line 5.

[51] Ibid., p. 273, line 3.

[52] Bahri, *'Arus-i 'Irfan*, fol. 17a.

doned by most Sufis. They have taken to plagiarism and sewing *khirqas*. In their involvement with mundane affairs they have even surpassed the men of the world themselves, and have acquired the worldly man's hairy armpit."[53] Although Bahri mentioned no individuals by name, there can be little doubt that he was referring here to Bijapur's many *inʿamdars* or *pirzadas* who, being securely tied to either a land endowment or a *dargah*, or both, had made a living out of being "professional" Sufis. He noted their low literary standard, and again there is the reference to sewing *khirqas*, i.e., the proliferation of Sufis whom Bahri considered unworthy and whose only claim to the title was an inherited frock.

On the other hand Bahri's sympathy with the *majzubs* of Bijapur sprang from his conviction that they were the only Sufis for whom love of God remained the paramount concern. He wrote that he would serve and support *majzubs* who had lost their senses from the wine of divine exhilaration, or who even suffered from mental disorders. He further wrote that if asked how he could sustain friendship with such people, he would reply:

A madman possessed by love and ebullient secrets
  Is a hundred times superior to the worldly man, Oh Friend.
For he has left the path of dissatisfaction for the seashore
  To drown himself in the ocean he longs for, Oh Friend.[54]

When asked what would happen if a dervish paid no heed to "established" religion, Bahri answered: "Unlike others he is not bound to it. If others are seen out of step they would be warned, which is quite fitting for a sultan, a shaikh, or a *qazi*—but not for a *faqir*. . . .

He who trods the path of mystic knowledge
  Bows to no religion.
Whatever comes to his attention contents him,
  And he speaks not of why.[55]

The place in society that Bahri perceived *majzubs* occupying lay not only ideologically beyond the pale of Islamic orthodoxy, but socially beneath the *ʿulama*, the soldiery, and the merchants.[56]

[53] Ibid., fol. 90a. [54] Ibid., fol. 62a-b. [55] Ibid., fol. 84b.

[56] Some passages suggest that the author associated the *majzubs*, at least those of Bijapur city, with the lumpenproletariat, i.e., the city's under-

Bahri also felt that *majzubs* of his time were persecuted at the hands of the orthodox elements of society. Referring to a fellow native of Gogi named Muhammad Waris, Bahri wrote: "Such men are not liked by worldly people, whose legs are tied with worldly chains."[57] Although he never explained exactly how the *'ulama* dealt with such dervishes, Bahri did observe that the tension between the *'ulama* and the dervishes was much greater in the capital city of Bijapur, where the upholders of Islamic orthodoxy were most heavily concentrated, than in the outlying districts. Thus he stated that in his home town of Gogi a *majzub* could be censured, but not killed. On the other hand he compared the city of Bijapur with tenth-century Baghdad where Mansur al-Hallaj, an early *majzub*, was sent to the gallows for declaring his identity with God in a moment of spiritual ecstasy. Bahri felt that the episode of Mansur would be reenacted if he were to leave Gogi for Bijapur.[58]

By his own account, Bahri's fears of persecution were quite well founded. Shortly after the city fell to Mughal armies in 1686, Aurangzeb, whose own strict interpretation of Islam in India is well known, inaugurated a purge of those Muslims in Bijapur who had demonstrated extreme deviation in matters of religion. Bahri wrote that a complaint against him had been lodged before one of the Mughal officers (*nawwab*):

> The *nawwab* then called for a certain Qazi Habib Allah, who in those days had already slain one dervish for saying things contrary to Islamic Law. Said the *nawwab*, "Go to the hospice of that *faqir* in Gogi and see if the complaint is true. If so, punish him so that he might be an example for others." The *qazi* arrived at my hospice in great pomp and with his own servants, greeted me, and sat down. In my heart I knew that to whatever he asked I would respond, "I have done only that

---

world of street people and prostitutes. For example, he wrote: "In the citadel of Bijapur there once was a paradise-like gathering of dancing street women. Somebody said, 'Although [some] men reject these women and suppose them to be polluting, to us they reflect God's purity' " (Bahri, *'Arus-i 'Irfan*, fol. 18a).

[57] Mahmud Bahri, *Masnawi* no. 107, ni M. Hafiz Syed, ed., *Kulliyat-i Bahri*, pp. 223 f.

[58] Bahri, *'Arus-i 'Irfan*, fol. 27b.

> which suited me for strengthening the dictates of Islam, and it is well that you do whatever suits you to the same end. What is the use of lengthy discussion?" God was benevolent—he asked nothing and left.[59]

The possibility of some exaggeration in the above story must be admitted, particularly when the writer was referring to events in which he was the central figure. Nonetheless, the passage illustrates the atmosphere of tension in late seventeenth century Bijapur between dervishes and the upholders of Islamic orthodoxy, i.e., the court, the *'ulama*, and the "worldly" Sufis.

Both Mahmud Bahri and Amin al-Din A'la, in different ways and in different degrees, opposed these pillars of Islamic society. In both one finds a consciousness of an anti-urban, anti-*'ulama* identity never explicitly expressed by other Sufis encountered in this study. Yet the two Sufis differed in important respects. While Bahri was mainly a spokesman for *majzubs*—even today he is remembered more as a poet than as a Sufi—Amin al-Din was himself a *majzub*. Still, Amin al-Din had inherited a *khirqa* and in fact passed many other *khirqas* to his *khalifas*, a practice despised by Bahri. Furthermore, as the only son of Burhan al-Din Janam, he was a legitimate *pirzada* residing at his grandfather's *khanaqah*. As such, even Amin al-Din, despite his doctrinal radicalism, his conflicts with representatives of Islamic orthodoxy, and the claim of both his admirers and detractors that he was a *majzub*, did not completely conform to Bahri's conception of a proper religious mendicant, utterly severed from worldly concerns.

THE *Majzubs* OF BIJAPUR

It is possible to argue that Mahmud Bahri's conception of the *majzub* as a wandering beggar absorbed in love of God might have represented an idealized prototype, a projection on to the society of his day of the sort of Sufi he wished to see. There is,

[59] Ibid., fol. 81b. An apocryphal version of this story has survived in at least one account, the *Waqi'at-i Mamlakat-i Bijapur*. According to this version Aurangzeb, on hearing of Bahri's unorthodox practices, personally went to Gogi to investigate the matter. On the Emperor's arrival Bahri offered him a glass of *bhang* (!), which when taken in Aurangzeb's hands miraculously turned to milk. Astonished at this demonstration of power, the Emperor refrained from punishing the Sufi (*Waqi'at*, III, p. 372).

however, considerable evidence that in the late seventeenth century there actually were a good many Sufis who, clad in rags and possessing little but a staff and a begging bowl, had abandoned the world of the *khanaqah* or the *dargah* in order to find God in their own chosen way.[60] Table 7 shows a list of Bijapuri Sufis

TABLE 7

MAJZUBS OF BIJAPUR

Name	*Death Date*	*Residence*	*Source*•
'Atiq Allah Qadiri	1614-15	Bijapur	R. 104-5
Majnun Qadiri Majzub	1650-1	Gogi	W. 367-74
Abu'l-Ma'ali	mid-17th	Bijapur	R. 215 f.
Muhammad Sibghat Allah II	1660	Bijapur	M. S. 19a-b
Amin al-Din A'la	1675	Shahpur Hillock	R. 172-76
Shah Baqar	1678-79	Gogi	W. 371-2
Nur al-Din Is-haq Qadiri	1687-88	Nilanga	M. 641b-42a
Shah Khaki	1692	Bijapur	M. 558b-59a
Mustafa s/o Burhan al-Din 'Alawi (d. 1674)	late 17th	Bijapur	T. 66b
Abu Muhammad s/o Burhan al-Din 'Alawi	late 17th	Bijapur	T. 66b
Abu Turab s/o Burhan al-Din 'Alawi	late 17th	Bijapur	T. 66b
'Abd al-Nabi s/o Burhan al-Din 'Alawi	late 17th	Bijapur	T. 66b

• A. I.—*'Arus-i 'Irfan*, by Mahmud Bahri
K.—*Kulliyat-i Bahri*, ed. by M. Hafiz Syed
M.—*Mishkat-i Nubuwat*, copy B
M. S.—*Malfuzat-i Shah Sibghat Allah*
R.—*Rauzat al-Auliya*, Persian MS, copy A
R. 2—*Rauzat al-Auliya*, Urdu edn.
R.A.—*Rauzat al-Aqtab*
T.—*Tuhfa az Kamtarin*
W.—*Waqi'at-i Mamlakat-i Bijapur*, III

[60] Miniature paintings of seventeenth-century dervishes of Bijapur reflect these features, and some also reveal the entranced expressions on their faces. See Figure 12, which has been definitely traced by art historians to seventeenth-century Bijapur.

TABLE 7 (*continued*)

Name	*Death Date*	*Residence*	*Source**
'Abd al-Qadir s/o Burhan al-Din 'Alawi	late 17th	Bijapur	T. 66b
Muhammad Waris	late 17th	Gogi	K. 223-24
Miyan Shah 'Abd al-Sattar	late 17th	Adoni	A. I. 106a
Miyan Khaksar	late 17th	Bijapur—Chincholi	R. A 242-43
Haidar Majzub	*c.* 1700	Kankal	R. 165
'Usman Majzub	*c.* 1700	Bijapur	R. 165
Alangi Majzub	early 18th	Bijapur	R. 227
Nangi Majzub	1713	Bijapur	R. 113, 227
Muhammad Majzub	1720	Bijapur—Chincholi	M. 576b
Tipu Auliya	1725	Shahpur Hillock—Arcot	R. 2 170 f.
Shah Jamal Allah	1727-28	Bijapur—Chincholi	M. 577b

who have been designated *majzubs* in the hagiographic literature. Unfortunately the extent of information on these Sufis is far less than that for most others considered in this study. None of them is known to have written anything himself, and the hagiographic biographies provide only the briefest sketches of their lives. Typical entries merely state the man's name, which is often suffixed with the word "*majzub*," his place of origin, and one or another aspect of his behavior that seemed particularly bizarre to the biographer. Their exact death dates are seldom given, and in many cases even the year of their death has not been recorded. Despite this paucity of source material, however, certain statements can be made about the *majzubs* of Bijapur.

The doctrinal positions of these Sufis were to varying degrees unorthodox. Because it was not their character to write books, far less to formulate theological systems, one cannot elaborate on the extent to which their religious thought might have deviated from strict orthodoxy. We have seen that Amin al-Din A'la, who was hailed as a *majzub* by his followers and condemned as one by his enemies, had his religious thoughts and experiences recorded, and that these quite explicitly reached the heretical position that Man and God were identical. One can assume that other *majzubs*, since they were frequently called *bi-shar'* or "unorthodox" in the hagiographic literature, reached similar states in their meditations. So alien to them were form and structure that they seem to have ignored even procedural exercises, the *zikrs*.

Regarding their behavior we have much more complete information. Indeed it was precisely their eccentric behavior that attracted attention to them in the seventeenth century, just as the unique dance ceremony of the Mevlevi Sufis of nineteenth-century Ottoman Turkey attracted the attention of contemporary European observers, who on this account forever associated the adjective "whirling" with "dervish." Below are descriptions of such Sufis as recorded by contemporary European and Indian observers. Referring to Indian dervishes in general, John Fryer noted in 1676,

> A Fakier is an Holy Man among the Moors . . . yet declaring for this kind of life, and wearing a patch'd Coat of a Saffron Colour, with a pretended careless neglect of the World, and no certain Residence, they have Immunity from all Apprehensions, and will dare the *Mogul* himself to his Face: Of this Order are many of the most Dissolute, Licentious, and Prophane Persons in the World, committing Sodomy, will be Drunk with *Bang*, and Curse God and Mahomet.[61]

With reference to North Indian dervishes, the Indian traveler Mohsan Fani (d. 1670) made similar observations:

> Among the most celebrated of [unorthodox Sufis] are, in the first line, the *Madarian*, who, like the Sanyasis Avadhuts, wear the hair entangled; and the ashes which they and the Sanyasis rub upon their bodies are called *bhasma*; besides, they carry iron chains on their heads and necks, and have black flags and black turbans; they know neither prayers nor fasts; they are always sitting at a fire; they drink a great deal of bang; and the most perfect among them go without any dress. . . . These also consume much bang, and to the praise of one of their sect they say: "Such a one takes two or three *seers* of bang."[62]

[61] Fryer, *East India and Persia*, II, p. 113.

[62] Mohsan Fani, *Dabistan, or School of Manners*, trans. by D. Shea and A. Troyer (3 vols.; Paris, 1843), II, p. 223. A *ser* is a unit of weight equal to about two pounds.

12. A *majzub* of Bijapur, seventeenth century, A.D.

Disregard for orthodox Muslim behavior and indulgence in *bhang*, noted in both of the above accounts, were certainly important traits of *majzubs* in Bijapur. A certain Shah Khaki (d. 1692), who had taken a *bai'at* from Qadir Linga of Shahpur Hillock, was associated with a house where *bhang* was drunk (*bhang-khana*), possibly on the model of the ubiquitous *chai-khana*, or tea-house.[63] Furthermore, there was evidently some consciousness among *majzubs* that the drinking of *bhang* violated the spirit (though not the letter) of Islamic Law. As Bahri advised, "Be not afraid of taking *bhangab*,/Even if someone beats you with many sticks."[64]

But *bhang*-drinking was not the only form of unorthodox behavior in which *majzubs* indulged. One also finds in the hagiographies of *majzubs* occasional references to wine-drinking, though this is usually played down because of its explicit illegality in Muslim Law. An account of Nur al-Din Is-haq Qadiri (d. 1687-88), a *majzub* of the town of Nilanga in the northern part of the kingdom, provides an example of the extremes to which some hagiographers went in order to rationalize, or possibly to compensate for, this unlawful behavior:

> It is related that he was a complete *majzub*, and fond of pleasures. At all times he had dancing women around him. [Yet] he would pray so hard as to lose all human senses. It is even said that nights when he became sleepy [from praying] he would place his hand in a bowl of scorpions, or sprinkle chili pepper in his eyes. The daylight hours he spent with the dancing girls. He would also request wine from anyone who came to see him. And in an ecstatic state he would pour the wine to his lips but allow all of it to drop through his beard on to his chest, ultimately spilling on the floor. Not one drop reached his mouth. Although it was believed that he was fond of wine, in truth he was pouring the forbidden drink to the floor.[65]

Some Bijapuri *majzubs* attracted attention by their nakedness. Among these was one of Amin al-Din A'la's *murids*, Tipu Auliya (d. 1725), who is said to have ignored the distinguished shaikhs of his time.[66] Another naked *majzub*, Shah Nangi Majzub (d.

[63] *Mishkat*, copy A, fol. 164a.
[64] Bahri, *Bangab-nama*, p. 267, line 8.
[65] *Mishkat*, copy B, fol. 641b.
[66] *Tarjama-yi Rauzat al-Auliya'-i Bijapur*, pp. 170 f.

1713), purportedly declared that he would invite the Mughals to Bijapur and give them the city as a gift. To this, another *majzub* replied that should the Mughals come they would surely clothe him. The austere Aurangzeb did come and, so the story concludes, did have the naked *majzub* clothed.[67]

Who, indeed, were these socially deviate Sufis, and why did they appear in Bijapur when they did? Any answers to these questions require an understanding of the social conditions in which they lived and the social origins from which they came. As Table 7 indicates, most *majzubs* lived in the late seventeenth or early eighteenth centuries, a period when the political and social disruptions accompanying the decline of the kingdom were followed by further disruptions after the Mughal conquest. Indeed, in some respects the latter period was characterized by even greater social dislocation than was the period preceding the Mughal conquest of 1686. First, a devastating cholera epidemic, which was said to have killed 150,000 people of the Bijapur plateau, commenced the year following Aurangzeb's conquest and lasted for three years.[68] Then in 1696 the Bhima River flooded, drowning many and ruining a year's harvest in one of the Bijapur plateau's most productive regions.[69] Worse still was the terrible famine that scourged the western Deccan in 1717 and plunged the economy of the area into severe instability.[70] As a result of these calamities both the city and much of the Bijapur plateau suffered widespread death and desertion. A census taken by Aurangzeb after the fury of the cholera epidemic had abated (around 1690) showed that the city of Bijapur had lost over half of its former population in just the several years following the Mughal conquest.[71]

In addition to these natural calamities were the political, cultural, and social disruptions that accompanied the Mughals' brief rule over the Bijapur plateau (1686-1724). From the perspective of Bijapur's historic feud between Deccani Muslims and Foreigner

[67] *Rauzat*, copy A, p. 227.

[68] *Basatin*, p. 549. The timing of the Mughal invasion and the epidemic was probably not coincidental. One Sufi hagiography blamed the Mughals for the plague, and gave as a chronogram for the epidemic's first year, which was A.H. 1099, *bud waba az Mughal*—"the cholera came from the Mughals" (*Sahifat*, Persian MS copy, p. 252).

[69] *Basatin*, p. 554. [70] Ibid., p. 566.

[71] Sathyan, ed., *Mysore State Gazetteer: Bijapur District*, p. 78.

Muslims, the Mughals, or the *ghair-mulkis* as they were contemptuously called by the Deccanis, followed the Iranians and the Afghans as the latest foreign element in Bijapur. A good deal of Bijapur's post-1686 disruptions can be understood in this perspective. Politically, the assimilation of the 'Adil Shahi nobility into the Mughal imperial structure met with only limited success, and in some instances with outright failure.[72] Culturally, the conquest resulted in the displacement of Dakhni by North Indian "Hindustani" as the language of urban Muslims.[73] This linguistic

[72] The aim of Aurangzeb's Deccan policy, after annexing Bijapur and Golconda, was to subdue the Marathas. It is therefore unlikely that the emperor succeeded in assimilating Marathas into the imperial service, though they had formed the most important non-Muslim pillar of the old 'Adil Shahi nobility. The Mughals seem to have had somewhat more success in winning over the Kannada *nayaks* of the Bijapur Karnatak. But even here they frequently met resistance, the most striking examples of which were the rebellions of the Berad *nayaks* of Sagar, a fortress located 10 miles south of Gogi and about 70 miles east of Bijapur. The *nayaks* of Sagar were descended from a race of aboriginal Kannadiga warriors, called the Berads, that had dominated the hilly Sagar region even when it was under the suzerainty of Vijayanagar. When that dynasty fell in 1565 the Berad *nayaks* of Sagar were allowed by Sultan 'Ali I to retain their independent position, and later Bijapur sultans continued the policy. These *nayaks* therefore remained among the most loyal subjects of the 'Adil Shahi dynasty and obstinately resisted the Mughal invasions that finally resulted in the conquest of 1686. After that conquest Aurangzeb gave a rank of 5,000 to Pam Nayak, the chieftain then dominant at Sagar. But the *nayak* was never reconciled to Mughal domination and retired to the fastness of his mountain fortress, where he soon died. His son, even more contemptuous of Mughal domination than his father had been, joined Maratha forces plundering the Mughal Deccan even to points as far as Golconda and Ahmadnagar. Failing to cajole the refractory *nayak* into submission, the aged but tireless emperor in 1705 launched an invasion of the Sagar stronghold in concert with the most part of his forces in the Deccan and the Karnatak. Though he succeeded in subduing the *nayak*, the incident is significant in revealing the persistence of anti-Mughal feeling in the Bijapur plateau. For in addition to a core of Berad warriors, the *nayak's* forces of 12,000 included many Deccani Muslims and Abyssinians formerly loyal to the 'Adil Shahi throne. For nineteen years after the fall of Bijapur these elements had evidently refused allegiance to Mughal authority. (See Taylor and Fergusson, *Architecture at Beejapoor*, pp. 51 f.)

[73] "The advent of Delhi 'Hindustani,'" wrote S. K. Chatterji, "brought in a conflict of dialects in the Deccan from the 17th century onwards, in which Delhi Hindustani . . . won, and is now reigning supreme as a literary language in the Deccan, the earlier dialect becoming reduced to a position of a broken *patois* confined to the homes of Deccan and South Indian

development reflects the extent to which the Deccanis as a class had been vanquished by these new Foreigners. The influx of North Indians following the Mughal conquest, as well as Deccani resentment to it, can be documented in Dakhni folk literature of the period. Woven into a contemporary *chakki-nama* was the following portrait of Bijapuri society in the late seventeenth century:

The twelfth century [A.H.] has arrived and Aurangzeb is king;
We have seen the sign
of the Day of Judgment.
The orthodox leaders explain that Aurangzeb's rule is just—
Outwardly there is benevolence,
but in hearts there is spite.
The regulations of Aurangzeb are with the officials themselves.
They give us envelopes
and keep the letters themselves.
Low people and money-lenders have become courtiers,
And in the houses of nobles
are only simple soldiers.
Under Aurangzeb's rule bribery is everywhere;
Mean people have become governors [*hākim*],
and the *qazi* himself is called a thief.
Young *pirzadas* have lost their social standing and respect;
Pawns have leaped to become queens.
Those who used to be nobles now have to serve these
mean people.
Khayasts, Khatris, and Brahmins of the army have gained much;
And *dhoti*-wearers, by virtue of their iron weapons,
have become an estranged retinue.
North Indian Leather-workers, Tanners, and Untouchables,
Washermen, Oil-sellers, and Gardeners—
all have become rulers.
May God damn the tyrant!
In this world he is an infidel;
in the next he shall be in Hell.[74]

Muslims who are *Mulkis* (that is, settled in the country for generations), and not *Ghair-mulkis* or newcomers, recent arrivals into the Deccan from North India" (Chatterji, *Indo-Aryan and Hindi*, pp. 207 f.).

[74] *Chakki-nama* (Hyderabad: Salar Jung Museum, Urdu MSS, Tasawwuf & Akhlaq no. 36), fol. 2b. While the general tone of this *chakki-nama*

The author of this *chakki-nama* seems to have been a *pirzada* attached to one of the city's *dargahs* and a contemporary of the Aurangzeb era of Mughal rule in Bijapur (1686-1707).[75]

The assertion that *pirzadas* had lost their social standing reflects the author's fear that the influx of Northerners in Bijapur was creating a new foreign elite threatening the *pirzadas'* own elite

---

conveys an anti-Northerner bias, its anti-Hindu sentiment is also present. The groups whose dominance the author deplores—Khayasts, Khatris, and Brahmins—are all non-Muslim. The *dhoti*—the cloth worn around the waist, passing between the legs and tucked in behind—was identified more with the Hindu population in both North India and the Deccan than it was with Northerners generally. John Platts has noted that the term *dhoti-walla*, or wearer of a *dhoti*, was used contemptuously for a Hindu, especially a Brahmin or a Baniya (John Platts, *A Dictionary of Urdu, Classical Hindi, and English* [London: Oxford University Press, 1968], p. 550).

[75] The twelfth century A.H. began in the year A.D. 1688, or just two years after Aurangzeb's conquest of Bijapur. Since the emperor remained in Bijapur from 1686 to 1688, when he himself was driven out by the cholera epidemic, the year 1688 might well have been the year of the writing of this *chakki-nama*. Its references to Aurangzeb suggest it was contemporary with the emperor's rule over Bijapur, and its archaic style furthermore belongs to the late seventeenth century. The authorship of the manuscript is somewhat less certain. It is catalogued as the work of Amin al-Din A'la (d. 1675), but it cannot be Amin al-Din's work because the Sufi had died eleven years before the Mughal conquest. Nevertheless the Sufi origin of this *chakki-nama*, like those discussed in chapter six above, is indicated by its many lines devoted to explanations of Sufi terms, *zikrs*, etc. (*ibid*., fols. 3a-6a). Such an origin is further suggested by the name and address of the manuscript's copyist, appended at the end of the work (fol. 6a):

> Faqir Miyan Shah Shattari, Sajjada, Miranji Sahib—
> Inhabitant adjacent to the tomb of Ibrahim 'Adil Shah.

This would seem to refer to the *sajjada-nishin* of the *dargah* of Miranji Shams al-'Ushshaq on Shahpur Hillock. But no *sajjada-nishin* of that *dargah* had the name Miyan Shah Shattari. Furthermore, the Miranji *dargah* is not located opposite the tomb of either Ibrahim I or Ibrahim II, the latter tomb being the more famous and probably the one referred to in the *chakki-nama*. But there is a *dargah* located near the tomb of Ibrahim II—that of Habib Allah Sibghat Allahi, who was a Shattari Sufi. Hence the copyist of this *chakki-nama*, Miyan Shah Shattari, was probably attached to the Habib Allah *dargah* whose *sajjada-nishin* at the time of the manuscript's copying was evidently named Miranji. The content of the *chakki-nama* and the identity of its copyist point to the probability that it was authored by some descendant of Habib Allah Sibghat Allahi toward the end of the seventeenth century, and very likely in the year 1688.

status. Whether or not such a fear was justified, it was precisely this kind of concern that contributed to making the *pirzadas*, from the *majzubs*' viewpoint, "worldly people." In earlier chapters we have noted that many *pirzadas* of the late 'Adil Shahi period had joined the *'ulama* as one of the pillars of Bijapur's ruling Muslim establishment, and also that the latter had become increasingly strident in its interpretation of Islamic orthodoxy from the reign of Muhammad 'Adil Shah through the Mughal conquest. The clustering in the late seventeenth and early eighteenth centuries of Sufis having unusually unorthodox tendencies suggests a reaction to the confining world of the *pirzadas* and the *'ulama*. The social origins of such Sufis, in addition to the timing of their appearance, further suggests this development.

Some *majzubs* were sons of orthodox urban Sufis. For example Muhammad Sibghat Allah II (d. 1660), as his name suggests, was descended spiritually from the Shattari followers of the zealous Reformist Sufi, Shah Sibghat Allah. His father, Habib Allah Sibghat Allahi (d. 1632), had accepted a *khilafat* from Shah Sibghat Allah and an *in'am* grant from Sultan Ibrahim II. The latter seems to have had the more lasting effect, for although Habib Allah kept a *khanaqah* and a circle of followers, he also developed a conspicuous taste for wealth and pomp in apparent contradiction to the austere principles of his *pir*. Habib Allah's son Muhammad thus probably grew up in relatively comfortable surroundings; and, as the Sufi's only son, he would seem to have had his future assured as the *sajjada-nishin* of his father's *khanaqah*. But instead of adopting this course, the *pirzada* became a *majzub*, a development about which his father later complained in his recorded discourses (*malfuzat*).[76] A similar development occurred with Shaikh 'Alam Allah Muhaddis (d. 1616) and his son, Shaikh Abu'l-Ma'ali. Shaikh 'Alam Allah, born in North India of a family descended from the Prophet, received a *khilafat* in the minor 'Aidarusi order, an orthodox order based in Hadramaut, Arabia. Eventually he settled in Burhanpur, Khandesh, where he acquired a reputation of an orthodox Sufi and an erudite teacher of Islamic theology. So great was his renown, in fact, that Sultan Ibrahim II personally invited him to Bijapur. The shaikh obliged the sultan's request, and in Bijapur he likewise established himself as a Sufi

[76] *Malfuzat-i Shah Sibghat Allah*, fol. 19a-b.

and a teacher of the orthodox Islamic sciences. Even the famous Shattari Sufi Shah Hashim Pir 'Alawi is said to have studied with him. But notwithstanding Shaikh 'Alam Allah's thorough integration with the city's Muslim establishment, his eldest son, Shaikh Abu'l-Ma'ali, adopted the heady life of a *majzub*.[77] Both Muhammad Sibghat Allah II and Abu'l-Ma'ali evidently turned their backs on the Sufi life as exemplified by their fathers.

A similar process operated among the descendants of Hashim Pir 'Alawi. Hashim Pir's grandson and *sajjada-nishin* at the *dargah*, Burhan al-Din 'Alawi (d. 1674), had five sons by his first wife: Shah Mustafa, Shah Abu Muhammad, Shah Abu Turab, Shah 'Abd al-Nabi, and Shah 'Abd al-Qadir. According to the custom then practiced at Bijapur's *dargahs* Burhan al-Din would have passed the successorship on to one of these sons, ordinarily the eldest one. But a family history records that all five of these sons became *majzubs* and not one had any offspring. The account then relates that Burhan al-Din married a second woman, a nobleman's daughter, by whom he had one son who became his successor at the Hashim *dargah*.[78] This son was a youth of only thirteen when, on his father's death, he became the *sajjada-nishin* at the *dargah*. His five half-brothers by his father's first wife, all of them older and therefore theoretically better qualified for the position, evidently rejected altogether the life of the professional *pirzada*.

Other *majzubs*, before adopting the staff and begging bowl of the dervish, either had been affiliated with Bijapur's Muslim establishment themselves, or had come from prominent families that were. A certain Shah Jamal Allah (d. 1727-28), whose behavior was so wildly eccentric that he was considered dangerous to be near, came from a family of 'Adil Shahi nobles (*mansabdars*).[79] Another dervish, Saiyid Muhammad Majzub (d. 1720), had been engaged in government service before becoming a *majzub*.[80] One of Amin al-Din A'la's *khalifas*, Shah Miranji Khudanama (d. 1675), had been a military officer (*jama'dar*) in Golconda before

[77] *Rauzat*, copy A, pp. 212-15.

[78] *Tuhfa az Kamtarin*, comp. by Kamtarin. Persian MS (Bijapur: Hashim Dargah), fols. 66b-68a.

[79] *Mishkat*, copy B, fol. 577a.

[80] Ibid., fol. 576b. He eventually migrated to Hyderabad, where he died. His tomb is located just north of the Chauk Mosque in the old city.

coming to Bijapur as an ambassador.[81] Once in Bijapur where he met Amin al-Din, he evidently underwent a dramatic change in his life, giving up everything to live on Shahpur Hillock as a Chishti devotee. The same was true for another of Amin al-Din's *khalifas*, Qadir Linga. This disciple had been a cavalryman in the Bijapur service when he first met Amin al-Din. "When his eyes fell upon his presence," recorded one early but undated account, "his heart turned cold to this world and his belief in [Amin al-Din] took strength. Then he went home, sold his horse and other such things, and, having applied himself to the Way of Truth, became a *murid* of Amin al-Din A'la."[82] The *Mishkat al-Nubuwat*, compiled in 1804-5, noted that like his *pir*, Qadir Linga frequently lost his senses during sessions of collective *zikrs*, adding that he also indulged in unlawful practices such as wine-drinking.[83] Thus we see again the theme of a sudden conversion in life styles resulting in an unrestrained quest for spiritual freedom even when that quest challenged orthodox Islamic Law and society.

Unfortunately the social origins of other Bijapuri *majzubs* were not recorded. But from those that were, it is evident that *majzubs* were not born into their style of life, as were *pirzadas* who had inherited a *dargah* or an *in'am*. Rather, they became dervishes, a process involving a significant transformation in their lives. Each of the individuals mentioned above had formerly been integrated either with Bijapur's orthodox Sufi establishment or with some arm of the ruling establishment. On the other hand, being a *majzub* necessarily involved embracing doctrines that were heretical from the standpoint of Islamic orthodoxy, adopting practices like drinking *bhang* or wine that were condemned by the orthodox, and flaunting behavioral eccentricities such as nakedness that were offensive to the "worldly people." Hence, it is possible to conclude that abandonment of one's former life for that of the *majzub* frequently involved a repudiation of the orthodox Sufi establishment, and necessarily involved a repudiation of the ruling establishment with which orthodox Sufis had become identified.

Owing to the *majzubs*' disinclination to write, it is difficult to ascertain their own viewpoint of the tensions existing between

[81] *Mishkat*, copy B, fol. 532b. [82] *Tazkirat al-Qadiri*, fol. 70a.

[83] *Mishkat*, copy A, fol. 153a.

them and the orthodox Sufi establishment. We do have the valuable remarks of a poet like Mahmud Bahri who expressed considerable sympathy for *majzubs* while hurling vitriolic invectives at "worldly" Sufis, but we have nothing written by the *majzubs* themselves. On the other hand, the arguments of orthodox Sufis and their protests at the rising phenomenon of *majzubs* are indeed well documented. Even in the first half of the seventeenth century the Reformist Sufi Abu'l-Hasan Qadiri (d. 1635) warned of the dangerous tendencies of "intoxicated" Sufis:

> There are many *pirs* who are like devils
>   Whom you should not follow.
> If you follow them
>   You would eventually regret it.
>
> . . . .
>
> They are awakened at the end of the night
>   To sing, play music, and dance.
> In this way their faces are very bright
>   And everyone beholds them.
> But the devil can come disguised as a cat
>   And can deceive us at any moment.
>
> . . . .
>
> *Pirs* of today, compared with us,
>   Are the deputies of the devil.
> Those ignorant people who are without a *pir*
>   Are surprised at seeing them.
> They are involved with various kinds of magic, like jugglers.
>   They change water to oil.
> They indulge in giving out prophecy;
>   Within a moment they change into a boy, or disappear.
> They are jugglers
>   And will tell us faulty information.
> They are snake-charmers,
>   And they use *bhang* for intoxication.
> As soon as they shut their eyes
>   Whatever they see they mistake for God.[84]

Though viewed from a hostile perspective, some of the most important attributes of the *majzubs* are indicated in the above

[84] Abu'l-Hasan Qadiri, *Sukh Anjan*, p. 127, lines 13-16; p. 128, lines 11-16; p. 140, lines 11-18; p. 141, lines 1-6.

passage: their use of music, dance, and *bhang* to achieve states of ecstasy, their illuminated nature while in these states, their indulgence in prophesying, trickery, or magic, and their pantheistic theosophy.

A similar indictment appeared in a book by Maulana Muhammad Zubairi II (d. 1677), a man who himself represented the marriage, so typical in late seventeenth century Bijapur, between institutional Sufism and the orthodox tradition of the *'ulama*: he had been instructed in the orthodox Muslim sciences by his paternal uncle, who was a *qazi*, and he was given a *khilafat* by his maternal uncle, the orthodox Shattari Sufi Saiyid Muhammad Mudarris.[85] In his *Kashf al-Asrar* Zubairi condemned those Sufis dominated by psychic states (*hal*) and urged his readers to follow only those Sufis dominated by exoteric knowledge (*'ilm*).[86] And with apparent reference to his dervish contemporary Amin al-Din A'la, Zubairi labeled as an atheist anyone who neglected the daily Muslim prayers, and asked how anybody could claim to have become God when even the Prophet of Islam had made no such claim.[87] Then referring to the *majzubs*, Zubairi asserted that such individuals were not fit to be shaikhs or to have followers, that they should be judged not only insane, but also heretical in light of the *shari'at*, and finally that any persons disagreeing with this judgment were themselves heretics and atheists (*zindiq* and *mulhid*).[88]

Summary

In late seventeenth century Bijapur a formidable social and ideological gulf separated the *majzubs* from the established Sufi community of *pirzadas* attached to *dargahs* or holding *in'am* grants. This development is perhaps best reflected in the strident nature of Maulana Muhammad Zubairi II's judgment of *majzubs* and in the fears expressed by other orthodox Sufis that even Qadiri shaikhs might defect to the heterodox following of Amin al-Din A'la. What had occurred in this period was essentially a

85 *Rauzat*, copy A, p. 222.

86 Maulana Muhammad Zubairi II, *Kashf al-Asrar*. Dakhni MS (Hyderabad: Personal collection of M. Akbaruddin Siddiqi), p. 16.

87 Ibid., pp. 7c, 8.

88 Ibid., p. 7b.

polarization of those Sufis who had accommodated themselves rather comfortably to the social and political world of the Muslim ruling elite, and those discontented individuals born of that class who rejected their former lives in favor of independent, more inner-directed forms of religious experience without reference to external authority. Indeed, so far apart were the world-views and life-styles of the *in'amdar-pirzada* and the *majzub* that neither one would likely have recognized in the other their common spiritual origins in Central Asia or Baghdad.

It is true that Sufis of the dervish variety were found in many times and places throughout Islamic history. While traveling along coastal Tamilnad around 1344, Ibn Battuta met a certain shaikh whom he described as "one of the crazy darwishes who let their hair hang loose over their shoulders."[89] Other foreign travelers like Battuta seldom failed to notice dervishes in various parts of the Muslim world at various times, precisely because their behavior or dress made them so conspicuous. At the same time, however, the fact remains that the preponderance of Bijapur's *majzubs*, as was also the case with its landed Sufis, appeared in the period of the kingdom's decline. As for the landed Sufis, we have seen that that class was wholly created by the state and appeared at a time when the government would have perceived reason to gather to the cause of orthodoxy all elements of the Muslim population. The *majzubs* also appeared at this time since fundamentally they arose in reaction to the values and life-styles of the landed Sufis, who in their opinion had compromised too much with this world.

The declining fortunes of Bijapur and its Muslim community in the late seventeenth century could only have reinforced the *majzubs*' negative response to "this world." As a result they withdrew, a phenomenon that was certainly not without parallel in India or elsewhere. Referring to the "decaying Mughal-Maratha-Rajput civilisation" of eighteenth-century North India, Hermann Goetz observed that "the retirement from worldly affairs into a life of pious devotion is not less remarkable in this age. The dervish and the jogini are likewise a favourite theme of art literature; the simple, sober life without many wants and fears, far

89 Battuta, *Travels in Asia and Africa*, p. 264.

from the vanities, the lies and the ferociousness of the courts became an almost sentimental desire."[90]

Although he was referring more to ascetic recluses than the heterodox dervishes we have been considering, Goetz recognized that the phenomenon of withdrawal from society on the part of certain individuals represented a response to certain historical conditions. It was their perception of these historical conditions that seems to have caused them to form what Victor Turner has called a "communitas of withdrawal or retreat." This involved, wrote Turner, "a total or partial withdrawal from participation in the structural relations of the world, which is, in any case, conceived of as sort of a permanent 'disaster area.' "[91]

Regarded in Turner's perspective, the *majzubs* of Bijapur find rather close parallel in the Anabaptist movement of sixteenth-century central Europe. The Anabaptists, wrote a social historian of the movement,

> were convinced that the existing society made it impossible to lead a Christian life . . . [they] condemned the existing political institutions as unchristian and withdrew from the world as much as possible. Even so, their position had dangerous implications. By condemning law courts, oaths, the legal use of force, and indeed, government itself as unchristian, this peaceful brethren became a potential threat to civilization.[92]

Similarly, the *majzubs*' deviation from orthodox doctrine and orthodox norms of behavior provoked persecution on at least several occasions. And there were other parallels between the two movements. Just as the *majzubs* condemned the *in'amdar-pirzadas* for compromising too much with the 'Adil Shahi government and its religious auxiliaries, so also did the Anabaptists condemn the Lutherans who in their opinion had compromised too much with the Roman Church. For what the Anabaptists wanted was a return to the pristine age of apostolic Christianity before the institution of the Church began to inhibit, in their view, man's

[90] Hermann Goetz, *The Crisis of Indian Civilisation in the Eighteenth and Early Nineteenth Centuries* (Calcutta: University of Calcutta, 1938), p. 18.

[91] Victor W. Turner, *The Ritual Process: Structure and Anti-Structure* (Chicago: Aldine Publishing Company, 1969), pp. 154 f.

[92] Claus-Peter Clasen, *Anabaptism: A Social History, 1525-1618* (Ithaca and London: Cornell University Press, 1972), p. 425.

direct communion with God. It was in this sense of desiring a return to the religion's original purity that the *majzubs* of seventeenth-century Bijapur most closely resembled the Anabaptists.

It was also in this sense that Bijapur's *majzubs* resembled the original Sufis of eighth-century Iraq and Khurasan. In the final analysis the dervishes of Bijapur represented something of a termination point in the evolution of Sufism, or perhaps more accurately, a return full circle to the point from which that evolution first sprang. Just as the first Sufis reacted to the hardened and worldly institutions that had crystallized around Abbasid Islam, so nine centuries later the dervishes of Bijapur reacted to the hardened and worldly institutions that had crystallized around not only Islam but also the Sufi movement itself. In relation to official Islam, then, Sufis had moved from an early position of revolt to one of accommodation, and now back to one of revolt. Both the early Sufis and Bijapur's *majzubs* were responding to a world they perceived as a "disaster area." Only the nature of their responses differed. Living in fear of God's wrath with His erring people, the early Sufis did not ridicule their contemporary society but rather withdrew from that society in a solitary quest for God by leading lives of pious asceticism, vigilance, and prayer. On the other hand the *majzubs*, while also seeking a solitary road to God and practicing rigorous austerities, emphasized more their repudiation of their contemporary society and its Muslim leadership by mocking and rebuking it in ways they knew to be offensive. It was perhaps inevitable that their bizarre display of contempt for the outward observances of Islam led some to rank charlatanism. But we should not deplore this development as evidence of the "decline" or "decay" of Sufism, as would classical scholars of Sufism such as Arberry.[93] Fundamentally, it merely signaled a change in life-style that some heirs of the tradition felt was necessary in order to adapt themselves and that tradition to a changing social, political, and psychological environment.

[93] See Arberry, *Sufism*, chap. 11.

Chapter Ten

CONCLUSION AND EPILOGUE

Section One

Between 1300 and 1700, especially during the seventeenth century, a great many Sufis lived in the city and kingdom of Bijapur. Some of them wielded a sword, others a pen, others a royal land grant, and still others a begging bowl. Some were introverted to the point of reclusive withdrawal, others extroverted to the point of militancy. Some were orthodox to the point of zealous puritanism, others unorthodox to the point of heresy. Indeed, this study demonstrates that the stereotyped conception of medieval Indian Sufis as pious and quietistic mystics patiently preaching Islam among Hindus is no longer valid. It is simply not possible to generalize about the Sufis of medieval Bijapur, much less of India as a whole, as any unitary group relating in any single or predictable way to the society in which they lived. They clearly played a variety of social roles.

This study has attempted to define and elucidate some of these roles by focusing attention on those behavior patterns that were unique to some Sufis but not to all. Some, whom we have termed the Warrior Sufis, were unique in affiliating themselves with Muslim armies and engaging in armed combat with non-Muslims. Others, the Reformist Sufis, differed from all others in their willingness, or in some cases eagerness, to guide the ʻAdil Shahi court toward a path of strict Islamic orthodoxy. Another type was unique in its propensity to write mystic or popular literature. Still others differed from the rest in their acceptance of government land grants, creating in Bijapur a petty gentry of Sufi *inʻamdars*. Finally, some Sufis rejected the orthodox Muslim society of their day and exhibited a fondness for spiritual and even narcotic exhilaration as a means of attaining a direct experience of God.

While the above characteristics were unique to each type, all of the types can be viewed with reference to common variables.

The three most fundamental of these, as stated in the Introduction to this study, are (1) how Sufis interacted with the Muslim religious establishment or *'ulama*; (2) how they interacted with the court; and (3) how they interacted with the non-Muslim population. Other variables include the Sufis' relation to Islamic doctrine, their affiliation by class (whether Deccani or Foreigner), their affiliation by order, their place of residence, and their literary mode, if any. Having identified the basic types of Sufis, it is possible to compare and contrast them in tabular form with reference to the above-mentioned variables. Table 8 thus illustrates many of the dominant themes of this study. But the limitations of this typological model must be admitted. One pitfall of any typology is the tendency to perceive the categories as rigid or exclusive units. In truth, some Sufis of Bijapur straddled several categories; others fit smoothly into none. Hashim Pir 'Alawi, for example, shared some attributes of Reformist Sufis (his close contact with the court) as well as of the Literati (his interest in the non-Muslim population). The effort has been not to force each Sufi into one or another exclusive category, but to suggest several clusterings of behavioral patterns around which most of those individuals under review coalesced, some more closely than others.

The social functions of the Sufis of Bijapur were, to an appreciable extent, shaped by the society in which they lived. And since Bijapur's society changed over time, some Sufi types were generally more characteristic of certain historical periods than others. Thus the Warrior Sufis appeared predominantly in the first half of the fourteenth century, a period when Muslim armies were for the first time penetrating the Bijapur plateau. There being no established tradition of urban Islamic culture in the plateau at that time, such Sufis could not relate to any court or *'ulama*. Indeed, in one sense they themselves functioned as the *'ulama*. In the absence of a Muslim court in the Deccan, Sufis, being in some instances the only representatives of Islamic organization accompanying the armies, declared and thereby legitimized the *jihad* against non-Muslims.

During the late fourteenth and fifteenth centuries the Bijapur plateau gradually passed from a fluid arena of conflicting Maharashtrian, Kannadiga, and Turkish Muslim culture groups to a more stabilized region in which an eclectic and urbanized Deccani Muslim culture began to coalesce precisely along the fault line

TABLE 8

COMPARATIVE CHARACTERISTICS OF SUFI TYPES

	Warrior Sufis	*Reformist Sufis*	*Literati, Mystical*	*Literati, Popular*	*Landed Sufis*	*Dervish Sufis*
Relation to Court:	n. r.					
integrated with		x			x	
indifferent to			x	x		
hostile to						x
Relation to 'Ulama:	n. r.					
integrated with		x			x	
indifferent to			x	x		
hostile to						x
Relation to Islam:	n. r.					
closely integrated		x			x	
generally orthodox			x	x		
unorthodox						x
Relation to non-Muslims:						
hostile	x				x	
indifferent		x				
accommodating			x	x		x
Affiliation by Order:						
Qadiri		x			x	
Shattari		x			x	
Chishti			x	x		x
none	x					x
Affiliation by Class:						
Foreigner	x	x				
Deccani			x	x	x	x
Literary Language:						
Persian			x			
Dakhni			x	x		
neither	x	x			x	x
Residence:	n. r.					
urban		x			x	
rural			x	x		x
Approximate Number Identified:	10	25	10	10	40	25
Period when Most Characteristic:	1275-1350	1575-1650	1500-1700	1650-1700	1650-1700	1650-1725

n. r.—not relevant. Warrior Sufis settled the Bijapur plateau prior to the formation of an urban environment with its accompanying religious and political institutions.

between Maharashtra and Karnataka. With the disappearance of a Muslim frontier and its replacement by an urban culture focused on Gulbarga and Bidar, the two successive capitals of the Bahmani Sultanate, the Warrior Sufis as a type vanished. In their place a number of urban Sufis were attracted to these seats of regional Muslim power: the Chishti Sufi Bandanawaz Gisudaraz migrated from Delhi to Gulbarga, and a number of Qadiri Sufis migrated from Arabia to Bidar. The city of Bijapur itself did not emerge as an important urban center until the end of the fifteenth century when the Bahmani Sultanate, in which Bijapur had been but a provincial outpost, began to dissolve. By the opening of the sixteenth century Bijapur had acquired all the royal apparatus of an independent Muslim sultanate (a royal family, a nobility, a court, and a class of *'ulama*) and under Sultan 'Ali I (1558-80) vastly expanded its political and territorial base at the expense of the Hindu warrior state to the south, Vijayanagar. But despite its fledgling importance as a regional Islamic center, Bijapur throughout most of the sixteenth century failed to attract Sufis. This was mainly because the court during most of this period was dominated by Shi'as, the sect of Muslims historically antagonistic to Sufis.

In the reign of Sultan Ibrahim II (1580-1627) a series of circumstances combined to attract to Bijapur the first significant number of Sufis since the Warrior Sufis. In a development reflecting a major shift in power balance from the foreign-born Iranian class to the native-born Deccani class, Ibrahim II's regent replaced *isna-'ashari* Shi'ism with Sunnism as the state religion. And while ruling in his own right, Sultan Ibrahim II took steps to make his kingdom the focus of a culture reflecting syncretic elements drawn from both Muslim and Hindu traditions. But if his desire to adorn his court with cultivated individuals and the cessation of Shi'a rule had attracted a good many Sufis to Bijapur, the sultan's personal religious experimentation drew their criticism. Indeed many of the migrants—Sufis of the Qadiri and Shattari orders—set for themselves the goal of reforming Islam in the kingdom and redirecting the sultan from what they considered his aberrant ways. As members of urban orders having close ties with the Arab Middle East, the Reformist Sufis easily accommodated themselves to the religious and political world of the city's *'ulama*. In fact, the orthodox reaction that characterized the reigns of

Ibrahim II's successors seems to have been influenced in part by these Arab-oriented Sufis.

The last two types of Sufis considered in this study, the Landed and Dervish Sufis, were also products of their social environments. Both appeared most typically in the latter half of the seventeenth century when the kingdom as a whole was undergoing social and political decay and the court had begun to adopt a pro-Muslim communal policy. The court's communal partisanship was first suggested in Sultan Muhammad's references to *jizya* and *jihad* in documents of state policy. Practical application of this policy appeared in royal orders levying taxes on the celebration of Hindu festivals and forbidding Muslims to participate in such celebrations. But the deepest wedge between Hindu and Muslim communities was driven by Afzal Khan who, at the head of 10,000 cavalry in 1659, desecrated the most sacred shrine of the Maharashtrian people—the temple of Vithoba at Pandharpur. This act was followed in the reigns of 'Ali II and Sikandar by the defection of many nobles from 'Adil Shahi service and eventually the disaffection of local officials, notably Maharashtrian *desais*, who had formed the foundation of the kingdom's local administration. Stricter application of Muslim Law, which only further aggravated Muslim-Hindu tensions in the kingdom, seems to have been the court's response to the political chaos in which it was engulfed.

As the court came increasingly to conceive the kingdom as a Muslim state and to act in such a way as to realize this conception, it became politically expedient to harness to state interests the one element of Bijapur's Muslim society believed to wield considerable influence among the kingdom's non-elite population —the prominent non-Chishti *pirs* and their sons, the *pirzadas*. And as land was one item universally valued in Indian society and absolutely monopolized by the 'Adil Shahi government, the grant in tax-free lands became the chief instrument by which the court absorbed such Sufis into its fold. Furthermore, by giving *in'am* grants both to Sufis and to members of the kingdom's *'ulama*, the court succeeded in gaining a measure of uniformity among, as well as control over, its Muslim establishment.

But the transformation of *pirzadas* into a petty landed gentry did not occur without profound effects on Sufi institutions. First, it encouraged the abandonment of the *khanaqah* as the basic unit of Bijapur's urban Sufis in favor of the *dargah*. For it was the tombs, not the hospices, that attracted the large crowds of common devotees and therefore fell within the orbit of court interest and court patronage. It was in favor of the attendants and *sajjada-nishins* of such tombs that *in'am* grants were normally issued. Second, the land grant served as a potent means of state intervention in the internal affairs of the *dargah*. Since the succession to a *dargah*'s leadership carried with it the lands granted to it by the state, any dispute over succession had necessarily to be resolved where any land disputes were properly litigated—the Bijapur court. In this way the court acquired the right to confirm or deny successors at the *dargahs*. Also, state dependency seems to have diminished many *in'amdars*' responsiveness to the non-Muslim population not affiliated with Sufi *dargahs*. Like the Warrior Sufis, some landed *pirzadas* of the late seventeenth century even raised the cry of *jihad* and participated directly in some of the communal conflicts that accompanied the final dissolution of the 'Adil Shahi state.

In the last years of the kingdom's history the pressures exerted on Muslims by the court and the *'ulama* to conform to their social mold, as the *in'amdars* had done, produced a counter-effect in the appearance of Dervish Sufis. Contemporary sources give the pejorative label *majzub* to a number of individuals ranging from a Chishti of respectable origins who espoused heretical notions (Amin al-Din A'la) to those spiritual nonconformists who exulted in their unorthodoxy, nakedness, or addiction to *bhang*—all of which were anathema to the orthodox Muslim establishment. As Table 8 indicates, the last type of Sufi contrasted with their landed contemporaries in most all of the indexes listed. While the landed Sufis were well integrated with the court, the *'ulama*, and with Islamic orthodoxy, *majzubs* were hostile to the institutions of urban Islam and unmindful of orthodoxy. Precisely because they held such opposing positions, the antagonisms between *in'amdars* and *majzubs* were greater than those between any other Sufi types of Bijapur. The former were perceived from the other's viewpoint as "worldly men" who had sold out to the structured and confining world of the city's orthodox establishment. On the other hand, the *majzubs* were perceived by the *in'amdars* and other *pirzadas* as "madmen" who had wandered from the path of correct belief and behavior. Indeed, many *majzubs* had repudiated their own origins in the world of the orthodox Muslim establishment. By the collapse of the dynasty the polarization between the two types had become so complete that neither would have acknowledged the other's claim to the title "Sufi."

Although the Warrior, Reformist, Landed, and Dervish types were all to varying degrees products of the social milieu in which they lived, the Literati Sufis were the least affected by the shifting fortunes of the dynasty. Aloof from the world of the court and the *'ulama*, the Chishtis of Shahpur Hillock spanned the entire two hundred years of 'Adil Shahi rule in Bijapur as a relatively continuous tradition. The *khalifas* and *murids* of Miranji Shams al-'Ushshaq, Burhan al-Din Janam, and Amin al-Din A'la can be further distinguished from most other Sufis of Bijapur by their propensity to write. Although their contributions in the field of Islamic mystic literature were not original, in two other respects their writings deserve attention. One of them was their pioneering role in stabilizing and giving literary respectability to the Dakhni language, the vernacular tongue spoken primarily by Deccani Muslims. That Dakhni Urdu achieved literary status long before North Indian Urdu has not been sufficiently appreciated, doubtless because the former was dislodged and rusticated by the latter following the Mughal conquests of the late seventeenth century.

In terms of Sufi contact with Hindus, the most important achievement of the Literati Sufis lay in their writing folk literature, especialy the *chakki-nama* and the *charkha-nama*. Because this literature formed the link between the mystic philosophy of Islam and the popular religion of a *pir's* devotee—many of whom were non-Muslims—its significance cannot be underestimated. For in it were combined the popularity of an existing folk medium, the imagery of the household chores performed by village women, the simplest precepts of the Islamic religion, and the elements of *pir*-worship. And although its esoteric content became considerably adulterated in the transfer from a mystic to a popular idiom, this literature represented an important link between the inner circles of Chishti *pirs* and their largely non-elite, female constituency. Such a constituency became integrated into the outer circles of a *pir's* following largely through this literature, which might therefore be termed the litany of folk Islam.

Section Two

The demise of the city of Bijapur as an important Indo-Muslim cultural center was as thorough as it was swift. "In a political sense," wrote Meadows Taylor in 1866, "Beejapoor ceased to exist after its capture by the Emperor Aurungzeeb. It is never again mentioned by historians of the period, nor in local memoirs. No event of remarkable character appears to have happened there, and thus silently and mournfully the great city passed to its decay, which was comparatively rapid."[1] The natural disasters that swept over the Bijapur plateau immediately after the Mughal conquest—the plagues, floods, and famines—contributed immensely to the abandonment of the city and to its eclipse as a focus of regional Muslim culture. From 1724 to 1795 a greatly depopulated city of Bijapur along with the eastern districts of the former kingdom fell under the administration of the Nizam of Hyderabad. In the late eighteenth century, when Maratha forces defeated the Nizam (1795) and the territories of the erstwhile 'Adil Shahi dynasty were wholly ceded to the Maratha Peshwa, the city was regularly plundered. By the beginning of the nineteenth century the countryside had become a desert, and the city itself a pile of plundered ruins.[2] Maratha spoliation of the city continued unabated even after the 1818 wars with the British, for Bijapur was allowed to remain in the revived Maratha kingdom.[3]

[1] Taylor and Fergusson, *Architecture at Beejapoor*, p. 51.

[2] Sir James Mackintosh, who visited Bijapur in 1808, described the country north of the city as a desert. "For fourteen miles," he wrote, "the only living creatures were some pretty parroquets, a partridge, a hare, and a herd of deer" (quoted in Sathyan, ed., *Mysore State Gazetteer: Bijapur District*, p. 83).

[3] " It is for ever to be regretted that this was done," complained Meadows Taylor in 1866, "and that Beejapoor was not made the permanent station of a large force, or at least an express stipulation in regard to the preservation of the royal edifices was not provided; thus the work of spoliation continued with renewed vigour, and the most perfect and deliberate impunity. Palaces and private houses were soon unroofed for the sake of their noble teak beams. The whole of the window and door frames, with their exquisitely carved lattice-work, were carried away in cartloads to Sattara [the Maratha capital], and to every other place of which the owner could get an order from the Sattara Rajah. There are persons still alive in Beejapoor who witnessed this devastation with a grief which is now outspoken, and accompanied by many a deep curse; and tell of it with mournful tears" (Taylor and Fergusson, *Architecture at Beejapoor*, p. 55).

These developments had serious effects for Sufism and Sufi institutions. With the physical basis of Muslim urban culture virtually obliterated, Sufis having an urban orientation would no longer immigrate to the region. And many of those already living in the city, particularly landed *pirzadas* whose livelihood depended on the court's patronage, fled to other centers of Muslim culture such as Hyderabad or Arcot as the fortunes of Bijapur itself ebbed. Even those Sufis or heirs to Sufis who were not dependent in any direct way upon Bijapur's political existence, such as the *majzubs*, were frequently forced to flee because of cholera or famines in the area.

Despite the turmoil of the eighteenth century, however, several legacies of the Sufis have survived to the present day. Both are characteristic of the third or *ta'ifa* phase of Sufism's evolution, as the *tariqa* systems ended with the disappearance of the Sufis themselves. One such legacy is the folk literature Sufis left behind them—*chakki-namas*, *charkha-namas*, and other devotional materials—which can be found in Deccan villages today in cheap lithograph editions. The other legacy is the great *dargahs* built over the Sufis' graves. Many of these tombs had been built during the 'Adil Shahi period, indicating that the transition from *tariqa* to *ta'ifa* Sufism in Bijapur was taking place even before the political demise of the state. There is no evidence that after the dynasty's collapse any *khanaqahs*, the central institution of *tariqa* Sufism, remained in Bijapur as functioning units. Even the *khanaqah* of Miranji Shams al-'Ushshaq, which had once been the focus of a vibrant and literarily active tradition of Chishti teaching, was swiftly replaced by the *dargah* of his grandson Amin al-Din A'la as the basic institution of Shahpur Hillock. This *dargah* was constructed in 1677-78, just two years after Amin al-Din's death. The rapid transition from *tariqa* to *ta'ifa* Sufism on Shahpur Hillock is further indicated in the careers of Amin al-Din's descendants. His son Baba Shah (d. 1707-8) is scarcely mentioned in the primary sources, and the later *pirzadas* of Shahpur Hillock appear to have achieved no recognition beyond being the *sajjada-nishins* or related functionaries of Amin al-Din's *dargah*.

Yet today this and other *dargahs* of Bijapur have immense importance as centers of folk Islam. The Amin al-Din *dargah* is perhaps unique in that it continues to induct *murids* into its formal organization by means of issuing them printed certificates. Such a certificate, a copy of which is found in Appendix II, provides the

13. Devotees at the *dargah* of ʿAbd al-Razzaq Qadiri

newly inducted *murid* with a spiritual genealogy linking himself or herself not only to Amin al-Din but to the Prophet of Islam.[4] At the head of the certificate is the Islamic credo. Beneath this is the name of the Prophet, followed by a spiritual genealogy extending through the Chishti Sufis of Delhi to Bandanawaz Gisudaraz of Gulbarga, and from him through Miranji Shams al-ʿUshshaq, Burhan al-Din Janam, Amin al-Din Aʿla, and each generation's successor at the *dargah* from Amin al-Din to the present. At the bottom is a blank space to be filled in with the name of the prospective *murid* and a second blank space for the day, month, and year that the *sajjada-nishin* formally enrolled him or her among the *dargah's murids*. The certificate, signed by the *sajjada-nishin*, is kept by the *murid*.

[4] I am indebted to Shah Faruq Husaini, brother of the current *sajjada-nishin* at the Amin al-Din *dargah*, for giving me a copy of the *dargah's* initiation certificate, of which this is a reproduction.

14. Devotees at the *dargah* of Hamīd Qadiri

Informal association with *dargahs*, meaning participation in the festivities that occur at *dargahs* on Thursdays and during *'urs* celebrations, is much more widespread in Bijapur than such formal association as that indicated in the giving of certificates. In the main, the kind of devotions performed by the devotees informally associated with the *dargahs* parallel those of Hindu pilgrims at Hindu shrines: circumambulation of the site, entrance into the main chamber, the touching of the clothes, turban, or other relics of the departed saint, and the general belief in the healing effect accruing to the devotee upon making these devotions.[5] The Thursday participation includes lighting candles around the Sufi's tomb, offering gifts (*nazr*) of flowers or coins to the *sajjada-nishin*, meeting and talking with fellow devotees at the *dargah*, or singing devotional songs individually or collectively (often with musical instruments) in praise of the Sufi and asking for his intercession with God.[6] The following lines, for example, are sung by women at the *dargah* of Bandanawaz Gisudaraz in Gulbarga:

> Having said "Allah, Allah," I have climbed the stairs,
> One by one.
> With my thread and flowers in hand
> I am standing here claiming my wishes.
> My *khwaja* is sleeping in the flower garden;
> Incense is burning in the flower garden.
> Oh *khwaja*, the little red bird is sitting over your tomb—
> Everyone sees the red bird sitting there.
> Yes, yes, Allah—my *pir*, my *murshid*.
> How are you sleeping in the tomb, my *murshid*?
> Oh *khwaja*, you know my heart's desire.
> Oh *khwaja*, please grant my desire:
> My yard is empty, my house deserted—
> Today fill my lap with child.[7]

As the final lines of the song indicate, a woman's desire for children can be one basis of her belief in the spirit of the departed saint and an important reason for her participation in the folk worship that takes place at a *dargah*. Other reasons for frequent-

[5] See Agehananda Bharati, "Pilgrimage in the Indian Tradition," *History of Religions*, 3 (Summer 1963), p. 142.

[6] See Figures 13 and 14, which illustrate some of these activities at two of Bijapur's *dargahs*: that of 'Abd al-Razzaq and that of Shah Hamīd Qadiri.

[7] Zinat Sajida, "Dakani Git," pp. 216 f.

ing *dargahs* are similarly votive in nature. Some *dargahs* are specialized in that visits or pilgrimages to them are believed to grant certain wishes or alleviate certain ills of the devotee. The *dargah* of 'Abd al-Razzaq Qadiri, for example, is believed to work special powers in healing mental disorders. Similarly the tomb of Hamīd Qadiri has a chain fixed on its gate that a sick person must pull five consecutive Thursdays in order to get well.

The major event at any *dargah* has always been the annual *'urs* ceremony commemorating the Sufi's marriage (*'urs*) with God, or his death date. We have noted above the extent to which the *'urs* at the *dargah* of Bandanawaz Gisudaraz had, even in the seventeenth century, become a major festival of the Deccan, attended by sultans and commoners alike. Today similar festivals mark many *dargahs* of Bijapur, the larger *'urs* celebrations being held at the tombs of 'Abd al-Razzaq Qadiri (attended by 10,000 to 15,000), Amin al-Din A'la (attended by 8,000 to 10,000), and Hashim Pir 'Alawi (attended by 4,000 to 5,000). Other major celebrations take place at the *dargahs* of Murtaza Qadiri, Habib Allah Sibghat Allahi, Hamza Husaini, Hamīd Qadiri, and Haji Rumi.[8] It is somewhat ironic that the largest *'urs* celebration today is held at the *dargah* of one of the least-conspicuous Sufis in this study—'Abd al-Razzaq Qadiri.[9] What this indicates is that

[8] Shah Burhan al-Din Husaini, *sajjada-nishin* at the Hashim Pir *dargah*, and 'Abd al-Qadir, Urdu teacher at the Government Teacher Training College, Bijapur. Interviews held in Bijapur on 27 and 29 October 1970.

[9] Little is known of 'Abd al-Razzaq Qadiri (d. 1641). He seems to have conformed to the Reformist type, having been a *khalifa* of Shah Mustafa Qadiri, a close friend of Hashim Pir 'Alawi, and the spiritual guide for Sultan Muhammad's Abyssinian *wazir*, Khan Muhammad (*Rauzat*, pp. 127 f.). A Qadiri biography further records that the Sufi had migrated from his native Baghdad to Bijapur via East Africa, where a local king out of gratitude to the Sufi presented him with his own son. This was the future Khan Muhammad, whom 'Abd al-Razzaq brought to Bijapur as a child and who eventually rose to become Sultan Muhammad's *wazir* (*Sahifat*, Urdu edn., pp. 16 f., note). It is possible that 'Abd al-Razzaq had been a slave merchant who, having brought the Abyssinian to Bijapur, remained his benefactor. The construction of 'Abd al-Razzaq's *dargah* is more easily explained. Khan Muhammad was the *wazir* who, in 1657, sixteen years after his *pir's* death, was treacherously murdered by the Bijapur nobility for having intrigued with the Mughals during Aurangzeb's first invasion of Bijapur. When Aurangzeb eventually conquered the city he constructed a mausoleum over the *wazir's* grave, probably in memory of the service Khan Muhammad had performed for the Mughals long before. At the same time, and in the same style, a companion mausoleum was constructed over the

over the past several centuries *dargahs* have acquired their own legends and spiritual power (this one is noted for its capacity to heal mentally disturbed persons) quite independent of the lives of those buried beneath them. Thus, the hiatus between the *tariqa* tradition of the Sufis themselves and the *ta'ifa* traditions that have focused on their *dargahs* is now complete.

For the past two or three centuries the *dargahs* and the class of *pirzadas* who manage them have been functioning as dynamic catalysts in deepening Islamic acculturation among the score of communities that are already self-confessed Muslims in Bijapur District. The Weavers, one of the largest of all Muslim communities in the district, and among convert communities, one of the most orthodox, were reported in an 1884 survey to have been converted to Islam by Hashim Pir 'Alawi and Bandanawaz Gisudaraz. We have seen in our discussion of Hashim Pir that he did in fact induct non-Muslims in his following as *murids*, though it was not specified that these included Weavers. But the survey went on to say that the Weavers "still pay special devotion to those two saints and show great respect to their descendants who are called *pirzadas*."[10] This suggests that although a few Hindus belonging to the Koshti or Sali castes may have become *murids* of Hashim Pir—representing an initial, formal step in becoming Muslim—it was the Sufi's *dargah* that over successive generations became the religious focus of the Weavers as a community and that has continued even to the present day to further the process of Islamic acculturation.[11]

These remarks would indicate that Henry Cousens in his 1890 description of Bijapur—"a lonely and deserted extent of ruins, the haunt of the jackal, the wolf, and the hyaena, and an elysium of bats and owls"—may have overlooked something. Sufi *dargahs* may have appeared physically crumbled to Cousens and hence dead. But in reality these stately tombs, though severed from the lives of the Sufis buried beneath them, have sustained a living tradition of folk Islam that has remained vibrant and responsive to the needs of many.

---

grave of the *wazir's pir*, 'Abd al-Razzaq (Cousens, *Bijapur and its Architectural Remains*, p. 113).

[10] *Gazetteer of Bombay Presidency*, p. 299.

[11] Shah Burhan al-Din Husaini, the present *sajjada-nishin* of the Hashim Pir *dargah*, asserts that Weavers are still predominant among the devotees of his *dargah*. Interview held at the *dargah* on 7 July 1970.

Appendix I

SPIRITUAL AND FAMILIAL GENEALOGIES

QADIRIS OF BIJAPUR

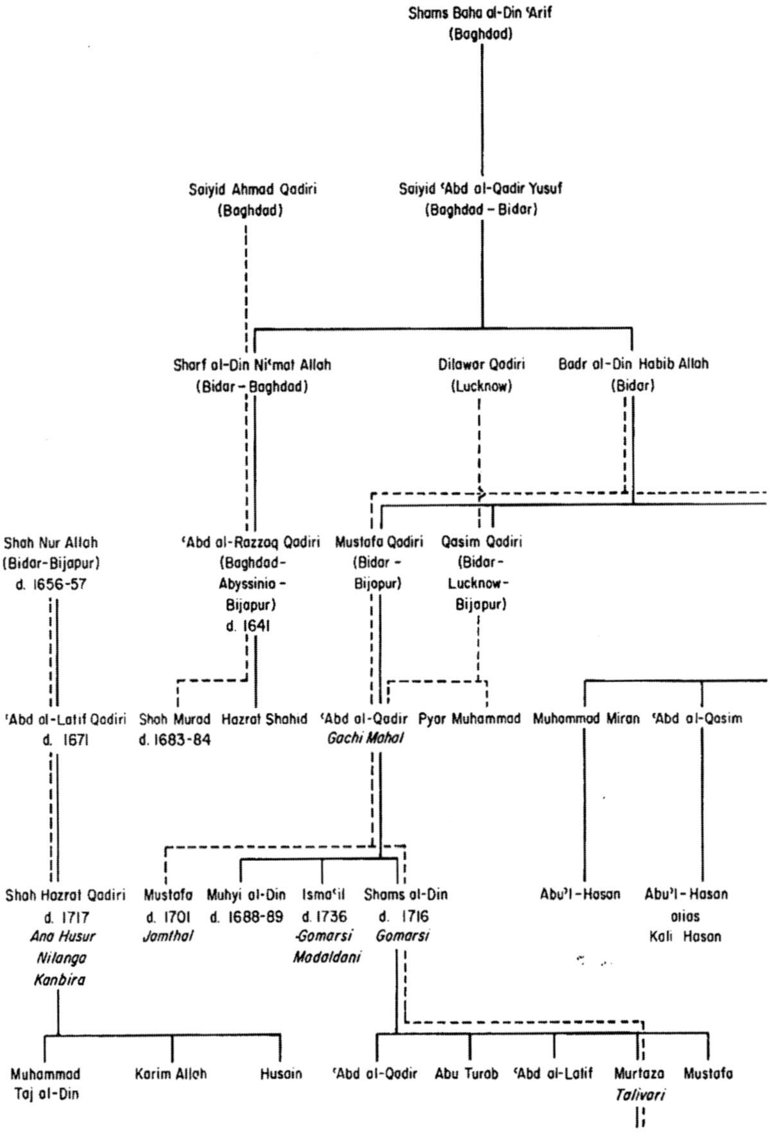

Note: Broken lines indicate spiritual lineage; unbroken lines indicate familial lineage.

Italicized place names indicate villages granted to the recipient in in'am, ma'ash, or jagir.

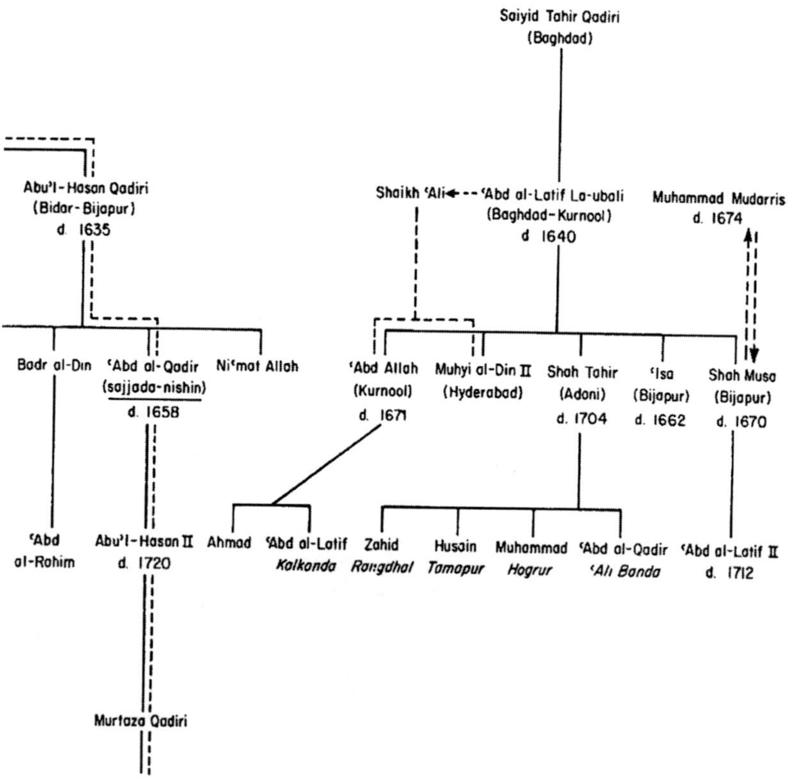

SHATTARIS OF BIJAPUR, THROUGH SHAH SIBGHAT ALLAH

Note: Broken lines indicate spiritual lineage; unbroken lines indicate familial lineage.

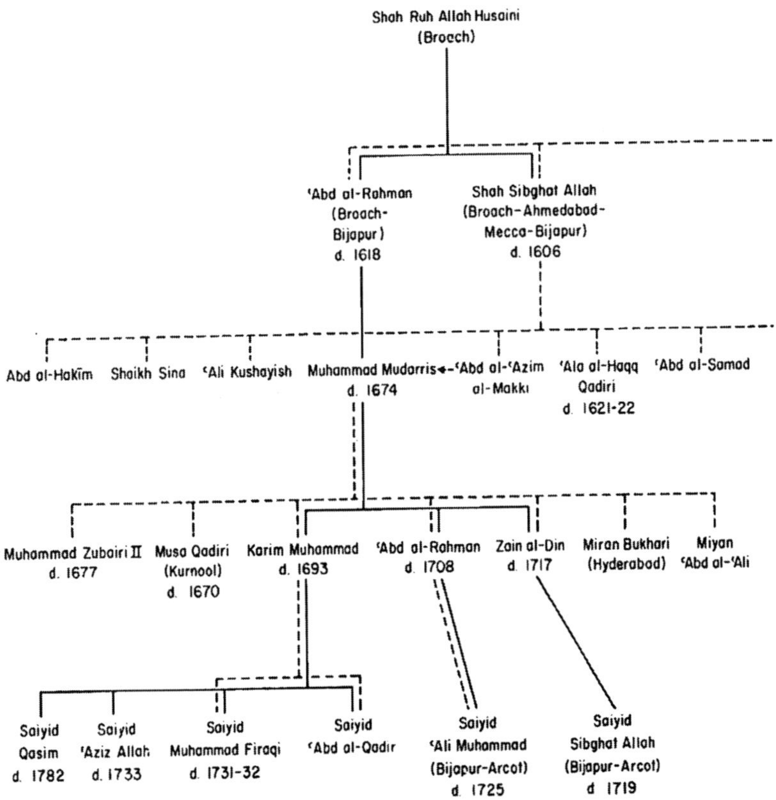

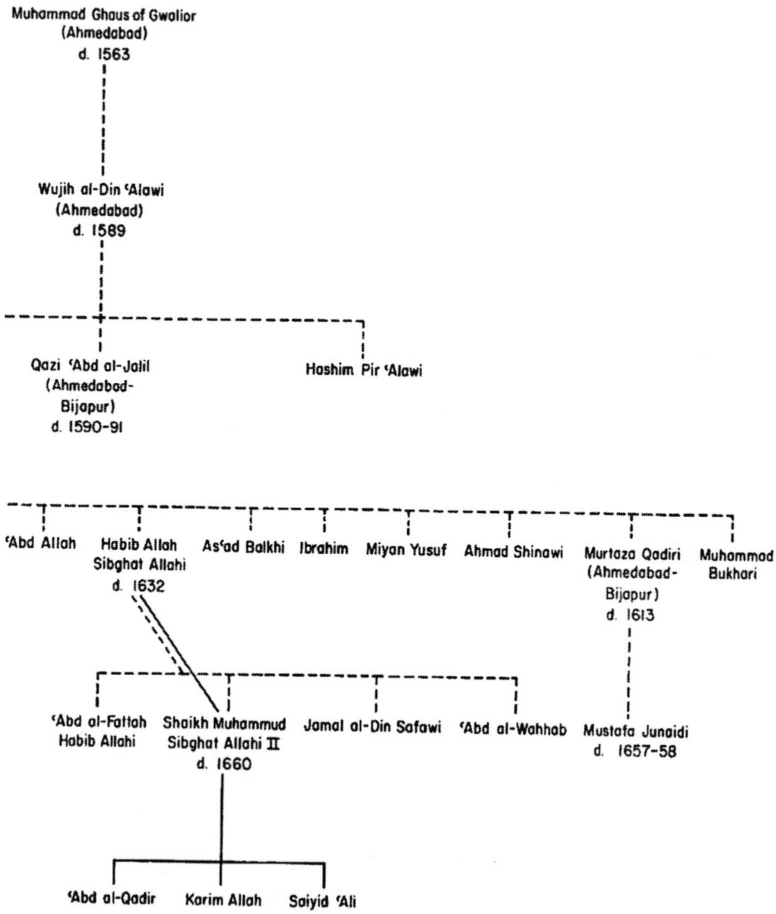

Muhammad Ghaus of Gwalior (Ahmedabad) d. 1563
Wujih al-Din ʿAlawi (Ahmedabad) d. 1589
Qazi ʿAbd al-Jalil (Ahmedabad-Bijapur) d. 1590-91
Hashim Pir ʿAlawi
ʿAbd Allah
Habib Allah Sibghat Allahi d. 1632
Asʿad Balkhi
Ibrahim
Miyan Yusuf
Ahmad Shinawi
Murtaza Qadiri (Ahmedabad-Bijapur) d. 1613
Muhammad Bukhari
ʿAbd al-Fattah Habib Allahi
Shaikh Muhammud Sibghat Allahi II d. 1660
Jamal al-Din Safawi
ʿAbd al-Wahhab
Mustafa Junaidi d. 1657-58
ʿAbd al-Qadir
Karim Allah
Saiyid ʿAli

SHATTARIS OF BIJAPUR, THROUGH SHAH HASHIM PIR ʿALAWI

Note: Broken lines indicate spiritual lineage; unbroken lines indicate familial lineage.

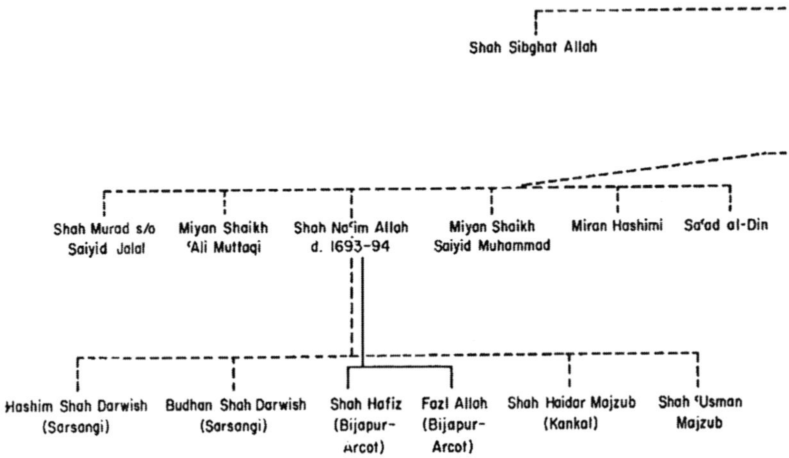

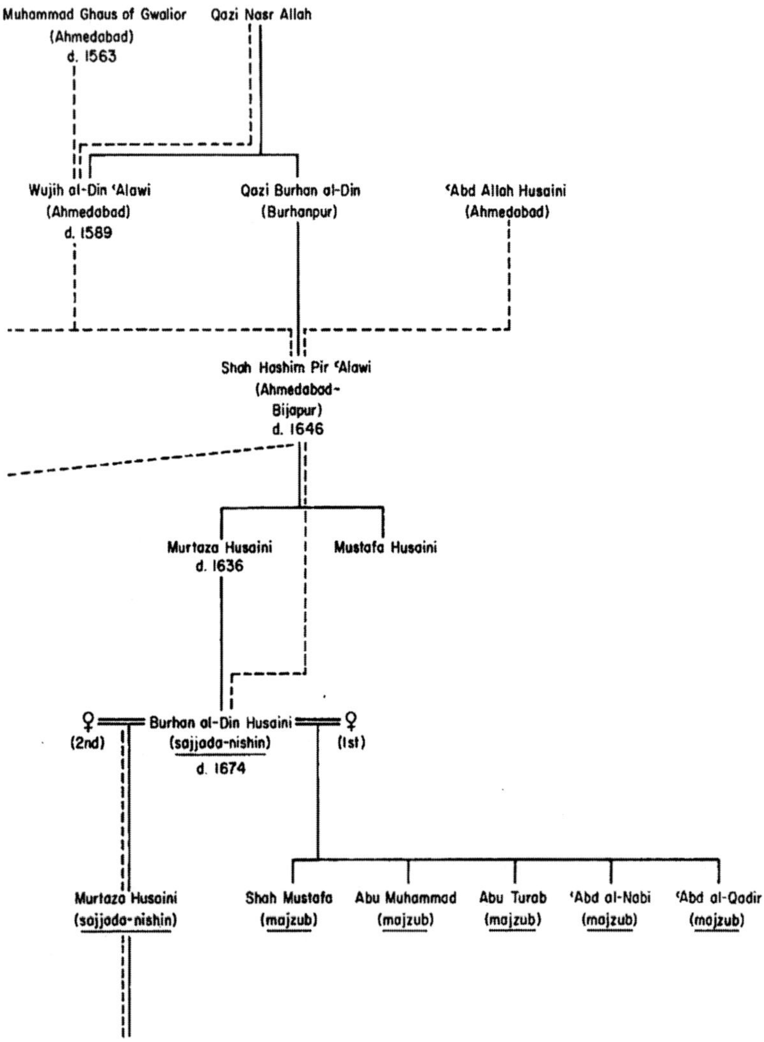
Muhammad Ghaus of Gwalior
(Ahmedabad)
d. 1563
Qazi Nasr Allah
Wujih al-Din 'Alawi
(Ahmedabad)
d. 1589
Qazi Burhan al-Din
(Burhanpur)
'Abd Allah Husaini
(Ahmedabad)
Shah Hashim Pir 'Alawi
(Ahmedabad-
Bijapur)
d. 1646
Murtaza Husaini
d. 1636
Mustafa Husaini
♀
(2nd)
Burhan al-Din Husaini
(sajjada-nishin)
d. 1674
♀
(1st)
Murtaza Husaini
(sajjada-nishin)
Shah Mustafa
(majzub)
Abu Muhammad
(majzub)
Abu Turab
(majzub)
'Abd al-Nabi
(majzub)
'Abd al-Qadir
(majzub)

CHISHTIS OF BIJAPUR

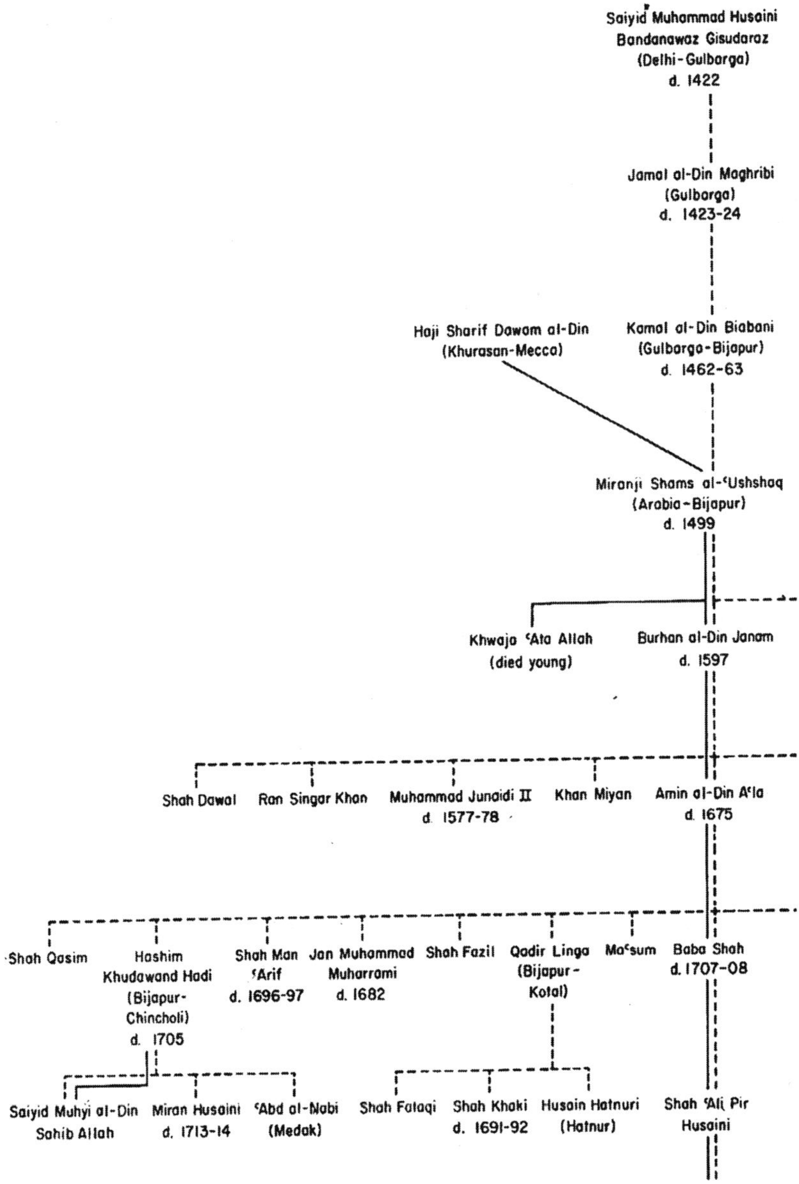

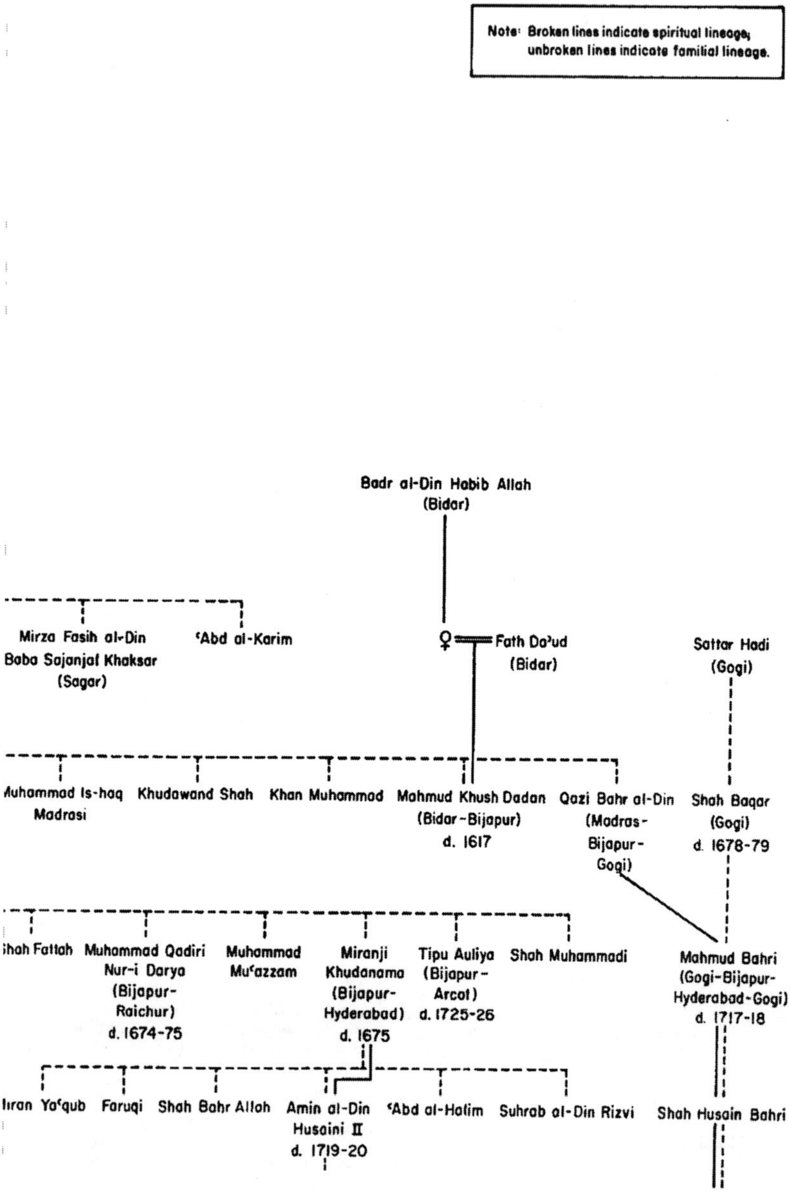
Note: Broken lines indicate spiritual lineage; unbroken lines indicate familial lineage.
Badr al-Din Habib Allah (Bidar)
Mirza Fasih al-Din Baba Sajanjal Khaksar (Sagar)
ʿAbd al-Karim
♀
Fath Daʾud (Bidar)
Sattar Hadi (Gogi)
Muhammad Is-haq Madrasi
Khudawand Shah
Khan Muhammad
Mahmud Khush Dadan (Bidar-Bijapur) d. 1617
Qazi Bahr al-Din (Madras-Bijapur-Gogi)
Shah Baqar (Gogi) d. 1678-79
Shah Fattah
Muhammad Qadiri Nur-i Darya (Bijapur-Raichur) d. 1674-75
Muhammad Muʿazzam
Miranji Khudanama (Bijapur-Hyderabad) d. 1675
Tipu Auliya (Bijapur-Arcot) d. 1725-26
Shah Muhammadi
Mahmud Bahri (Gogi-Bijapur-Hyderabad-Gogi) d. 1717-18
Imran Yaʿqub
Faruqi
Shah Bahr Allah
Amin al-Din Husaini II d. 1719-20
ʿAbd al-Halim
Suhrab al-Din Rizvi
Shah Husain Bahri

Appendix II

CERTIFICATE INDUCTING DEVOTEES AT THE AMIN AL-DIN *DARGAH*

بسم اللہ الرحمن الرحیم

لا الٰہ الا اللہ محمد رسول اللہ

الٰہی بحرمت حضرت خواجہ انبیا ابوالقاسم محمد مصطفےٰ رسول خدا صلی اللہ علیہ وسلم

الٰہی بحرمت حضرت خواجہ صدر الدین ابوالفتح ولی الاکبر الصادق جعفر الثانی محمد یوسف الحسینی الملقب گیسو دراز بندہ نواز قدس اللہ سرہٗ العزیز

الٰہی بحرمت حضرت خواجہ شاہ جمال الدین مغربی قدس اللہ سرہٗ العزیز

الٰہی بحرمت حضرت خواجہ شاہ کمال الدین بیابانی قدس اللہ سرہٗ العزیز

الٰہی بحرمت حضرت خواجہ میرانجی شمس العشاق قدس اللہ سرہٗ العزیز

الٰہی بحرمت حضرت خواجہ شاہ برہان الدین قطب الآفاق قدس اللہ سرہٗ العزیز

الٰہی بحرمت حضرت خواجہ امین الدین اعلیٰ معشوق ربانی قدس اللہ سرہٗ العزیز

الٰہی بحرمت حضرت خواجہ پیر باباشاہ حسینی قدس اللہ سرہٗ العزیز

الٰہی بحرمت حضرت خواجہ مولا علی پیر صاحب قدس اللہ سرہٗ العزیز

الٰہی بحرمت حضرت خواجہ پیر دستگیر حسینی بادشاہ قدس اللہ سرہٗ العزیز

الٰہی بحرمت حضرت خواجہ امین الدین علی ثانی قدس اللہ سرہٗ العزیز

الٰہی بحرمت حضرت خواجہ سید محمد امین قدس اللہ سرہٗ العزیز

الٰہی بحرمت حضرت خواجہ سید ثانی امین الدین علی صاحب قدس اللہ سرہٗ العزیز

الٰہی بحرمت حضرت خواجہ سید شاہ اسد اللہ حسینی قدس اللہ سرہٗ العزیز

الٰہی بحرمت حضرت خواجہ سید بادشاہ حسینی صاحب قدس اللہ سرہٗ العزیز

الٰہی بحرمت حضرت خواجہ سید شاہ عطاء اللہ حسینی صاحب کعبہ و قبلہ مدظلہٗ العالی

الٰہی بحرمت حضرت خواجہ سید شاہ فاروق حسینی چشتی قدس اللہ سرہٗ العزیز

این شجرہ خواجگان چشت واہلِ بہشت باسم

مرحمت گردیدہ مورخہ ماہ سنہ

غلام خواجہ خواجگان چشت اہل بہشت

سید محمد فاروق حسینی برادر سجادہ

خواجہ امین درگاہ بیجاپور

Appendix III

MUSLIM COMMUNITIES OF BIJAPUR DISTRICT IN 1884

MUSLIM COMMUNITIES OF BIJAPUR DISTRICT IN 1884

Name	*Occupation*	*Origin*	*Language*	*Religious Customs*
I. COMMUNITIES OF FOREIGN ORIGIN				
A. General Classes				
* 1. Saiyid	*Pirzadas*, *jagirdars*, and husbandmen	Descendants of Middle Eastern Sufis	Urdu	Strict Sunni
* 2. Shaikh	Constables, soldiers, messengers, and servants	Claim Arab descent	Urdu	Strict Sunni
3. Mughal	Constables, messengers, and servants	North Indian, came with Aurangzeb	Urdu	Strict Sunni
* 4. Pathan	Constables, soldiers, messengers, servants	Afghans who had migrated in ʿAdil Shahi period	Urdu	Lax Sunni
B. Special Classes				
1. Kakar	Laborers, servants, pony-keepers	Afghanistan	Mixed Marathi, Urdu and Malwi	Sunni
2. Labbey	Traders in skins and hides	Arab trading enclaves on coastal India	Tamil, Arabic, and Urdu	Strict Sunni

SOURCE: *Gazetteer of Bombay Presidency: Bijapur District*, 23 (Bombay: 1884), pp. 282-305.
* Communities of considerable size.

Name	*Occupation*	*Origin*	*Language*	*Religious Customs*
3. Jat	Cultivators and servants	Punjab and Sindh, came in 16th and 17th centuries	Urdu and Marathi	Strict Sunni
II. COMMUNITIES OF CONVERTS FROM HINDU POPULATION				
• 1. Momin	Weavers	Koshti or Sali caste, converted by Sufi saints, among them Hashim Pir	Urdu with strong Kannada accent	Sunni
• 2. Bakar Kasab	Mutton butchers	Lad Khatik caste	Kannada among villagers; Urdu among townsmen	Worship local Hindu deities, avoid beef, keep Hindu festivals, and do not mix with other Muslims, yet practice circumcision and have funerals and marriages in the Muslim style
• 3. Bagban	Fruit and vegetable dealers	Mali and Kunbi castes	Urdu mixed with Kannada and Marathi	Lax Sunni; avoid beef and worship Hindu deities
4. Attar	Perfumers	Jain converts	Urdu and Kannada	Lax Sunni; avoid beef and worship Hindu deities
5. Manyar	Bracelet and hardware dealers	unspecified	Urdu, mixed with Kannada and Marathi	Strict Sunni

MUSLIM COMMUNITIES OF BIJAPUR DISTRICT IN 1884 (*continued*)

Name	*Occupation*	*Origin*	*Language*	*Religious Customs*
6. Kagzi	Paper-makers	unspecified	Urdu	Strict Sunni
7. Kalaigar	Tinners	unspecified	Urdu	Lax Sunni; addicted to alcohol and opium
8. Nalband	Farriers	unspecified	Urdu	Lax Muslims, fond of alcohol
9. Hakim	Physicians	unspecified	Urdu	unspecified
10. Mahawat	Elephant drivers	Rajput converts	Urdu and Kannada	unspecified
11. Chaparband	Thatchers	Hindu converts from Gujarat (16th and 17th centuries)	Urdu mixed with much Gujarati	Lax Sunni; worship Hindu deities and avoid beef
12. Bhadbhunja	Grain-parchers	Bhoi, or Fisher caste	Rough Urdu with much Kannada	Lax Sunni; offer vows to Hindu deities and keep Hindu festivals
13. Gaundi	Bricklayers	Ghandi caste	Urdu, with much Kannada and Marathi	Lax Sunni; avoid beef, worship Hindu deities and keep Hindu festivals
14. Pinjara	Cotton-cleaners	Pinjari caste	Kannada, and some Urdu	Lax Sunni; avoid beef, worship Hindu deities and keep Hindu festivals

Name	*Occupation*	*Origin*	*Language*	*Religious Customs*
15. Patvegar	Tassel-winders	Patvegar caste	Urdu, mixed with much Kannada	Lax Sunni
16. Saikalgar	Armorers and tinkers	Ghisadi caste	Kannada	Lax Sunni; seldom go to mosque, worship Hindu deities and avoid beef
17. Pakhali	Water-carriers	Pakhali caste	Kannada and Urdu	Lax Sunni; avoid beef, worship Hindu deities and keep Hindu festivals
18. Hajam	Barbers	Hajam caste	Kannada and Urdu	Lax Sunni
19. Bhatyara	Cooks for low-class Muslims and low-caste Hindus (Mahars, Bhangis and Mangs)	unspecified	Urdu	unspecified
20. Kanjar	Poulterers and hemp-rope makers	Pardhi tribals	Mixed Urdu, Marathi and Kannada	Lax Sunni; worship Hindu deities
21. Pindhara	Grass-cutters	Pindhari caste	Mixed Urdu, Malwi, and Marathi	Lax Sunni; avoid beef, keep Hindu festivals and worship Hindu deities, especially the goddess Yellama, whose temple is at Kaladgi

GLOSSARY

This is a selected glossary of important terms that have appeared at least once in the text. All words are Perso-Arabic unless otherwise indicated. The system of transliteration used in this glossary follows, with slight modifications, the system employed by John T. Platts in his *Dictionary of Urdu, Classical Hindi, and English*. The modifications are as follows: (1) the Persian letter *che* has been rendered "ch," (2) the Arabic letters *ghain* and *khe* have been rendered "g̲h̲" and "k̲h̲" respectively, (3) the silent *waw* when appearing after the letter *khe* in Persian words has not been transliterated, (4) the Persian *izafat* has been indicated by "-i-" after consonants and "-yi" after vowels, and (5) the Arabic definite article has been rendered "al-" in all cases except when following a word ending in a vowel, in which case it is rendered "ʾl-."

abhang (Marathi)	a Marathi verse form used and popularized by the poet-saints of Pandharpur to express religious longing.
ahl-i bihisht	(literally "people of heaven")—a phrase used by Sufis to describe themselves.
ahl-i dunyā	(literally "people of the world")—a phrase used by some Sufis to describe the lay population.
ʿālim	a man learned in religious sciences; a member of the *ʿulama* class.
ʿāshūrā	the tenth day of the month of Muharram, when Shiʿas commemorate the martyrdom of Imam Husain.
ʿāshūrā-k̲h̲āna	the building in which Shiʿas set up the bier and banners used in their *ʿAshura* ceremony.
baiʿat	a vow of spiritual allegiance to a *pir*, usually accompanied by a simple ceremony. The vow bound the follower to the *pir* as a *murid* and, in a formal sense, inducted him into the institutional structure of Sufism.

bairāgī (Hindi)	a Hindu religious mendicant, usually a worshipper of Vishnu.
bang (Persian)	see "bhāng."
bangāb	an intoxicating drink prepared by mixing *bhang* with water or milk.
baqā	abiding eternally in God.
barakat	blessing, holiness. The spiritual power inherent in a saint giving him his charisma, transferable after his death to his tomb and to his descendants.
bā-sharʿ	orthodox, conforming to Islamic Law.
bhākta (Sanskrit)	a devotee of a *bhakti* cult.
bhakti (Sanskrit)	the theistic and devotional principle in Hinduism, manifested in a number of cults to deities which are adored and worshiped as personal gods.
bhāng (Hindi)	a narcotic intoxicant prepared from the leaves of hemp (*cannabis sativa*), which was either eaten or smoked.
bīghā (Hindi)	a measurement of land area used by the Bijapur government, equivalent to about nine-tenths of an acre. There were 120 *bighas* to a *chawar*.
bi-k͟hūdī	senseless rapture.
bī-sharʿ	unorthodox, not conforming to Islamic Law.
chakkī (Hindi)	the grindstone found throughout the Deccan, used for grinding *juwar* or other food grains.
chakkī-nāma (Hindi)	any form of folk poetry sung by women to accompany their work at the grindstone.
chark͟ha	a spinning wheel.
chark͟ha-nāma	any form of folk poetry sung by women to accompany their work at the spinning wheel.
chāwal (Marathi)	a silver coin worth one-eighth of a rupee.
chāwar (Marathi)	a Marathi measurement of land used by the Bijapur government, equivalent to about 109 acres.

chillā	a forty-day period of solitary seclusion, spent in fasting and prayer.
Dār al-Ḥarb	(literally "the abode of war")—that part of the world not under Islamic rule.
Dār al-Islām	(literally "the abode of Islam")—that part of the world under Islamic rule.
dargāh	(literally "court")—a tomb of a Sufi, which in Bijapur was typically a structure of about twenty feet in height having a square or octagonal base supporting a nearly spherical dome.
darwīsh	any Sufi, as used in Persian sources. When anglicized to "dervish," however, the word carries the more restricted connotation of the Sufi who stresses ecstasy over knowledge, even at the risk of violating Islamic Law.
desāī (Marathi)	the hereditary and principal revenue officer of a *pargana.* He was by far the most important figure in the ʻAdil Shahi local administration, being responsible not only for the collection of revenue, but also for the defense and security of his *pargana*, and the litigation of disputes.
deshkulkarnī, or deshpānde (Marathi)	the accountant of a *pargana*'s revenue records, and assistant to the *desai.*
deshmukh	see "desāī."
fanā	"passing away" or absorption of the individual self into the divine.
faqīr	(a) a Muslim mendicant who wanders about subsisting on alms; (b) a term used by Bijapuri Sufis of all types when referring to themselves, doubtless because the word literally means "a poor man," and poverty was held as an ideal by even the most worldly Sufis; (c) a term including those persons of the lower classes or the lumpenproletariat who are informally attached to a Sufi *dargah* and compose its outer circle of musicians, jugglers, monkey trainers, flagellants, beggars, petty traders, etc.

farmān	a written command issued by the court and bearing the royal seal.
fātiḥa	(a) the opening chapter of the Koran, which consists of the fundamental prayer of Islam; (b) any prayer offered up in the name of saints, and hence frequently associated with *dargahs.*
fiqh	religious jurisprudence; Islamic Law codified.
g͟hair-mulkī	a Deccani's term for a Foreigner, especially a North Indian who had accompanied or followed the Mughals to the Deccan.
g͟hazal	a stylized form of poem found in Arabic, Persian, and Urdu verse.
g͟hāzī	a warrior, especially a religious fighter in the cause of Islam.
g͟hulāt (sing. g͟hālī)	adherents to a variety of Shi'ism holding that 'Ali and the imams descended from him were incarnations of God.
gurū (Sanskrit)	a Hindu spiritual guide or religious teacher.
gusāīn (Hindi)	(a) a Hindu mendicant in general; (b) a member of a group of Hindu ascetics organized around a leader (*guru*) and attached to hospices (*math*).
gōsha-nishīn	a recluse, "one who sits in a corner."
ḥadīs̤	traditional sayings or deeds of the Prophet Muhammad, based on the authority of a chain of transmitters.
ḥajj	the pilgrimage to Mecca, one of the five fundamental duties of all Muslims.
ḥāl	a "state" of spiritual exhilaration.
ḥaqīqat	(a) truth, reality; (b) the third stage on the Chishti Path.
hūn (Sanskrit)	the gold coin that served as the 'Adil Shahi standard of monetary exchange, about 50 grains in weight.

ʿilm	knowledge; especially the revealed or exoteric knowledge that the non-Sufi laity is capable of acquiring, and which Sufis must acquire before moving to the higher stages of the Path.
imām	(a) a leader of the public prayers at a mosque; (b) among Shiʿas, one of the spiritual and temporal leaders of Islam after the death of the Prophet.
inʿām	a grant in tax-free land given by the government in perpetuity to an individual or an institution.
inʿāmdār	a holder of an *inʿam*.
is̱nā-ʿasharī	the majority sect among Shiʿas, which accords special veneration to ʿAli and the Twelve Imams.
jāgīr	lands in which revenue collection was farmed out to a high-ranking noble, in return for which the noble owed military service to the government. This was a Mughal term occasionally used in Bijapur even before Aurangzeb's conquest, and paralleled the ʿAdil Shahi *mukhasa*.
jāgīrdār	a holder of a *jagir*.
jihād	(a) a Sufi's inward or spiritual struggle against the temptations of this world; (b) war against non-Muslims.
jizya	a poll-tax levied on non-Muslims.
juwār (Hindi)	the species of millet that constitutes the principal food grain of the Bijapur plateau.
kāfir	a non-Muslim.
kalima	the Muslim confession of faith: "There is no god but Allah, and Muhammad is His prophet."
karāmat	a miracle believed to have been performed by a Sufi.
kār-kun	a clerk, writer, or any minor official in the local revenue administration.

khalīfa	one who receives the *khilafat* from a *pir* and is thereby permitted to induct others into the order. A *pir* frequently had one or several *khalifas*.
khānaqāh	the humble structure in which a *pir* taught his disciples, frequently his own house.
khaṭīb	a preacher; a reader of the prayers in the mosque.
khilāfat	(literally "successorship")—permission granted by a *pir* to one of his disciples to go out and induct others in the name of the order.
khilāfat-nāma	the "letter of succession" that formalized the granting of a *khilafat*.
khirqa	the patched frock worn by Sufis, often passed from a *pir* to a *khalifa* to symbolize the latter's legitimate succession.
khuṭba	the Friday sermon in which the secular ruler's name was mentioned and prayed for.
khwāja	a title of respect for any man of distinction, especially a deceased saint.
kos (Hindi)	a measure of distance equivalent to about two miles.
langar-khāna	an almshouse (literally "anchor-house") where food and alms were distributed to the poor. Some were operated by the Bijapur government; others were attached to a Sufi *dargah* and were operated by its attendants.
linga (Sanskrit)	the emblem, a symbol of Siva, which Lingayats carry with them at all times, usually around the neck.
lorī-nāma (Hindi)	a lullaby.
maʿāsh	a grant of a means of subsistence, frequently in the form of land revenue from reserved villages, in such cases identical to an *inʿam*.

mahdī	generally, a spiritual personage who will appear on the last day and establish Islam over all unrighteous forces; among Shi'as this personage is the twelfth or "hidden" Imam.
majẕūb	(literally "attracted")—(a) a Sufi drawn immediately to God without his own effort or guidance from a *pir*; (b) a Sufi willing to risk social disapprobation in order to attain states of ecstatic rapture.
malfūẓāt (sing. malfūẓ)	(literally "words")—the sayings of a *pir* as collected and recorded by one of his disciples.
maqām	a station on the Sufi Path, differing from *hal* (state) in that it can be attained through the Sufi's own efforts, while the latter is God-given.
maqām-i qurb	(literally "the place of nearness")—the goal of the Chishti Sufi. It signified the place either of companionship with God or of unity with God, depending on the Sufi.
maʻrifat	(a) mystic or esoteric knowledge, as opposed to *ʻilm*; (b) the fourth stage on the Chishti Path.
maṭh (Sanskrit)	the hospice at which Lingayat ascetics, or Hindu ascetics, generally congregate and study under the direction of a *guru*.
mauẓaʻ	a village, including the lands farmed by its inhabitants, having known limits.
muʻāmala	a district, varying in size from 10 to 200 villages, located in strategically important or particularly fertile regions and hence administered by bureaucrats (*hawaldar*) directly appointed by the sultan.
mujāhid	(a) one who struggles against the temptations of this world, a Sufi; (b) one who engages in religious war (*jihad*).

mukhāṣa — lands in which revenue collection was farmed out to a high-ranking noble, in return for which the noble owed the government military service. It paralleled what in Mughal terminology was a *jagir*.

mulḥid — an atheist.

murīd — a novice, or pupil of a *pir*. A *murid* would have received a *bai'at* inducting him into the order, but he was not given the right to initiate other followers, as was the *khalifa*.

murshid — a spiritual guide. The term can refer to the master of a *khanaqah*, or the *pir*, with emphasis more on the master as instructor than as mediator with God.

murtadd — an apostate from Islam.

nafs — the lower self, the animal-spirit "soul."

naql — a written or oral tradition about the life, and especially the miracles, of a Sufi.

nawwāb — a title of any man of high rank in Mughal service.

nāyak (Sanskrit) — after 1565, any Telugu or Kannadiga military chief formerly loyal to Vijayanagar; hence, the indigenous nobility in the sub-Tungabhadra Karnatak.

naẕr, or naẕar — any present or offering given by an inferior to a superior. At the *dargahs*, this refers to the gifts of flowers, coins, sweets, etc., given as votive offerings by female devotees to the *sajjada-nishin*.

pargana — a district, varying in size from 10 to 200 villages, administered by an indigenous and hereditary class of local officials, frequently given by the government to a prominent noble for over-all administration.

pīr — (literally "elder")—the master Sufi of a hospice, the teacher of the Sufi Way.

pīrzāda — the son, or any familial descendant, of a *pir*.

pūjā (Sanskrit)	prayer, or any form of veneration before Hindu deities; in Muslim hagiographies, idol-worship.
qalʿa	a fort; also, a directly administered district having a fort.
qaṣba	a town, somewhat larger than a *mauza* (village).
qāẓī	a Muslim judge, appointed by the government to enforce Islamic Law.
rāfiẓ (plural, rafaẓa)	one who rejects; a group of Shiʿa.
rāga (Sanskrit)	a musical mode conveying one of several emotions.
rāginī (Sanskrit)	a modification of the *raga*.
rāg-mālā (Sanskrit)	a treatise on music, including pictures illustrating the subjects appropriate to the various modes.
rāh	the Path, or Way, of the Sufi's spiritual journey.
raqṣ	dancing, especially when used to induce a state of spiritual ecstasy.
rauẓa	the mausoleum and surrounding garden of a Sufi or any learned, pious man.
ribāṯ	the hospice of early Sufis, especially those of the Islamic frontiers in the early centuries of Islam.
rūḥ	the higher self, the human spirit or soul.
sādhū (Sanskrit)	a Hindu mendicant leading a pious and ascetic life.
ṣadr	a high employee in the government's judicial or revenue administration.
ṣadr al-ṣudūr	the chief judge of the realm, responsible for appointing *qazis* and administering religious endowments.
sajjāda-nishīn	the successor to the leadership of a *khanaqah* or a *dargah* (literally "one who sits upon the prayer-carpet").
sākā (Hindi)	the Hindu solar calendar. An equivalent Christian year can be calculated by adding 78¼ to a *saka* year.

sālik	a traveler on the Way; hence a Sufi.
samā'	musical sessions held by Sufis, with the object of inducing a state of spiritual ecstasy.
samt (samatu, or simt)	a subdistrict, into which both *mu'amalas* and *jagirs* were divided, and consisting of several villages.
sanad	a document conveying a government order, bearing the royal seal.
sannyāsi (Sanskrit)	a Hindu of the fourth order (*ashram*) who abandons all worldly connections and wanders about as a mendicant.
sā'ir	all miscellaneous taxes other than the land tax.
saiyid	anyone professing blood descent from the family of the Prophet Muhammad.
shādī-nāma	a wedding song.
Shahur San (corruption of "shuhūr sinn")	a solar calendar devised by the Bahmani government and used by the 'Adil Shahi revenue bureaucracy for reconciling the lunar Muslim calendar with the harvests, which follow solar years.
shaikh	(a) a title of respect given to various Sufis, or to elderly Muslims in general; (b) a Muslim professing Arab descent.
sharī'at	the law of God; the revealed and canonized body of Islamic Law.
sijda	prostration performed either in worship or in respect.
silsila	(literally "chain")—(a) a term denoting all Sufis living or deceased who are linked together by a common spiritual descent from a single founder; (b) in India, the term for a Sufi order, like the term *ta'ifa* in the Arab world.
suhāgan-nāma (Hindi)	a married woman's song.
ṭā'ifa	(a) a people, tribe, company, band, or group; (b) the collection of common devotees spiritually affiliated with a Sufi, usually through devotions made to that Sufi's tomb.

ṭālib	one who seeks, pursues or inquires; hence, a Sufi.
ṭarīqa	(a) a road, path, or way; (b) the system or doctrine associated with particular Sufis or a school of Sufis.
taṣawwuf	mysticism, equivalent to the English "Sufism."
tauḥīd	the doctrine of Divine Unity; the culmination of the Sufi Path, at which God is perceived as without qualities or attributes.
ta'wīẕ	(a) any gift given by a *pir* to a *murid*, originally a written *zikr* for the follower to memorize; (b) an amulet or charm given by a *pirzada* to the followers at a *dargah*.
taẕkira, or taẕkirat (plural taẕkirāt)	(literally "mentionings")—a collection of biographical accounts, compiled from both written and oral traditions.
'ulamā	(a) plural of *'alim*, a man trained in the (Islamic) religious sciences; (b) the class of state-supported judges, theologians, and preachers who were collectively responsible for upholding Islamic orthodoxy in the kingdom.
'urs	(literally "marriage with God")—the festival commemorating the death date of a *pir*, normally the most important festival at a *dargah*.
vachana (Sanskrit)	a form of vernacular Kannada literature that was instrumental in the early spread of Lingayat devotionalism in the Karnatak.
virakta (Sanskrit)	In the Karnatak, a Lingayat ascetic from the caste of Jangams, or Lingayat priests.
waḥdat al-wujūd	the doctrine of the Unity of Being, positing that all Reality is a borrowed fragment from the being of God.
wazīr, pīshwā, wakīl	in Bijapur, the first or prime minister of the realm, appointed by the sultan.
yaumīya	a daily allowance granted by the government.

yogī, or jogī (Hindi) — (a) one who practices *yoga*, the system of Hindu thought intended to unite the individual with the universal soul; (b) a Hindu professing superhuman abilities, appearing in a variety of forms: ascetic, magician, fortune-teller, or most frequently, a wandering mendicant.

zamīndār — any Kannadiga or Telugu chieftain in the sub-Tungabhadra Karnatak. This was how the term was generally used in Bijapur. In Mughal usage, however, the term *zamindar* more closely resembled what in Bijapur was the *desai*.

ẕikr — the mentioning of God, sometimes in combination with other ritual activities or spiritual exercises, with the aim of bringing the Sufi closer to God.

zindīq — a heretic, or a dualist.

BIBLIOGRAPHY

This is a select bibliography in which are listed not every source cited in the text, but only those most central to the study. The sources are listed topically rather than by language or by facts of publication. This scheme, with its subcategories, is as follows:

1. Works by Prominent Sufis
   A. Mystical Literature
   B. Popular Literature
   C. Other
2. Contemporary Works About Prominent Sufis
   A. Discourses
   B. Biographies
   C. Eulogistic Literature
3. Contemporary Histories, Narratives, and Memoirs
4. State Documents
5. Epigraphic Sources
6. Travel Accounts
7. Secondary Sources
8. Reference Works

All works are listed by author except those included in category 2, Contemporary Works about Prominent Sufis. Those works are mostly biographies, which are better known and more easily locatable by their title than by the name of their compiler.

In the case of manuscripts, the dates of composition and/or copying have been included when available. Manuscripts for which neither date is known are indicated by "n.d."

Works by Prominent Sufis

A. Mystical Literature

Abu'l-Hasan Qadiri. *Sukh Anjan.* Edited by Saiyida Ja'far. (Dakhni lithograph.) Hyderabad: Lutf al-Daula Research Institute, 1968.

An important work by one of the few Qadiri Sufis of Bijapur who engaged in writing.

Amin, Saiyid. *Majzub al-Salikin.* (Urdu MS.) Hyderabad: Idara-e-Adabiyat-e-Urdu, no. 680. n.d. 65 fols.

One of the more syncretic Sufi works to be produced at Bijapur, this tract was written by a fifth-generation descendant (spiritual and familial) of Amin al-Din A'la.

Amin al-Din A'la, Shah. *Irshadat.* (Dakhni MS.) Hyderabad: Asafiyah Library, Jadid no. 790. n.d. fols. 11a-13b.

———. *Khiyal-i Rikhta.* (Dakhni MS.) Hyderabad: Personal collection of Professor M. Akbaruddin Siddiqi.

———. *Muhibb-nama.* (Dakhni MS.) Karachi: Anjuman-i Taraqqi-yi Urdu, vol. 1/151. n.d. pp. 71-73.

———. *Phul-ban.* (Dakhni MS.) Karachi: Anjuman-i Taraqqi-yi Urdu, vol. 2/28. n.d. pp. 135-36.

———. *Qurbiya.* (Dakhni MS.) Hyderabad: Salar Jung Museum, Urdu MSS, Tasawwuf & Akhlaq no. 99. n.d. fols. 69b-73a.

———. *Risala-yi Tasawwuf.* (Dakhni MS.) Hyderabad: Salar Jung Museum, Tasawwuf & Akhlaq no. 59. n.d. fols. 73b-74a.

———. *Risala-yi Tasawwuf.* (Dakhni MS.) Hyderabad: Salar Jung Museum, Urdu MSS, Tasawwuf & Akhlaq no. 60. n.d. fols. 34b-39a.

———. *Wujudiya.* (Dakhni MS.) Hyderabad: Salar Jung Museum, Urdu MSS, Tasawwuf & Akhlaq no. 102, n.d. fols. 1b-13a.

———. *Wujudiya.* (Mixed Persian and Dakhni MS.) Karachi: Anjuman-i Taraqqi-yi Urdu, vol. 1/151. n.d. pp. 3-16.

Amin al-Din A'la II. *Makhzan al-Amin.* (Persian MS.) Hyderabad: Asafiyah Library. Tasawwuf no. 1722. Copied 1888-89. 198 pp.

Although he lived in Hyderabad and not Bijapur, Amin al-Din II was the son of Miranji Khudanama, who in turn was a close disciple of Amin al-Din A'la. This work is probably contemporary with Amin al-Din's life since the younger Amin al-Din died in the late seventeenth century.

Bahri, Mahmud. *'Arus-i 'Irfan.* (Persian MS.) Hyderabad: Salar Jung Museum, Tasawwuf no. 114. Composed 1704-5; copied 1846-47. 132 fols.

———. *Bangab-nama.* (Dakhni lithograph.) In M. Hafiz Syed, ed., *Kulliyat-i Bahri.* Lucknow: Nawal Kishor, A.H. 1339.

———. *Man Lagan.* (Dakhni print.) Edited by M. Sakhawat Mirza. Karachi: Anjuman-i Taraqqi-yi Urdu, 1955.

———. *Masnawis.* (Dakhni lithograph.) In M. Hafiz Syed, *Kulliyat-i Bahri.* Lucknow: Nawal Kishor, A.H. 1339.

Burhan al-Din Janam. *Basharat al-Zikr.* (Dakhni MS.) Hyderabad: Salar Jung Museum, Urdu MSS, Tasawwuf & Akhlaq no. 9. n.d. fols. 7b-10a. Another copy is in Karachi: Anjuman-i Taraqqi-yi Urdu, vol. 1/151. n.d. pp. 133-36.

———. *Hujjat al-Baqa.* (Dakhni MS.) Karachi: Anjuman-i Taraqqi-yi Urdu, vol. 1/151. Copied 1658. pp. 260-99.

———. *Irshad al-Talibin.* (Persian MS.) Karachi: Anjuman-i Taraqqi-yi Urdu, vol. 1/151. n.d. pp. 23-27. Another copy is in vol. 2/27. n.d. pp. 58-70.

———. *Irshad-nama.* (Dakhni MS.) Hyderabad: Idara-e-Adabiyat-e-Urdu no. 124. Composed 1582-83. 69 pp. An unpublished lithograph copy of this work is in the Idara-e-Adabiyat-e-Urdu, no. v 6, #4. Another manuscript copy is in Karachi: Anjuman-i Taraqqi-yi Urdu, vol. 1/151. Copied 1657. pp. 363-479.

———. *Kalimat al-Haqayiq.* Edited by M. Akbaruddin Siddiqi. (Persian and Dakhni lithograph.) Hyderabad: Idara-e-Adabiyat-e-Urdu, 1961.

An abridged and simplified summary of the *Irshad-nama.*

———. *Makhzan-i Salikin.* (Persian MS.) Hyderabad: Asafiyah Library, Tasawwuf no. 197. n.d. pp. 137-43. Another copy is in Karachi: Anjuman-i Taraqqi-yi Urdu, vol. 1/151. Copied 1657. pp. 300-24.

———. *Manfa'at al-Iman.* (Dakhni MS.) Hyderabad: Personal collection of Professor M. Akbaruddin Siddiqi. Another copy is in Karachi: Anjuman-i Taraqqi-yi Urdu, vol. 1/151. n.d. pp. 139-42.

———. *Nasim al-Kalam.* (Dakhni MS.) Hyderabad: Personal collection of Professor M. Akbaruddin Siddiqi.

———. *Nukta-yi Wahid.* (Dakhni MS.) Hyderabad: Personal collection of Professor M. Akbaruddin Siddiqi.

———. *Rumuz al-Wasilin.* (Dakhni MS.) Karachi: Anjuman-i Taraqqi-yi Urdu, vol. 2/43. n.d. pp. 1-25.

———. "*Suk-Sahela* of Shah Burhan-uddin Janam." Edited and translated by Muhammad Hafiz Syed. *Allahabad University Studies*, VI, part 1 (1930), pp. 487-509. A manuscript copy of this work is in Karachi: Anjuman-i Taraqqi-yi Urdu, vol. 1/151. n.d. pp. 136-39.

———. *Wasiyat al-Hadi.* (Dakhni MS.) Hyderabad: Salar Jung Museum, Urdu MSS, Tasawwuf & Akhlaq no. 54. Composed 1582-83. fols. 6b-11a. Another copy is in Karachi: Anjuman-i Taraqqi-yi Urdu, vol. 1/151. n.d. pp. 127-32.

———. *Wujudiya.* (Mixed Dakhni and Persian MS.) Karachi: Anjuman-i Taraqqi-yi Urdu, vol. 2/17. n.d. pp. 27-36.

Dawal, Saiyid Shah. *Kashf al-Anwar.* (Dakhni MS.) Karachi: Anjuman-i Taraqqi-yi Urdu, vol. 1/151, n.d. pp. 497-503. Another copy is in vol. 2/12. n.d. pp. 615-25.

———. *Kashf al-Wujud.* (Dakhni lithograph.) Edited by M. Akbaruddin Siddiqi. Hyderabad: M. Akbaruddin Siddiqi, n.d.

Kamal al-Din Biabani. *Chahar Shahadat.* (Dakhni lithograph.) In Hashim ʿAli, ed., *Maghz-i Marghub & Chahar Shahadat.* Hyderabad: Urdu Academy, 1966.

Khush Dahan, Shaikh Mahmud. *Asrar al-Haqq.* (Persian MS.) Karachi: Anjuman-i Taraqqi-yi Urdu, vol. 1/151. Copied 1658. pp. 163-201.

———. *Maʿrifat al-Suluk.* (Persian lithograph.) Lucknow: Nawal Kishor, 1898. A manuscript copy of this work is in Hyderabad: Salar Jung Museum, Tasawwuf no. 185.

A summary and lucid statement of Chishti doctrine at Bijapur.

———. *Risala-yi Mukhtasar dar Bab-i Kasb Kardan-i Wujudiya.* (Dakhni MS.) Karachi: Anjuman-i Taraqqi-yi Urdu, vol. 2/18. n.d. pp. 6-9.

———. *Salat-i ʿAshiqin* (Persian MS.) Karachi: Anjuman-i Taraqqi-yi Urdu, vol. 2/19. n.d. pp. 273-75.

Miranji Khudanama. *Basharat al-Anwar.* (Dakhni lithograph.) In ʿAbd al-Hafiz Qatil, *Miranji Khudanama.* Hyderabad: Urdu Academy, 1961.

———. *Chahar Wujud.* (Dakhni MS.) Karachi: Anjuman-i Taraqqi-yi Urdu, vol. 2/9. n.d. pp. 245-51.

Miranji Shams al-ʿUshshaq. *Khush Naghz.* (Dakhni lithograph.) In Hashim ʿAli, ed., *Maghz-i Marghub & Chahar Shahadat.* Hyderabad: Urdu Academy, 1966.

———. *Maghz-i Marghub.* (Dakhni lithograph.) In Hashim ʿAli, ed., *Maghz-i Marghub & Chahar Shahadat.* Hyderabad: Urdu Academy, 1966.

Qasim, Muhammad. *Nafayis al-Anfas.* (Persian MS.) Hyderabad: Salar Jung Museum, Tasawwuf no. 255. Composed 1669-70. 29 fols.

Sufi poetry composed by a *murid* of Habib Allah Sibghat Allahi.

Sadiq, Mir Muhammad. *Shams al-Haqayiq.* (Dakhni MS.) Hyderabad: Salar Jung Museum, Tasawwuf & Akhlaq no. 136. n.d. 92 pp. Another copy is in Bijapur: Gachi Mahal.

An exposition on Sufi terminology, including an attack on Amin al-Din Aʿla.

Tahir La-ubali, Saiyid Shah. *Kanz al-Nafayis.* (Persian MS.) Bijapur: Gachi Mahal. n.d.

Orthodox Sufi poetry, containing considerable praise for one of Bijapur's nobles, Masʿud Khan.

Zubairi, Maulana Muhammad II. *Kashf al-Asrar.* (Dakhni MS.) Hyderabad: Personal collection of Professor M. Akbaruddin Siddiqi. Copied 1712-13. 79 pp.

One of the few works by a Bijapur Sufi of the Qadiri order.

B. Popular Literature

'Ali Pir Husaini, Shah. *Suhaila.* (Dakhni lithograph.) In M. Akbaruddin Siddiqi, *Bujhte Chiragh.* Hyderabad: National Fine Printing Press, 1975. pp. 56-58.

Amin al-Din A'la. *Chakki-nama.* (Dakhni MS.) Hyderabad: Salar Jung Museum, Urdu MSS, Tasawwuf & Akhlaq no. 36. n.d. 11 pp.

A work spuriously attributed to Amin al-Din, it being rather the work of a late-seventeenth-century Shattari Sufi of Bijapur. It throws much light on the changing social order of that period.

Bandanawaz Gisudaraz, Khwaja Muhammad Husaini. *Chakki-nama.* (Dakhni MS.) Hyderabad: Salar Jung Museum, Urdu MSS, Tasawwuf & Akhlaq no. 37.

Spuriously attributed to the renowned saint of Gulbarga.

———. *Chakki-nama.* (Dakhni MS.) Hyderabad: Idara-e-Adabiyat-e-Urdu, no. 120 B. Copied 1807-8. 2 pp.

Spuriously attributed to Bandanawaz.

Chakki-nama, Charkha-nama, Lori-nama, Harini-nama. Author unknown. (Urdu lithograph.) Hyderabad: Matba' Muzaffari. n.d. 24 pp.

A recent lithograph of popular Sufi literature.

Faruqi. *Chakki-nama.* (Dakhni MS.) Hyderabad: Adara-e-Adabiyat-e-Urdu, no. 657. n.d. fols. 1b-2b.

Substantially identical in content to the *chakki-nama* of Hashim Khudawand Hadi.

Ghausi. *Chakki-nama.* (Dakhni MS.) Hyderabad: Salar Jung Museum, Urdu MSS, Tasawwuf & Akhlaq no. 37. n.d. fols. 1a-3a.

Hashim Khudawand Hadi, Saiyid. *Chakki-nama 'Irfan.* (Dakhni MS.) Hyderabad: Idara-e-Adabiyat-e-Urdu no. 93b. Composed 1659-60. Copied 1743-44. fols. 126b-128a.

Kamal. *Chakki-nama.* (Dakhni MS.) Hyderabad: Salar Jung Museum, Urdu MSS, Pand & Nasayih no. 4. n.d. 4 pp. Published in Sakhawat Mirza, "Saiyid Shah Kamal al-Din." *Urdu* (April 1939), pp. 263-87.

Kamtar. *Charkha-nama.* (Dakhni MS.) Hyderabad: Salar Jung Museum, Urdu MSS, Pand & Nasayih no. 3. n.d. 3 pp.

Salar. *Charkha-nama.* (Dakhni MS.) Hyderabad: Salar Jung Museum, Urdu MSS, Tasawwuf & Akhlaq no. 35. n.d. 1 fol.

Shah Raju. *Suhagan-nama.* (Dakhni MS.) Hyderabad: Salar Jung Museum, Urdu MSS, Pand & Nasayih no. 144. n.d. fols. 1a-5a.

C. Other

Abu'l-Hasan Qadiri II. *Bayaz-i Abu'l-Hasan II.* (Persian and Dakhni MSS.) Bijapur: Gachi Mahal. n.d. fols. 69-104.

Abu'l-Hasan Qadiri II. *Makhzan al-Salasil al-Hasaniya.* (Arabic MS.) Bijapur: Gachi Mahal.

Spiritual genealogies of all orders in Bijapur until the early 1700s.

———. *Maktubat-i Abu'l-Hasan II.* (Persian and Arabic MS.) Bijapur: Gachi Mahal. Composed 1707-8. fols. 113-20.

Includes three letters from the Sufi to Mughal authorities in Bijapur, dated 1707-8.

Bahri, Mahmud. *Lashkar-nama.* (Persian MS.) In Mahmud Bahri, *Majmu'a.* (Persian, Dakhni, and Arabic MSS.) Bijapur: Gachi Mahal, fols. 141-43.

Burhan al-Din Janam. *Marsiyat-i Hazrat Burhan al-Din Janam.* (Dakhni MS.) Hyderabad: Personal collection of Professor M. Akbaruddin Siddiqi.

An elegy to his father, Miranji Shams al-'Ushshaq.

Hasan Muhyi al-Din Qadiri, Saiyid. *Makhzan al-Ansab wa A'ras.* (Persian MS.) Bijapur: Gachi Mahal. Compiled 1823-24.

Genealogies of the families of Abu'l-Hasan Qadiri and Shah Sibghat Allah, including lists of villages given to their descendants in *in'am* or *jagir.*

Karim Allah, Shah. Letter to Shah Hashim Shattari and 'Abd al-Razzaq. (Persian MS.) Inserted loosely in Mir Muhammad Sadiq, *Shams al-Haqayiq.* (Dakhni MS.) Bijapur: Gachi Mahal.

The letter complains of Amin al-Din A'la's growing popularity in the Deccan.

Miranji Shams al-'Ushshaq. *Khud-niwisht wa Nasl-nama.* (Persian MS.) Hyderabad: Idara-e-Adabiyat-e-Urdu, no. 863. n.d. fols. 21a-22b.

Autobiography of Miranji Shams al-'Ushshaq.

Sumam, Saiyid s/o Shah Dawal. *Bai'-nama.* (Persian MS.) Hyderabad: Personal collection of Professor M. Akbaruddin Siddiqi.

A bill of sale for Shah Dawal's house, signed by his son, Saiyid Sumam.

Contemporary Works about Prominent Sufis

A. Discourses (*malfuzat*)

Ganj-i Asrar. Compiled by Shah Na'im Allah. (Persian MS.) Hyderabad: Salar Jung Museum, Tasawwuf no. 134. Composed 1664-65; copied 1877-78. 114 fols.

Sayings of Shah Hashim Pir 'Alawi, to which is appended a short biography of his grandson, Burhan al-Din 'Alawi.

Ganj-i Makhfi. Compiler unknown. (Dakhni MS.) Hyderabad: Asafiyah Library, Shamilat no. 58. n.d. 5 fols.

Sayings of Amin al-Din A'la as taken down by a disciple.

Guftar-i Hazrat Mahbub Allah Shah Amin. Compiler unknown. (Dakhni MS.) Karachi: Anjuman-i Taraqqi-yi Urdu, vol. 1/151. n.d. pp. 256-57. Another copy is in vol. 2/16. n.d. pp. 415-18.

Guftar-i Khara . . . Baba Shah Husaini. Compiled by Saiyid Muhammad Hasan Chishti. (Dakhni MS.) Karachi: Anjuman-i Taraqqi-yi Urdu, vol. 2/18. Compiled 1790. pp. 41-47.

Discourses of Baba Shah Husaini, son of Amin al-Din A'la.

Guftar-i Shah Amin. Compiler unknown. (Dakhni MS.) Hyderabad: Personal collection of Professor M. Akbaruddin Siddiqi. Other copies can be found in the Idara-e-Adabiyat-e-Urdu, no. 883, and in the Asafiyah Library, Shamilat no. 16.

The sayings of Amin al-Din A'la as taken down by a disciple.

Guftar-i Shah Amin. Compiler unknown. (Persian MS.) Karachi: Anjuman-i Taraqqi-yi Urdu, vol. 2/16. n.d. pp. 410-18.

Another short compilation of sayings of Amin al-Din A'la, differing from manuscripts of the same title in Hyderabad.

Guftar-i Shah Burhan. Compiler unknown. (Dakhni MSS.) Karachi: Anjuman-i Taraqqi-yi Urdu, vol. 2/28, pp. 134-35; vol. 1/151, p. 66; vol. 1/151, p. 81.

Three different works having the same title, each one apparently the words of Burhan al-Din as taken down by different *murids*. None is dated.

Kalam-i Shah Amin al-Din A'la. Compiler unknown. (Dakhni MS.) Karachi: Anjuman-i Taraqqi-yi Urdu, vol. 2/6. n.d. pp. 339-61.

A *malfuzat* of Amin al-Din A'la in question and answer form, composed in Dakhni verse apparently by a *murid*.

Kalam-i Shah Burhan. Compiler unknown. (Dakhni MS.) Karachi: Anjuman-i Taraqqi-yi Urdu, vol. 2/7. n.d. pp. 208-21.

Kalimat al-Asrar. Compiler unknown. (Dakhni MS.) Karachi: Anjuman-i Taraqqi-yi Urdu, vol. 1/154. Copied 1891. pp. 1-50.

Teachings of Amin al-Din A'la, recorded by an unknown *murid*.

Malfuzat-i Shah Sibghat Allah. Compiled by Habib Allah 'Abd al-Fattah. (Persian MS.) Hyderabad: Asafiyah Library, Tasawwuf no. 1420. Composed 1606-7; copied 1631-32. 44 fols.

Also includes some sayings of Habib Allah Sibghat Allahi.

Malfuzat-i Shah Wajih al-Din Gujarati. Compiler unknown. (Persian MS.) Hyderabad: Asafiyah Library, Tasawwuf no. 547. Copied 1878. 20 pp.

Maqsud al-Murad. Compiled by Shah Murad s/o Saiyid Jalal. (Persian MS.) Hyderabad: Asafiyah Library, Tasawwuf no. 335. n.d. 141 pp.

Sayings of Shah Hashim Pir 'Alawi as recorded by a prominent *murid*.

Tashrih-i Malfuzat-i Hazrat Shah Burhan. Compiled by Saiyid Muhammad Hasan Chishti. (Dakhni MS.) Karachi: Anjuman-i Taraqqi-yi Urdu, vol. 1/180. pp. 1-9.

A commentary on the discourses of Burhan al-Din Janam.

B. *Biographies* (*tazkirat*)

Anwar al-Qandhar Tariqa-yi Rifa'iya. Compiled by Ghulam Rifa'i. (Persian MS.) Hyderabad: Personal collection of Husain Yafia, no. 84. n.d. 29 fols.

Mentions Sufis of the Rifa'i order in various parts of the Deccan plateau, especially in the town of Qandhar, in the Kingdom of Ahmadnagar near the 'Adil Shahi border.

Armaghan-i Sultani, or *Sair-i Gulbarga*. Compiled by Muhammad Sultan. (Urdu lithograph.) Agra: Mufid-i 'Am, 1902.

A recent biography of Sufis of Gulbarga, mainly Bandanawaz Gisudaraz and Siraj al-Din Junaidi.

Gulzar-i Abrar fi Sair al-Akhyar. Compiled by Muhammad Ghausi s/o Husain s/o Musawi Shattari. (Persian MS.) Hyderabad: State Archives of Andhra Pradesh, Oriental Manuscripts Library, Tasawwuf no. 258. Compiled *c*. 1613; copied 1748-49. Another copy of the same work, not used in this study, is located in Hyderabad: Salar Jung Museum, Tasawwuf no. 27.

The famous biography of Indian Sufis of the Shattari order, containing occasional references to Deccani Sufis.

Latayif al-Latif. Compiled by 'Ali Musawi al-Qadiri. (Persian MS.) Hyderabad: Asafiyah Library, Tasawwuf no. 681. n.d. 225 pp.

Biography of Shah 'Abd al-Latif La-ubali of Kurnool and his five sons. At the end are appended some letters of Shah Tahir and the *khilafat-nama* of 'Abd al-Latif.

Ma'asir al-Kiram. Compiled by Ghulam 'Ali Azad Bilgrami. (Persian lithograph.) 2 vols. Agra: Mufid-i 'Am Press, 1910.

Mirat-i Ahmadi. Compiled by Qazi 'Abd al-Karim. (Persian lithograph.) 2 vols. Bombay: Fath al-Karim, A.H. 1306.

Biographies of mostly Gujarati Sufis.

Mishkat-i Nubuwat. Compiled by 'Ali Musawi al-Qadiri. (Persian MS.) Copy A, Hyderabad: Asafiyah Library, Tazkira no. 21. Composed 1804-5 (autographed copy). 229 fols. Copy B, Hyderabad: Asafiyah Library, Tazkira no. 194. Copy date unknown. 673 fols.

The most complete and reliable of the general biographies of

Deccani Sufis, also containing much information on North Indian Sufis. There are two copies in the Asafiyah Library. The first, Copy A, is the author's original, written in 1804-5 in sprawling *shikasta*. The second, Copy B, was written in excellent *nasta'liq* at some later date, which is not known. Both copies were used in this study, for while the original included some details omitted in Copy B, the latter included whole entries of Sufis excluded by the compiler.

Nizam al-Ansab. Compiled by Muhammad Mansur 'Ali. (Persian MS.) 2 vols. Hyderabad: Asafiyah Library, Mutafarriqat no. 406. Compiled 1909-10. vol. I, 445 pp.; vol. II, 616 pp.

Lineage charts for Deccani Sufis, poets, monarchs, and nobles.

Notes copied from the Amin al-Din Dargah. Compiled by Ahmad Khan Darwish. Hyderabad: Personal collection of Ahmad Khan Darwish.

Chronograms of the major Chishti Sufis of Bijapur.

Rauzat al-Aqtab. Compiled by Raunaq 'Ali. (Urdu lithograph.) Aurangabad: Mu'in-i Dakan Press, 1908-9.

A short work of biographies of Sufis of North India and Aurangabad.

Rauzat al-Auliya, Tazkira-yi Auliya'-i Dar al-Zafar Bijapur. Compiled by Muhammad Ibrahim Zubairi. (Persian MS.) Copy A, Hyderabad: Asafiyah Library, Tazkira no. 266. Compiled 1825-26; copied 1882-83. 243 pp. Copy B, Hyderabad: State Archives of Andhra Pradesh, Oriental Manuscripts Library no. 196. Copied 1868-69. 79 fols.

The only biography dealing exclusively with the Sufis of Bijapur, compiled largely from sources no longer extant by the author of the *Basatin al-Salatin*. Copy B contained some material not included in Copy A, most of it appended at the end.

Sahifat-i Ahl-i Huda. Compiled by Muhyi al-Din b. Saiyid Mahmud Qadiri. Translated to Urdu and edited by M. Akbaruddin Siddiqi. (Urdu lithograph.) Hyderabad: National Fine Printing Press, 1966. Persian MS copy is in Bijapur: Gachi Mahal. Compiled 1796-97; copied 1965. 288 pp.

An important biography of Bijapur's Qadiri Sufis, compiled in 1796-97 from notes collected by Abu'l-Hasan Qadiri II in 1684-85. The manuscript copy in Gachi Mahal, Bijapur, is the work of two scribes. The first and much earlier half was copied shortly after the work's compilation in the late eighteenth century. The second half, a continuation of the first half, was copied from an original by Murtaza Qadiri, the present *sajjada-nishin* at Gachi Mahal. Professor Akbaruddin Siddiqi's Urdu translation was made from the Gachi Mahal copy.

Sair-i Muhammadi. Compiled by Muhammad 'Ali Samani. (Persian MS.) Hyderabad: Asafiyah Library, Tasawwuf no. 1728. Compiled 1427-28. 63 fols.

An early narrative of Muhammad Husaini Bandanawaz Gisudaraz.

Samarat al-Quds min Shajarat al-Uns. Compiled by Mirza La'l Beg. (Persian MS.) 2 vols. Hyderabad: Salar Jung Museum, Tarajim-i Sufiya no. 5. Vol. I, fols. 9-310; vol. II, fols. 311-658.

Shajarat al-Atqiya. Compiled by Muhammad Mu'azzam Bijapuri. (Dakhni MS.) Hyderabad: Salar Jung Museum, Urdu MSS, Tasawwuf & Akhlaq no. 131. n.d. 41 pp.

A contemporary narrative of Bijapur's Chishti Sufis, and the only biographical work devoted exclusively to those Sufis.

Siraj al-'Ishq. Translated by Hazrat 'Ali Sahib s/o Shah Sahib s/o Amin al-Din A'la. (Persian MS.) Hyderabad: Asafiyah Library, Philosophy no. 169. pp. 259-73.

A slightly abridged Persian translation of the *Shajarat al-Atqiya* by Muhammad Mu'azzam Bijapuri.

Tajalliyat-i Rahmani. Compiled by Saiyid 'Ali Muhammad Husaini. (Persian MS.) Hyderabad: Salar Jung Museum, Tasawwuf no. 28. Copied 1747-48. 107 fols.

Contains information on Saiyid Muhammad Mudarris.

Tarjama-yi Rauzat al-Auliya'-i Bijapur. Translated by Shah Saif Allah. (Urdu lithograph.) Raichur: Sibghat Allahi Press, A.H. 1315.

A good translation of the *Rauzat*, including some additional notes collected by the translator.

Tazkira-yi Auliya'-i Dakan. Compiled by 'Abd al-Jabbar Mulkapuri. (Urdu lithograph), 2 vols. Hyderabad: Hasan Press, 1912-13.

A recent collection of biographies of Deccan Sufis.

Tazkirah-e-Makhtutat. Compiled by Saiyid Muhiuddin Qadri Zore. (Urdu lithograph.) 5 vols. Hyderabad: Idara-e-Adabiyat-e-Urdu, 1957.

Biographical notes on Sufis and other writers whose manuscripts are catalogued in the Idara-e-Adabiyat-e-Urdu, Hyderabad.

Tazkirat al-Qadiri. Compiled by Munshi Qadir Khan Bidari. (Persian MS.) Hyderabad: Asafiyah Library, Tazkirat-i Jadid, no. 1086. n.d. 98 fols.

An early biography of both Qadiri and Chishti Sufis of Bijapur.

Tuhfa az Kamtarin. Compiled by Kamtarin. (Persian MS.) Bijapur: Hashim Dargah. n.d. 75 fols.

A biography of Shah Hashim Pir 'Alawi and his family is found on fols. 54-75, following a biography of the Prophet.

Waqi'at-i Mamlakat-i Bijapur. Compiled by Bashir al-Din Ahmad. (Urdu lithograph.) 3 vols. Agra: Mufid-i 'Am Press, 1915.

The first two volumes are essentially an Urdu translation of the *Basatin al-Salatin*, but the third volume contains many details of Sufis and is written in *tazkira* form.

C. *Eulogistic Literature*

Madh-i Shah Burhan al-Din. By Amin al-Din A'la. (Dakhni MS.) Karachi: Anjuman-i Taraqqi-yi Urdu, vol. 1/151. n.d. pp. 69-71.

Qasida. Authorship unknown. (Dakhni MS.) Karachi: Anjuman-i Taraqqi-yi Urdu, vol. 2/45. n.d. pp. 10-12.

A *qasida* or eulogistic poem praising the major Chishti Sufis of Shahpur Hillock, from Jamal al-Din Maghribi to Baba Shah Husaini.

Tawallud-nama-yi Hazrat Amin al-Din A'la. Authorship unknown. (Dakhni MS.) Karachi: Anjuman-i Taraqqi-yi Urdu, vol. 2/55. n.d. pp. 1-5.

A short *masnawi* in praise of Amin al-Din A'la, composed probably by one of his *murids.*

Wiladat-nama-yi Shah Amin al-Din. By Saiyid 'Ali and Mahmud Khush Dahan. (Dakhni MS.) Karachi: Anjuman-i Taraqqi-yi Urdu, vol. 2/17. n.d. pp. 149-55.

A *masnawi* in praise of Amin al-Din A'la.

Contemporary Histories, Narratives, and Memoirs

Ahmad 'Ali Khan, Mir. *Guldasta-yi Bijapur.* (Urdu MS.) Hyderabad: State Archives of Andhra Pradesh, Oriental Manuscripts Library, no. 852. Composed 1862-63. 62 fols.

Amir Khusrau. *Khaza'in al-Futuh.* Edited by Syed Moinul Haq. (Persian lithograph.) Aligarh: Muslim University, 1927. Abridged English edition in vol. 3 of H. M. Elliot and J. Dowson, eds., *The History of India as Told by its Own Historians.* 8 vols. Allahabad: Kitab Mahal, 1964.

Asad Beg. *Wikaya-yi Asad Beg.* Abridged translation by B. W. Chapman in vol. 6 of H. M. Elliot and J. Dowson, eds., *The History of India as Told by its Own Historians.* 8 vols. Allahabad: Kitab Mahal, 1964.

Astarabadi, Hashim Beg "Fuzuni." *Futuhat-i 'Adil Shahi.* (Persian MS.) London: British Museum, Add. 26,234.

Writing under the patronage of Mustafa Khan, one of Bijapur's powerful nobles, the author describes chiefly the military-diplomatic history of the sultanate, and particularly 'Adil Shahi-Mughal relations in the period 1600-44.

Barani, Ziya al-Din. *Tarikh-i Firuz Shahi.* Edited by S. Ahmad Khan. (Persian printed edn.) Calcutta: Asiatic Society of Bengal, 1862.

Abridged English edition in vol. 3 of H. M. Elliot and J. Dowson, eds., *The History of India as Told by its Own Historians*. 8 vols. Allahabad: Kitab Mahal, 1964.

Fani, Mohsan. *Dabistan, or School of Manners*. Translated by D. Shea and A. Troyer. 3 vols. Paris, 1843.

Firishta, Muhammad Qasim. *Tarikh-i Firishta*. (Persian lithograph.) 2 vols. Lucknow: Nawal Kishor, 1864-65. English edition: John Briggs, trans., *History of the Rise of the Mahomedan Power in India*. 4 vols. London, 1829. Reprinted in 3 vols. Calcutta: Editions Indian, 1966.

Born in Iran, Firishta traveled to India and resided in Bijapur from 1591 to his death in 1623. The famous historian was thus a contemporary of Sultan Ibrahim ʿAdil Shah II and an eyewitness to an important phase of Bijapur's history. His account of Bijapur, as is true of his account of Indian history generally, is a reliable one.

Ibrahim ʿAdil Shah II, Sultan. *Kitab-i Nauras*. Edited by Nazir Ahmad. Lucknow, 1955.

Jahangir, Emperor. *The Tuzuk-i-Jahangiri, or Memoirs of Jahangir*. Translated into English by Alexander Rogers. Edited by Henry Beveridge. 2 vols. 2nd edn. Delhi: Munshiram Manoharlal, 1968.

Nizam al-Din Ahmad. *Tabaqat-i Akbari*. (Persian lithograph.) Lucknow: Nawal Kishor, 1879. Abridged English edition in vol. 5 of H. M. Elliot and J. Dowson, eds., *The History of India as Told by its Own Historians*. 8 vols. Allahabad: Kitab Mahal, 1964.

Sen. Surendranath, ed. and trans. *Siva Chhatrapati*. Volume 1 of *Extracts and Documents Relating to Maratha History*. Calcutta: University of Calcutta, 1920.

Shirazi, Rafiʿ al-Din Ibrahim. *Tazkirat al-Muluk*. (Persian MS.) Hyderabad: Salar Jung Museum, Tarikh no. 142. Composed 1608-9; copied 1735-36. 184 fols. Another copy is in Hyderabad: Asafiyah Library, Tarikh no. 1081. Still another is in London: British Museum, Add. 23,883.

A graphic history of sixteenth-century Bijapur by an Iranian adventurer and diplomat.

Tabataba'i, Saiyid ʿAli. *Burhan-i Ma'asir*. (Persian printed edition.) Delhi: Jamʿi Press, 1936.

The standard history of the Bahmani Kingdom and the Nizam Shahi dynasty of Ahmadnagar.

Wassaf, ʿAbd Allah. *Tazjiyat al-Amsar wa Tajriyat al-Asrar* (*Tarikh-i Wassaf*). (Persian lithograph.) Bombay, 1853. Abridged English edition in vol. 3 of H. M. Elliot and J. Dowson, eds., *The History of India as Told by its Own Historians*. 8 vols. Allahabad: Kitab Mahal, 1964.

Zubairi, Muhammad Ibrahim. *Basatin al-Salatin*. (Persian lithograph.) Hyderabad: Saiyidi Press, 1892-93.

Although compiled as late as 1811, this is the most authoritative general history of Bijapur available. In his preface to this work, Zubairi lists and describes his various sources, which were mostly Persian chronicles and state documents contemporary with the 'Adil Shahi period.

Zuhuri, Muhammad Zuhur bin. *Muhammad-nama*. (Persian MS.) Patiala: Punjab State Archives, no. M/727. Copied 1781. 490 pp. Partially translated to English by Bhagwat D. Verma, "History in Muhammad Nama," in *Shivaji—Nibandhavali 2*. Poona: Shri Shivacharitrakaryalaya, 1930. pp. 73-134.

Composed in the reign of Sultan Muhammand 'Adil Shah, this work is mainly concerned with chronicling that sultan's campaigns in the Karnatak.

State Documents

Farmans. (Persian MSS.) Bijapur: Archeological Museum of Bijapur.

Farmans. (Persian MSS.) Bijapur: Gachi Mahal. *Farman* of Sikandar 'Adil Shah (12 Rajab, A.H. 1087); *farman* of Muhammad 'Adil Shah (14 Rabi' II, A.H. 1066); *farman* of Aurangzeb (11 Ramazan, A.H. 1117).

Khan, Yusuf Husain, trans. and ed. *Farmans and Sanads of the Deccan Sultans*. Hyderabad: State Archives, Government of Andhra Pradesh, 1963.

Khwaja Bandanawaz Collection. 'Adil Shahi *farmans*. (Persian MSS.) Hyderabad: State Archives of Andhra Pradesh.

Walter Elliot Collection. *Farmans*. (English MSS.) London: India Office Library, European MSS, no. F. 50.

Rough translations of forty-nine *farmans* of Bijapur and Golconda (forty-four of which are of Bijapur), collected and translated between 1821 and 1860 by Sir Walter Elliot, who was then serving in the Madras Presidency.

Epigraphic Sources

Fleet, J. F. "Sanskrit and Old-Canarese Inscriptions." *The Indian Antiquary* 10 (May 1881), pp. 126-31.

Nazim, Muhammad. "Bijapur Inscriptions." *Memoirs of the Archeological Survey of India*. No. 49. Delhi: Manager of Publications, 1936. pp. 1-110.

———. "An Inscription from Dabol." *Epigraphia Indo-Moslemica* (1933-34), pp. 9-10.

Siddiqi, M. Akbaruddin. "The Dakani Inscription on the Amin Dargah in Bijapur." *Epigraphia India. Arabic & Persian Supplement* (1968), pp. 79-92.

South Indian Inscriptions, xx. Subtitled *Bombay-Karnatak Inscriptions*, iv. Delhi: Manager of Publications, 1964.

Yazdani, G. "Inscriptions of Shahpur, Gogi and Sagar." *Epigraphia Indo-Moslemica* (1931-32), pp. 1-25.

Travel Accounts

Carré, Abbé. *The Travels of the Abbé Carré in India and the Near East. 1672 to 1674.* Translated by Lady Fawcett. Edited by Charles Fawcett. 3 vols. London: Hakluyt Society, 1947.

Correia-Afonso, John. "Bijapur Four Centuries Ago as Described in a Contemporary Letter." *Indica* 1 (March 1964), pp. 81-88.

Fryer, Dr. John. *A New Account of East India and Persia.* Edited by W. Crooke. 3 vols. London: Hakluyt Society, 1909-15.

Ibn Battuta. *Travels in Asia and Africa, 1325-54.* Translated by H. A. R. Gibb. London: Routledge & Sons, 1929.

Linschoten, John Hughen von. *The Voyage of John Hughen von Linschoten to the East Indies.* Vol. 1 edited by A. C. Burnell; vol. 2 edited by P. A. Tiele. 2 vols. London: Hakluyt Society, 1884. Reprint. New York: Burt Franklin, 1970.

Masʿudi. *Les Prairies d'Or.* Translated into French by C. Barbier de Maynard and Pavet de Courteille. 9 vols. Paris: l'Imprimerie Imperiale, 1861-1917.

Pyrard, François. *The Voyage of François Pyrard of Laval to the East Indies.* Translated into English by Albert Gray. 2 vols. in 3. London: Hakluyt Society, 1887-90. Reprint. New York: Burt Franklin, n.d.

Sen, Surendranath, ed. *The Indian Travels of Thevenot and Careri.* New Delhi: National Archives of India, 1949.

Secondary Sources

Ahmad, Aziz. *Studies in Islamic Culture in the Indian Environment.* Oxford: Clarendon Press, 1964.

———."The Sufi and the Sultan in Pre-Mughal India." *Der Islam* (1955), pp. 142-53.

Ahmad, Nazir, ed. Introduction to *Kitab-i Nauras* by Sultan Ibrahim ʿAdil Shah II (Urdu). Lucknow, 1955.

———. *Kitab-i Nauras, by Ibrahim ʿAdil Shah II.* New Delhi: Bharatiya Kala Kendra, 1956.

Apte, D. V. "Shivakalin Adilshahi" (Marathi). *Bharata Itihasa Sanshodhaka Mandal* 2 (June 1922), pp. 20-29.

Arberry, A. J. *Sufism.* 5th edn. London: Allen & Unwin, Ltd., 1969.

Arnold, Thomas W. *The Preaching of Islam: A History of the Propagation of the Muslim Faith.* 2nd edn. London: Constable & Co., Ltd., 1913.

Bailey, T. Grahame *A History of Urdu Literature.* London: Oxford University Press, 1932.

Basu, K. K. "The Dasturu'l-amal of the Bijapur Court." *Indian Historical Records Commission, Proceedings* 17 (1941), pp. 123-29.

Bilgrami, Saiyid 'Ali. *Tarikh-i Dakan* (Urdu). 3 vols. Agra: Mufid-i 'Am, 1897-1903.

Chaghatai, M. A. "'Adil Shahi grants to Shaikh Muhammad Abu Turab Mudarris." *Indian Historical Records Commission, Proceedings* 21 (1944), pp. 7-9.

———. "Dargah-i Khwaja Amin Bijapur" (Urdu). In S. A. J. Zaidi, ed., *Malik Ram Felicitation Volume,* II, pp. 611-22. New Delhi: Malik Ram Felicitation Committee, 1971.

Chatterji, S. K. *Indo-Aryan and Hindi.* 2nd edn. Calcutta: Firma K. L. Mukhopadhyay, 1960. Reprinted 1969.

Cousens, Henry. *Bijapur and Its Architectural Remains.* Bombay: Government Central Press, 1916.

———. *Notes on the Buildings and Other Antiquarian Remains at Bijapur.* Bombay: Government Central Press, 1890.

Dhere, R. C. *Musalman Marathi Santa Kavi* (Marathi). Poona, 1967.

Fukazawa, Hiroshi. "A Study of the Local Administration of Adilshahi Sultanate (A.D. 1489-1686)." *Hitotsubashi Journal of Economics* 3 (June 1963), pp. 37-67.

Gayani, B. G. "Kitab-i Nauras." *Islamic Culture* 19 (1945), pp. 140-52.

Gazetteer of Bombay Presidency. Bijapur District 23 (Bombay, 1884).

Ghauri, Iftikhar Ahmad. "Central Structure of the Kingdom of Bijapur." *Islamic Culture* 44 (January 1970), pp. 19-33.

———. "Kingship in the Sultanates of Bijapur and Golconda." *Islamic Culture* 46 (January 1972), pp. 39-52.

———. "Local Government under the Sultanates of Bijapur and Golconda." *Journal of the Research Society of Pakistan* 3 (January and April 1966), pp. 43-62.

———. "Muslims in the Deccan: A Historical Survey." *Islamic Literature* 13 (May 1967), pp. 25-38.

———. "Organization of the Army under the Sultanates of the Deccan." *Journal of the Pakistan Historical Society,* 14 (July 1966), pp. 147-72.

Goetz, Hermann. "The Fall of Vijayanagar and the Nationalization of Muslim Art in the Dakhan." *Journal of Indian History* 19 (1940), pp. 249-55.

Habib, Mohammad. "Chishti Mystics Records of the Sultanate Period." *Medieval India Quarterly* 1 (October 1950), pp. 1-42.

———. "Shaikh Nasir ud-din Mahmud Chiragh-i Delhi as a Great Historical Personality." *Islamic Culture* 20 (1946), pp. 129-53.

Hafīz Syed, M., ed. Introduction to *Kulliyat-i Bahri* (Urdu). Lucknow: Nawal Kishor, 1939.

———. "Qazi Mahmud Bahri: A Mystic Poet of the 11th Century A.H. and His Poetical Works." *Allahabad University Studies* 5 (1928), pp. 445-78.

———. "Qazi Mahmud Bahri and his Contemporaries." *Allahabad University Studies*, 12 (1936), pp. 267-99.

Hamīd al-Din Shāhid, ed. Introduction to *Risala-yi Mahmud Khush Dahan Bijapuri* (Urdu). Karachi: Aiwan-i Urdu, 1969.

Haq, Abdul. *Qadim Urdu* (Urdu). Karachi: Anjuman-i Taraqqi-yi Urdu, 1961.

———. *Urdu ki Ibtidai Nashv-o-nama men Sufiya-i Kiram ka Kam* (Urdu) [Sufis' Work in the Early Development of Urdu Language]. Delhi: Anjuman-i Taraqqi-yi Urdu, 1939.

———. "Urdu Nasr ki ek Bahut Qadim Kitab" (Urdu). *Urdu* (April 1928), pp. 153-58.

Hashim ʿAli, ed. Introduction to *Maghz-i Marghub* by Miranji Shams al-ʿUshshaq (Urdu). Hyderabad: Aʿjaz Printing Press, 1966.

Hashimi, Nasir al-Din. *Dakani Culture* (Urdu). Lahore: Majlis-i Taraqqi-yi Adab, 1963.

———. *Dakan men Urdu* (Urdu). 6th edn. Lucknow: Nasim Book Depot, 1963.

———. "Khwaja Bandanawaz ki Urdu Shaʿiri" (Urdu). *Hindustan* (October 1934), pp. 443-53.

Hashimi, Saiyid Mustafa Husaini ʿAlawi. *Tazkira-yi Qutb-i Dakan* (Urdu). Hyderabad: Taj Press, 1947-48.

Jaʿfar, Saiyida, ed. Introduction to *Sukh Anjan* by Abu'l-Hasan Qadiri (Urdu). Hyderabad: Lutf al-Daula Research Institute, 1968.

———. "Mahmud Khush Dahan" (Urdu). *Naya Daur* (January 1969), pp. 3-7.

Jalibi, Jamil. *Tarikh-i Adab-i Urdu*, vol. i, *Aghaz se 1750 tak* (Urdu). Lahore: Majlis-i Taraqqi-yi Adab, 1975.

Joshi, P. M. "Asad Beg's Mission to Bijapur, 1603-1604," in Sen, S. N., ed., *Professor D. V. Potdar Commemoration Volume*. Poona: D. K. Sathe, 1950. pp. 184-96.

———. "The Kingdom of Bijapur." Ph.D. dissertation, University of London, 1935.

———. "The Reign of Ibrahim ʿAdil Shah II of Bijapur." *Bharatiya Vidya* (Bombay, 1949), IX, pp. 284-309.

———. "Some Notes on the Textile Industry and Trade of the Kingdom of Bijapur." *Proceedings, 7th Indian Historical Congress* (1944), pp. 262-64.

Kazimi Shattari al-Qadiri. *Sirat-i Hashimi* (Urdu). Hyderabad: Aʿjaz Printing Press, 1961.

Khare, G. H. "Archives from the Deshmukh and Deshpande Families of Kasegaon Sholapur, Bombay." *Indian Historical Records Commission, Proceedings* 31 (1955), pp. 77-80.

———. "The Archives of the Deshmukh Family of Sholapur." *Indian History Congress, Proceedings* 16 (1953), pp. 273-75.

Khrishnaswami Aiyangar, S. *South India and Her Muhammadan Invaders*. London: Oxford University Press, 1921.

Kulkarni, A. R. "Social Relations in the Maratha Country in the Medieval Period." *Indian History Congress, Proceedings*. 32nd session (Jabalpur, 1970), pp. 231-68.

Nayeem, M. A. *The External Relations of the Bijapur Kingdom (1489-1686 A.D.)*. Hyderabad, A. P.: Bright Publishers, 1974.

Nilakanta Sastri, K. A. *Development of Religion in South India*. Madras: Orient Longmans, Ltd., 1963.

———. *A History of South India*. 3rd edn. Madras: John Brown, Oxford University Press, 1966.

Nizami, Khaliq Ahmad. "The Shattari Saints and Their Attitude towards the State." *Medieval India Quarterly*, I (October 1950), pp. 56-70.

———. *Some Aspects of Religion and Politics in India during the 13th Century*. Aligarh: S. Nural Hasan, 1961.

———. *Studies in Medieval Indian History and Culture*. Allahabad: Kitab Mahal, 1966.

Potdar, D. V. "Sri Moraya Dev Sansthan Chinchwad Sambandhi Kahin Junat Assal Kagad" (Marathi). *Bharata Itihasa Sanshodhaka Mandal* 2 (June 1922), pp. 52-69.

Qatil, ʿAbd al-Hafiz. *Miranji Khudanama* (Urdu). Hyderabad: Urdu Academy, 1961.

Rafiʿa Sultana. *Urdu Nasr ka Aghaz aur Irtiqa* (Urdu). Hyderabad: Majlis-i Tahqiqat-i Urdu, n.d.

Rifiʿat, Saiyid Mubariz al-Din. "Dakani Adab ka ek ʿAzim Markiz" (Urdu). *Majallai Osmania. Deccani Adab Number*, no. 65 (1963-64), pp. 62-69.

Rizvi, Saiyid A. A. *Muslim Revivalist Movements in Northern India in the Sixteenth and Seventeenth Centuries*. Agra: Agra University, 1965.

Sakhawat Mirza, Muhammad, ed. Introduction to *Man Lagan* by Mahmud Bahri (Urdu). Karachi: Anjuman-i Taraqqi-yi Urdu, 1955.

———. "Saiyid Shah Kamal al-Din" (Urdu). *Urdu* (April 1939), pp. 263-86.

———. "Shaikh Mahmud Chishti al-Mulaqqab ba Khush Dahan Bijapuri" (Urdu). *Urdu-nama* (January-March 1962), pp. 71-75.

Salim, Mohammad. "The Attitude of the Chishti Saints towards Political Power." *Proceedings, Pakistan Historical Conference* 2 (1952), pp. 225-29.

Sarkar, Jadunath. *History of Aurangzib*. 5 vols. Calcutta: S. C. Sarkar & Sons, 1925-30.

———. *House of Shivaji*. 3rd edn. Calcutta: M. C. Sarkar, 1955.

———. *Shivaji and His Times*. 5th edn. Calcutta: M. C. Sarkar & Sons, Ltd., 1952.

Sathyan, B. N. Sri, ed. *Mysore State Gazetteer, Bijapur District*. Bangalore: Government Press, 1966.

Schimmel, Annemarie. "The Influence of Sufism on Indo-Muslim Poetry." In Joseph P. Strelka, ed., *Anagogic Qualities of Literature*, pp. 181-210. University Park, Pa.: Pennsylvania State University Press, 1971.

———. *Islamic Literatures of India*. Wiesbaden: Otto Harrossowitz, 1973.

Shāhid, Husaini. "Shah Amin al-Din 'Ali A'la aur unke Khulfa" (Urdu). 2 vols. Ph.D. dissertation, Osmania University, 1966.

Shams Allah Qadiri. *Urdu-i Qadim* (Urdu). Lucknow: Nawal Kishor, 1925.

Sharma, Sri Ram. *Dakani Zaban ka Aghaz aur Irtiqa* (Urdu). Translated from Hindi to Urdu by Ghulam Rasul. Hyderabad: Andhra Pradesh Sahitia Academy, 1967.

Sherwani, H. K. *The Bahmanis of the Deccan*. Hyderabad: Manager of Publications, 1953.

———. "Cultural Synthesis in Medieval India." *Journal of Indian History* 41 (April 1963), pp. 239-59.

Sherwani, H. K. and Joshi, P. M., eds. *History of Medieval Deccan, 1295-1724*. 2 vols. Hyderabad: Government of Andhra Pradesh, 1973-74.

Siddiqi, M. Akbaruddin. *Bujhte Chiragh: Dakani Adab par Mazamin ka Majmu'a* (Urdu). Hyderabad: National Fine Press, 1975.

———. "Firaqi Bijapuri" (Urdu). *Sab Ras* (September 1965), pp. 17-32.

———, ed. Introduction to *Kalimat al-Haqayiq* by Burhan al-Din Janam (Urdu). Hyderabad: Idara-e-Adabiyat-e-Urdu, 1961.
———, ed. Introduction to *Kashf al-Wujud* by Shah Dawal (Urdu). Hyderabad: M. Akbaruddin Siddiqi, n.d.
Subhan, John A. *Sufism, Its Saints and Shrines*. Lucknow: Lucknow Publishing House, 1960.
Taylor, Meadows, and Fergusson, James. *Architecture at Beejapoor*. London: J. Murray, 1866.
Trimingham, J. Spencer. *The Sufi Orders in Islam*. Oxford: Oxford University Press, 1971.
Venkata Ramanayya, N. *The Early Muslim Expansion in South India*. Madras: University of Madras, 1942.
Verma, D. C. *History of Bijapur*. New Delhi: Kumar Brothers, 1974.
Yazdani, G. *Bidar, Its History and Monuments*. Oxford: Oxford University Press, 1947.
Zinat Sajida. "Dakani Git" (Urdu). *Majallai Osmania. Deccani Adab Number*, no. 65 (1963-64), pp. 201-7.
Zore, S. Muhiuddin Qadri. *Dakan Adab ki Tarikh, 1350-1750* (Urdu). Karachi: Urdu Akadami-yi Sindh, 1960.
———, ed. Introduction to *Irshad-nama* by Burhan al-Din Janam (Urdu). Unpublished proof in Hyderabad: Idara-e-Adabiyat-e-Urdu, no. v 6, #4.

Reference Works

Arberry, A. J., trans. *The Koran Interpreted*. New York: Macmillan Co., 1970.
Freeman-Grenville, G. S. P. *The Muslim and Christian Calendars*. London: Oxford University Press, 1963.
Platts, John T. *A Dictionary of Urdu, Classical Hindi, and English*. London: Oxford University Press, 1968.
Steingass, F. *A Comprehensive Persian-English Dictionary*. Beirut: Librarie du Liban, 1970.
Storey, G. A. *Persian Literature, a Bio-Bibliographic Survey*. 2 vols. London: Luzac & Co., 1927-71.
Wehr, Hans. *A Dictionary of Modern Written Arabic*. Edited by J. Milton Cowan. Wiesbaden: Otto Harrossowitz, 1966.
Wilson, H. H. *A Glossary of Judicial and Revenue Terms . . . of British India*. 2nd edn. Delhi: Munshiram Manoharlal, 1968.

INDEX